500 WAYS TO COOK CHICKEN

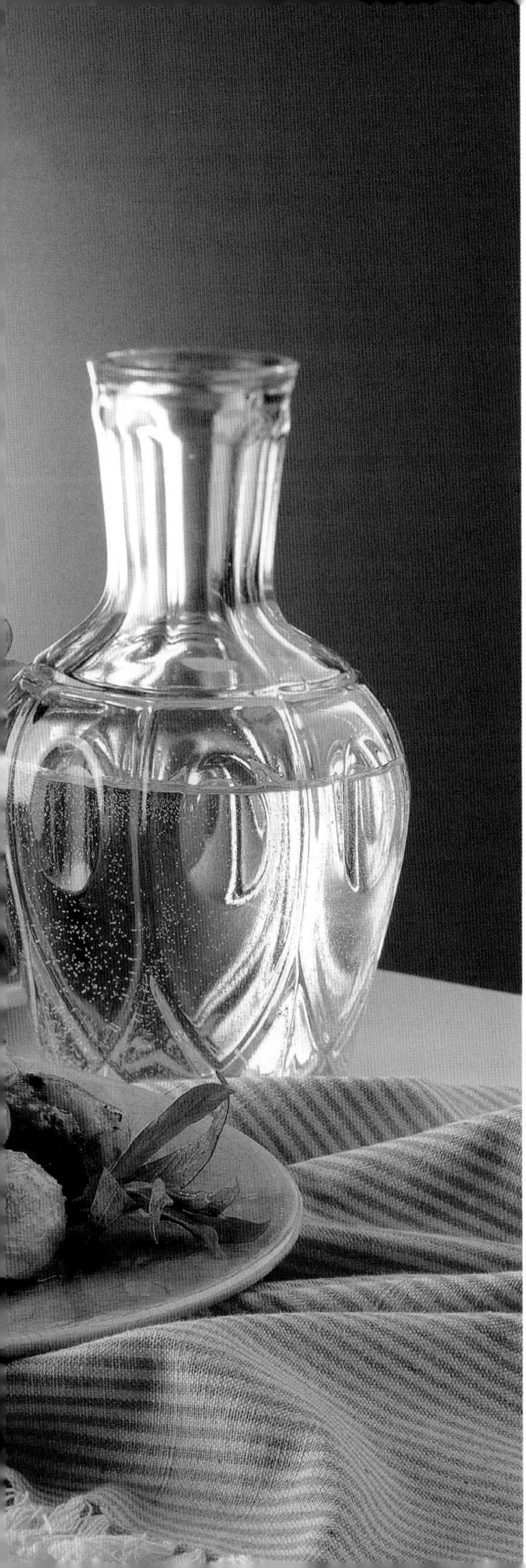

500 WAYS TO COOK CHICKEN

THE ULTIMATE POULTRY AND GAME BIRD COOKBOOK, WITH EASY-TO-FOLLOW IDEAS FOR EVERY OCCASION

VALERIE FERGUSON

This edition is published by Southwater, an imprint of Anness Publishing Ltd,
Hermes House, 88–89 Blackfriars Road, London SE1 8HA;
tel. 020 7401 2077; fax 020 7633 9499

www.southwaterbooks.com; www.annesspublishing.com

If you like the images in this book and would like to investigate using them for publishing, promotions or advertising, please visit our website www.practicalpictures.com for more information.

UK agent: The Manning Partnership Ltd
tel. 01225 478444; fax 01225 478440; sales@manning-partnership.co.uk
UK distributor: Grantham Book Services Ltd
tel. 01476 541080; fax 01476 541061; orders@gbs.tbs-ltd.co.uk
North American agent/distributor: National Book Network
tel. 301 459 3366; fax 301 429 5746; www.nbnbooks.com
Australian agent/distributor: Pan Macmillan Australia
tel. 1300 135 113; fax 1300 135 103; customer.service@macmillan.com.au
New Zealand agent/distributor: David Bateman Ltd
tel. (09) 415 7664; fax (09) 415 8892

Publisher: Joanna Lorenz
Consultant Editor: Valerie Ferguson
Designer: Carole Perks
Editorial Reader: Richard McGinlay
Production Controller: Claire Rae
Recipes contributed by: Catherine Atkinson, Alex Barker, Angela Boggiano, Kathy Brown, Carla Capalbo, Lesley Chamberlain, Kit Chan, Maxine Clarke, Frances Cleary, Carole Clements, Trisha Davies, Roz Denny, Michelle Derrie-Johnson, Patrizia Diemling, Matthew Drennan, Sarah Edmonds, Joanna Farrow, Rafi Fernandez, Christine France, Silvano Franco, Sarah Gates, Shirley Gill, Rosamund Grant, Carole Handslip, Rebekah Hassan, Deh-Ta Hsuing, Shehzad Husain, Christine Ingram, Judy Jackson, Sheila Kimberley, Masaki Ko, Ruby Le Bois, Lesley Mackley, Norma MacMillan, Sue Maggs, Kathy Man, Maggie Mayhew, Norma Miller, Sallie Morris, Elizabeth Lambert Ortiz, Maggie Pannell, Katherine Richmond, Anne Sheasby, Jenny Stacey, Liz Trigg, Hilaire Walden, Laura Washburn, Steven Wheeler, Judy Williams, Polly Wreford, Jeni Wright, Elizabeth Wolf-Cohen
Photography: Karl Adamson, Edward Allwright, David Armstrong, Steve Baxter, James Duncan, John Freeman, Ian Garlick, Michelle Garrett, John Heseltine, Amanda Heywood, Ferguson Hill, Janine Hosegood, David Jordan, Don Last, William Lingwood, Patrick McLeavey, Thomas Odulate, Juliet Piddington, Peter Reilly

ETHICAL TRADING POLICY

Because of our ongoing ecological investment programme, you, as our customer, can have the pleasure and reassurance of knowing that a tree is being cultivated on your behalf to naturally replace the materials used to make the book you are holding. For further information about this scheme, go to www.annesspublishing.com/trees

Previously published as *500 Greatest-Ever Chicken Recipes*

NOTES

For all recipes, quantities are given in both metric and imperial measures and, where appropriate, in standard cups and spoons.
Follow one set of measures, but not a mixture, because they are not interchangeable.
Standard spoon and cup measures are level. 1 tsp = 5ml, 1 tbsp = 15ml, 1 cup = 250ml/8fl oz.
Australian standard tablespoons are 20ml. Australian readers should use 3 tsp in place of 1 tbsp for measuring small quantities.
American pints are 16fl oz/2 cups. American readers should use 20fl oz/2.5 cups in place of 1 pint when measuring liquids.
Electric oven temperatures in this book are for conventional ovens. When using a fan oven, the temperature will probably need to be reduced by about 10–20°C/20–40°F. Since ovens vary, you should check with your manufacturer's instruction book for guidance.
Medium (US large) eggs are used unless otherwise stated.

Main front cover image shows Chicken with Lemon & Garlic – for recipe, see page 36.

Publisher's Note

Although the advice and information in this book are believed to be accurate and true at the time of going to press, neither the authors nor the publisher can accept any legal responsibility or liability for any errors or omissions that may be made nor for any inaccuracies nor for any harm or injury that comes about from following instructions or advice in this book.

Contents

Introduction

Chicken is an extremely popular food. It is versatile and economical, and can be cooked with a wide variety of ingredients and flavourings. It is low in fat and quick to cook, with very little wastage.

Chicken can be bought in many forms: whole, quartered or jointed into thighs, drumsticks, breasts and wings, with or without bones and skin, which makes preparation very easy. Minced chicken can be found at some large supermarkets, but the skinned flesh can be minced quickly at home in a food processor. Although it is convenient to buy portions individually packed, it can be expensive. It is much cheaper to buy a whole chicken and prepare it yourself, and cheaper still to buy a frozen chicken and defrost it thoroughly before using. The added bonus of a frozen bird are the giblets (neck, heart, liver and gizzard) found inside the cavity which can be used for making stock. To get the best results from a frozen chicken, allow it to thaw slowly in a cool place overnight or until completely defrosted.

Many types of chicken are available, such as free-range and corn-fed (with yellow skin), and all are full of flavour. Some have added herbs and flavourings, and others are

self-basting with either butter or olive oil injected into the flesh. This helps to keep the flesh succulent. Chicken is available all year round, although some of the more expensive types are raised only in limited numbers. Baby chickens are called poussins and can be bought to serve whole or halved, depending on their size and your appetite. In fact, chicken can be bought at any weight ranging from 450g to 2.75kg (1lb to 6lb).

When buying, look for a firm, plump bird with no signs of damage to the limbs, flesh or skin. Unwrap the bird, immediately store it in the fridge and use as soon as possible, as all poultry deteriorates very rapidly.

This book offers chicken, turkey and game recipes from all corners of the world and for every occasion, from simple snacks, starters and light meals, through substantial family suppers, to luxurious dishes for celebrations and entertaining. Soups, salads and pâtés; roasts, casseroles and pies; stir-fries and sautés; hot and spicy dishes in profusion; and low-fat recipes for people who are watching their cholesterol levels or weight – there is truly something here for every taste and requirement. You need never again be at a loss for an inspiring chicken recipe.

Choosing a Chicken

When choosing a fresh chicken for cooking, it should have a plump breast and the skin should be creamy in colour. The tip of the breastbone should be pliable when pressed. A bird's dressed weight is taken after plucking and drawing, and may include the giblets (neck, gizzard, heart and liver). A frozen chicken must be thawed slowly in the fridge or a cool room before cooking. Never try to thaw it in hot water, as this will toughen the flesh.

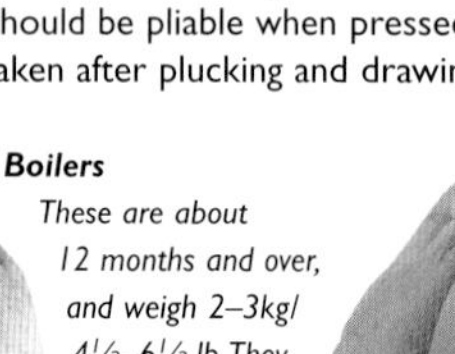

Boilers
These are about 12 months and over, and weigh 2–3kg/ 4½–6½ lb. They require long, slow cooking, around 2–3 hours, to make them tender.

Corn-fed Chickens
These are free-range birds and are generally more expensive. They usually weigh 1.2–1.5kg/ 2½ – 3½ lb.

Roasters
These birds are about 6–12 months old and weigh 1.5–2kg/ 3½ – 4½ lb. They will feed a family.

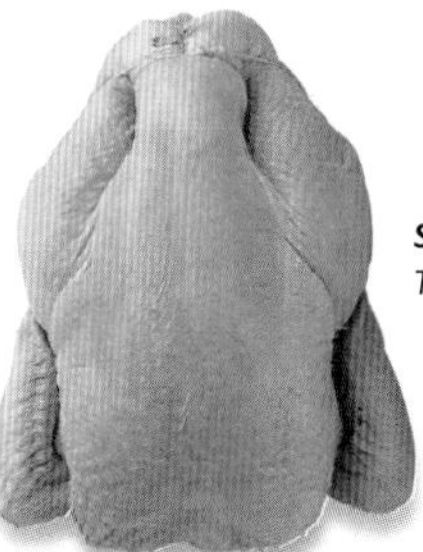

Spring Chickens
These birds are about 3 months old and weigh 900g–1.2kg/2–2½ lb. They will serve three to four people.

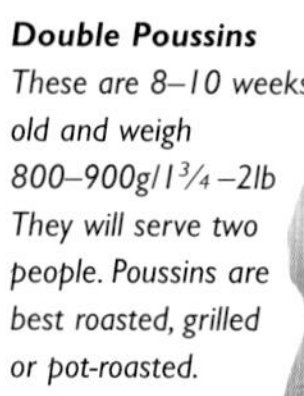

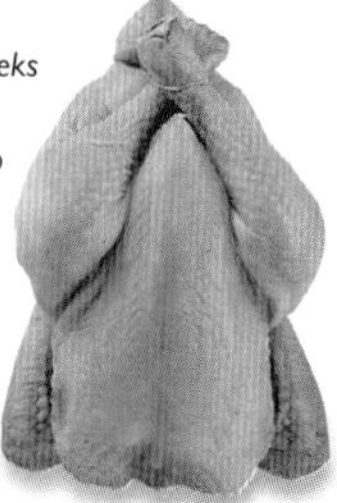

Double Poussins
These are 8–10 weeks old and weigh 800–900g/1¾–2lb They will serve two people. Poussins are best roasted, grilled or pot-roasted.

Poussins
These are 4–6 weeks old and weigh 450–500g/1–1¼ lb. They are sufficient for one person.

Cuts of Chicken

Chicken pieces today are available pre-packaged in a variety of different ways. If you do not want to buy a whole bird, you can choose from the many selected cuts on the market. Most cooking methods are suitable for all cuts, but some are especially suited to specific cuts of meat. These are ideal for frying, grilling and barbecuing.

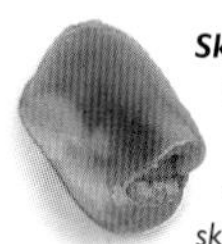

Skinless Boneless Thigh
This makes tasks such as stuffing and rolling much quicker, as it is already skinned and jointed.

Liver
This makes a wonderful addition to pâtés or to salads.

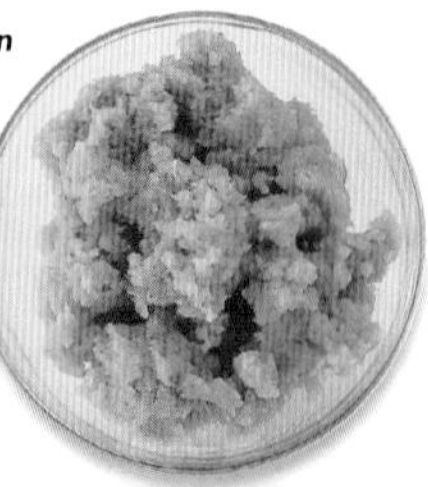

Minced Chicken
This is not as strongly flavoured as, say, minced beef, but may be used as a substitute in some recipes.

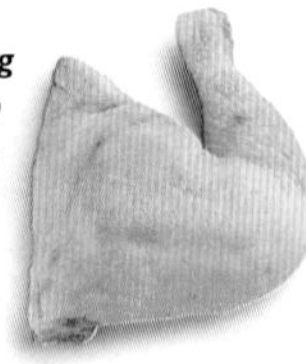

Leg
The leg comprises the thigh and drumstick. Large pieces with bones, such as this, are suitable for slow-cooking, such as casseroling or poaching.

Wing
The wing does not supply much meat. It is often barbecued or fried.

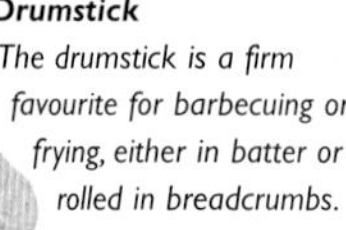

Drumstick
The drumstick is a firm favourite for barbecuing or frying, either in batter or rolled in breadcrumbs.

Breast
This comprises tender white meat and can be simply cooked in butter, as well as stuffed.

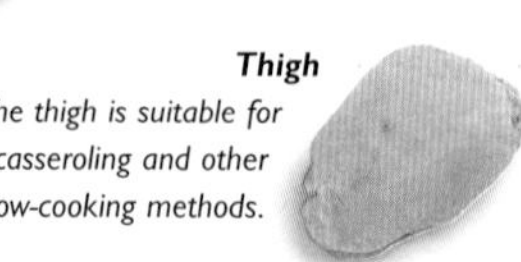

Thigh
The thigh is suitable for casseroling and other slow-cooking methods.

Jointing a Chicken

For recipes that call for chicken joints, it is often cheaper to buy a whole chicken and joint it yourself, particularly if you are cooking for a large number of people. It is important to have a portion of bone with the wing and breast joints, otherwise the flesh shrinks during cooking.

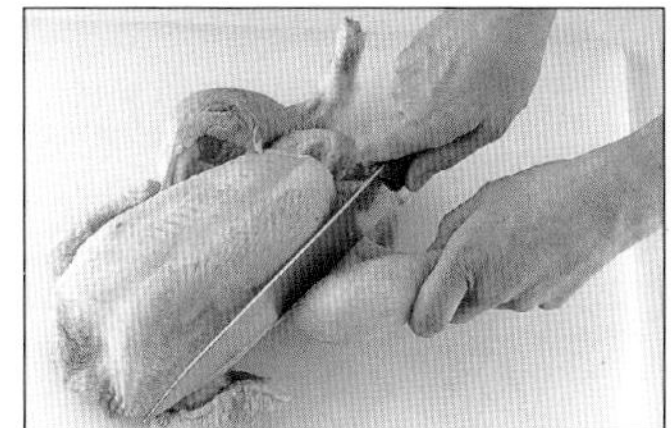

1 Hold the leg firmly with one hand. Using a sharp knife, cut the skin between the leg and breast.

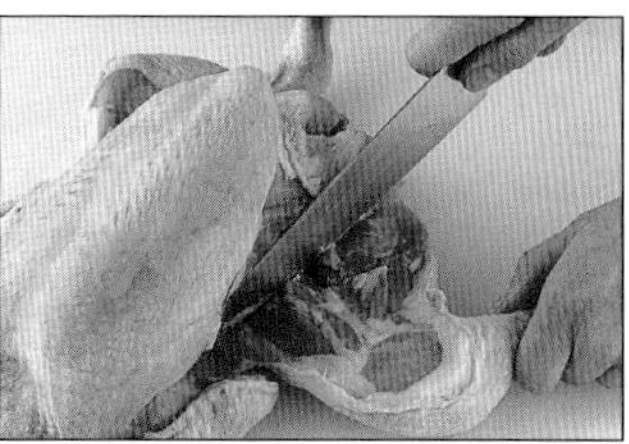

2 Then press the leg down to expose the ball-and-socket joint, cut or break the joint apart and cut down towards the parson's nose.

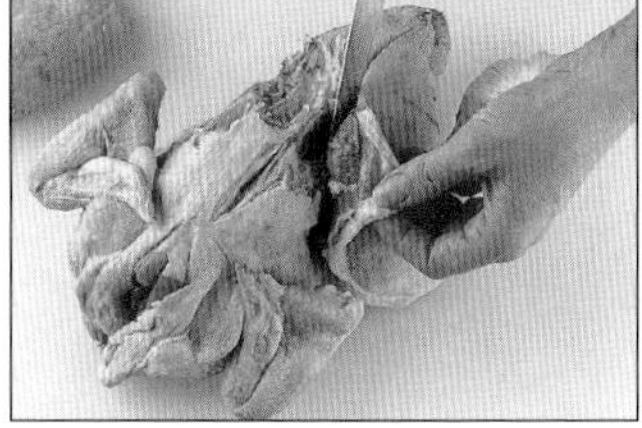

3 Turn the chicken over and loosen the "oyster" from the underside (this lies embedded alongside the backbone). Repeat with the other leg.

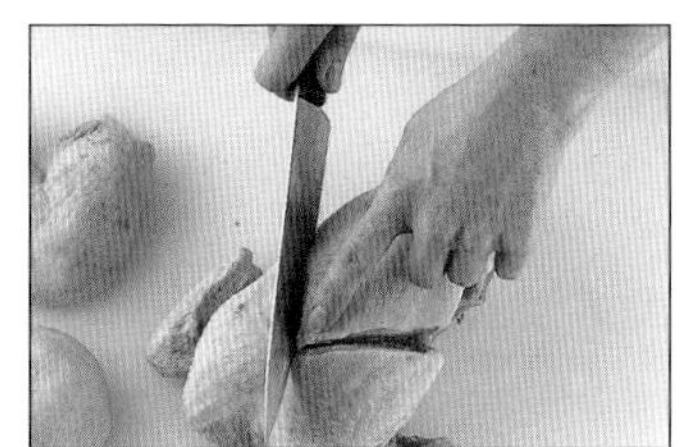

4 Now, with your finger, feel for the end of the breastbone, and, using a sharp knife, cut diagonally through the flesh to the rib cage.

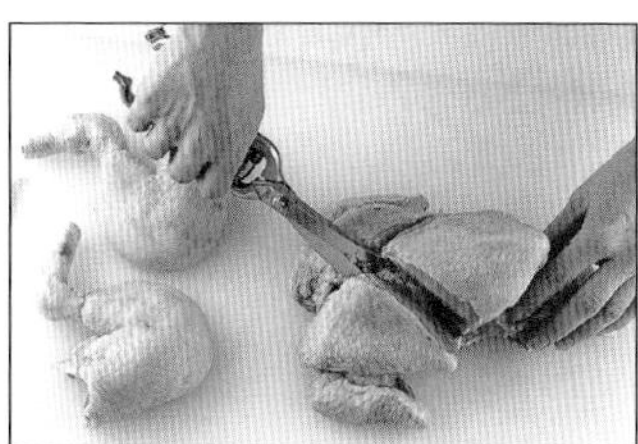

5 Using strong kitchen scissors, cut through the rib cage and wishbone, separating the two wing joints.

6 Twist the wing tip and tuck it under the breast meat so that the joint is held flat. This will ensure that it has a good shape for cooking.

7 Using strong kitchen scissors, cut the breast meat from the carcass in one piece. (All that remains of the carcass is half of the rib cage and the backbone.)

8 The legs can be cut in half through the joint to give a thigh joint and a drumstick. The breast can also be cut into two pieces through the breastbone.

Spatchcocking a Chicken

This is a good way to prepare chickens for grilling or barbecuing, especially the smaller sizes such as poussins. By removing their backbones, poussins can be opened out and flattened ready for even and fast cooking.

1 Using a very sharp pair of kitchen scissors, cut the poussin on either side of its backbone.

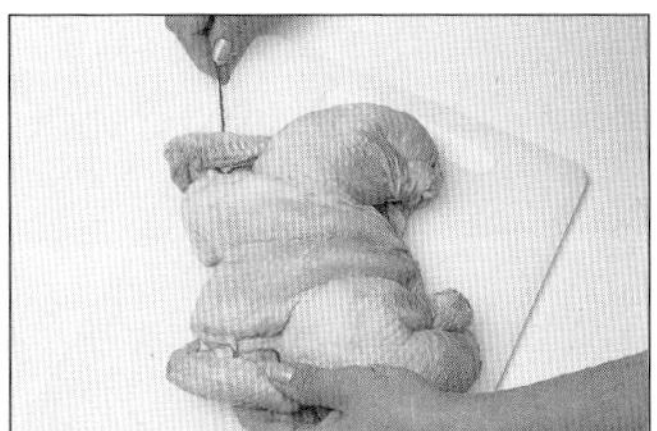

2 Flatten the bird with the palm of your hand or a rolling pin. Turn it over and cut away the fine rib cage, leaving the rest of the carcass intact to hold its shape. Thread thin skewers through the wings.

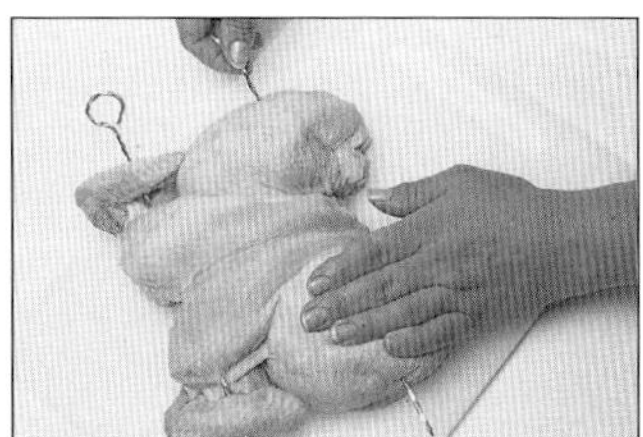

3 Then thread thin skewers through the legs to hold them in position and keep the bird flat. Brush liberally with melted butter. It will take 10–15 minutes on each side, depending on the heat.

Stuffing a Chicken

Stuffing helps to keep chickens moist during cooking, which is important because they have very little fat. The stuffing also helps to make the meal go further. There are many different flavours of stuffing that may be used to enhance the taste of chicken, without detracting from its own delicate flavour. Bread, rice or potatoes can be used as the basis to which other ingredients may be added. Fat is important in stuffing because it prevents it from becoming dry and crumbly.

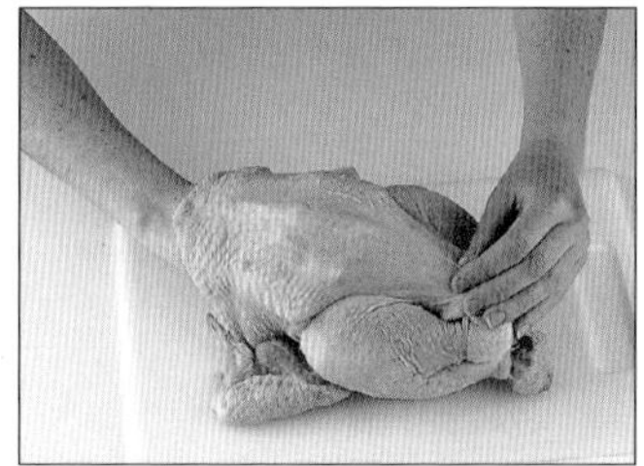

1 Only stuff the small neck-end of the chicken and not the large cavity inside the carcass, as the heat from the oven will not penetrate all the way through the chicken. Any leftover stuffing should be made into small balls and fried separately or put into a shallow, buttered ovenproof dish, baked in the oven with the chicken and cut into squares for serving with the chicken.

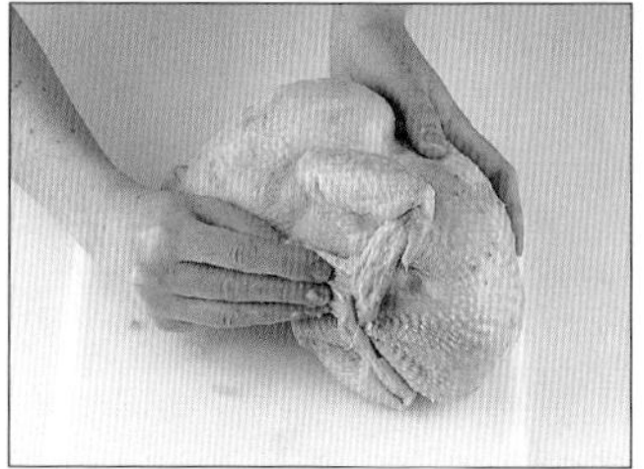

2 Never pack the stuffing too tightly, as breadcrumbs will expand during cooking and this may cause the skin to burst open. The flap of neck skin should then be tucked under the chicken and secured with the wing tips or sewn into place with a needle and fine trussing thread. Remember to weigh the chicken after it has been stuffed to calculate the cooking time accurately.

Casseroling

This slow-cooking method is good for large chicken joints with bones, or more mature meat.

1 Heat some olive oil in a flameproof casserole and fry the chicken joints until they are browned on all sides.

2 Add stock, wine or a mixture of both to a depth of 2.5cm/1in. Add seasonings and herbs, cover and cook on top of the stove or in the oven for 1½ hours or until the chicken is tender.

3 Add a selection of lightly fried vegetables such as button onions, mushrooms, carrots and small new potatoes about halfway through the cooking time.

Braising

This method can be used for whole chickens or pieces and is ideal for strongly flavoured meat.

1 Heat some olive oil in a flameproof casserole and lightly fry a whole bird or chicken joints until golden on all sides.

2 Remove the chicken from the casserole and fry 450g/1lb diced vegetables, such as carrots, onions, celery and turnips, until soft.

3 Replace the chicken, cover with a tight lid and cook very slowly on the top of the stove or in the oven, preheated to 160°C/325°F/Gas 3, until tender.

Carving a Chicken

It is best to allow the chicken to stand (or "rest") for 10–15 minutes before carving (while the gravy is being made). This allows the meat to relax, so the flesh will not tear while carving. Use a sharp carving knife and work on a plate that will catch any juices that can be added to the gravy. The leg can be cut into two for a thigh and a drumstick.

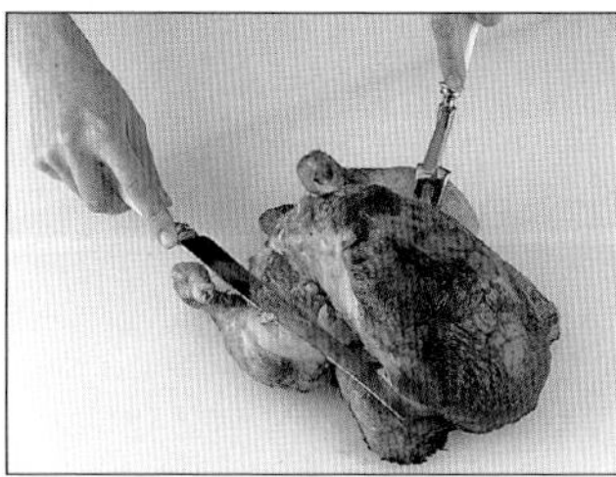

1 Hold the chicken firmly with a carving fork, between the breast and one of the legs, down to the backbone. Cut the skin around the opposite leg, press gently outwards to expose the ball-and-socket joint and cut through. Slip the knife under the back to remove the "oyster" with the leg.

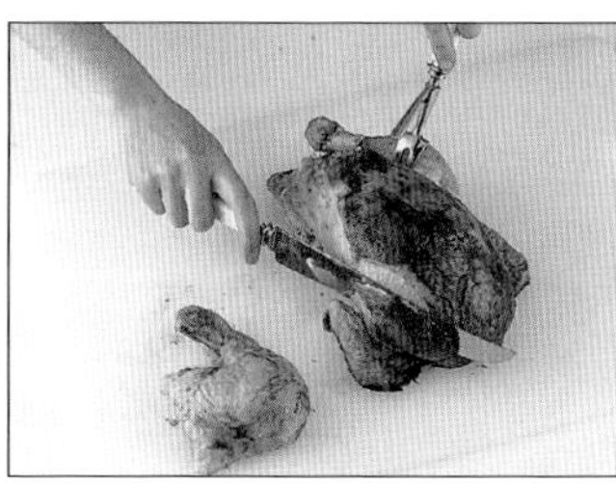

2 With the knife at the top end of the breastbone, cut down parallel on one side of the wishbone to take a good slice of breast meat with the wing joint.

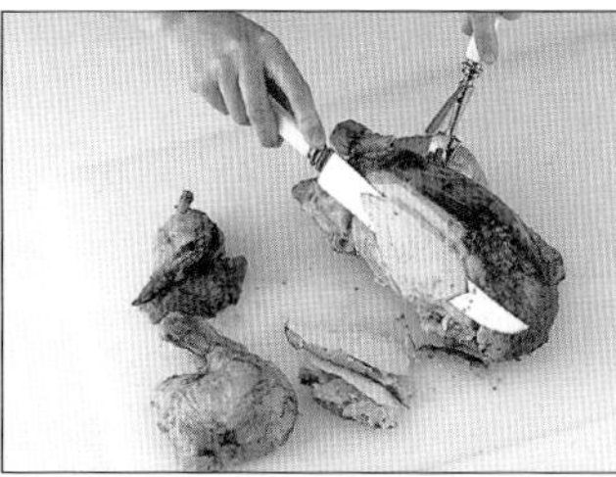

3 With the knife at the end of the breastbone, cut down the front of the carcass, removing the wishbone. Carve the remaining breast into slices.

Chicken Stock

A good chicken stock is called for in many dishes, so make a large quantity and freeze it in small batches.

1 onion
4 cloves
1 carrot
2 leeks
2 celery sticks
1 chicken carcass, cooked or raw
1 bouquet garni
8 black peppercorns
2.5ml/ ½ tsp salt

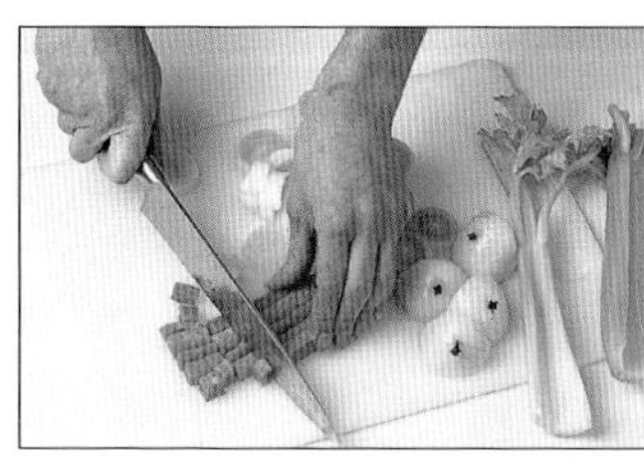

1 Peel the onion, cut into quarters and spike each quarter with a clove. Scrub and roughly chop the other vegetables.

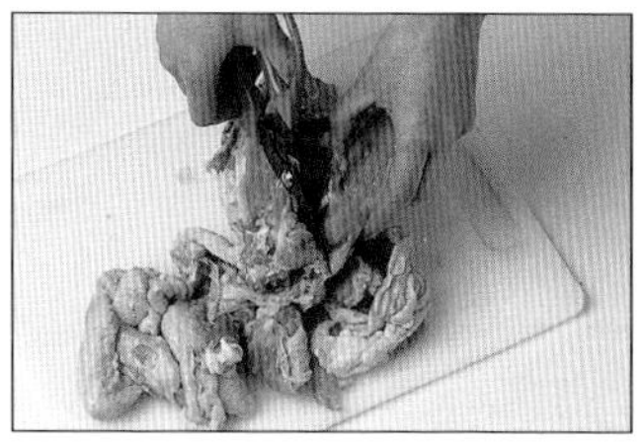

2 Break up the chicken carcass into several pieces and place in a large saucepan with the remaining ingredients.

3 Cover with 1.75 litres/3 pints/7½ cups water. Bring to the boil, skim and simmer, partially covered, for 2 hours. Strain the stock and allow to cool. When cold, remove the hardened fat before using.

How to Make Gravy

After roasting, transfer the chicken to a serving dish and remove any trussing string. Cover loosely with foil and leave to rest in a warm place before carving. Meanwhile, spoon the fat from the juices left in the roasting tin. Stirring constantly, blend 15ml/ 1 tbsp flour into the juices and cook gently on top of the stove until golden brown. Add 300ml/½ pint/1¼ cups chicken stock or vegetable cooking water and bring to the boil, to thicken. Season to taste. Strain into a jug or gravy boat to serve.

Roasting Times for Poultry

Note: Birds should be weighed after stuffing.

Poussin	450–675g/1–1½lb	1–1¼ hours at 180°C/350°F/Gas 4
Chicken	1.2–1.3kg/2½–3lb	1–1¼ hours at 190°C/375°F/Gas 5
	1.5–1.75kg/3½–4lb	1¼–1¾ hours at 190°C/375°F/Gas 5
	2–2.25kg/4½–5lb	1½–2 hours at 190°C/375°F/Gas 5
	2.25–2.75kg/5–6lb	1¾–2½ hours at 190°C/375°F/Gas 5
Duck	1.3–2.25kg/3–5lb	1¾–2¼ hours at 200°C/400°F/Gas 6
Goose	3.6–4.5kg/8–10lb	2½–3 hours at 180°C/350°F/Gas 4
	4.5–5.4kg/10–12lb	3–3½ hours at 180°C/350°F/Gas 4
Turkey *(whole bird)*	2.75–3.6kg/6–8lb	3–3½ hours at 160°C/325°F/Gas 3
	3.6–5.4kg/8–12lb	3–4 hours at 160°C/325°F/Gas 3
	5.4–7.2kg/12–16lb	4–5 hours at 160°C/325°F/Gas 3
Turkey *(whole breast)*	1.75–2.75kg/4–6lb	1½–2¼ hours at 160°C/325°F/Gas 3
	2.75–3.6kg/6–8lb	2¼–3¼ hours at 160°C/325°F/Gas 3

Mexican Chicken Soup

For a hearty version of this simple soup, add some cooked chick-peas or rice.

Serves 6

1.5 litres/2½ pints/6¼ cups Chicken Stock
2 cooked chicken breast fillets, skinned and cut into large strips
1 canned chipotle chilli or jalapeño chilli, drained and rinsed
1 avocado
salt and freshly ground black pepper

1 Heat the stock in a large saucepan, and add the chicken and chilli. Simmer over a very gentle heat for 5 minutes to heat the chicken and release the flavour from the chilli.

2 Cut the avocado in half, remove the stone and peel off the skin. Slice the avocado flesh neatly.

3 Remove the chilli from the stock, using a slotted spoon, and then discard it. Taste the soup for seasoning, and add salt and pepper as necessary.

4 Pour the soup into warmed serving bowls, distributing the chicken evenly among them. Carefully add a few avocado slices to each bowl and serve immediately.

Cook's Tip

When using canned chillies, it is important to rinse them very thoroughly before adding them to the pan in order to remove the flavour of any pickling liquid.

Chicken Stellette Soup

The pasta shapes are the stars of this gently flavoured soup in two senses since despite their small size, they attract the eye and capture the interest.

Serves 4–6

900ml/1½ pints/3¾ cups Chicken Stock
1 bay leaf
4 spring onions
225g/8oz/3 cups button mushrooms, sliced
115g/4oz cooked chicken breast
50g/2oz/½ cup stellette (tiny soup pasta)
150ml/¼ pint/⅔ cup dry white wine
15ml/1 tbsp chopped fresh parsley
salt and freshly ground black pepper

1 Put the stock and bay leaf into a large saucepan and bring to the boil over a medium heat.

2 Thinly slice the spring onions and add to the pan of stock. Add the mushrooms.

3 Remove the skin from the chicken and discard. Slice the chicken thinly. Transfer to a plate and set aside.

4 Add the pasta to the pan, cover and simmer for 7–8 minutes. Just before serving, add the chicken, wine and parsley, season to taste and heat through for 2–3 minutes. Serve in warmed bowls.

Chicken Soup Lebanese-style

A substantial soup with a hint of cinnamon and cumin.

Serves 6

175g/6oz/¾ cup chick-peas, soaked in water overnight
2 litres/3½ pints/9 cups Chicken Stock
90g/3½oz/½ cup long-grain rice
1 onion, chopped
2 garlic cloves, crushed
30ml/2 tbsp olive oil
2.5ml/½ tsp ground cumin
5ml/1 tsp ground cinnamon
350g/12oz/2½ cups cooked chicken, diced
salt and freshly ground black pepper

1 Simmer the drained chick-peas in the stock for about 1 hour until tender but not mushy. Add the rice and cook for 15 minutes until the rice is just tender.

2 Meanwhile, gently fry the onion and garlic in the oil for 10 minutes until soft but not browned. Stir in the spices and cook gently for 5 minutes more.

3 Add the onion mixture and the cooked chicken to the soup at the end of its cooking time, and simmer long enough to heat the chicken thoroughly. Season to taste and serve.

Chicken & Asparagus Soup

A very delicate and delicious soup. When fresh asparagus is not in season, canned white asparagus is an acceptable substitute.

Serves 4

150g/5oz chicken breast fillet
5ml/1 tsp egg white
5ml/1 tsp cornflour
115g/4oz asparagus
750ml/1¼ pints/3 cups Chicken Stock
salt and freshly ground black pepper
fresh coriander leaves, to garnish

1 Cut the chicken meat into thin slices, each about the size of a postage stamp. Season with a pinch of salt and stir in the egg white. Mix the cornflour to a thin paste with a little water and add to the chicken.

2 Trim and discard the tough stems of the asparagus. Diagonally cut the tender spears into short lengths.

3 In a wok or saucepan, bring the stock to a rolling boil. Add the asparagus, return to the boil and cook for 2 minutes. (This is not necessary if using canned asparagus.)

4 Add the chicken, stir to separate and bring back to the boil once more. Taste the soup and adjust the seasoning as necessary. Serve hot, garnished with fresh coriander leaves.

Cook's Tip
When buying asparagus, look for tight buds and firm, unwrinkled stems that are evenly coloured.

Pasta Soup with Chicken Livers

A soup that can be served as either a first or main course. The fried chicken livers are so delicious that even if you do not normally like them, you will love them in this soup.

Serves 4–6

15ml/1 tbsp olive oil
knob of butter
4 garlic cloves, crushed
3 sprigs each fresh parsley, marjoram and sage, chopped
leaves from 1 fresh thyme sprig, chopped
5–6 fresh basil leaves, chopped
175g/6oz/⅔ cup chicken livers, thawed if frozen, cut into small pieces
15–30ml/1–2 tbsp dry white wine
2 × 300g/11oz cans condensed chicken consommé
225g/8oz/2 cups frozen peas
50g/2oz/½ cup small pasta shapes, e.g. farfalle
2–3 spring onions, diagonally sliced
salt and freshly ground black pepper
toasted slices of French bread, to serve

1 Heat the oil and butter in a frying pan, add the garlic and herbs, with salt and pepper to taste, and fry gently for a few minutes.

2 Add the livers, increase the heat to high and stir-fry for a few minutes until they change colour and become dry. Pour the wine over the livers, cook until the wine evaporates, then remove the pan from the heat. Season to taste.

3 Pour both cans of condensed chicken consommé into a large saucepan and add water as directed on the labels. Add an extra can of water, season to taste and bring to the boil.

4 Add the peas to the pan and simmer for about 5 minutes, then add the pasta and bring the soup back to the boil, stirring. Simmer, stirring frequently, until the pasta is just *al dente*: about 5 minutes or according to the instructions on the packet.

5 Add the fried chicken livers and the spring onions, and heat through for 2–3 minutes. Taste and adjust the seasoning as necessary. Serve hot in warm bowls, accompanied by toasted slices of French bread.

Chinese Chicken Soup

Sweetcorn, spring onions, carrots and egg noodles combine with chicken to create this tasty Eastern-style soup.

Serves 4–6

15ml/1 tbsp sesame oil
4 spring onions, roughly chopped
225g/8oz chicken breast fillets, skinned and cut into small cubes
1.2 litres/2 pints/5 cups Chicken Stock
15ml/1 tbsp soy sauce
115g/4oz/1 cup frozen sweetcorn kernels
115g/4oz medium thread egg noodles
1 carrot
salt and freshly ground black pepper
prawn crackers, to serve (optional)

1 Heat the oil in a large, heavy-based saucepan, add the spring onions and chicken and fry, stirring constantly, until the meat has browned all over.

2 Pour in the stock and soy sauce, and bring to the boil. Stir in the sweetcorn.

3 Add the noodles, breaking them up roughly, and simmer for a few minutes. Season to taste with salt and pepper.

4 Thinly slice the carrot lengthways. Use small cutters to stamp out shapes from the slices of carrot. Add them to the soup and simmer for 5 minutes.

5 Pour the soup into warmed bowls and serve, accompanied by prawn crackers if you wish.

Chicken & Buckwheat Noodle Soup

This satisfying soup is given body with buckwheat or soba noodles, which are widely enjoyed in Japan.

Serves 4

225g/8oz chicken breast fillets, skinned
120ml/4fl oz/ ½ cup soy sauce
15ml/1 tbsp sake
1 litre/1¾ pints/4 cups Chicken Stock
2 pieces young leek, cut into 2.5cm/1in pieces
175g/6oz spinach leaves
300g/11oz buckwheat or soba noodles
sesame seeds, toasted, to garnish

1 Slice the chicken diagonally into bite-size pieces. Combine the soy sauce and sake in a saucepan and bring to a simmer. Add the chicken and cook gently for about 3 minutes until it is tender. Keep hot.

2 Bring the stock to the boil in another saucepan. Add the leek and simmer for 3 minutes, then add the spinach. Remove from the heat but keep warm.

3 Cook the noodles in a large saucepan of boiling water until just tender, following the instructions on the packet.

4 Drain the noodles and divide among warmed individual serving bowls. Ladle the hot soup into the bowls, then add a portion of chicken to each. Serve at once, sprinkled with sesame seeds.

Cook's Tip

Sake is a Japanese rice wine widely available from supermarkets and specialist stores. Do not confuse it with rice vinegar.

Chicken Soup with Garlic Croûtons

A thick, chunky chicken and vegetable soup served with crisp fried croûtons: a meal in itself.

Serves 4

4 chicken thighs, boned and skinned
15g/½oz/1 tbsp butter
2 small leeks, thinly sliced
15ml/1 tbsp long-grain rice
900ml/1½ pints/3¾ cups Chicken Stock
15ml/1 tbsp mixed chopped fresh parsley and mint
salt and freshly ground black pepper
crusty bread, to serve (optional)

For the garlic croûtons

30ml/2 tbsp olive oil
1 garlic clove, crushed
4 slices bread, cut into cubes

1 Cut the chicken into 1cm/½in cubes. Melt the butter in a saucepan, add the leeks and cook them until they are tender. Add the rice and chicken, and cook for a further 2 minutes.

2 Pour in the stock, then cover and simmer for 15–20 minutes or until the rice is cooked and the chicken is tender.

3 To make the garlic croûtons, heat the oil in a large frying pan. Add the crushed garlic clove and bread cubes, and cook until golden brown, stirring all the time to prevent burning. Drain on kitchen paper and sprinkle with a pinch of salt.

4 Add the parsley and mint to the soup and adjust the seasoning to taste. Serve hot in warmed bowls and hand the garlic croûtons round separately for sprinkling over the soup. Accompany with crusty bread if you wish.

Cock-a-Leekie

This traditional soup recipe – it is known from as long ago as 1598 – originally included beef as well as chicken. In the past it would have been made from an old cock bird, hence the name.

Serves 4–6

1.2 litres/2 pints/5 cups Chicken Stock
2 chicken portions, about 275g/10oz each
1 bouquet garni
4 leeks
8–12 prunes, soaked overnight in water
salt and freshly ground black pepper
buttered soft rolls, to serve

1 Bring the stock to the boil in a large saucepan. Add the chicken and bouquet garni, and simmer gently for 40 minutes.

2 Cut the white part of the leeks into 2.5cm/1in slices and thinly slice a little of the green part. Drain the prunes.

3 Add the white parts of the leeks and the prunes to the saucepan and cook gently for 20 minutes, then add the green part of the leeks and cook for a further 10–15 minutes.

4 Discard the bouquet garni. Remove the chicken from the pan, discard the skin and bones, and chop the flesh. Return the chicken to the pan and season the soup to taste. Heat the soup through, then serve hot with buttered soft rolls.

Cook's Tip

Bouquet garni traditionally consists of fresh herbs – usually a bay leaf, thyme sprigs and parsley stalks. Ready-made dried bouquets garnis are also available.

Chicken Vermicelli Soup

This soup is very quick and easy – you can add all sorts of extra ingredients to vary the taste, using up leftovers.

Serves 4–6

3 large eggs
30ml/2 tbsp chopped fresh coriander or parsley
1.5 litres/2½ pints/6¼ cups Chicken Stock or canned consommé
115g/4oz/1 cup dried vermicelli or angel hair pasta
115g/4oz cooked chicken breast, sliced
salt and freshly ground black pepper

1 First make the egg shreds. Whisk the eggs together in a small bowl and stir in the coriander or parsley.

2 Heat a small, non-stick frying pan and pour in 30–45ml/ 2–3 tbsp egg, swirling to cover the base evenly. Cook until set. Repeat until all the mixture is used up.

3 Roll up each egg pancake and slice thinly into shreds using a sharp knife. Set aside until serving.

4 Bring the stock or consommé to the boil in a large saucepan and add the pasta, breaking it up into short lengths. Cook for 3–5 minutes until the pasta is almost tender, then add the chicken, salt and pepper.

5 Heat through for 2–3 minutes, then stir in the egg shreds. Serve immediately in warmed bowls.

Variation

To make a Thai variation of this soup, use Chinese rice noodles instead of pasta. Stir 2.5ml/ ½ tsp dried lemon grass, two small whole fresh chillies and 60ml/4 tbsp coconut milk into the chicken stock or consommé. Add four sliced spring onions and chopped fresh coriander.

Chicken Broth with Cheese Toasts

A really filling, hearty soup that makes excellent use of a chicken carcass and vegetables left over from the weekend roast.

Serves 4

1 roasted chicken carcass
1 onion, quartered
2 celery sticks, finely chopped
1 garlic clove, crushed
a few fresh parsley sprigs
2 bay leaves
225g/8oz can chopped tomatoes
200g/7oz canned chick-peas
30–45ml/2–3 tbsp leftover vegetables, chopped, or 1 large carrot, finely chopped
15ml/1 tbsp chopped fresh parsley
2 slices toast
25g/1oz/ ¼ cup grated cheese
salt and freshly ground black pepper

1 Pick off any little bits of flesh from the chicken carcass, especially from the underside where there is often some very tasty dark meat. Set aside.

2 Break the carcass in half and place in a large saucepan with the onion, half the celery, the garlic, parsley sprigs, bay leaves and sufficient water to cover. Cover the pan, bring to the boil and simmer for about 30 minutes or until you are left with about 300ml/ ½ pint/1¼ cups of liquid.

3 Strain the stock and return to the pan. Add the chicken flesh, the remaining celery, the tomatoes, chick-peas (and their liquid), leftover vegetables or carrot and chopped parsley. Season to taste and simmer for another 7–10 minutes.

4 Meanwhile, sprinkle the toast with the cheese and grill until bubbling, then cut into fingers or triangles. Serve the soup hot in warmed bowls with the cheese toasts floating on top or handed separately.

Sweetcorn & Chicken Soup

This popular classic Chinese soup is delicious and very easy to make.

Serves 4–6

115g/4oz chicken breast fillet, skinned and cubed
10ml/2 tsp light soy sauce
15ml/1 tbsp Chinese rice wine
5ml/1 tsp cornflour
60ml/4 tbsp cold water
5ml/1 tsp sesame oil
30ml/2 tbsp groundnut oil
5ml/1 tsp grated fresh root ginger
1 litre/1¾ pints/4 cups Chicken Stock
425g/15oz can creamed sweetcorn
225g/8oz can sweetcorn kernels
2 eggs, beaten
2–3 spring onions, green parts only, cut into tiny rounds
salt and freshly ground black pepper

1 Mince the chicken in a food processor, taking care not to over-process. Transfer the chicken to a bowl and stir in the soy sauce, rice wine, cornflour, water, sesame oil and seasoning. Cover and leave for about 15 minutes to absorb the flavours.

2 Heat a wok over a medium heat. Add the groundnut oil and swirl it around. Add the ginger and stir-fry for a few seconds. Add the stock, creamed sweetcorn and sweetcorn kernels. Bring to just below boiling point.

3 Spoon about 90ml/6 tbsp of the hot liquid into the chicken mixture until it forms a smooth paste, and stir. Return to the wok. Slowly bring to the boil, stirring constantly, then simmer for 2–3 minutes until cooked.

4 Pour the beaten eggs into the soup in a slow, steady stream, using a fork or chopsticks to stir the top of the soup in a figure-of-eight pattern. The eggs should set in lacy shreds. Serve immediately in warmed individual soup bowls with the spring onions sprinkled over.

Pumpkin, Rice & Chicken Soup

A warm, comforting soup which, despite the spice and basmati rice, is quintessentially English. For an even more substantial meal, add a little extra rice and make sure you use all the chicken from the stock.

Serves 4

1 pumpkin wedge, about 450g/1lb
15ml/1 tbsp sunflower oil
25g/1oz/2 tbsp butter
6 green cardamom pods
2 leeks, chopped
115g/4oz/½ cup basmati rice, soaked in water
350ml/12fl oz/1½ cups milk
salt and freshly ground black pepper
generous strips of pared orange rind, to garnish
Granary or wholemeal bread, to serve

For the chicken stock

2 chicken quarters
1 onion, quartered
2 carrots, chopped
1 celery stick, chopped
6–8 peppercorns
900ml/1½ pints/3¾ cups water

1 First, to make the chicken stock, place the chicken quarters, onion, carrots, celery and peppercorns in a large saucepan. Pour in the water and bring to the boil over a moderate heat. Skim the surface if necessary, then lower the heat, cover and simmer gently for 1 hour.

2 Strain the chicken stock into a clean, large bowl, discarding the vegetables. Skin and bone one or both chicken pieces and cut the flesh into strips. (If not using both chicken pieces for the soup, reserve the other piece for another recipe.)

3 Peel the pumpkin, and remove and discard all the seeds and pith, so that you have about 350g/12oz flesh. Cut the flesh into 2.5cm/1in cubes.

4 Heat the oil and butter in a saucepan and fry the cardamom pods for 2–3 minutes until slightly swollen. Add the leeks and pumpkin. Cook, stirring, for 3–4 minutes over a medium heat, then lower the heat, cover and sweat for 5 minutes more or until the pumpkin is quite tender, stirring once or twice.

5 Measure 600ml/1 pint/2½ cups of the stock and add to the pumpkin mixture. Bring to the boil, lower the heat, cover and simmer for 10–15 minutes until the pumpkin is soft.

6 Pour the remaining stock into a measuring jug and make up with water to 300ml/½ pint/1¼ cups. Drain the rice and put it into a saucepan. Pour in the stock, bring to the boil, then simmer for about 10 minutes until the rice is tender. Add seasoning to taste.

7 Remove the cardamom pods, then process the soup in a blender or food processor until smooth. Pour back into a clean saucepan and stir in the milk, chicken and rice (with any stock that has not been absorbed). Heat until simmering. Pour into warmed bowls and garnish with the strips of pared orange rind and freshly ground black pepper. Serve with Granary or wholemeal bread.

Chicken Soup with Lockshen

To achieve the best results with this traditional Jewish dish, follow two rules: make it the day before and try to find a boiling fowl, which has much more flavour than a roasting bird.

Serves 6–8

3kg/6½lb boiling chicken, including the giblets, but not the liver
1 litre/1¾ pints/4 cups cold water
2 onions, halved
2 carrots
5 celery sticks
handful of fine vermicelli (lockshen), about 115g/4oz
salt and freshly ground black pepper
fresh bread, to serve (optional)

1 Put the chicken into a very large saucepan, together with the giblets. Add the water and bring to the boil over a high heat. Skim off the white froth that comes to the top and then add the halved onions, the carrots and celery. Season to taste with ground black pepper only.

2 Bring the liquid to the boil again, then turn the heat to low, cover and simmer for at least 2 hours. Keep an eye on the water level and add a little more as needed so that the chicken is always covered.

3 When the chicken is tender, remove from the pan and take the meat off the bones, reserving it for another use. Put the bones back in the soup and continue cooking for a further 1 hour. There should be at least 1 litre/1¾ pints/4 cups of soup.

4 Strain the soup into a large bowl and chill overnight. When it is quite cold, it may form a jelly and a pale layer of fat will have settled on the top. Remove the fat with a spoon and discard.

5 Bring the soup to the boil again, season to taste and add the vermicelli. Boil for about 8 minutes and serve in warmed large bowls, with fresh bread, if using.

Chicken Soup with Matzo Kleis Balls

Another classic Jewish recipe, in which herby dumplings are cooked in delicious home-made soup.

Serves 4

2 matzot (sheets of unleavened bread)
30ml/2 tbsp oil
1 onion, chopped
handful of parsley
2 eggs
pinch of ground ginger
15–30ml/1–2 tbsp medium ground matzo meal
1 litre/1¾ pints/4 cups Chicken Soup
salt and freshly ground black pepper

1 Soak the matzot in cold water for about 5 minutes, and then drain and squeeze them dry.

2 Heat the oil in a frying pan and fry the onion until golden. Chop the parsley, reserving a few sprigs for the garnish. Whisk the eggs slightly.

3 Mix together the soaked matzot, fried onion, parsley and eggs. Season with salt, pepper and ginger, and add about 15ml/1 tbsp matzo meal. Chill for at least 1 hour.

4 Bring the soup to the boil in a large saucepan. Roll the dumpling mixture into small balls, drop them into the fast-boiling soup and cook for about 20 minutes. Serve the soup in warmed bowls, garnished with the reserved parsley.

Cook's Tip

You can make the dumplings well in advance, but they should be kept chilled. They also freeze well, so it is a good idea to make a double quantity, and cook half and freeze half. To use frozen dumplings, leave them to defrost for about 1 hour before cooking in the soup.

Chicken Soup with Vermicelli

This traditional Moroccan soup is injected with an extra burst of flavour in the form of lemon, parsley, coriander and saffron just before serving.

Serves 4–6

30ml/2 tbsp sunflower oil
15g/½oz/1 tbsp butter
1 onion, chopped
2 chicken legs or breasts, halved or quartered
seasoned flour, for dusting
2 carrots, cut into 4cm/1½in pieces
1 parsnip, cut into 4cm/1½in pieces
1.5 litres/2½ pints/6¼ cups Chicken Stock
1 cinnamon stick
good pinch of paprika
pinch of saffron
2 egg yolks
juice of ½ lemon
30ml/2 tbsp chopped fresh coriander
30ml/2 tbsp chopped fresh parsley
150g/5oz vermicelli
salt and freshly ground black pepper
Moroccan bread, to serve

1 Heat the oil and butter in a saucepan or flameproof casserole and fry the onion for 3–4 minutes until softened. Dust the chicken pieces in seasoned flour, add to the pan or casserole and fry gently until evenly browned.

2 Transfer the chicken to a plate and add the carrots and parsnip to the pan. Cook over a gentle heat for 3–4 minutes, stirring frequently, then return the chicken to the pan. Add the chicken stock, cinnamon stick and paprika, and season to taste with salt and pepper.

3 Bring the soup to the boil, cover and simmer for 1 hour or until the vegetables are very tender.

4 While the soup is cooking, blend the saffron in 30ml/2 tbsp boiling water. Beat the egg yolks with the lemon juice in a separate bowl and add the chopped coriander and parsley. When the saffron water has cooled, stir into the egg and lemon mixture until thoroughly blended.

5 When the vegetables are tender, transfer the chicken to a plate. Spoon away any excess fat from the soup, then increase the heat a little and stir in the vermicelli. Cook for 5–6 minutes until the noodles are tender.

6 Meanwhile, remove the skin from the chicken and, if liked, bone and chop the meat into bite-size pieces. If you prefer, simply skin the chicken and leave the pieces whole.

7 When the vermicelli is cooked, reduce the heat and stir in the chicken pieces and the egg, lemon and saffron mixture. Cook over a very low heat for 1–2 minutes, stirring all the time. Adjust the seasoning and serve with Moroccan bread.

Rich Minestrone

A special minestrone made with chicken. Served with crusty Italian bread, it makes a hearty meal.

Serves 4–6

15ml/1 tbsp olive oil
2 chicken thighs
3 lean bacon rashers, rinded and chopped
1 onion, finely chopped
a few fresh basil leaves, shredded
a few fresh rosemary leaves, finely chopped
15ml/1 tbsp chopped fresh flat-leaf parsley
2 potatoes, cut into 1cm/½in cubes
1 large carrot, cut into 1cm/½in cubes
2 small courgettes, cut into 1cm/½in cubes
1–2 celery sticks, cut into 1cm/½in cubes
1 litre/1¾ pints/4 cups Chicken Stock
200g/7oz/1¾ cups frozen peas
115g/4oz/1 cup stellette or other tiny soup pasta
salt and freshly ground black pepper
coarsely shaved Parmesan cheese, and fresh basil leaves, to garnish

1 Heat the oil in a large saucepan and fry the chicken for about 5 minutes on each side. Remove and set aside. Lower the heat, add the bacon, onion, shredded basil, rosemary and parsley to the pan and stir well. Cook gently, stirring constantly, for about 5 minutes. Add all the vegetables except the frozen peas and cook for 5–7 minutes more, stirring frequently.

2 Return the chicken thighs to the pan, add the stock and bring to the boil. Cover and cook over a low heat for 35–40 minutes, stirring the soup occasionally.

3 Remove the chicken thighs using a slotted spoon. Stir the peas and pasta into the soup, and bring back to the boil. Simmer, stirring frequently, until the pasta is *al dente*: 7–8 minutes or according to the instructions on the packet.

4 Meanwhile, skin the chicken and cut the meat into 1cm/½in pieces. Return it to the soup and heat through. Adjust the seasoning and serve, sprinkled with Parmesan and basil leaves.

Chicken, Tomato & Christophene Soup

An unusual soup from Africa which includes smoked haddock and christophene, a vegetable available from ethnic food shops.

Serves 4

225g/8oz chicken breast fillets, skinned
1 garlic clove, crushed
pinch of freshly grated nutmeg
25g/1oz/2 tbsp butter or margarine
½ onion, finely chopped
15ml/1 tbsp tomato purée
400g/14oz can tomatoes, puréed
1.2 litres/2 pints/5 cups Chicken Stock
1 fresh chilli, seeded and chopped
1 christophene, peeled and diced, about 350g/12oz
5ml/1 tsp dried oregano
2.5ml/ ½ tsp dried thyme
50g/2oz smoked haddock fillet, skinned and diced
salt and freshly ground black pepper
fresh snipped chives, to garnish

1 Dice the chicken, place in a bowl and season with salt, pepper, garlic and nutmeg. Mix well to flavour the chicken and then set aside for about 30 minutes.

2 Melt the butter or margarine in a large saucepan, add the chicken and sauté over a moderate heat for 5–6 minutes. Stir in the onion and fry gently for a further 5 minutes until the onion is slightly softened.

3 Add the tomato purée, puréed tomatoes, stock, chilli, christophene and herbs. Bring to the boil, cover and simmer gently for 35 minutes until the christophene is tender.

4 Add the smoked fish and simmer for a further 5 minutes or until the fish is cooked through. Taste the soup and adjust the seasoning as necessary. Pour into warmed soup bowls, garnish with a scattering of snipped chives and serve.

Tortilla Soup

You can make this Mexican-style soup as mild or as fiery as you wish.

Serves 4–6

vegetable oil, for frying
1 onion, finely chopped
1 large garlic clove, crushed
2 medium tomatoes, peeled, seeded and chopped
2.5ml/ ½ tsp salt
1.75 litres/3 pints/7½ cups Chicken Stock
1 carrot, diced
1 small courgette, diced
1 chicken breast fillet, skinned, cooked and shredded
25–50g/1–2oz canned green chillies, chopped

For the garnish

4 corn tortillas
1 small ripe avocado
2 spring onions, chopped
chopped fresh coriander
grated Cheddar cheese (optional)

1 Heat 15ml/1 tbsp oil in a large saucepan. Add the onion and garlic, and cook over a medium heat for 5–8 minutes until just softened. Add the tomatoes and salt, and cook for 5 minutes more. Stir in the stock. Bring to the boil, then lower the heat and simmer, covered, for about 15 minutes.

2 Meanwhile, to make the garnish, trim the tortillas into squares, then cut them into strips. Pour 1cm/ ½in depth of oil into a frying pan and heat until hot but not smoking. Add the tortilla strips, in batches, and fry until just beginning to brown, turning occasionally. Remove with a slotted spoon and drain on kitchen paper.

3 Add the carrot to the soup. Cook, covered, for 10 minutes. Add the courgette, shredded chicken and green chillies, and continue cooking, uncovered, for about 5 minutes until the vegetables are just tender.

4 Meanwhile, peel and stone the avocado. Cut the flesh into fine dice. Divide the tortilla strips among warmed soup bowls. Sprinkle with the avocado. Ladle in the soup, then scatter the spring onions and coriander on top. Serve immediately, with grated Cheddar if desired.

Chicken & Almond Soup

This rich and creamy soup makes an excellent appetizer for an Indian meal or, served with naan bread, a satisfying lunch or supper dish.

Serves 4

75g/3oz/6 tbsp unsalted butter
1 medium leek, chopped
2.5ml/ ½ tsp grated fresh root ginger
75g/3oz/1 cup ground almonds
5ml/1 tsp salt
2.5ml/ ½ tsp crushed black peppercorns
1 fresh green chilli, chopped
1 medium carrot, sliced
50g/2oz/ ½ cup frozen peas
115g/4oz chicken, skinned, boned and cubed
15ml/1 tbsp chopped fresh coriander
450ml/¾ pint/scant 2 cups water
250ml/8fl oz/1 cup single cream
4 coriander sprigs, to garnish

1 Melt the butter in a large karahi or deep, round-based frying pan and sauté the leek with the ginger until soft.

2 Lower the heat and add the ground almonds, salt, peppercorns, chilli, carrot, peas and chicken. Fry for about 10 minutes or until the chicken is completely cooked, stirring constantly. Add the chopped coriander.

3 Remove from the heat and allow to cool slightly. Transfer the mixture to a food processor or blender and process for about 1½ minutes. Pour in the water and process for a further 30 seconds.

4 Pour the soup back into the saucepan and bring to the boil, stirring occasionally. Once it has boiled, lower the heat and gradually stir in the cream. Cook gently for a further 2 minutes, stirring occasionally.

5 Serve the soup immediately in warmed bowls, garnished with the fresh coriander sprigs.

Spicy Chicken & Mushroom Soup

A creamy chicken soup which makes a hearty meal for a winter's night. Serve it piping hot with lots of fresh garlic bread.

Serves 4

225g/8oz chicken, skinned and boned
75g/3oz/6 tbsp unsalted butter
2.5ml/ ½ tsp crushed garlic
5ml/1 tsp garam masala
5ml/1 tsp crushed black peppercorns
5ml/1 tsp salt
1.5ml/ ¼ tsp grated nutmeg
1 medium leek, sliced
75g/3oz/generous 1 cup mushrooms, sliced
50g/2oz/ ⅓ cup sweetcorn kernels
300ml/ ½ pint/1 ¼ cups water
250ml/8fl oz/1 cup single cream
15ml/1 tbsp chopped fresh coriander
5ml/1 tsp crushed dried red chillies (optional)

1 Cut the chicken pieces into very fine, even-size strips.

2 Melt the butter in a medium saucepan. Lower the heat slightly and add the garlic and garam masala. Lower the heat even further and add the black peppercorns, salt and nutmeg. Finally add the chicken pieces, leek, mushrooms and sweetcorn, and cook for 5–7 minutes or until the chicken is cooked through, stirring constantly.

3 Remove from the heat and allow to cool slightly. Transfer three quarters of the mixture into a food processor or blender. Add the water and process for about 1 minute.

4 Pour the resulting purée back into the saucepan with the rest of the mixture and bring to the boil over a medium heat. Lower the heat and stir in the cream.

5 Add the fresh coriander. Taste the soup and adjust the seasoning as necessary. Serve hot, garnished with the crushed red chillies if wished.

Chicken Wonton Soup with Prawns

This Indonesian version of wonton soup is more luxurious than the more widely known basic recipe and is almost a meal in itself.

Serves 4

300g/11oz chicken breast fillet, skinned
200g/7oz prawn tails, fresh or cooked
5ml/1 tsp finely chopped fresh root ginger
2 spring onions, finely chopped
1 egg
10ml/2 tsp oyster sauce (optional)
15ml/1 tbsp cornflour
1 packet wonton skins
900ml/1½ pints/3¾ cups Chicken Stock
¼ cucumber, peeled and diced
salt and freshly ground black pepper

For the garnish

1 spring onion, roughly shredded
4 sprigs coriander leaves
1 tomato, peeled, seeded and diced

1 Place the chicken breast, 150g/5oz of the prawn tails, the ginger and spring onions in a food processor and process for 2–3 minutes. Add the egg, oyster sauce (if using) and seasoning and process briefly. Set aside.

2 Mix the cornflour with a little water to form a thin paste. Place eight wonton skins at a time on a work surface, moisten the edges with the cornflour paste and place 2.5ml/ ½ tsp of the filling in the centre of each. Fold in half and pinch to seal.

3 Bring the chicken stock to the boil, add the remaining prawn tails and the cucumber, and simmer for 3–4 minutes. Add the wontons and simmer to warm through.

4 Ladle the soup into warmed bowls and garnish with shredded spring onion, coriander leaves and diced tomato. Serve immediately in warmed bowls.

Chicken Mulligatawny

Using the original pepper water – mulla-ga-tani – this famous dish was created by the non-vegetarian chefs during the British Raj and imported to the United Kingdom.

Serves 4–6

900g/2lb chicken, boned, skinned and cubed
600ml/1 pint/2½ cups water
6 green cardamom pods
5cm/2in cinnamon stick
4–6 curry leaves
15ml/1 tbsp ground coriander
5ml/1 tsp ground cumin
2.5ml/½ tsp ground turmeric
3 garlic cloves, crushed
12 peppercorns
4 cloves
1 onion, finely chopped
115g/4oz coconut cream block
juice of 2 lemons
salt
deep-fried onions and chopped fresh coriander, to garnish

1 Place the chicken in a large saucepan with the water and cook until tender. Skim the surface, then strain, reserving the stock. Keep the chicken warm.

2 Return the stock to the pan and reheat. Add the cardamom, cinnamon, curry leaves, ground coriander, cumin and turmeric, garlic, peppercorns, cloves and onion. Add the creamed coconut, grated or chopped if you wish, the lemon juice and salt to taste. Simmer for 10–15 minutes.

3 Strain the soup again and return the chicken to the pan. Simmer for a few minutes to reheat thoroughly.

4 Taste the soup and adjust the seasoning as necessary. Divide among warmed bowls, garnish with deep-fried onions and chopped fresh coriander, and serve.

Thai-style Chicken Soup

A fragrant blend of coconut milk, lemon grass, ginger and lime makes a delicious soup, with just a hint of chilli.

Serves 4

5ml/1 tsp oil
1–2 fresh red chillies, seeded and chopped
2 garlic cloves, crushed
1 large leek, thinly sliced
600ml/1 pint/2½ cups Chicken Stock
400ml/14fl oz/1⅔ cups coconut milk
450g/1lb boneless, skinless chicken thighs, cut into bite-size pieces
30ml/2 tbsp fish sauce
1 lemon grass stalk, split
2.5cm/1in piece fresh root ginger, peeled and finely chopped
5ml/1 tsp sugar
4 kaffir lime leaves (optional)
75g/3oz/¾ cup frozen peas, thawed
45ml/3 tbsp chopped fresh coriander

1 Heat the oil in a large saucepan, and cook the chillies and garlic for about 2 minutes. Add the leek and cook for a further 2 minutes.

2 Stir in the stock and coconut milk, and bring to the boil.

3 Add the chicken, with the fish sauce, lemon grass, ginger, sugar and lime leaves, if using. Simmer, covered, for 15 minutes or until the chicken is tender, stirring occasionally.

4 Add the peas and cook for a further 3 minutes. Remove the lemon grass and stir in the coriander just before serving.

Cook's Tip

Kaffir lime leaves are aromatic and used frequently in South-east Asian cooking. They are available from specialist shops.

Spiced Vegetable Soup with Chicken & Prawns

Aubergine, French beans, red pepper and cabbage, succulent chicken and prawns are given a truly exotic flavour with a fabulous mixture of spices.

Serves 6–8

1 onion
2 garlic cloves, crushed
1 fresh red or green chilli, seeded and sliced
1cm/½in cube terasi
3 macadamia nuts or 6 almonds
1cm/½in piece galangal, peeled and sliced
5ml/1 tsp sugar
oil, for frying
225g/8oz chicken breast fillet, skinned and cut into 1cm/½in cubes
300ml/½ pint/1¼ cups coconut milk
1.2 litres/2 pints/5 cups Chicken Stock
1 aubergine, diced
225g/8oz French beans, chopped
small wedge of white cabbage, shredded
1 red pepper, seeded and finely sliced
115g/4oz cooked peeled prawns
salt and freshly ground black pepper

1 Halve the onion; slice one half and set aside; cut the other half in two and place in a mortar. Add the garlic, chilli, terasi, nuts, galangal and sugar, and grind to a paste using a pestle. Alternatively, grind in a food processor.

2 Heat a wok, add the oil and fry the paste, without browning, until it gives off a rich aroma. Add the reserved onion and chicken, and cook for 3–4 minutes. Stir in the coconut milk and stock. Bring to the boil and simmer for a few minutes.

3 Add the diced aubergine to the soup, with the beans, and cook for only a few minutes, until the beans are almost cooked.

4 A few minutes before serving, stir in the cabbage, red pepper and prawns. The vegetables should be cooked so that they are still crunchy and the prawns merely heated through. Taste the soup and adjust the seasoning as necessary. Serve in warmed bowls.

Ginger, Chicken & Coconut Soup

The ginger flavour in this aromatic soup is provided by galangal, which belongs to the same family as the more familiar fresh root ginger.

Serves 4–6

750ml/1¼ pints/3 cups coconut milk
475ml/16fl oz/2 cups Chicken Stock
4 lemon grass stalks, bruised and chopped
2.5cm/1in piece galangal, thinly sliced
10 black peppercorns, crushed
10 kaffir lime leaves, torn
300g/11oz boneless chicken, cut into thin strips
115g/4oz/1½ cups button mushrooms
50g/2oz/½ cup baby sweetcorn
60ml/4 tbsp lime juice
45ml/3 tbsp fish sauce

For the garnish

2 fresh red chillies, chopped
a few spring onions, chopped
fresh coriander leaves

1 Bring the coconut milk and chicken stock to the boil in a medium saucepan. Add the lemon grass, galangal, peppercorns and half the kaffir lime leaves, reduce the heat and simmer gently for 10 minutes.

2 Strain the stock into a clean pan. Return to the heat, then add the chicken, button mushrooms and baby sweetcorn. Simmer for about 5–7 minutes or until the chicken is cooked.

3 Stir in the lime juice, fish sauce to taste and the rest of the kaffir lime leaves.

4 Serve the soup hot in warmed bowls, garnished with chopped red chillies, spring onions and coriander.

Chiang Mai Noodle Soup

A signature dish of the Thai city of Chiang Mai, this delicious noodle soup, in fact, has Burmese origins.

Serves 4–6

600ml/1 pint/2½ cups coconut milk
30ml/2 tbsp red curry paste
5ml/1 tsp ground turmeric
450g/1lb chicken thighs, boned and cut into bite-size chunks
600ml/1 pint/2½ cups Chicken Stock
60ml/4 tbsp fish sauce
15ml/1 tbsp dark soy sauce
juice of ½–1 lime
450g/1lb fresh egg noodles, blanched briefly in boiling water
salt and freshly ground black pepper

For the garnish

3 spring onions, chopped
4 fresh red chillies, chopped
4 shallots, chopped
60ml/4 tbsp sliced pickled mustard leaves, rinsed
30ml/2 tbsp fried sliced garlic
fresh coriander leaves
4 fried noodle nests (optional)

1 Pour about one third of the coconut milk into a large saucepan and bring to the boil, stirring often with a wooden spoon until it separates.

2 Add the curry paste and ground turmeric, stir to mix completely and cook gently until fragrant.

3 Add the chicken and stir-fry for about 2 minutes, ensuring that all the chunks are coated with the paste.

4 Add the remaining coconut milk, the chicken stock, fish sauce and soy sauce. Season with salt and pepper to taste. Simmer over a low heat for 7–10 minutes. Remove from the heat and stir in the lime juice.

5 Reheat the noodles in boiling water, drain and divide among warmed individual bowls. Divide the chicken between the bowls and ladle in the hot soup. Top each bowl with a few of each of the garnishes and serve.

Turkey & Lentil Soup

A fairly substantial soup, ideal for a cold day and a great way of using up leftover cooked turkey, or other poultry, at the end of the festive season.

Serves 4

25g/1oz/2 tbsp butter or margarine
1 large carrot, chopped
1 onion, chopped
1 leek, white part only, chopped
1 celery stick, chopped
115g/4oz/1½ cups mushrooms, chopped
45ml/3 tbsp dry white wine
1 litre/1¾ pints/4 cups Chicken Stock
10ml/2 tsp dried thyme
1 bay leaf
115g/4oz/½ cup brown or green lentils
225g/8oz cooked turkey, diced
salt and freshly ground black pepper

1 Melt the butter or margarine in a large saucepan. Add the carrot, onion, leek, celery and mushrooms. Cook for 3–5 minutes until the vegetables are softened.

2 Stir in the wine and chicken stock. Bring to the boil and skim off any foam that rises to the surface. Add the thyme and bay leaf. Reduce the heat, cover and simmer for 30 minutes.

3 Add the lentils and continue cooking, covered, for 30–40 minutes more until they are just tender. Stir the soup from time to time.

4 Stir in the diced turkey and season to taste with salt and pepper. Cook until the turkey is just heated through. Ladle the soup into warmed bowls and serve hot.

Cook's Tip
Lentils are one of the few pulses that do not need to be soaked before cooking. Puy lentils have the best flavour and retain their shape well.

Oriental Duck Consommé

Though a little time-consuming to make, this wonderful soup, light and rich at the same time, is well worth the effort.

Serves 4

1 duck carcass (raw or cooked), plus 2 legs or any giblets, trimmed of as much fat as possible
1 large onion, unpeeled, with root end trimmed
2 carrots, cut into 5cm/2in pieces
1 parsnip, cut into 5cm/2in pieces
1 leek, cut into 5cm/2in pieces
2–4 garlic cloves, crushed
2.5cm/1in piece fresh root ginger, peeled and sliced
15ml/1 tbsp black peppercorns
4–6 fresh thyme sprigs
1 small bunch fresh coriander (6–8 sprigs), leaves and stems separated

For the garnish

1 small carrot
1 small leek, halved lengthways
4–6 shiitake mushrooms, thinly sliced
soy sauce
2 spring onions, thinly sliced
shredded Chinese leaves
freshly ground black pepper

1 Put the duck carcass, the legs or giblets, the vegetables, spices, thyme and coriander stems in a large saucepan, cover with cold water and bring to the boil over a medium-high heat, skimming any foam that rises to the surface.

2 Reduce the heat and simmer gently for 1½–2 hours, then strain through a muslin-lined sieve into a bowl.

3 Allow the stock to cool, then chill for several hours or overnight. Skim off any congealed fat and blot the surface with kitchen paper to remove any traces of fat.

4 To make the garnish, cut the carrot and leek into julienne strips. Place in a large saucepan with the mushrooms. Pour over the stock, add a few dashes of soy sauce and some pepper. Bring to the boil, skimming off any foam. Stir in the spring onions and Chinese leaves. Ladle into warmed bowls, sprinkle with coriander leaves and serve.

Chicken Liver Pâté

This is a really quick and simple pâté to make, yet it has a delicious, rich flavour. It is sealed with clarified butter, which helps maintain its freshness.

Serves 6

50g/2oz butter
1 onion, finely chopped
350g/12oz chicken livers, trimmed
60ml/4 tbsp medium sherry
25g/1oz full-fat soft cheese
15–30ml/1–2 tbsp lemon juice
2 hard-boiled eggs, shelled and chopped
50–75g/2–3oz/4–6 tbsp Clarified Butter
salt and freshly ground black pepper
bay leaves, to garnish
toast or savoury biscuits, to serve

1 Melt the butter in a frying pan. Add the onion and livers, and cook until the onion is soft and the livers are lightly browned and no longer pink in the centre.

2 Add the sherry and boil until reduced by half. Cool slightly.

3 Turn the mixture into a food processor or blender and add the soft cheese and 15ml/1 tbsp lemon juice. Process until thoroughly blended and smooth.

4 Add the hard-boiled eggs and blend briefly. Season with salt and pepper. Taste and add more lemon juice if liked.

5 Pack the liver pâté into a mould or into individual ramekins. Smooth the surface.

6 Spoon a layer of clarified butter over the surface of the pâté. Chill until firm and garnish with bay leaves. Serve at room temperature, with hot toast or savoury biscuits.

Clarified Butter

This is butter from which the milk solids have been removed.

Makes about 175g/6oz
225g/8oz butter

1 Put the butter in a heavy saucepan over a low heat. Melt gently. Skim off all the froth from the surface. You will then see a clear yellow layer on top of a milky layer: carefully pour the clear fat into a bowl or jug, leaving the milky residue in the pan.
2 Discard the milky residue, or add it to soups.

3 The clarified butter may be stored in the fridge for several weeks and for longer in the freezer.

Chicken Liver Pâté with Marsala

A more sophisticated version of chicken liver pâté which contains Marsala, a soft and pungent fortified wine from Sicily, and a generous quantity of garlic.

Serves 4–6

225g/8oz/1 cup butter, softened
350g/12oz chicken livers, trimmed
2 garlic cloves, crushed
15ml/1 tbsp Marsala
5ml/1 tsp chopped fresh sage
salt and freshly ground black pepper
8 sage leaves, to garnish
Melba toast, to serve

1 Melt 25g/1oz/2 tbsp of the butter in a frying pan, add the chicken livers and garlic, and fry over a medium heat for about 5 minutes or until the livers are lightly browned but still pink in the middle.

2 Transfer the livers to a blender or food processor, using a slotted spoon, and add the Marsala and chopped sage.

3 Melt 150g/5oz/10 tbsp of the remaining butter in the frying pan, stirring to loosen any sediment, then pour into the blender or processor and process until smooth. Season well.

4 Spoon the pâté into individual pots and smooth the surface. Melt the rest of the butter in a separate pan and pour over the pâtés. Garnish with sage leaves and chill until set. Serve with triangles of Melba toast.

Cook's Tip
Sage has a special affinity with liver. However, it is very powerfully flavoured and should be used sparingly.

Chicken & Pistachio Pâté

This version of a classic of French charcuterie can be made using a whole boned bird or chicken pieces.

Serves 10–12

900g/2lb boneless chicken meat
1 chicken breast fillet, about 175g/6oz, skinned
25g/1oz/ ½ cup fresh white breadcrumbs
120ml/4fl oz/½ cup whipping cream
1 egg white
4 spring onions, finely chopped
1 garlic clove, finely chopped
75g/3oz/½ cup cooked ham, cut into 1cm/½in cubes
50g/2oz/½ cup shelled pistachio nuts
45ml/3 tbsp chopped fresh tarragon
pinch of grated nutmeg
3.5ml/¾ tsp salt
7.5ml/1½ tsp freshly ground black pepper
oil, for greasing
green salad, to serve

1 Trim the chicken meat and cut into 5cm/2in cubes. Put in a food processor and pulse to chop the meat to a smooth purée, in two or three batches. Alternatively, pass the meat through the medium or fine blade of a mincer.

2 Preheat the oven to 180°C/350°F/Gas 4. Cut the chicken breast fillet into 1cm/ ½in cubes.

3 In a large mixing bowl, soak the breadcrumbs in the whipping cream. Add the puréed chicken, egg white, spring onions, garlic, ham, pistachio nuts, tarragon, nutmeg, salt and pepper.
Using a wooden spoon or your fingers, stir the mixture until very well combined.

4 Lay out a piece of foil about 45cm/18in long on a work surface and lightly brush oil on a 30cm/12in square in the centre. Spoon the chicken mixture on to the foil to form a log shape about 30cm/12in long and about 9cm/3½in thick. Bring together the long sides of the foil and fold over securely. Twist the ends and tie with string.

5 Transfer to a baking tray and bake for 1½ hours. Leave to cool, then chill overnight. Serve sliced with green salad.

Chicken Liver Mousse

This mousse makes an elegant yet easy first course. The onion marmalade makes a delicious accompaniment, along with a salad of bitter leaves.

Serves 6–8

175g/6oz/¾ cup butter, diced
1 small onion, finely chopped
1 garlic clove, finely chopped
450g/1lb chicken livers, trimmed
2.5ml/½ tsp dried thyme
30–45ml/2–3 tbsp brandy
salt and freshly ground black pepper

For the onion marmalade

25g/1oz/2 tbsp butter
450g/1lb red onions, thinly sliced
1 garlic clove, finely chopped
2.5ml/½ tsp dried thyme
30–45ml/2–3 tbsp raspberry or red wine vinegar
15–30ml/1–2 tbsp clear honey
40g/1½oz/¼ cup sultanas

1 In a heavy-based frying pan, melt 25g/1oz/2 tbsp of the butter over a medium heat. Add the onion and cook for 5–7 minutes until soft and golden, then add the chopped garlic and cook for 1 minute more.

2 Increase the heat to medium-high and add the chicken livers, thyme, salt and pepper. Cook for 3–5 minutes until the livers are coloured, stirring frequently; the livers should remain pink inside. Add the brandy and cook for a further minute.

3 Using a slotted spoon, transfer the livers to a food processor fitted with the metal blade. Pour in the cooking juices and process for 1 minute or until smooth, scraping down the sides once. With the machine running, add the remaining butter, a few pieces at a time, until it is incorporated.

4 Press the mousse mixture through a fine sieve with a wooden spoon or rubber spatula.

5 Line a 475ml/16fl oz/2 cup loaf tin with clear film, smoothing out as many wrinkles as possible. Pour the mousse mixture into the lined tin. Cool, then cover and chill until firm.

6 To make the onion marmalade, heat the butter in a heavy frying pan over a medium-low heat, add the onions, and cook for 20 minutes until softened and just coloured, stirring frequently. Stir in the garlic, thyme, vinegar, honey and sultanas and cook, covered, for 10–15 minutes until the onions are completely soft and jam-like, stirring occasionally. Spoon into a bowl and cool to room temperature.

7 To serve, dip the loaf tin into hot water for 5 seconds, wipe dry and invert on to a board. Lift off the tin, peel off the clear film and smooth the surface with a knife. Serve sliced with a little of the onion marmalade.

Cook's Tip

The mousse will keep for 3–4 days. If made ahead, cover and chill until ready to use. The onion marmalade can be made up to 2 days ahead and gently reheated over a low heat or in the microwave until just warm.

Chicken & Mushroom Terrine

Ideal as a starter or light lunch, this delicious dish proves that low-fat cooking need not sacrifice flavour.

Serves 4

2 shallots, chopped
175g/6oz/generous 2 cups mushrooms, chopped
45ml/3 tbsp Chicken Stock
2 chicken breast fillets, skinned and chopped
1 egg white
30ml/2 tbsp wholemeal breadcrumbs
30ml/2 tbsp chopped fresh parsley
30ml/2 tbsp chopped fresh sage
oil, for greasing
salt and freshly ground black pepper
fresh sage sprigs, to garnish
tomatoes, to serve

1 Preheat the oven to 180°C/350°F/Gas 4. Place the shallots, mushrooms and stock in a saucepan, and cook over a low heat, stirring occasionally, until the vegetables have softened and the mixture is dry.

2 Transfer to a food processor and add the chicken, egg white, breadcrumbs and seasoning, and chop coarsely. Add the chopped herbs and process briefly.

3 Spoon into a greased 900ml/1½ pint/3¾ cup ovenproof terrine dish and smooth the surface. Cover with foil and bake for 35–40 minutes until the juices are no longer pink.

4 Remove from the oven and place a weight on top. Leave to cool, then chill. Serve sliced, garnished with sage and accompanied by tomatoes.

Potted Chicken

A simple-to-make starter using cooked chicken, this looks good served in attractive individual pots.

Serves 4–6

350g/12oz skinless boneless cooked chicken
115g/4oz/½ cup Clarified Butter
25ml/1½ tbsp dry sherry
ground cinnamon
ground mace
salt and freshly ground black pepper

1 Put the cooked chicken through the fine blade of a mincer or chop finely in a food processor.
2 Heat the butter and blend half with the chicken. Add the sherry with cinnamon, mace, salt and pepper to taste.
3 Pack into individual containers and seal the tops with the remaining butter.

Chicken, Bacon & Walnut Terrine

A luxurious dish, richly textured and lightly spiced, this would make a perfect starter for a special occasion dinner or buffet.

Serves 8–10

2 chicken breast fillets
1 large garlic clove, crushed
½ slice bread
1 egg
350g/12oz bacon chops (the fattier the better), minced or finely chopped
225g/8oz chicken livers, trimmed and finely chopped
25g/1oz/¼ cup chopped walnuts, toasted
30ml/2 tbsp sweet sherry or Madeira
2.5ml/½ tsp ground allspice
2.5ml/½ tsp cayenne pepper
pinch each grated nutmeg and ground cloves
8 long rashers streaky bacon, rinded and stretched
oil, for greasing
salt and freshly ground black pepper
chicory leaves, chives and chopped walnuts, to garnish

1 Cut the chicken into thin strips and season lightly. Mash the garlic, bread and egg together. Work in the chopped bacon (using your hands is really the best way) and then the finely chopped livers. Stir in the chopped walnuts, sherry or Madeira, spices and seasoning to taste.

2 Preheat the oven to 200°C/400°F/Gas 6. Line a 675g/1½lb loaf tin with the bacon rashers and pack in half the meat mixture. Lay the chicken strips on the top and spread the rest of the mixture over. Cover the loaf tin with lightly greased foil, seal well and press down firmly.

3 Place the terrine in a roasting tin half full of hot water and bake for 1–1½ hours or until firm to the touch. Remove from the oven, place a weight on top and leave to cool, draining off any excess fat or liquid while the terrine is still warm. Chill.

4 To serve, turn out the terrine and cut into thick slices. Garnish with a few chicory leaves and chives, and a scattering of chopped walnuts.

Chicken & Pork Terrine

A delicate-flavoured, smooth pâté with a contrasting strip of coarser-textured meat in the centre.

Serves 6–8

225g/8oz rindless streaky bacon
375g/13oz chicken breast fillet, skinned
15ml/1 tbsp lemon juice
225g/8oz lean minced pork
½ small onion, finely chopped
2 eggs, beaten
30ml/2 tbsp chopped fresh parsley
5ml/1 tsp salt
5ml/1 tsp green peppercorns, crushed
oil, for greasing
green salad, radishes and lemon wedges, to serve

1 Preheat the oven to 160°C/325°F/Gas 3. Put the bacon on a board and stretch it using the back of a heavy knife so that it can be arranged in overlapping slices over the base and sides of a 900g/2lb loaf tin.

2 Cut 115g/4oz of the chicken into strips about 10cm/4in long. Sprinkle with lemon juice. Put the rest of the chicken in a food processor or blender with the minced pork and the onion. Process until fairly smooth.

3 Add the eggs, parsley, salt and peppercorns to the meat mixture, and process again briefly. Spoon half the mixture into the loaf tin and then level the surface.

4 Arrange the chicken strips on top, then spoon in the remaining meat mixture and smooth the top. Give the tin a couple of sharp taps to knock out any pockets of air.

5 Cover with a piece of oiled foil and put in a roasting tin. Pour in enough hot water to come halfway up the sides of the loaf tin. Bake for about 45–50 minutes, until firm.

6 Allow the terrine to cool in the tin before turning out and chilling. Serve sliced, with a green salad, radishes and wedges of lemon to squeeze over.

Turkey, Juniper & Green Peppercorn Terrine

This is an ideal dish for entertaining as it can be made several days in advance and looks beautiful.

Serves 10–12

225g/8oz chicken livers, trimmed
450g/1lb minced turkey
450g/1lb minced pork
225g/8oz cubetti pancetta
50g/2oz/½ cup shelled pistachio nuts, roughly chopped
5ml/1 tsp salt
2.5ml/½ tsp ground mace
2 garlic cloves, crushed
5ml/1 tsp green peppercorns in brine, drained
5ml/1 tsp juniper berries
120ml/4fl oz/½ cup dry white wine
30ml/2 tbsp gin
finely grated rind of 1 orange
8 large vacuum-packed vine leaves in brine
oil, for greasing
pickle or chutney, to serve

1 Chop the chicken livers finely. Put them in a bowl and add the turkey, pork, pancetta, pistachio nuts, salt, mace and garlic. Mix well. Lightly crush the peppercorns and juniper berries, and add them to the mixture. Stir in the wine, gin and orange rind. Cover and chill overnight.

2 Preheat the oven to 160°C/325°F/Gas 3. Rinse the vine leaves under cold running water. Drain them thoroughly. Lightly oil a 1.2 litre/2 pint/5 cup ovenproof terrine dish or loaf tin. Line the terrine or tin with the leaves, letting the ends hang over the sides. Pack the meat mixture into the terrine or tin and fold the leaves over to enclose. Brush lightly with oil.

3 Cover the terrine. Place it in a roasting tin and pour in boiling water to come halfway up the sides of the terrine. Bake for 1¾ hours, checking the level of the water occasionally.

4 Leave the terrine to cool, then pour off the surface juices. Cover with clear film, then foil, and place a weight on top. Chill overnight.

5 Serve in slices, at room temperature, with pickle or chutney.

Country Terrine

The terrine must have a lid, to seal in all the flavours during the cooking time.

Serves 8

225g/8oz unsmoked streaky bacon, rinded
225g/8oz chicken liver, minced
450g/1lb minced pork
1 small onion, finely chopped
2 garlic cloves, crushed
10ml/2 tsp dried mixed herbs
225g/8oz game (e.g. hare, rabbit, pheasant or pigeon)
60ml/4 tbsp port or sherry
1 bay leaf
50g/2oz/4 tbsp plain flour
300ml/ ½ pint/1 ¼ cups aspic jelly, made up as packet instructions
salt and freshly ground black pepper
fresh parsley and thyme sprigs, to garnish

1 Stretch each bacon rasher with the back of a heavy knife. Use to line a 1 litre/1¾ pint/4 cup ovenproof terrine dish.

2 In a bowl, mix together the minced liver and pork with the onion, garlic and dried herbs. Season with salt and pepper. Cut the game into thin strips and put it into another bowl with the port or sherry. Season with salt and pepper.

3 Put one-third of the minced mixture into the terrine. Cover with half the game and repeat the layers, ending with a minced layer. Level and lay the bay leaf on top.

4 Preheat the oven to 160°C/325°F/Gas 3. Put the flour into a bowl and mix to a dough with 30ml/2 tbsp cold water. Cover the terrine with a lid and seal it with the flour paste.

5 Place the terrine in a roasting tin and pour around enough hot water to come halfway up the sides of the dish. Cook in the oven for 2 hours.

6 Remove the lid and place a weight on top of the terrine. Leave to cool. Remove any fat, then cover with warmed aspic jelly. Cool, then chill. To serve, turn out, cut into slices and garnish with parsley and thyme.

Duck & Calvados Terrine

This classic dish from Normandy uses the regional apple brandy.

Serves 4

oil, for greasing
500g/1 ¼lb boneless duck meat, coarsely chopped
225g/8oz belly pork, minced
2 shallots, chopped
grated rind and juice of 1 orange
30ml/2 tbsp calvados
10 rindless streaky bacon rashers
2 eggs, beaten
30ml/2 tbsp chopped fresh parsley
salt and freshly ground black pepper
mixed salad and hot toast, to serve

1 Grease and base-line a 900g/2lb loaf tin or ovenproof terrine dish. Place the chopped duck meat in a bowl with the minced pork, shallots, orange rind and juice, calvados and seasoning. Mix well, cover and chill for 1–2 hours.

2 Preheat the oven to 180°C/350°F/Gas 4. Stretch the bacon rashers with the back of a heavy knife and use them to line the loaf tin or dish, leaving any excess hanging over the edge.

3 Stir the eggs and parsley into the meat mixture, then spoon it into the prepared tin or dish. Smooth the surface, fold the bacon over, then cover with foil.

4 Stand the terrine in a roasting tin and pour in boiling water to come about two thirds of the way up the sides.

5 Bake for 1¼ hours, then remove the terrine from the water bath, lift off the foil and leave to cool. Cover with clean foil and a weight, and chill for 3–4 hours until firm.

6 Turn out the terrine and cut it into slices. Serve with a mixed salad and hot toast.

Cook's Tip
Marinating the meat for a few hours will develop the flavours.

Chicken Livers in Sherry

This dish, which could hardly be quicker to prepare, makes an excellent simple starter. Serve with crusty bread.

Serves 4

225g/8oz chicken livers
1 small onion
2 small garlic cloves
15ml/1 tbsp olive oil
5ml/1 tsp fresh thyme leaves
30ml/2 tbsp sweet sherry
30ml/2 tbsp soured or double cream
salt and freshly ground black pepper
fresh thyme sprigs, to garnish

1 Trim any green spots and sinews from the chicken livers. Finely chop the onion and garlic.

2 Heat the oil in a frying pan and fry the onion, garlic, chicken livers and thyme leaves for 3 minutes or until the livers are coloured on the outside but still slightly pink in the middle.

3 Stir in the sherry and cook gently for 1 minute. Add the soured or double cream and cook over a low heat for 1–2 minutes more.

4 Stir in salt and pepper to taste, and serve at once, garnished with thyme sprigs.

Fresh Tomato Sauce

Adding a little tomato purée gives extra strength of flavour to this sauce.

Makes 300ml/½ pint/1¼ cups

1 onion, chopped
1 garlic clove, crushed
15ml/1 tbsp olive oil
450g/1lb tomatoes, peeled and chopped
10ml/2 tsp tomato purée
5ml/1 tsp sugar (optional)
salt and freshly ground black pepper

1 Cook the onion and garlic in the oil for about 5 minutes until softened but not brown. Add the tomatoes, tomato purée, sugar (if using imported tomatoes, out of season) and seasoning.

2 Cover and simmer for 15–20 minutes, stirring occasionally. If the sauce seems a little thin, remove the lid and simmer for a few more minutes to reduce slightly.

Polenta with Chicken Livers

The richness of the livers is perfectly balanced here by the mild-flavoured polenta and fresh tomato sauce.

Serves 4

750ml/1¼ pints/3 cups Chicken Stock or water
130g/4½oz/generous 1 cup polenta
about 50g/2oz/4 tbsp butter
30ml/2 tbsp olive oil
450g/1lb chicken livers, trimmed and cut in half
1–2 garlic cloves, finely chopped
60ml/4 tbsp chopped fresh parsley, preferably flat leaf
5ml/1 tsp chopped fresh oregano or 2.5ml/½ tsp dried oregano
squeeze of lemon juice
salt and freshly ground black pepper
350ml/12fl oz/1½ cups Fresh Tomato Sauce, heated

1 Bring the stock or water to the boil in a large saucepan. If using water, add a little salt. Gradually stir in the polenta and cook over a low heat until very thick, stirring constantly. Pour the polenta into a buttered 20cm/8in round tin. Set aside for at least 30 minutes to firm up.

2 Invert the block of polenta on to a board. Cut it into four wedges. Fry in 40g/1½oz of the butter until golden brown on both sides, turning once.

3 Heat the remaining butter and the oil in a frying pan over moderately high heat. Add the livers and fry for 2–3 minutes or until they are starting to brown, turning once. Add the garlic, herbs, lemon juice and seasoning. Continue cooking for a further 1–2 minutes or until the livers are lightly browned on the outside but still pink in the centre.

4 Place a wedge of polenta on each warmed plate. Spoon the tomato sauce over and put the chicken livers on top.

Variation
Use 450g/1lb/6 cups sliced mushrooms sautéed in 40g/1½oz butter in place of the chicken livers.

Thai-style Chicken Livers

This dish is full of the flavours of Thailand.

Serves 4–6
45ml/3 tbsp vegetable oil
450g/1lb chicken livers, trimmed
4 shallots, chopped
2 garlic cloves, chopped
15ml/1 tbsp roasted ground rice
45ml/3 tbsp fish sauce
45ml/3 tbsp lime juice
5ml/1 tsp sugar
2 lemon grass stalks, bruised and finely chopped
30ml/2 tbsp chopped fresh coriander
10–12 fresh mint leaves and 2 fresh red chillies, chopped, to garnish

1 Heat the oil in a wok or large frying pan. Add the livers and fry over a medium-high heat for about 4 minutes until the livers are golden brown and cooked, but still slightly pink inside.

2 Move the livers to one side of the pan, and add the shallots and garlic. Fry for about 1–2 minutes.

3 Add the ground rice, fish sauce, lime juice, sugar, lemon grass and coriander. Stir and remove from the heat, and discard the lemon grass. Serve garnished with mint leaves and chillies.

Chicken Livers with Chinese Chives

This popular Thai dish is simplicity itself.

Serves 4
450g/1lb chicken livers, trimmed
3 garlic cloves, finely chopped
45ml/3 tbsp groundnut oil
450g/1lb Chinese chives, cut into 4cm/1½in lengths
15–30ml/2–3 tbsp fish sauce
30ml/2 tbsp oyster sauce
15ml/1 tbsp sugar

1 Cut the livers into thin strips using a sharp knife.
2 Stir-fry the garlic in the oil for 1–2 minutes until golden. Add the livers and stir-fry over a high heat for 3–4 minutes. Add the Chinese chives, fish and oyster sauces and sugar, and cook for 1 minute more.

Spiced Chicken Livers

Chicken livers combine brilliantly with ground coriander, cumin, cardamom, paprika and nutmeg to make this tasty first course or light meal.

Serves 4
350g/12oz chicken livers, trimmed
115g/4oz/1 cup plain flour
2.5ml/½ tsp ground coriander
2.5ml/½ tsp ground cumin
2.5ml/½ tsp ground cardamom seeds
1.25ml/¼ tsp ground paprika
1.25ml/¼ tsp grated nutmeg
90ml/6 tbsp olive oil
salt and freshly ground black pepper
salad and garlic bread, to serve

1 Dry the chicken livers on kitchen paper. Cut any large livers in half and leave the smaller ones whole.

2 Mix the flour with the coriander, cumin, cardamom, paprika, nutmeg, salt and pepper.

3 Coat a small batch of livers with spiced flour, separating each piece. Heat the oil in a large frying pan and fry the livers in batches. (This helps to keep the oil temperature high and prevents the flour from becoming soggy.)

4 Fry quickly, stirring frequently, until crispy. Keep warm and repeat with the remaining livers. Serve immediately with salad and warm garlic bread.

Cook's Tip
Although always milder than chilli or cayenne pepper, paprika varies in strength from mild, (sometimes called sweet), to hot.

Tandoori Chicken Sticks

This aromatic chicken dish is traditionally baked in a clay oven called a tandoor.

Makes about 25
450g/1lb chicken breast fillets, skinned

For the coriander yogurt
250ml/8fl oz/1 cup plain yogurt
30ml/2 tbsp whipping cream
½ cucumber, peeled, seeded and finely chopped
15–30ml/1–2 tbsp fresh chopped coriander or mint
salt and freshly ground black pepper

For the marinade
175ml/6fl oz/¾ cup plain yogurt
5ml/1 tsp garam masala or curry powder
1.25ml/¼ tsp ground cumin
1.25ml/¼ tsp ground coriander
1.25ml/¼ tsp cayenne pepper (or to taste)
5ml/1 tsp tomato purée
1–2 garlic cloves, finely chopped
2.5cm/½in piece fresh root ginger, peeled and finely chopped
grated rind and juice of ½ lemon
15–30ml/1–2 tbsp fresh chopped coriander or mint

1 First, make the coriander yogurt. Mix all the ingredients and season with salt and pepper. Cover and chill.

2 To make the marinade, place all the ingredients in a food processor and process until smooth. Pour into a shallow dish.

3 Freeze the chicken fillets for 5 minutes to firm them, then slice in half horizontally. Cut the slices into 2cm/¾in strips and add to the marinade. Toss to coat well. Cover and chill for 6–8 hours or overnight.

4 Preheat the grill and line a baking sheet with foil. Using a slotted spoon, remove the chicken from the marinade and arrange the pieces in a single layer on the baking sheet. Scrunch up the chicken slightly so it makes wavy shapes. Grill for 4–5 minutes until brown and just cooked, turning once.

5 Thread 1–2 pieces of cooked chicken on to cocktail sticks or short skewers and serve immediately with the bowl of coriander yogurt as a dip.

Sesame Seed Chicken Bites

Best served warm, these crunchy bites are delicious accompanied by a glass of chilled dry white wine.

Makes 20
175g/6oz chicken breast fillet
2 garlic cloves, crushed
2.5cm/1in piece fresh root ginger, peeled and grated
1 small egg white
5ml/1 tsp cornflour
25g/1oz/¼ cup shelled pistachio nuts, roughly chopped
60ml/4 tbsp sesame seeds
30ml/2 tbsp grapeseed oil
salt and freshly ground black pepper

For the dipping sauce
45ml/3 tbsp hoisin sauce
15ml/1 tbsp sweet chilli sauce

For the garnish
finely shredded fresh root ginger
roughly chopped pistachios
fresh dill sprigs

1 Place the chicken, garlic, grated ginger, egg white and cornflour in a food processor, and process to a smooth paste. Stir in the pistachios, and season well with salt and pepper.

2 Place the sesame seeds in a bowl. Form the chicken mixture into 20 balls between the palms of the hands and roll in the sesame seeds to coat them completely.

3 Heat a wok and add the oil. When the oil is hot, stir-fry the chicken bites in batches, turning regularly until golden. Drain on kitchen paper and keep warm.

4 To make the dipping sauce, mix together the hoisin and chilli sauces in a small bowl.

5 Place the chicken bites on a serving platter and garnish with shredded ginger, chopped pistachios and dill. Serve with the dipping sauce.

Spicy Chicken Canapés

These little cocktail sandwiches have a spicy filling, finished with different flavours of toppings.

Makes 18

75g/3oz/generous ½ cup finely chopped cooked chicken
2 spring onions, finely chopped
30ml/2 tbsp chopped red pepper
90ml/6 tbsp Curry Mayonnaise
5 slices white bread
15ml/1 tbsp paprika
15ml/1 tbsp chopped fresh parsley
30ml/2 tbsp chopped salted peanuts

1 Mix the chicken with the chopped spring onions and red pepper and half the curry mayonnaise.

2 Spread the mixture over both sides of three of the bread slices and sandwich with the remaining bread, pressing well together. Spread the remaining curry mayonnaise over the top and cut into 4cm/1½in circles using a plain cutter.

3 Dip into paprika, chopped parsley or chopped nuts and arrange on a serving platter.

Curry Mayonnaise

Makes about 300ml/½ pint/1¼ cups

2 egg yolks
5ml/1 tsp French mustard
15–20ml/3–4 tbsp curry paste
150ml/5fl oz/⅔ cup extra virgin olive oil
150ml/5fl oz/⅔ cup groundnut or sunflower oil
10ml/2 tsp white wine vinegar
salt and freshly ground black pepper

1 Place the egg yolks, mustard and curry paste in a food processor and blend smoothly.

2 Add the olive oil a little at a time while the processor is running. When the mixture is thick, add the remainder of the oil in a slow, steady stream. Add the vinegar and season to taste with salt and pepper.

Chicken & Avocado Mayonnaise

You need quite firm 'scoops' or forks to eat this starter, so don't be tempted to pass it round as finger food.

Serves 4

30ml/2 tbsp mayonnaise
15ml/1 tbsp fromage frais
2 garlic cloves, crushed
115g/4oz/scant 1 cup chopped cooked chicken
1 large ripe but firm avocado
30ml/2 tbsp lemon juice
salt and freshly ground black pepper
nacho chips or tortilla chips, to serve

1 Mix together the mayonnaise, fromage frais, garlic and seasoning to taste in a small bowl. Stir in the chopped chicken.

2 Peel, stone and chop the avocado and immediately toss in the lemon juice, then stir gently into the chicken mixture. Taste and adjust the seasoning as necessary. Chill until required.

3 Serve in small dishes, with nacho or tortilla chips as scoops.

Cook's Tip

This mixture also makes a great, chunky filling for sandwiches, baps or pitta bread. Alternatively, serve it as a main-course salad, heaped on to a base of mixed salad leaves.

Chicken Cigars

These small, crispy rolls can be served warm as canapés with a drink before a meal, or as a first course with a crisp, colourful salad.

Serves 4

275g/10oz packet filo pastry
45ml/3 tbsp olive oil
fresh flat leaf parsley, to garnish

For the filling

350g/12oz minced chicken
1 egg, beaten
2.5ml/½ tsp ground cinnamon
2.5ml/½ tsp ground ginger
30ml/2 tbsp raisins
15ml/1 tbsp olive oil
1 small onion, finely chopped
salt and freshly ground black pepper

1 To make the filling, mix all the ingredients, except the oil and onion, together in a bowl. Heat the oil in a large frying pan and cook the onion until tender. Leave to cool, then stir into the chicken mixture.

2 Preheat the oven to 180°C/350°F/Gas 4. Once the filo pastry packet has been opened, keep the pastry covered at all times with a damp dish towel. Work fast, as the pastry dries out very quickly when exposed to the air. Unravel the pastry and cut into 10 x 25cm/4 x 10in strips.

3 Take one strip (cover the remainder), brush with a little oil and place a small spoonful of the filling about 1cm/½in from the end.

4 To encase the filling, fold the sides inwards to a width of 5cm/2in and roll into a cigar shape. Place on a greased baking tray and brush with oil. Bake for about 20–25 minutes until golden brown and crisp. Garnish with parsley and serve.

Aubergine with Sesame Chicken

Sweet, delicate-tasting, small aubergines are stuffed with seasoned chicken and deep fried in a crispy sesame seed coating.

Serves 4

175g/6oz chicken, breast or thigh, skinned
1 spring onion, green part only, finely chopped
15ml/1 tbsp dark soy sauce
15ml/1 tbsp mirin or sweet sherry
2.5ml/½ tsp sesame oil
1.5ml/¼ tsp salt
4 small aubergines, about 10cm/4in long
15ml/1 tbsp sesame seeds
flour, for dusting
vegetable oil, for deep frying

For the dipping sauce

60ml/4 tbsp dark soy sauce
60ml/4 tbsp dashi or vegetable stock
45ml/3 tbsp mirin or sweet sherry

1 Remove the chicken meat from the bone and mince it finely in a food processor. Add the spring onion, soy sauce, mirin or sherry, sesame oil and salt.

2 Make four slits in each aubergine, leaving them joined at the stem. Spoon the minced chicken mixture into the aubergines, opening them slightly to accommodate the mixture. Dip the fat end of each stuffed aubergine in the sesame seeds, then dust in flour. Set aside.

3 To make the dipping sauce, combine the soy sauce, dashi or stock and mirin or sherry. Pour into a shallow serving bowl and set aside.

4 Heat the vegetable oil in a deep-fat fryer to 196°C/385°F. Fry the aubergines, two at a time, for 3–4 minutes. Lift out using a slotted spoon on to kitchen paper to drain. Serve hot, accompanied by the dipping sauce.

Chicken with Lemon & Garlic

This succulent dish is simplicity itself to cook and will disappear from the serving plates even more quickly.

Serves 4

225g/8oz chicken breast fillets, skinned
30ml/2 tbsp olive oil
1 shallot, finely chopped
4 garlic cloves, finely chopped
5ml/1 tsp paprika
juice of 1 lemon
30ml/2 tbsp chopped fresh parsley
salt and freshly ground black pepper
lemon wedges, to serve
flat leaf parsley, to garnish

1 Sandwich the chicken breast fillets between two sheets of clear film or greaseproof paper. Beat with a rolling pin until the fillets are about 5mm/ ¼in thick, then cut into strips about 1cm/ ½in wide.

2 Heat the oil in a large frying pan. Stir-fry the chicken strips with the shallot, garlic and paprika over a high heat for about 3 minutes until lightly browned and cooked through.

3 Add the lemon juice and parsley with salt and pepper to taste. Serve hot with lemon wedges, garnished with flat leaf parsley.

Variation
Try using strips of turkey breast instead for this dish.

Nutty Chicken Balls

Serve these as a first course with the lemon sauce, or make into smaller balls and serve on cocktail sticks as canapés with drinks.

Serves 4

350g/12oz boneless chicken
50g/2oz/ ½ cup pistachio nuts, finely chopped
15ml/1 tbsp lemon juice
2 eggs, beaten
plain flour, for shaping
75g/3oz/ ¾ cup blanched chopped almonds
75g/3oz/generous 1 cup dried breadcrumbs
oil, for greasing
salt and freshly ground black pepper

For the lemon sauce

150ml/ ¼ pint/ ⅔ cup Chicken Stock
225g/8oz/1 cup cream cheese
15ml/1 tbsp lemon juice
15ml/1 tbsp chopped fresh parsley
15ml/1 tbsp snipped fresh chives

1 Skin the chicken and mince or chop finely. Mix with salt and pepper to taste, plus the pistachio nuts, lemon juice and 1 of the beaten eggs.

2 Shape into 16 small balls using floured hands (use a spoon as a guide, so that all the balls are roughly the same size). Roll the balls in the remaining beaten egg and coat with the almonds first and then the dried breadcrumbs, pressing on firmly. Chill until ready to cook.

3 Preheat the oven to 190°C/375°F/Gas 5. Place the chicken balls on a greased baking tray and bake for about 15 minutes or until golden brown and crisp.

4 To make the lemon sauce, gently heat the chicken stock and cream cheese together in a pan, whisking until smooth. Add the lemon juice, herbs and seasoning to taste. Serve hot with the chicken balls.

Chicken Kofta Balti with Paneer

This rather unusual appetizer looks most elegant when served in small individual karahis.

Serves 6

450g/1lb boneless chicken, skinned and cubed
5ml/1 tsp crushed garlic
5ml/1 tsp grated fresh root ginger
7.5ml/1½ tsp ground coriander
7.5ml/1½ tsp chilli powder
2.5ml/½ tsp ground fenugreek
1.5ml/¼ tsp ground turmeric
5ml/1 tsp salt
30ml/2 tbsp chopped fresh coriander
2 fresh green chillies, chopped
600ml/1 pint/2½ cups water
corn oil, for frying
1 dried red chilli, crushed (optional), and fresh mint sprigs, to garnish

For the paneer mixture

1 medium onion, sliced
1 red pepper, seeded and cut into strips
1 green pepper, seeded and cut into strips
175g/6oz paneer, cubed
175g/6oz/1 cup sweetcorn kernels

1 Put the chicken, garlic, spices, salt, fresh coriander, chillies and water into a medium saucepan. Bring slowly to the boil over a medium heat and cook until all the liquid has evaporated.

2 Remove from the heat and allow to cool slightly. Put the mixture into a food processor or blender and process for 2 minutes, stopping once or twice to loosen the mixture with a spoon or spatula.

3 Scrape the mixture into a large mixing bowl using a wooden spoon. Taking a little of the mixture at a time, shape it into small even-size balls using your hands. You should be able to make about 12 koftas.

4 Heat 1cm/½in oil in a karahi or deep, round-bottomed frying pan over a high heat. Turn the heat down slightly and drop the koftas carefully into the oil. Move them around gently to ensure that they cook evenly.

5 When the koftas are lightly browned, remove them from the oil with a slotted spoon and drain on kitchen paper. Set aside.

6 Reheat the oil still remaining in the karahi and flash fry all the ingredients for the paneer mixture. This should take about 3 minutes over a high heat.

7 Divide the paneer mixture evenly between six small individual karahis, if using. Add two koftas to each serving and garnish with crushed red chilli, if using, and mint sprigs.

Cook's Tip
Paneer is a smooth white cheese available from Asian foodstores and some supermarkets.

Buffalo-style Chicken Wings

A fiery-hot fried chicken recipe, said to have originated in the town of Buffalo, New York, after which it is named. Serve it with traditional blue-cheese dip and celery sticks.

Makes 48

24 plump chicken wings, tips removed
vegetable oil, for frying
75g/3oz/6 tbsp butter
50ml/2oz/¼ cup hot pepper sauce, or to taste
15ml/1 tbsp white or cider vinegar
salt

For the blue-cheese dip

115g/4oz blue cheese, such as Danish blue
120ml/4fl oz/½ cup mayonnaise
120ml/4fl oz/½ cup soured cream
2–3 spring onions, finely chopped
1 garlic clove, finely chopped
15ml/1 tbsp white or cider vinegar
salad leaves, to garnish
celery sticks, to serve

1 To make the dip, use a fork to mash the blue cheese gently against the side of a bowl. Add the mayonnaise, soured cream, spring onions, garlic and vinegar, and stir together until well blended. Chill until ready to serve.

2 Using kitchen scissors or a sharp knife, cut each wing in half at the joint to make 48 pieces in all.

3 In a large saucepan or wok, heat 5cm/2in of oil until hot but not smoking. Fry the chicken wing pieces in small batches for 8–10 minutes until crisp and golden, turning once. Drain on kitchen paper. Season with salt to taste and arrange in a bowl.

4 In a small saucepan over a medium-low heat, melt the butter. Stir in the hot pepper sauce and vinegar, and immediately pour over the chicken, tossing to combine. Serve the wings hot, garnished with salad leaves and accompanied by the blue-cheese dip and celery sticks.

Bon-bon Chicken with Sesame Sauce

For this popular Sichuan Chinese dish the chicken meat is tenderized by being beaten with a stick (called a *bon*) – hence its name.

Serves 6–8

1 chicken, about 1kg/2¼lb
1.2 litres/2 pints/5 cups water
15ml/1 tbsp sesame oil
shredded cucumber, to garnish

For the sauce

30ml/2 tbsp light soy sauce
5ml/1 tsp sugar
15ml/1 tbsp finely chopped spring onions
5ml/1 tsp red chilli oil
2.5ml/½ tsp ground Sichuan peppercorns
5ml/1 tsp white sesame seeds
10ml/2 tbsp sesame paste or 30ml/2 tbsp peanut butter creamed with a little sesame oil

1 Clean the chicken well. In a wok or saucepan, bring the water to a rolling boil, add the chicken, reduce the heat and cook, covered, for 40–45 minutes. Remove the chicken from the pan and immerse in cold water to cool.

2 After at least 1 hour, remove the chicken from the water and drain; dry well with kitchen paper and brush on a coating of sesame oil. Carve the meat off the legs, wings and breast, and pull the meat off the rest of the bones.

3 On a flat work surface, pound the meat with a rolling pin, then tear it into shreds with your fingers.

4 To make the sauce, mix together all the ingredients in a bowl, reserving a little chopped spring onion for the garnish.

5 Place the shredded chicken in a serving dish and arrange the cucumber around the edge. Pour the sauce over the chicken, garnish with the reserved spring onion and serve.

Lettuce Parcels

This popular "assemble-it-yourself" treat is based on a recipe from Hong Kong. The filling – an imaginative blend of textures and flavours – is served with crisp lettuce leaves, which are used as wrappers.

Serves 6

2 chicken breast fillets, about 350g/12oz total weight
4 Chinese dried mushrooms, soaked for 30 minutes in warm water to cover
vegetable oil, for stir-frying and deep frying
2 garlic cloves, crushed
6 canned water chestnuts, drained and thinly sliced
30ml/2 tbsp light soy sauce
5ml/1 tsp Sichuan peppercorns, dry fried and crushed
4 spring onions, finely chopped
5ml/1 tsp sesame oil
50g/2oz cellophane noodles
salt and freshly ground black pepper
1 crisp lettuce and 60ml/4 tbsp hoisin sauce, to serve

1 Remove the skin from the chicken fillets, pat dry and set aside. Cut the chicken into thin strips. Drain the soaked mushrooms. Cut off and discard the mushroom stems; slice the caps finely and set aside.

2 Heat 30ml/2 tbsp of the oil in a wok or large frying pan. Add the garlic, then add the chicken and stir-fry until the pieces are cooked through and no longer pink.

3 Add the sliced mushrooms, water chestnuts, soy sauce and peppercorns. Toss for 2–3 minutes, then taste and add salt and pepper if necessary. Stir in half of the spring onions and the sesame oil. Remove from the heat and set aside.

4 Heat the oil for deep frying to 190°C/375°F. Cut the chicken skin into strips, deep fry until very crisp and drain on kitchen paper. Add the noodles to the hot oil and deep fry until crisp. Transfer to a plate lined with kitchen paper.

5 Crush the noodles and place in a serving dish. Top with the chicken skin, chicken and vegetable mixture and the remaining spring onions. Wash the lettuce leaves, pat dry and arrange on a large platter.

6 Toss the chicken and noodles to mix. Invite guests to take one or two lettuce leaves, spread the inside with hoisin sauce and add a spoonful of filling, turning in the sides of the leaves and rolling them into a parcel. The parcels are traditionally eaten in the hand.

Cook's Tip

Sichuan peppercorns are wild red peppers from Sichuan province in China. They are more aromatic but less hot than either white or black peppercorns, yet give a unique flavour.

Chicken Croquettes

These tasty bites are a great way to "stretch" a small quantity of chicken to make a starter for four people.

Serves 4

25g/1oz/2 tbsp butter
25g/1oz/¼ cup plain flour
150ml/¼ pint/⅔ cup milk
15ml/1 tbsp olive oil
1 chicken breast fillet with skin, about 75g/3oz, diced
1 garlic clove, finely chopped
1 small egg, beaten
50g/2oz/1 cup fresh white breadcrumbs
vegetable oil, for deep frying
salt and freshly ground black pepper
flat leaf parsley, to garnish
lemon wedges, to serve

1 Melt the butter in a small saucepan. Add the flour and cook over a low heat, stirring, for 1 minute. Gradually beat in the milk to make a smooth, very thick sauce. Cover with a lid and remove from the heat.

2 Heat the olive oil in a frying pan and cook the chicken with the garlic for 5 minutes, until the chicken is lightly browned and cooked through.

3 Tip the contents of the frying pan into a food processor and process until finely chopped. Stir into the sauce. Add plenty of salt and pepper to taste, then leave to cool completely.

4 Shape the chicken mixture into eight small sausages using moistened hands. Dip each one in beaten egg and then in breadcrumbs.

5 Heat the oil in a heavy-based pan or deep-fat fryer. It is ready when a cube of bread tossed into the oil sizzles on the surface. Deep fry the croquettes in the oil for 4 minutes or until crisp and golden. Drain on kitchen paper.

6 Pile the croquettes on to a serving plate, garnish with flat leaf parsley and serve with lemon wedges.

Chicken Goujons

Serve as a first course for eight people or as a filling main course for four.

Serves 4–8

4 chicken breast fillets, skinned
175g/6oz/3 cups fresh breadcrumbs
5ml/1 tsp ground coriander
10ml/2 tsp ground paprika
2.5ml/½ tsp ground cumin
45ml/3 tbsp plain flour
2 eggs, beaten
oil, for deep frying
salt and freshly ground black pepper
lemon wedges and fresh coriander sprigs, to garnish

For the dip

300ml/½ pint/1¼ cups Greek yogurt
30ml/2 tbsp lemon juice
60ml/4 tbsp chopped fresh coriander
60ml/4 tbsp chopped fresh parsley

1 Divide the chicken breasts into two natural fillets. Place them between two sheets of clear film and, using a rolling pin, flatten each one to a thickness of 5mm/¼in. Cut on the diagonal into 2.5cm/1in strips.

2 Mix the breadcrumbs with the spices and seasoning in a bowl. Place the flour and beaten eggs in separate bowls.

3 Toss the chicken fillet pieces (goujons) in the flour, keeping them separate. Dip the goujons into the beaten egg and finally coat in the breadcrumb mixture.

4 To make the dip, thoroughly mix all the ingredients together and season to taste. Pour into a serving bowl and chill.

5 Heat the oil in a heavy-based pan or deep-fat fryer. It is ready when a cube of bread tossed into the oil sizzles on the surface. Fry the goujons in batches until golden and crisp. Drain on kitchen paper and keep warm in the oven.

6 Arrange the goujons on a warmed serving plate and garnish with lemon wedges and sprigs of coriander. Serve with the dip.

Chicken Roulades

These attractive chicken rolls, stuffed with a nutty spinach filling, make an impressive hot first course for a dinner party.

Makes 4

4 chicken thighs, boned and skinned
115g/4oz chopped frozen spinach
15g/½oz/1 tbsp butter
25g/1oz/2 tbsp pine nuts
pinch of grated nutmeg
25g/1oz/½ cup fresh white breadcrumbs
4 rashers rindless streaky bacon
30ml/2 tbsp olive oil
150ml/¼ pint/⅔ cup white wine or Chicken Stock
10ml/2 tsp cornflour
30ml/2 tbsp single cream
15ml/1 tbsp snipped fresh chives
salt and freshly ground black pepper
salad leaves, to garnish

1 Preheat the oven to 180°C/350°F/Gas 4. Place the chicken thighs between clear film and flatten with a rolling pin.

2 Put the spinach and butter into a saucepan, heat gently until the spinach has defrosted, then increase the heat and cook rapidly, stirring occasionally, until all the moisture has been driven off. Add the pine nuts, seasoning, nutmeg and breadcrumbs.

3 Divide the spinach mixture between the chicken pieces and roll up neatly. Wrap a rasher of bacon around each piece and secure with string.

4 Heat the oil in a large frying pan and brown the roulades all over. Drain through a slotted spoon and place in a shallow, ovenproof dish.

5 Pour over the wine or stock, cover and bake for about 15–20 minutes or until tender. Transfer the chicken to a serving plate and remove the string. Strain the cooking liquid into a saucepan. Mix the cornflour to a thin, smooth paste with a little cold water and add to the juices in the pan, along with the cream. Bring to the boil to thicken, stirring all the time. Adjust the seasoning and add the chives. Pour the sauce round the chicken and serve with a garnish of salad leaves.

Mini Spring Rolls

Eat these light, crispy parcels with your fingers. If you like slightly spicier food, sprinkle them with a little cayenne pepper before serving.

Makes 20

1 fresh green chilli
120ml/4fl oz/½ cup vegetable oil
1 small onion, finely chopped
1 garlic clove, crushed
75g/3oz cooked chicken breast
1 small carrot, cut into fine matchsticks
1 spring onion, thinly sliced
1 small red pepper, seeded and cut into fine matchsticks
25g/1oz beansprouts
5ml/1 tsp sesame oil
4 large sheets filo pastry
1 small egg white, lightly beaten
fresh chives, to garnish (optional)
light soy sauce, to serve

1 Carefully remove the seeds from the chilli and chop finely, wearing rubber gloves to protect your hands, if necessary.

2 Heat a wok or heavy-based frying pan, then add 30ml/2 tbsp of the vegetable oil. When hot, add the onion, garlic and chilli. Stir-fry for 1 minute.

3 Slice the chicken thinly, then add to the wok and fry over a high heat, stirring constantly until browned.

4 Add the carrot, spring onion and red pepper, and stir-fry for 2 minutes. Add the beansprouts, stir in the sesame oil, then remove from the heat and leave to cool.

5 Cut each sheet of filo pastry into five short strips. Place a small amount of filling at one end of each strip, then fold in the long sides and roll up the pastry to make a neat parcel. Seal and glaze the parcels with the egg white, then chill, uncovered, for 15 minutes before frying.

6 Wipe out the wok with kitchen paper, heat it again and add the remaining vegetable oil. When the oil is hot, fry the rolls in batches until crisp and golden brown. Drain on kitchen paper and keep warm. Serve garnished with chives, if liked, accompanied by light soy sauce for dipping.

Chicken & Sticky Rice Balls

These balls can either be steamed or deep fried. The fried versions are crunchy and are excellent for serving at drinks parties.

Makes about 30

450g/1lb minced chicken
1 egg
15ml/1 tbsp tapioca flour
4 spring onions, finely chopped
30ml/2 tbsp chopped fresh coriander
30ml/2 tbsp fish sauce
pinch of granulated sugar
225g/8oz cooked sticky rice
banana leaves
oil, for brushing
freshly ground black pepper
shredded carrot, strips of red pepper and snipped chives, to garnish
sweet chilli sauce, to serve

1 In a bowl, combine the chicken, egg, flour, spring onions and coriander. Mix and season with fish sauce, sugar and pepper.

2 Spread the cooked sticky rice on a large plate or flat tray.

3 Place 5ml/1 tsp of the chicken mixture on the bed of rice. With damp hands, roll and shape the mixture in the rice to make a ball about the size of a walnut. Repeat using the rest of the chicken mixture and rice.

4 Line a bamboo steamer with banana leaves and lightly brush them with oil. Place the chicken balls on the leaves, spacing them well apart to prevent them sticking together. Steam over a high heat for about 10 minutes or until cooked.

5 Remove the balls from the steamer and arrange on serving plates. Garnish with shredded carrot, red pepper strips and snipped chives. Serve with sweet chilli sauce for dipping.

Cook's Tip

Sticky rice, also known as glutinous rice, has a very high starch content. It is so called because the grains stick together when it is cooked. It is very popular in Thailand and can be eaten both as a savoury and as a sweet dish.

San Francisco Chicken Wings

A mouth-watering dish that reflects the influence of Chinese immigrants on American cuisine.

Serves 8

75ml/5 tbsp soy sauce
15ml/1 tbsp light brown sugar
15ml/1 tbsp rice vinegar
30ml/2 tbsp dry sherry
juice of 1 orange
5cm/2in strip orange rind
1 star anise
5ml/1 tsp cornflour
50ml/2fl oz/¼ cup water
15ml/1 tbsp grated fresh root ginger
15ml/1 tbsp crushed garlic
1.5–5ml/¼–1 tsp chilli sauce
24 chicken wings, about 1.5kg/3–3½lb, tips removed
salad leaves and chives, to garnish

1 Preheat the oven to 200°C/400°F/Gas 6. Combine the soy sauce, brown sugar, vinegar, sherry, orange juice and rind, and star anise in a saucepan. Bring to the boil over a medium heat.

2 Combine the cornflour and water in a small bowl and stir until blended. Add to the boiling soy sauce mixture, stirring well. Boil for 1 minute, stirring constantly.

3 Remove the soy sauce mixture from the heat and stir in the ginger, garlic and chilli sauce.

4 Arrange the chicken wings, in a single layer, in a large ovenproof dish. Pour over the soy sauce mixture and stir thoroughly to coat the wings evenly.

5 Bake the wings for 30–40 minutes until tender and browned, basting occasionally. Serve hot or warm, garnished with salad leaves and chives.

Turkey Sticks with Soured Cream Dip

Crisp morsels of turkey with a quick-to-prepare dip.

Serves 4

350g/12oz turkey breast fillets, skinned
50g/2oz/1 cup fine fresh breadcrumbs
1.5ml/¼ tsp paprika
1 small egg, lightly beaten
salt and freshly ground black pepper

For the soured cream dip
45ml/3 tbsp soured cream
15ml/1 tbsp ready-made Tomato Sauce
15ml/1 tbsp mayonnaise

1 Preheat the oven to 190°C/375°F/Gas 5. Cut the turkey into strips. In a bowl, mix the breadcrumbs and paprika, and season with salt and pepper. Put the beaten egg into another bowl.

2 Dip the turkey strips into the egg, then into the breadcrumbs, turning until evenly coated. Place on a greased baking sheet.

3 Cook the turkey at the top of the oven for 20 minutes until crisp and golden. Turn once during the cooking time.

4 To make the dip, mix all the ingredients together and season to taste. Serve the turkey sticks accompanied by the dip.

Basic Pasta Dough

200g/7oz/1¾ cups plain flour
pinch of salt
2 eggs
10ml/2 tsp cold water

1 Sift the flour and salt on to a work surface. Make a well in the centre. Break the eggs and add the water into the well.

2 Using a fork, beat the eggs gently together, then draw in the flour to make a thick paste.

3 Use your hands to mix to a firm dough.

4 Knead the dough for 5 minutes, until smooth. Wrap the pasta in clear film and leave to rest for 20–30 minutes.

Pasta Bonbons

These little pasta parcels are filled with a turkey stuffing.

Serves 4–6

1 quantity of Basic Pasta Dough
flour, for dusting
1 egg white, beaten
salt and freshly ground black pepper

For the filling
1 small onion, finely chopped
1 garlic clove, crushed
150ml/¼ pint/⅔ cup Chicken Stock
225g/8oz minced turkey
2–3 fresh sage leaves, chopped
2 canned anchovy fillets, drained

For the sauce
150ml/¼ pint/⅔ cup Chicken Stock
200g/7oz cream cheese
15ml/1 tbsp lemon juice
5ml/1 tsp caster sugar
2 tomatoes, peeled, seeded and finely diced
½ red onion, finely chopped
6 small cornichons (pickled gherkins), sliced

1 To make the filling, put the onion, garlic and stock into a saucepan. Cover and simmer for 5 minutes. Uncover and boil for 5 minutes, or until the stock has reduced to 30ml/2 tbsp.

2 Add the turkey and stir until it is no longer pink. Add the sage and anchovies, and season. Cook, uncovered, for 5 minutes until all the liquid has been absorbed. Leave to cool.

3 Divide the pasta dough in half. Roll into thin sheets and cut into 9 × 6cm/3½ × 2½in rectangles. Lay on a lightly floured dish towel. Repeat with the remaining dough. Place a teaspoon of the filling on the centre of each rectangle, brush around the meat with egg white and roll up the pasta, pinching in the ends. Transfer to a floured dish towel and rest for 1 hour.

4 To make the sauce, put the stock, cream cheese, lemon juice and sugar into a saucepan. Heat gently and whisk until smooth. Add the tomatoes, onion and cornichons. Keep warm.

5 Cook the pasta bonbons in a large pan of boiling, salted water for 5 minutes. Remove with a slotted spoon, drain well and serve immediately with the sauce poured over.

Chicken Liver Salad

An inspired combination of flavours and textures: warm, succulent livers; cool, refreshing grapefruit; smooth, rich avocado and crisp salad leaves.

Serves 4
mixed salad leaves, e.g. frisée and oakleaf lettuce or radicchio
1 avocado, peeled, stoned and diced
2 pink grapefruit, segmented
350g/12oz chicken livers
30ml/2 tbsp olive oil
1 garlic clove, crushed
salt and freshly ground black pepper
fresh chives, to garnish
crusty bread, to serve

For the dressing
30ml/2 tbsp lemon juice
60ml/4 tbsp olive oil
2.5ml/ ½ tsp wholegrain mustard
2.5ml/ ½ tsp clear honey
15ml/1 tbsp snipped fresh chives

1 To make the dressing, put all the ingredients into a screw-top jar with salt and pepper, and shake vigorously to emulsify. Taste and adjust the seasoning as necessary.

2 Wash the salad leaves and spin dry. Arrange attractively on a serving plate with the avocado and grapefruit.

3 Dry the chicken livers on kitchen paper and remove any unwanted pieces. Cut the larger livers in half and leave the smaller ones whole.

4 Heat the oil in a large frying pan. Stir-fry the livers and garlic briskly until the livers are brown all over but still slightly pink on the inside. Season with salt and pepper. Remove the livers from the pan using a slotted spoon and drain briefly on kitchen paper.

5 Place the warm livers on the salad and spoon over the dressing. Garnish with snipped fresh chives and serve immediately with crusty bread.

Chicken Liver, Bacon & Tomato Salad

Warm salads are especially welcome during the autumn months when the evenings are growing shorter and a little cooler.

Serves 4
225g/8oz young spinach, stems removed
1 frisée lettuce
105ml/7 tbsp groundnut oil
175g/6oz rindless unsmoked bacon, cut into strips
75g/3oz day-old bread, crusts removed and cut into short fingers
450g/1lb chicken livers, trimmed
115g/4oz cherry tomatoes
salt and freshly ground black pepper

1 Wash the salad leaves and spin dry. Place in a salad bowl. Heat 60ml/4 tbsp of the oil in a large frying pan. Add the bacon and cook for 3–4 minutes or until crisp and brown. Remove the bacon with a slotted spoon and drain on kitchen paper.

2 Fry the bread fingers in the bacon-flavoured oil, tossing them until crisp and golden. Drain the croûtons on kitchen paper.

3 Heat the remaining oil in the frying pan, add the chicken livers and fry briskly for 2–3 minutes. They should be coloured on the outside but still slightly pink in the middle. Turn the livers out over the salad leaves and add the bacon, croûtons and tomatoes. Season, toss and serve immediately.

French Dressing

French vinaigrette is appreciated for its simplicity.

Makes about 120ml/ 4fl oz/½ cup
90ml/6 tbsp extra virgin olive oil
15ml/1 tbsp white wine vinegar
5ml/1 tsp French mustard
pinch of caster sugar

1 Place the olive oil and vinegar in a screw-top jar.
2 Add the mustard and sugar. Replace the lid and shake well.

Pan-fried Chicken Liver Salad

The hot dressing includes vin santo, a sweet dessert wine from Tuscany, but this is not essential – any dessert wine will do, or a sweet or cream sherry.

Serves 4

75g/3oz baby spinach leaves
75g/3oz lollo rosso leaves
75ml/5 tbsp olive oil
15ml/1 tbsp butter
225g/8oz chicken livers, trimmed and thinly sliced
45ml/3 tbsp vin santo
50–75g/2–3oz Parmesan cheese, shaved into curls
salt and freshly ground black pepper

1 Wash the spinach and lollo rosso, and spin dry. Tear the leaves into a large bowl, season with salt and pepper to taste, and toss gently to mix.

2 Heat 30ml/2 tbsp of the oil with the butter in a large, heavy-based frying pan. When foaming, add the chicken livers and toss over a medium to high heat for 5 minutes or until the livers are browned on the outside but still pink in the centre. Remove from the heat.

3 Remove the livers from the pan using a slotted spoon, drain them on kitchen paper, then place on top of the salad.

4 Return the pan to a medium heat, add the remaining oil and the vin santo, and stir until sizzling.

5 Pour the hot dressing over the spinach and livers, and toss to coat. Transfer the salad to a serving bowl and sprinkle over the Parmesan shavings. Serve at once.

Warm Chicken Salad with Shallots & Mangetouts

Succulent cooked chicken pieces are combined with vegetables in a lightly spiced chilli dressing.

Serves 6

50g/2oz mixed salad leaves
50g/2oz baby spinach leaves
50g/2oz watercress
30ml/2 tbsp chilli sauce
30ml/2 tbsp dry sherry
15ml/1 tbsp light soy sauce
15ml/1 tbsp tomato ketchup
10ml/2 tsp olive oil
8 shallots, finely chopped
1 garlic clove, crushed
350g/12oz chicken breast fillets, skinned and cut into thin strips
1 red pepper, seeded and sliced
175g/6oz mangetouts, trimmed
400g/14oz can baby sweetcorn, drained and halved
275g/10oz cooked brown rice
salt and freshly ground black pepper
fresh flat leaf parsley sprig, to garnish

1 Wash the salad leaves and spinach, and spin dry. Arrange the salad leaves, tearing up any large ones, and the spinach on a serving dish. Add the watercress and toss to mix.

2 In a small bowl, mix together the chilli sauce, sherry, soy sauce and tomato ketchup. Set aside.

3 Heat the oil in a large, non-stick frying pan or wok. Add the shallots and garlic, and stir-fry over a medium heat for 1 minute.

4 Add the sliced chicken to the pan and stir-fry for a further 4–5 minutes until the chicken pieces are nearly cooked.

5 Add the red pepper, mangetouts, sweetcorn and cooked rice, and stir-fry for 2–3 minutes.

6 Pour in the chilli sauce mixture and stir-fry for 2–3 minutes until hot and bubbling. Season to taste. Spoon the chicken mixture over the salad leaves, toss together to mix and serve immediately, garnished with a sprig of flat leaf parsley.

Warm Chicken Salad with Sesame & Coriander Dressing

This salad needs to be served warm to make the most of the wonderful sesame, lemon and coriander flavourings.

Serves 6

4 medium chicken breast fillets, skinned
225g/8oz mangetouts
2 heads decorative lettuce, e.g. lollo rosso or oakleaf
3 carrots, cut into small matchsticks
175g/6oz/generous 2 cups button mushrooms, sliced
6 bacon rashers, fried and chopped
15ml/1 tbsp chopped fresh coriander leaves, to garnish

For the dressing

120ml/4fl oz/½ cup lemon juice
30ml/2 tbsp wholegrain mustard
250ml/8fl oz/1 cup olive oil
75ml/5 tbsp sesame oil
5ml/1 tsp coriander seeds, crushed

1 To make the dressing, mix all the ingredients together in a bowl, beating well to blend. Place the chicken breasts in a shallow dish and pour on half the dressing. Chill overnight, and chill the remaining dressing also.

2 Cook the mangetouts for 2 minutes in boiling water, then cool under cold running water to stop them cooking any further, so they remain crisp.

3 Wash and spin dry the lettuces. Tear the leaves into small pieces and place in a large bowl. Add the mangetouts, carrots, mushrooms and bacon, and toss to mix thoroughly. Divide among individual serving dishes.

4 Grill the chicken until cooked through, then slice on the diagonal into quite thin pieces. Divide between the bowls of salad and sprinkle some dressing over the top. Combine quickly, scatter fresh coriander over each bowl and serve.

Chicken Salad with Cranberry Dressing

The unusual fruity dressing lifts this deceptively simple salad to a higher plane.

Serves 4

4 chicken breast fillets, about 675g/1½lb total weight
300ml/½ pint/1¼ cups Chicken Stock or a mixture of stock and dry white wine
fresh herb sprigs
200g/7oz mixed salad leaves
50g/2oz/½ cup chopped walnuts or hazelnuts

For the dressing

30ml/2 tbsp olive oil
15ml/1 tbsp walnut or hazelnut oil
15ml/1 tbsp raspberry or red wine vinegar
30ml/2 tbsp cranberry relish
salt and freshly ground black pepper

1 Skin the chicken breast fillets. Pour the stock, or stock and wine mixture, into a large, shallow saucepan. Add the herbs and bring the liquid to simmering point. Add the chicken and poach for about 15 minutes until cooked through. Alternatively, leave the skin on the breasts and grill or roast them until tender, then remove the skin.

2 Wash and spin dry the salad leaves and arrange them on four plates. Slice each chicken breast neatly, keeping the slices together, then place each breast on top of a portion of salad, fanning the slices out slightly.

3 To make the dressing, place all the ingredients in a screw-top jar and shake vigorously.

4 Spoon a little dressing over each salad and sprinkle with the chopped walnuts or hazelnuts. Serve.

Lemon & Tarragon Chicken Salad

Warm cooked chicken is tossed with salad leaves as soon as it comes out of the pan.

Serves 4

4 chicken breast fillets, skinned and cut into strips
4 rindless smoked bacon rashers, chopped (optional)
15ml/1 tbsp oil
25ml/5 tsp chopped fresh tarragon
juice of 1 lemon
mixed salad leaves, washed
French Dressing
salt and freshly ground black pepper

1 Cook the chicken and bacon, if using, in the oil with half the tarragon for about 5 minutes until lightly browned. Add the lemon juice, season to taste and cook for about 5 minutes more.

2 Meanwhile, put the salad leaves in a large bowl, add a little French dressing, and toss. Stir the remaining tarragon into the chicken and add to the salad bowl. Serve at once.

Warm Chicken Salad with Hazelnut Dressing

This quickly prepared, warm salad combines pan-fried chicken and spinach with a light, nutty dressing.

Serves 4

45ml/3 tbsp olive oil
30ml/2 tbsp hazelnut oil
15ml/1 tbsp white wine vinegar
1 garlic clove, crushed
15ml/1 tbsp chopped fresh mixed herbs
225g/8oz baby spinach leaves
250g/9oz cherry tomatoes, halved
1 bunch spring onions, chopped
2 chicken breast fillets, skinned and cut into pieces
salt and freshly ground black pepper

1 Place 30ml/2 tbsp of the olive oil, the hazelnut oil, vinegar, garlic and chopped herbs in a small bowl or jug and whisk together until thoroughly mixed. Set aside.

2 Wash and spin dry the spinach leaves and trim any long stalks. Place the spinach in a large serving bowl with the tomatoes and spring onions, and toss together to mix.

3 Heat the remaining olive oil in a frying pan, add the chicken and stir-fry over a high heat for 7–10 minutes until the chicken is cooked, tender and lightly browned.

4 Scatter the cooked chicken pieces over the salad, give the dressing a quick whisk to blend, then drizzle it over the salad and gently toss all the ingredients together to mix. Season to taste with salt and pepper, and serve immediately

Variation

You could substitute walnut oil for the hazelnut oil and chicory for the spinach leaves.

Peanut Chicken Salad in a Pineapple Boat

This beautiful dish would go down well as part of a celebration meal.

2 small ripe pineapples
225g/8oz cooked chicken breast, cut into bite-size pieces
2 celery sticks, diced
50g/2oz spring onions, chopped
225g/8oz seedless green grapes
40g/1½oz/6 tbsp salted peanuts, coarsely chopped

For the dressing

75g/3oz/6 tbsp smooth peanut butter
120ml/4fl oz/½ cup mayonnaise
30ml/2 tbsp cream or milk
1 garlic clove, finely chopped
5ml/1 tsp mild curry powder
15ml/1 tbsp apricot jam
salt and freshly ground black pepper
fresh mint sprigs, to garnish

1 Make four pineapple boats (see box) from the pineapples. Cut the flesh removed from the boats into bite-size pieces.

2 Combine the pineapple flesh, cooked chicken, celery, spring onions and grapes in a bowl.

3 To make the dressing, put all the ingredients in another bowl and mix with a wooden spoon or whisk until evenly blended. Season with salt and pepper. (The dressing will be thick at this point, but will be thinned by the juices from the pineapple.)

4 Add the dressing to the pineapple and chicken mixture. Fold together gently but thoroughly.

5 Divide the chicken salad among the pineapple boats. Sprinkle the chopped peanuts over the top before serving, garnished with mint sprigs.

Making a Pineapple Boat

1 Trim off any browned ends from the green leaves of the crown. Trim the stalk end if necessary. Using a long, sharp knife, cut the pineapple lengthways in half, through the crown. Cut a thin slice from the underside of each "boat" so it has a flat surface and will not rock.

2 Using a small sharp knife, cut straight across the top and bottom of the central core in each pineapple half.

3 Cut lengthways at a slant on either side of the core. This will cut out the core in a V-shape.

4 Using a curved, serrated grapefruit knife, cut out and reserve the flesh from each half.

Orange Chicken Salad

For this delicious dish the rice is cooked with thinly pared orange rind for a more intense flavour.

Serves 4

3 large seedless oranges
175g/6oz long-grain rice
475ml/16fl oz/2 cups water
175ml/6fl oz/⅔ cup French Dressing, made with red wine vinegar and a mixture of olive and vegetable oils
10ml/2 tsp Dijon mustard
2.5ml/½ tsp caster sugar
450g/1lb cooked chicken, diced
45ml/3 tbsp snipped fresh chives
75g/3oz cashew nuts, toasted
salt and freshly ground black pepper
cucumber slices and chives, to garnish

1 Thinly peel 1 orange, taking only the coloured part of the rind and leaving the white pith.

2 Combine the orange rind, rice and water in a saucepan. Add a pinch of salt. Bring to the boil, cover and cook over very low heat for 15–18 minutes or until the rice is tender and all the water has been absorbed.

3 Peel all the oranges and cut out the segments, reserving the juice. Add the orange juice to the French dressing, then add the Dijon mustard and sugar and whisk to combine well. Taste and add more salt and freshly ground black pepper if needed.

4 When the rice is cooked, remove it from the heat and cool slightly, uncovered. Discard the orange rind.

5 Turn the rice into a serving bowl and add half of the dressing. Toss well and leave to cool completely.

6 Add the cooked chicken, the chives, cashew nuts and orange segments to the rice with the remaining dressing. Toss gently. Serve at room temperature, garnished with cucumber slices and chives.

Chicken & Fruit Salad

An ideal party dish as the chickens may be cooked in advance and the salad finished off on the day. Serve with warm garlic bread.

Serves 8

4 fresh tarragon or rosemary sprigs
2 × 1.75kg/3½lb chickens
65g/2½oz/5 tbsp softened butter
150ml/¼ pint/⅔ cup Chicken Stock
150ml/¼ pint/⅔ cup white wine
115g/4oz/1 cup walnut pieces
1 small cantaloupe melon
450g/1lb seedless grapes or stoned cherries
salt and freshly ground black pepper
mixed lettuce, to serve

For the dressing

30ml/2 tbsp tarragon vinegar
120ml/4fl oz/½ cup light olive oil
30ml/2 tbsp chopped mixed fresh herbs, e.g. parsley, mint and tarragon

1 Preheat the oven to 200°C/400°F/Gas 6. Put the sprigs of tarragon or rosemary inside the chickens and season. Tie the chickens in a neat shape with string. Spread them with 50g/2oz/4 tbsp of the butter, place in a roasting tin and add the stock. Cover loosely with foil and roast for about 1½ hours, basting twice, until browned and the juices run clear. Remove the chickens from the roasting tin and leave to cool.

2 Add the wine to the juices in the tin. Boil until syrupy. Strain and cool. Heat the remaining butter in a frying pan and fry the walnuts until lightly browned. Drain on kitchen paper and cool. Scoop the melon into balls. Joint the chickens.

3 To make the dressing, whisk the vinegar and oil together with a little salt and pepper. Remove all the fat from the cooled chicken juices and add these to the dressing with the herbs.

4 Wash and spin dry the lettuce and arrange on a serving platter. Put the chicken pieces on top and scatter over the grapes or cherries and the melon. Spoon over the dressing, sprinkle with the walnuts and serve.

Chinese-style Chicken Salad

A spicy peanut sauce accompanies this salad of crunchy vegetables and tender chicken.

Serves 4

4 chicken breast fillets, about 175g/6oz each
60ml/4 tbsp dark soy sauce
pinch of Chinese five spice powder
good squeeze of lemon juice
½ cucumber, peeled and cut into matchsticks
5ml/1 tsp salt
45ml/3 tbsp sunflower oil
30ml/2 tbsp sesame oil
15ml/1 tbsp sesame seeds
30ml/2 tbsp dry sherry
2 carrots, cut into matchsticks
8 spring onions, shredded
75g/3oz/scant ½ cup beansprouts

For the sauce

60ml/4 tbsp crunchy peanut butter
10ml/2 tsp lemon juice
10ml/2 tsp sesame oil
1.5ml/¼ tsp hot chilli powder
1 spring onion, finely chopped

1 Put the chicken portions into a large saucepan and just cover with water. Add 15ml/1 tbsp of the soy sauce, the Chinese five spice powder and lemon juice. Cover and bring to the boil, then simmer for about 20 minutes.

2 Meanwhile, place the cucumber matchsticks in a colander, sprinkle with the salt and cover with a plate with a weight on top. Leave to drain for 30 minutes – set the colander in a bowl or on a deep plate to catch the drips.

3 Lift out the poached chicken with a draining spoon and leave until cool enough to handle. Remove and discard the skin, and bash the chicken lightly with a rolling pin to loosen the fibres. Slice into thin strips and reserve.

4 Heat the oils in a large frying pan or wok. Add the sesame seeds, fry for 30 seconds and then stir in the remaining soy sauce and the sherry. Add the carrots and stir-fry for 2–3 minutes until tender. Remove from the heat and reserve.

5 Rinse the cucumber well, pat dry with kitchen paper and place in a bowl. Add the shredded spring onions, beansprouts, cooked carrots, pan juices and shredded chicken, and mix together. Transfer to a shallow dish. Cover and chill for about 1 hour, turning the mixture in the juices once or twice.

6 To make the sauce, cream the peanut butter with the lemon juice, sesame oil and chilli powder, adding a little hot water to form a paste, then stir in the chopped spring onion. Arrange the chicken mixture on a serving dish and serve with the peanut sauce.

Tangy Chicken Salad

This fresh and lively dish is bursting with the flavours of Thailand. It is ideal for a starter or light lunch.

Serves 4–6

4 chicken breast fillets, skinned
2 garlic cloves, crushed and roughly chopped
30ml/2 tbsp soy sauce
30ml/2 tbsp vegetable oil
120ml/4fl oz/½ cup coconut cream
30ml/2 tbsp fish sauce
juice of 1 lime
30ml/2 tbsp palm sugar
1 head lettuce
115g/4oz water chestnuts, sliced
50g/2oz cashew nuts, toasted
4 shallots, finely sliced
4 kaffir lime leaves, finely sliced
1 lemon grass stalk, finely sliced
5ml/1 tsp chopped galangal
1 large red fresh chilli, seeded and thinly sliced
2 spring onions, thinly sliced
10–12 mint leaves, torn
fresh coriander sprigs and sliced red chillies, to garnish

1 Trim the chicken breasts of any excess fat and put them in a large, shallow dish. Rub with the garlic, soy sauce and 15ml/1 tbsp of the oil. Leave to marinate for 1–2 hours.

2 Grill or pan-fry the chicken for 3–4 minutes on both sides or until cooked. Remove from the heat and set aside to cool.

3 In a small saucepan, heat the coconut cream, fish sauce, lime juice and palm sugar. Stir until all of the sugar has dissolved and then remove from the heat. Wash and spin dry the lettuce.

4 Cut the cooked chicken into strips and combine in a bowl with the water chestnuts, cashew nuts, shallots, kaffir lime leaves, lemon grass, galangal, red chilli, spring onions and mint leaves. Pour over the coconut dressing, toss and mix well.

5 Spread out the lettuce leaves on a large serving platter or individual plates. Arrange the chicken salad on top, garnish with sprigs of coriander and sliced red chillies, and serve.

Chicken & Broccoli Salad

Gorgonzola makes a tangy dressing that goes well with both chicken and broccoli. Serve this salad for lunch or a light supper.

Serves 4

175g/6oz broccoli, divided into small florets
225g/8oz/2 cups farfalle
2 large cooked chicken breasts
salt and freshly ground black pepper
fresh sage leaves, to garnish

For the dressing

90g/3½oz Gorgonzola cheese
15ml/1 tbsp white wine vinegar
60ml/4 tbsp extra virgin olive oil
2.5–5ml/½–1 tsp finely chopped fresh sage

1 Cook the broccoli florets in a large saucepan of boiling salted water for 3 minutes. Remove with a slotted spoon and rinse under cold running water, then spread out on kitchen paper to drain and dry.

2 Add the farfalle to the broccoli cooking water, then bring back to the boil and cook according to the packet instructions until *al dente*. When it is cooked, drain the pasta into a colander, rinse well under cold running water until cold, then allow to drain and dry, shaking the colander occasionally.

3 Remove the skin from the cooked chicken breasts and cut the meat into bite-size pieces.

4 To make the dressing, put the cheese in a large bowl and mash with a fork, then whisk in the wine vinegar, followed by the oil, chopped sage, and salt and pepper to taste.

5 Add the pasta, chicken and broccoli to the bowl. Toss well, then taste and adjust the seasoning as necessary. Serve garnished with sage leaves.

Chicken & Pasta Salad

This is a delicious way to use up leftover cooked chicken and makes a really filling meal.

Serves 4

225g/8oz/2 cups tri-coloured pasta twists
30ml/2 tbsp bottled pesto sauce
15ml/1 tbsp olive oil
1 beefsteak tomato
225g/8oz cooked French beans
12 stoned black olives
350g/12oz cooked chicken, cubed
salt and freshly ground black pepper
fresh basil, to garnish

1 Cook the pasta in plenty of boiling salted water according to the packet instructions until *al dente*. Drain, rinse in plenty of cold running water, then drain again.

2 Put the pasta into a large bowl and stir in the pesto sauce and olive oil, mixing well.

3 Peel the tomato: place it in boiling water for about 10 seconds and then into cold water to loosen the skin, which you can then slip off easily. Cut the tomato into small cubes. Cut the French beans into 4cm/1½in lengths.

4 Add the tomato and beans to the pasta with the olives and seasoning to taste. Add the cubed chicken. Toss gently together and transfer to a serving platter. Garnish with basil and serve.

Penne Salad with Chicken & Peppers

A rainbow-hued salad that tastes as good as it looks.

Serves 4

350g/12oz/3 cups penne
45ml/3 tbsp olive oil
225g/8oz/1½ cups cooked chicken, cut into bite-size pieces
1 small red pepper, seeded and diced
1 small yellow pepper, seeded and diced
50g/2oz/½ cup stoned green olives
4 spring onions, chopped
45ml/3 tbsp mayonnaise
5ml/1 tsp Worcestershire sauce
15ml/1 tbsp wine vinegar
salt and freshly ground black pepper

1 Cook the pasta in a large pan of boiling salted water according to the packet instructions until *al dente*.
2 Drain and rinse under cold water. Drain again well and turn into a large bowl.
3 Toss with the olive oil and allow to cool completely.
4 Combine all the remaining ingredients, then mix into the pasta and serve immediately.

Dijon Chicken Salad

An attractive and elegant dish to serve for lunch with herb and garlic bread.

Serves 4

4 chicken breast fillets, skinned
mixed salad leaves, e.g. frisée and oakleaf lettuce or radicchio, to serve

For the marinade

30ml/2 tbsp Dijon mustard
3 garlic cloves, crushed
15ml/1 tbsp grated onion
60ml/4 tbsp white wine

For the mustard dressing

30ml/2 tbsp tarragon wine vinegar
5ml/1 tsp Dijon mustard
5ml/1 tsp clear honey
90ml/6 tbsp olive oil
salt and freshly ground black pepper

1 To make the marinade, mix all the ingredients together in a shallow glass or earthenware dish that is large enough to hold the chicken in a single layer.

2 Add the chicken to the marinade and turn several times to coat completely. Cover with clear film and chill overnight.

3 Preheat the oven to 190°C/375°F/Gas 5. Transfer the chicken and the marinade into an ovenproof dish, cover with foil and bake for about 35 minutes or until tender. Remove from the oven and leave to cool in the liquid.

4 To make the mustard dressing, put all the ingredients into a screw-top jar and shake vigorously to emulsify. (This can be made several days in advance and stored in the fridge.)

5 Slice the chicken thinly, fan out the slices and arrange on a serving dish with the salad leaves. Spoon over some of the mustard dressing and serve.

French Chicken Salad

A light first course for eight people or a substantial main course for four, this is served with large, crisp, garlic-flavoured croûtons.

Serves 8

1.5kg/3½lb free-range chicken
300ml/½ pint/1¼ cups white wine and water, mixed
24 slices French bread, 5mm/¼in thick
1 garlic clove, peeled
225g/8oz green beans
115g/4oz young spinach leaves
2 celery sticks, thinly sliced
2 spring onions, thinly sliced
2 sun-dried tomatoes, chopped
fresh chives and parsley, to garnish

For the vinaigrette

30ml/2 tbsp red wine vinegar
90ml/6 tbsp olive oil
15ml/1 tbsp wholegrain mustard
15ml/1 tbsp clear honey
30ml/2 tbsp chopped mixed fresh herbs, e.g. thyme, parsley and chives
10ml/2 tsp finely chopped capers
salt and freshly ground black pepper

1 Preheat the oven to 190°C/375°F/Gas 5. Put the chicken into a casserole with the wine and water. Roast for 1½ hours until tender. Remove from the oven and leave to cool in the liquid. Discard the skin and bones and cut the flesh into small pieces.

2 To make the vinaigrette, put all the ingredients into a screw-top jar and shake vigorously to emulsify.

3 Toast the French bread under the grill or in the oven until dry and golden brown, then lightly rub with the peeled garlic clove.

4 Trim the green beans, cut into 5cm/2in lengths and cook in boiling water for a few minutes until just tender. Drain and rinse under cold running water.

5 Wash the spinach thoroughly and spin dry. Remove the stalks and tear the leaves into small pieces. Arrange on serving platter with the celery, beans, spring onions, chicken and tomatoes. Spoon over the vinaigrette dressing. Arrange the toasted croûtons on top, garnish with chives and parsley, and serve the salad immediately.

Grilled Chicken Salad with Lavender & Sweet Herbs

Lavender may seem like an odd salad ingredient, but its delightful scent has a natural affinity with orange, sweet garlic and other wild herbs. The inclusion of polenta makes this salad both filling and delicious.

Serves 4

4 chicken breast fillets
750ml/1½ pints/3¾ cups light Chicken Stock
175g/6oz/1½ cups fine polenta or cornmeal
50g/2oz/4 tbsp butter
450g/1lb young spinach
175g/6oz lamb's lettuce
8 fresh lavender sprigs
8 small tomatoes, halved
salt and freshly ground black pepper

For the lavender marinade

6 fresh lavender flowers
10ml/2 tsp finely grated orange rind
2 garlic cloves, crushed
10ml/2 tsp clear honey
30ml/2 tbsp olive oil
10ml/2 tsp chopped fresh thyme
10ml/2 tsp chopped fresh marjoram

1 To make the marinade, strip the lavender flowers from the stems and combine with the orange rind, garlic, honey and a pinch of salt. Add the olive oil and herbs. Slash the chicken deeply, spread the mixture over the chicken and leave to marinate in a cool place for at least 20 minutes.

2 To make the polenta, bring the chicken stock to the boil in a heavy saucepan. Add the meal in a steady stream, stirring all the time for 2–3 minutes until thick. Turn the cooked polenta out into a wide 2.5cm/1in-deep buttered tin and allow to cool.

3 Heat the grill to a moderate temperature. (If using a barbecue, let the embers settle to a steady glow.) Grill the chicken for about 15 minutes, turning once.

4 Cut the polenta into 2.5cm/1in cubes using a wet knife. Heat the butter in a large frying pan and fry the polenta until golden, turning once.

5 Wash the salad leaves and spin dry, then divide among four large plates. Slice each chicken breast and lay over the salad. Place the polenta among the salad, arrange the sprigs of lavender and tomatoes decoratively on top, season and serve.

Cook's Tip
Be sure to use culinary lavender, not that sold by the cosmetics industry as it will have been treated and will not be edible.

Maryland Salad

Barbecue-grilled chicken, sweetcorn, bacon, banana and watercress combine here in a sensational main-course salad. Serve with jacket potatoes and a knob of butter.

Serves 4

4 chicken breast fillets
oil, for brushing
225g/8oz rindless unsmoked bacon
4 sweetcorn cobs
40g/1½oz/3 tbsp softened butter
4 ripe bananas, peeled and halved
4 firm tomatoes, halved
1 escarole or butterhead lettuce
1 bunch watercress
salt and freshly ground black pepper

For the dressing

75ml/5 tbsp groundnut oil
15ml/1 tbsp white wine vinegar
10ml/2 tsp maple syrup
10ml/2 tsp mild mustard

1 Season the chicken fillets, brush with oil and barbecue or grill for 15 minutes, turning once. Barbecue or grill the bacon for 8–10 minutes or until crisp.

2 Bring a large saucepan of salted water to the boil. Shuck and trim the corn cobs or leave the husks on if you prefer. Boil for 20 minutes. For extra flavour, brush with butter and brown over the barbecue or under the grill.

3 Barbecue or grill the bananas and tomatoes for 6–8 minutes: you can brush these with butter too if you wish.

4 To make the dressing, combine the oil, vinegar, maple syrup and mustard with 15ml/1 tbsp water in a screw-top jar and shake well to emulsify.

5 Wash the salad leaves and spin dry. Place in a large bowl, pour over the dressing and toss to coat thoroughly.

6 Distribute the salad leaves among four large plates. Slice the chicken and arrange over the leaves with the bacon, banana, sweetcorn and tomatoes. Serve immediately.

Coronation Chicken

A dish that never fails to please, this was invented for the coronation of Queen Elizabeth II.

Serves 8

½ lemon
2.25kg/5lb chicken
1 onion, quartered
1 carrot, quartered
1 large bouquet garni
8 black peppercorns, crushed
salt
watercress sprigs, to garnish

For the sauce

15g/½oz/1 tbsp butter
1 small onion, chopped
15ml/1 tbsp curry paste
15ml/1 tbsp tomato purée
120ml/4fl oz/½ cup red wine
1 bay leaf
juice of ½ lemon, or more to taste
10–15ml/2–3 tbsp apricot jam
300ml/½ pint/1¼ cups mayonnaise
120ml/4fl oz/½ cup whipping cream, whipped
freshly ground black pepper

1 Put the lemon half in the chicken cavity, then place the chicken in a saucepan that it just fits. Add the vegetables, bouquet garni, peppercorns and salt.

2 Add sufficient water to come two-thirds of the way up the chicken, bring to the boil, then cover and cook gently for 1½ hours or until the chicken juices run clear.

3 Transfer the chicken to a large bowl, pour over the cooking liquid and leave to cool. When cold, lift the chicken from the liquid, discard the skin and bones and chop into bite-size pieces.

4 To make the sauce, heat the butter in a saucepan and cook the onion until soft. Add the curry paste, tomato purée, wine, bay leaf and lemon juice, and cook for 10 minutes. Add the jam, heat gently, stirring until it is incorporated, then remove the pan from the heat. Strain the sauce and leave to cool.

5 Beat the cooled sauce into the mayonnaise. Fold in the whipped cream. Add salt and pepper to taste, plus a little more lemon juice if needed. Stir in the chicken and serve garnished with watercress.

Swiss Cheese, Chicken & Tongue Salad with Apple & Celery

The rich, sweet flavours of this salad marry well with the tart, peppery nature of watercress. A minted lemon dressing combines to freshen the overall effect. Serve with warm new potatoes.

Serves 4

2 chicken breast fillets, skinned
½ chicken stock cube
225g/8oz sliced ox tongue or ham, 5mm/¼in thick
225g/8oz Gruyère cheese
1 lollo rosso lettuce
1 butterhead or Batavian endive lettuce
1 bunch watercress
2 green-skinned apples, cored and sliced
3 celery sticks, sliced
60ml/4 tbsp sesame seeds, toasted
salt, freshly ground black pepper and grated nutmeg

For the dressing

75ml/5 tbsp groundnut or sunflower oil
5ml/1 tsp sesame oil
45ml/3 tbsp lemon juice
10ml/2 tsp chopped fresh mint
3 drops Tabasco sauce

1 Place the chicken breasts in a shallow saucepan, cover with 300ml/½ pint/1¼ cups water, add the ½ stock cube and bring to the boil. Put the lid on the pan and simmer for 15 minutes. Drain, reserving the stock for another occasion, then cool the chicken under cold running water.

2 To make the dressing, put all the ingredients into a screw-top jar and shake vigorously. Cut the chicken, tongue and cheese into strips. Moisten with a little dressing and set aside.

3 Wash and spin dry the salad leaves and place in a large bowl. Add the apple and celery. Pour in some dressing and toss to coat thoroughly.

4 Distribute the salad leaves among four large plates. Pile the chicken, tongue and cheese in the centre, and scatter with toasted sesame seeds. Season with salt, freshly ground black pepper and grated nutmeg, and serve.

Chicken, Vegetable & Chilli Salad

This Vietnamese salad is full of surprising textures and flavours. Serve it as a light lunch dish or for supper with crusty French bread.

Serves 4

225g/8oz Chinese leaves
2 carrots, cut into matchsticks
½ cucumber, cut into matchsticks
2 fresh red chillies, seeded and cut into thin strips
1 small onion, sliced into thin rings
4 pickled gherkins, sliced, plus 45ml/3 tbsp of the liquid
50g/2oz/ ½ cup peanuts, lightly ground
225g/8oz cooked chicken, thinly sliced
1 garlic clove, crushed
5ml/1 tsp sugar
30ml/2 tbsp cider or white wine vinegar
salt

1 Thinly slice the Chinese leaves and spread out on a large board with the carrot and cucumber matchsticks. Sprinkle the vegetables with salt and set aside for 15 minutes.

2 In a bowl, mix together the chillies and onion rings, and add the sliced gherkins and ground peanuts. Tip the salted vegetables into a colander, rinse well with cold water and pat dry with kitchen paper.

3 Put the vegetables into a salad bowl and add the chilli mixture and cooked chicken. In a small jug or bowl, mix the gherkin liquid with the garlic, sugar and vinegar. Pour over the salad and toss lightly, then serve immediately.

Cook's Tip
Add a little more cider or white wine vinegar to the dressing if a sharper taste is preferred.

Hot-and-sour Chicken Salad

Another salad from Vietnam, in which deliciously spiced chicken is served hot on crisp vegetables.

Serves 4–6

2 chicken breast fillets, skinned
1 small fresh red chilli, seeded and finely chopped
1cm/ ½in piece fresh root ginger, peeled and finely chopped
1 garlic clove, crushed
15ml/1 tbsp crunchy peanut butter
30ml/2 tbsp chopped fresh coriander
5ml/1 tsp sugar
2.5ml/ ½ tsp salt
15ml/1 tbsp rice or white wine vinegar
60ml/4 tbsp vegetable oil
10ml/2 tsp fish sauce (optional)
115g/4oz/ ½ cup beansprouts
1 head Chinese leaves, roughly shredded
2 medium carrots, cut into matchsticks
1 red onion, cut into thin rings
2 large pickled gherkins, sliced

1 Slice the chicken thinly, place in a shallow bowl and set aside.

2 Grind the chilli, ginger and garlic in a mortar with a pestle. Add the peanut butter, coriander, sugar and salt. Add the vinegar, 30ml/2 tbsp of the oil and the fish sauce, if using. Combine well.

3 Cover the chicken with the spice mixture and leave to marinate for at least 2–3 hours.

4 Heat the remaining oil in a wok or frying pan. Add the chicken and cook for 10–12 minutes, tossing occasionally.

5 Arrange the beansprouts, Chinese leaves, carrots, onion and gherkins on a serving platter or individual plates and place the chicken on top. Pour over the pan juices and serve at once.

Turkey, Rice & Apple Salad

A flavoursome, healthy and crunchy salad to use up leftover turkey and fruit during the holiday festivities.

Serves 8

225g/8oz/1 1/4 cups brown rice
50g/2oz/ 1/3 cup wild rice
2 red-skinned apples, quartered, cored and chopped
2 celery sticks, coarsely sliced
115g/4oz seedless grapes
45ml/3 tbsp lemon or orange juice
150ml/ 1/4 pint/ 2/3 cup thick mayonnaise
350g/12oz cooked turkey, chopped
salt and freshly ground black pepper
frisée lettuce leaves, to serve

1 Cook the brown and wild rice together in plenty of boiling salted water for about 30 minutes or until tender. Rinse under cold running water and drain thoroughly.

2 Turn the rice into a large bowl and add the apples, celery and grapes. In another bowl, beat the lemon or orange juice into the mayonnaise, season with salt and pepper, and pour over the rice, mixing thoroughly.

3 Add the cooked turkey and mix well to coat completely with the mayonnaise.

4 Arrange the lettuce over the base and around the sides of a large serving dish. Spoon the turkey and rice mixture on top and serve immediately.

Cook's Tip
This is a good choice for a summer buffet party, but keep the salad in the fridge until ready to serve.

Wild Rice & Turkey Salad

An attractive fanned pear garnish complements this salad, which is tossed in a walnut oil dressing.

Serves 4

175g/6oz/scant 1 cup wild rice, boiled or steamed
2 celery sticks, thinly sliced
50g/2oz spring onions, chopped
115g/4oz/1 1/2 cups small button mushrooms, quartered
450g/1lb cooked turkey breast, diced
120ml/4fl oz/ 1/2 cup French Dressing made with walnut oil
5ml/1 tsp fresh thyme leaves
2 pears, peeled, halved and cored
25g/1oz/ 1/4 cup walnut pieces, toasted
fresh parsley sprigs, to garnish

1 Combine the cooled cooked wild rice with the celery, spring onions, mushrooms and turkey in a bowl.

2 Add the dressing and thyme leaves to the salad, and toss together well to mix.

3 Thinly slice the pear halves lengthways without cutting through the stalk end and spread the slices like a fan.

4 Divide the salad among four plates. Arrange a fanned pear half alongside each salad and sprinkle with walnuts. Garnish with parsley sprigs and serve.

Cooking Wild Rice

Although called "rice", this is actually an aquatic grass. Its deliciously nutty flavour and firm, chewy texture make it a perfect complement to many meat and poultry dishes. It is also an excellent partner for vegetables such as courgettes and mushrooms. It can be cooked like white rice, by boiling or steaming, needing only about 20 minutes longer cooking.

Warm Duck Salad with Orange

The distinct, sharp flavour of radicchio, curly endive and fresh oranges is a perfect foil for the rich taste of duck. Serve with steamed new potatoes for an elegant main course.

Serves 4
2 duck breast fillets
2 oranges
curly endive, radicchio and lamb's lettuce leaves
30ml/2 tbsp medium-dry sherry
10–15ml/2–3 tsp dark soy sauce
salt

1 Rub the skin of the duck breast fillets with salt and then slash the skin several times with a sharp knife.

2 Heat a heavy, cast-iron frying pan and fry the duck breasts, skin side down at first, for 20–25 minutes, turning once, until the skin is well browned and the flesh is cooked through. Transfer to a plate to cool slightly and pour off the excess fat from the pan, leaving behind the meat juices.

3 Peel the oranges. Separate the oranges into segments and use a sharp knife to remove all the pith, working over a small bowl to catch the juice.

4 Wash and spin dry the salad leaves and arrange in a wide, shallow serving bowl.

5 Heat the cooking juices remaining in the pan and stir in 45ml/3 tbsp of the reserved orange juice. Bring to the boil over a medium heat, add the sherry and then just enough soy sauce to give a piquant, spicy flavour.

6 Cut the duck into thin slices and arrange over the salad with the orange segments. Pour over the warm dressing and serve immediately.

Apricot Duck Breasts with Beansprout Salad

The duck stays beautifully moist when cooked on a barbecue.

Serves 4
4 plump duck breasts, with skin
1 small red onion, thinly sliced
115g/4oz/½ cup ready-to-eat dried apricots
15ml/1 tbsp clear honey
5ml/1 tsp sesame oil
10ml/2 tsp ground star anise
salt and freshly ground black pepper

For the salad
½ head Chinese leaves, finely shredded
150g/5oz/3 cups beansprouts
2 spring onions, shredded

For the dressing
15ml/1 tbsp light soy sauce
15ml/1 tbsp groundnut oil
5ml/1 tsp sesame oil
5ml/1 tsp clear honey

1 Place a duck breast, skin side down, on a board and cut a long slit down one side, cutting not quite through, to form a large pocket. Tuck some slices of onion and apricots inside the pocket and press the breast firmly back into shape. Secure with a metal skewer. Repeat with the other breasts.

2 Mix together the honey and sesame oil, and brush over the duck. Sprinkle over the ground star anise and season with salt and pepper.

3 To make the salad, mix together the shredded Chinese leaves, beansprouts and spring onions in a bowl.

4 To make the dressing, put all the ingredients in a screw-top jar with salt and pepper to taste and shake vigorously. Toss into the salad, mixing well.

5 Cook the duck over a medium-hot barbecue for about 12–15 minutes, turning once, until golden brown on the outside and cooked through. Divide the salad among four plates, place a duck breast on top of each portion and serve at once.

Chicken Teriyaki

A bowl of boiled rice is the ideal accompaniment to this Japanese-style chicken dish.

Serves 4

450g/1lb chicken breast fillets, skinned
mustard and cress, to garnish

For the marinade

5ml/1 tsp sugar
15ml/1 tbsp sake
15ml/1 tbsp dry sherry
30ml/2 tbsp dark soy sauce
grated rind of 1 orange

1 Thinly slice the chicken fillets.

2 To make the marinade, mix the sugar, sake, sherry, soy sauce and orange rind together in a small bowl, stirring until the sugar has dissolved.

3 Place the chicken in another bowl, pour over the marinade and leave to marinate for 15 minutes.

4 Heat a wok or heavy-based frying pan, add the chicken and marinade and stir-fry for 4–5 minutes. Serve garnished with mustard and cress.

Cook's Tip

Make sure the marinade is brought to the boil and cooked for 4–5 minutes, because it has been in contact with raw chicken.

Lemon Chicken Stir-fry

It is essential to prepare all the ingredients before you begin so they are ready to cook. This dish can then be cooked in minutes.

Serves 4

4 chicken breast fillets, skinned
15ml/1 tbsp light soy sauce
175ml/5 tbsp cornflour
1 bunch spring onions
1 lemon
1 garlic clove, crushed
15ml/1 tbsp caster sugar
30ml/2 tbsp sherry
150ml/ ¼ pint/ ⅔ cup Chicken Stock
60ml/4 tbsp olive oil
lemon wedges, to garnish
salad leaves, to serve

1 Divide each chicken breast into two natural fillets. Place each between two sheets of clear film and flatten to a thickness of 5mm/¼in with a rolling pin. Cut into 2.5cm/1in strips across the grain of the fillets. Put the chicken into a bowl with the soy sauce and toss to coat. Sprinkle over 60ml/4 tbsp cornflour to coat each piece.

2 Trim the roots off the spring onions and cut diagonally into 1cm/ ½in pieces. With a swivel peeler, remove the lemon rind in thin strips, without cutting into the white pith, and cut into fine shreds. Squeeze the juice from the lemon into a small bowl. Have ready the garlic, sugar, sherry, stock, lemon juice and remaining cornflour blended to a thin paste with water.

3 Heat the oil in a wok or large, heavy-based frying pan and cook the chicken very quickly in small batches for 3–4 minutes until lightly coloured. Remove and keep warm while frying the rest of the chicken. Remove the final batch of chicken.

4 Add the spring onions and garlic to the pan and cook for 2 minutes. Add the sugar, sherry, stock and cornflour paste and bring to the boil, stirring until thickened. Add more sherry or stock if the sauce seems a little too thick.

5 Return the chicken to the pan and stir until it is evenly covered with sauce. Reheat for 2 more minutes. Garnish with lemon wedges, and serve immediately on a bed of salad leaves.

Glazed Chicken with Cashew Nuts

Hoisin sauce lends a sweet yet slightly hot note to this chicken dish, while cashew nuts add a pleasing contrast of texture.

Serves 4

75g/3oz/ ¾ cup cashew nuts
1 red pepper
450g/1lb chicken breast fillets, skinned
45ml/3 tbsp groundnut oil
4 garlic cloves, finely chopped
30ml/2 tbsp rice wine or medium-dry sherry
45ml/3 tbsp hoisin sauce
10ml/2 tsp sesame oil
5–6 spring onions, green parts only, cut into 2.5cm/1in lengths
cooked rice or noodles, to serve

1 Heat a wok or heavy-based frying pan until hot, add the cashew nuts and stir-fry over a low to medium heat for 1–2 minutes until golden brown. Remove from the heat and set the cashews aside.

2 Halve the red pepper and remove the seeds. Slice the pepper and chicken into finger-length strips.

3 Heat the wok again until hot, add the oil and swirl it around. Add the garlic and let it sizzle in the oil for a few seconds. Add the red pepper and chicken, and stir-fry for 2 minutes.

4 Add the rice wine or sherry and hoisin sauce. Continue to stir-fry until the chicken is tender and all the ingredients are evenly glazed.

5 Stir in the sesame oil, reserved toasted cashew nuts and the spring onion tips. Serve immediately with rice or noodles.

Variation
Use blanched almonds instead of cashew nuts if you prefer.

Yellow Chicken

A super-fast version of an all-time Chinese favourite stir-fry.

Serves 4

30ml/2 tbsp oil
75g/3oz/ ¾ cup salted cashew nuts
4 spring onions
450g/1lb chicken breast fillets
165g/5½oz jar yellow bean sauce
cooked rice, to serve

1 Heat 15ml/1 tbsp of the oil in a wok or frying pan and fry the cashew nuts until browned. Remove from the pan with a slotted spoon and set aside.

2 Roughly chop the spring onions. Skin and thinly slice the chicken fillets. Heat the remaining oil and fry the spring onions and chicken for 5–8 minutes until the meat is browned all over and cooked.

3 Return the nuts to the pan and pour the jar of sauce over. Stir well and cook gently until hot. Serve at once, accompanied by cooked rice.

Cook's Tip
Yellow bean sauce is made from salted, fermented yellow soya beans crushed with sugar and flour to make a thick paste. It is available from supermarkets and Chinese foodstores.

Stir-fried Chicken with Pineapple

An Indonesian-inspired dish in which pineapple adds an extra dimension to chicken and the usual stir-fry flavourings.

Serves 4–6

500g/1¼lb chicken breast fillets
30ml/2 tbsp cornflour
60ml/4 tbsp sunflower oil
1 garlic clove, crushed
5cm/2in piece fresh root ginger, peeled and cut into matchsticks
1 small onion, thinly sliced
1 fresh pineapple, peeled, cored and cubed, or 425g/15oz can pineapple chunks in natural juice
30ml/2 tbsp dark soy sauce
1 bunch spring onions, white bulbs left whole, green tops sliced
salt and freshly ground black pepper

1 Skin the chicken fillets and slice thinly on the diagonal. Toss the strips of chicken in the cornflour with a little seasoning.

2 Heat the oil in a wok or heavy-based frying pan and stir-fry the chicken for 5–8 minutes until lightly browned and cooked through. Lift the chicken out of the wok using a slotted spoon and keep warm.

3 Reheat the oil and fry the garlic, ginger and onion until soft but not browned. Add the fresh pineapple and 120ml/4fl oz/½ cup water, if using, or the canned pineapple pieces together with their juice.

4 Stir in the soy sauce and return the chicken to the pan to heat through. Taste and adjust the seasoning as necessary.

5 Stir in the whole spring onion bulbs and half of the sliced green tops. Toss well together and then turn the chicken stir-fry on to a serving platter. Serve garnished with the remaining sliced green spring onion tops.

Thai Chicken & Vegetable Stir-fry

An all-in-one midweek main course that needs only boiled or steamed rice as an accompaniment.

Serves 4

30ml/2 tbsp sunflower oil
1 lemon grass stalk, thinly sliced
1cm/½in piece fresh root ginger, peeled and chopped
1 large garlic clove, chopped
275g/10oz lean chicken, thinly sliced
½ red pepper, seeded and sliced
½ green pepper, seeded and sliced
4 spring onions, chopped
2 medium carrots, cut into matchsticks
115g/4oz/¾ cup fine green beans
30ml/2 tbsp oyster sauce
pinch of sugar
salt and freshly ground black pepper
25g/1oz/¼ cup salted peanuts, lightly crushed, and fresh coriander leaves, to garnish
cooked rice, to serve

1 Heat the oil in a wok or heavy-based frying pan over high heat. Add the lemon grass, ginger and garlic, and stir-fry for 30 seconds until lightly browned.

2 Add the chicken and stir-fry for 2 minutes. Then add the vegetables and stir-fry for 4–5 minutes until the chicken is cooked and the vegetables are almost cooked.

3 Stir in the oyster sauce, sugar and seasoning to taste, and stir-fry for another minute to mix and blend well.

4 Serve at once, sprinkled with the peanuts and coriander leaves, and accompanied by rice.

Variations

If lemon grass is unavailable, you can substitute the thinly pared and chopped rind of ½ lemon, although the citrus flavour will not be as intense.
Make this quick supper dish a little hotter by adding more fresh root ginger, if you wish.

Chinese Chicken with Cashew Nuts

The roasted cashew nuts provide additional proteins as well as extra texture and flavour to this dish.

Serves 4

4 chicken breast fillets, about 175g/6oz each, skinned and cut into strips
3 garlic cloves, crushed
60ml/4 tbsp soy sauce
30ml/2 tbsp cornflour
225g/8oz dried egg noodles
45ml/3 tbsp groundnut or sunflower oil
15ml/1 tbsp sesame oil
115g/4oz/1 cup cashew nuts, roasted
6 spring onions, cut into 5cm/2in pieces and halved lengthways
spring onion curls and a little chopped red chilli, to garnish

1 Place the chicken in a bowl with the garlic, soy sauce and cornflour, and mix until the chicken is well coated. Cover and chill for about 30 minutes.

2 Meanwhile, bring a large saucepan of water to the boil and add the egg noodles. Turn off the heat and leave to stand for 5 minutes. Drain well and reserve.

3 Heat the oils in a wok or large heavy-based frying pan and add the chilled chicken and marinade juices. Stir-fry over a high heat for about 3–4 minutes or until the chicken is golden brown all over.

4 Add the cashew nuts and spring onions to the pan, and stir-fry for 2–3 minutes.

5 Add the drained noodles and stir-fry for a further 2 minutes. Toss well to mix everything thoroughly. Serve immediately, garnished with spring onion curls and chopped red chilli.

Stir-fried Rice Noodles with Chicken & Prawns

This Thai recipe combines chicken with prawns and has the characteristic sweet, sour and salty flavours.

Serves 4

225g/8oz dried flat rice noodles
120ml/4fl oz/½ cup water
60ml/4 tbsp fish sauce
15ml/1 tbsp sugar
15ml/1 tbsp fresh lime juice
5ml/1 tsp paprika
pinch of cayenne pepper
45ml/3 tbsp oil
2 garlic cloves, finely chopped
1 chicken breast fillet, skinned and finely sliced
8 raw prawns, peeled, deveined and cut in half
1 egg
50g/2oz roasted peanuts, coarsely crushed
3 spring onions, cut into short lengths
175g/6oz/¾ cup beansprouts
fresh coriander leaves and lime wedges, to garnish

1 Place the rice noodles in a large bowl, cover with warm water and soak for 30 minutes until soft. Drain well. Combine the water, fish sauce, sugar, lime juice, paprika and cayenne in a small bowl. Set aside until required.

2 Heat the oil in a wok or heavy-based frying pan. Add the garlic and fry for 30 seconds until it starts to brown. Stir in the chicken and prawns, and stir-fry for 3–4 minutes until cooked.

3 Push the chicken and prawn mixture to the sides of the wok. Break the egg into the centre, then quickly stir to break up the yolk and cook over a medium heat until lightly scrambled.

4 Add the noodles and the fish sauce mixture to the wok. Add half the crushed peanuts and cook, stirring frequently, until the noodles are soft and most of the liquid has been absorbed.

5 Add the spring onions and half of the beansprouts. Cook, stirring for 1 minute more. Spoon on to a serving platter. Sprinkle with the remaining peanuts and beansprouts. Garnish with coriander and lime wedges, and serve.

Shredded Chicken with Celery

The tender chicken breast makes a fine contrast with the crunchy texture of the celery, and the red chillies add colour and flavour.

Serves 4

275g/10oz chicken breast fillet, skinned
5ml/1 tsp salt
½ egg white, lightly beaten
10ml/2 tsp cornflour
about 475ml/16fl oz/2 cups vegetable oil
1 celery heart, thinly shredded
1–2 fresh red chillies, seeded and thinly shredded
1 spring onion, thinly shredded
few strips of fresh root ginger, peeled and thinly shredded
5ml/1 tsp light brown sugar
15ml/1 tbsp Chinese rice wine or dry sherry
few drops of sesame oil

1 Using a sharp knife, thinly shred the chicken. Place in a bowl and add a pinch of the salt and the egg white. Mix the cornflour to a thin paste with a little water and add to the bowl, stirring well to coat.

2 Heat the oil in a wok or heavy-based frying pan until warm, add the chicken and stir to separate the shreds. When the chicken turns white, remove with a slotted spoon and drain on kitchen paper. Keep warm.

3 Pour all but 30ml/2 tbsp of the oil from the wok. Add the celery, chillies, spring onion and ginger, and stir-fry for 1 minute.

4 Return the chicken to the wok and add the remaining salt, the sugar and rice wine or sherry. Stir-fry for 1 minute, then add the sesame oil. Serve immediately.

Cook's Tip

Sesame oil is not often used for frying in Chinese cooking. More usually, it is added towards the end of the cooking time for extra flavour.

Chicken with Chinese Vegetables

Shiitake mushrooms, bamboo shoots and mangetouts combine with chicken in this tasty stir-fry.

Serves 4

225–275g/8–10oz chicken, boned and skinned
5ml/1 tsp salt
½ egg white, lightly beaten
10ml/2 tsp cornflour
60ml/4 tbsp vegetable oil
6–8 small dried shiitake mushrooms, soaked in water and drained
115g/4oz canned sliced bamboo shoots, drained
115g/4oz mangetouts, trimmed
1 spring onion, cut into short sections
few small pieces of fresh root ginger, peeled
5ml/1 tsp light brown sugar
15ml/1 tbsp light soy sauce
15ml/1 tbsp Chinese rice wine or dry sherry
few drops of sesame oil

1 Using a sharp knife, cut the chicken into thin slices, each about the size of an oblong postage stamp. Place in a bowl and mix with a pinch of the salt and the egg white. Mix the cornflour to a thin paste with a little water and add to the bowl.

2 Heat a wok or heavy-based frying pan and add the oil. When the oil is hot, add the chicken and stir-fry over a medium heat for about 30 seconds, then remove with a slotted spoon and drain on kitchen paper. Keep warm.

3 Add the mushrooms, bamboo shoots, mangetouts, spring onion and ginger to the wok, and stir-fry over a high heat for about 1 minute.

4 Return the chicken to the wok, and add the remaining salt and the sugar. Blend, then add the soy sauce and rice wine or sherry. Stir a few more times. Sprinkle with the sesame oil and serve immediately.

Chicken with Mangetouts & Coriander

Delicate and fresh-tasting mangetouts are excellent in stir-fries and also give additional colour to paler ingredients, such as chicken.

Serves 4

4 chicken breast fillets, skinned
225g/8oz mangetouts
vegetable oil, for deep frying
15ml/1 tbsp vegetable oil
3 garlic cloves, finely chopped
2.5cm/1in piece fresh root ginger, freshly grated
5–6 spring onions, cut into 4cm/1½in lengths
10ml/2 tsp sesame oil
30ml/2 tbsp chopped fresh coriander
salt
cooked rice, to serve

For the marinade

5ml/1 tsp cornflour
15ml/1 tbsp light soy sauce
15ml/1 tbsp medium-dry sherry
15ml/1 tbsp vegetable oil

For the sauce

5ml/1 tsp cornflour
10–15ml/2–3 tsp dark soy sauce
120ml/4fl oz/½ cup Chicken Stock
30ml/2 tbsp oyster sauce

1 Cut the chicken into strips about 1 × 4cm/½ × 1½in and place in a wide, shallow dish. To make the marinade, blend together the cornflour and soy sauce in a small bowl. Stir in the sherry and oil. Pour over the chicken, turning the pieces to coat them evenly, and leave for 30 minutes.

2 Trim the mangetouts and plunge into a pan of boiling salted water. Bring back to the boil, then drain and refresh under cold running water.

3 To make the sauce, mix together the cornflour, soy sauce, stock and oyster sauce in a bowl. Set aside.

4 Heat the oil in a deep-fat fryer. Drain the chicken strips and fry, in batches if necessary, for about 30 seconds until brown. Remove using a slotted spoon and drain on kitchen paper.

5 Heat 15ml/1 tbsp oil in a wok or heavy-based frying pan and add the garlic and ginger. Stir-fry for 30 seconds. Add the mangetouts and stir-fry for 1–2 minutes. Transfer to a plate and keep warm.

6 Heat a further 15ml/1 tbsp oil in the wok, add the spring onions and stir-fry for 1–2 minutes. Add the chicken and stir-fry for 2 minutes. Pour in the sauce, reduce the heat and cook until it thickens and the chicken is cooked through.

7 Return the mangetouts to the wok, and stir in the sesame oil and chopped coriander. Serve with rice.

Variation

If mangetouts are not available you could use broccoli or French beans.

Fu-yung Chicken

Because the egg whites (*Fu-yung* in Chinese) mixed with milk are deep fried, they have prompted some rather imaginative cooks to refer to this dish as "deep fried milk"!

Serves 4

175g/6oz chicken breast fillet
5ml/1 tsp salt
4 egg whites, lightly beaten
15ml/1 tbsp cornflour
30ml/2 tbsp milk
vegetable oil, for deep frying
1 lettuce heart, separated into leaves
about 120ml/4fl oz/½ cup Chicken Stock
15ml/1 tbsp Chinese rice wine or dry sherry
15ml/1 tbsp garden peas
few drops of sesame oil
5ml/1 tsp very finely chopped ham, to garnish

1 Finely mince the chicken meat and place in a bowl. Add a pinch of the salt and the egg whites. Mix the cornflour to a thin paste with a little water and add to the bowl with the milk. Blend well until smooth.

2 Heat the oil in a very hot wok, but before the oil gets too hot, gently spoon the chicken mixture into the oil in batches. Do not stir, otherwise it will scatter. Stir the oil from the bottom of the wok so that the chicken pieces rise to the surface. Remove the chicken as soon as the colour turns bright white. Drain.

3 Pour off the excess oil, leaving about 15ml/1 tbsp in the wok. Add the lettuce leaves and remaining salt, and stir-fry for 1 minute. Add the stock and bring to the boil.

4 Return the chicken to the wok, add the rice wine or sherry and peas, and blend well. Sprinkle with the sesame oil, garnish with the ham and serve.

Pasta with Chicken Livers

Chicken livers and smoked bacon seem made for each other in this surprisingly rich-tasting dish. If orecchiette pasta is unavailable, use another medium-size pasta.

Serves 4

225g/8oz chicken livers
30ml/2 tbsp olive oil
2 garlic cloves, crushed
175g/6oz smoked back bacon, rinded and roughly chopped
400g/14oz can chopped tomatoes
150ml/ ¼ pint/ ⅔ cup Chicken Stock
15ml/1 tbsp tomato purée
15ml/1 tbsp dry sherry
30ml/2 tbsp chopped fresh mixed herbs, e.g. parsley, rosemary and basil
350g/12oz dried orecchiette
salt and freshly ground black pepper
Parmesan cheese shavings, to serve

1 Trim the chicken livers and cut into bite-size pieces. Heat the olive oil in a sauté pan and fry the livers for 3–4 minutes until lightly browned.

2 Add the garlic and bacon to the pan, and fry until golden brown. Add the tomatoes, chicken stock, tomato purée, sherry, herbs and seasoning.

3 Bring to the boil and simmer gently, uncovered, for about 5 minutes until the sauce has thickened.

4 Meanwhile, cook the pasta in boiling salted water for about 12 minutes or according to the packet instructions until *al dente*. Drain well, then toss into the sauce. Serve hot, sprinkled with Parmesan cheese shavings.

Cook's Tip
You'll find orecchiette, a dried pasta shaped like ears – it means "little ears" – in most large supermarkets.

Noodles with Aubergines & Chicken Livers

A modern Jewish pasta recipe with an unusual and tasty sauce.

Serves 4

2 large aubergines, about 350g/12oz each
2 garlic cloves
1 large onion
90–120ml/6–8 tbsp oil
500g/1¼lb carton creamed tomatoes
250ml/8fl oz/1 cup boiling water
350g/12oz flat noodles
275g/10oz chicken livers
salt and freshly ground black pepper
chopped flat leaf parsley, to garnish

1 Peel and dice the aubergines. Crush the garlic and roughly chop the onion.

2 Put half the oil in a frying pan and sauté the onion for about 1 minute. Add the garlic and cook until the onion starts to brown. Transfer to a plate.

3 Add the remaining oil to the pan and heat. Add the aubergines and fry briskly, turning occasionally, until browned.

4 Return the onion to the pan, and add the creamed tomatoes, boiling water and seasoning. Simmer for 30 minutes.

5 Preheat the grill. Cook the noodles in boiling salted water or according to the packet instructions until *al dente*. Meanwhile, grill the chicken livers on oiled foil for 3–4 minutes on each side. Snip into strips.

6 Drain the noodles and arrange on serving plates. Spoon over the aubergine sauce and top with the chicken livers. Serve immediately, garnished with flat leaf parsley.

Conchiglie with Chicken Livers & Herbs

Fresh sage and flat leaf parsley are a superb foil to chicken livers, here cooked in a tasty sauce and tossed with pasta shells.

Serves 4

50g/2oz/4 tbsp butter
115g/4oz pancetta or lean bacon, diced
250g/9oz chicken livers, trimmed and diced
2 garlic cloves, crushed
10ml/2 tsp chopped fresh sage
350g/12oz conchiglie
150ml/¼ pint/⅔ cup dry white wine
4 ripe Italian plum tomatoes, peeled and diced
15ml/1 tbsp chopped fresh flat leaf parsley
salt and freshly ground black pepper

1 Melt half the butter in a medium frying pan or saucepan, add the pancetta or bacon and fry over a medium heat for a few minutes until lightly coloured but not crisp.

2 Add the chicken livers, garlic, half the sage and plenty of pepper. Increase the heat and toss the livers for about 5 minutes until they change colour all over but remain slightly pink in the centre.

3 Meanwhile, bring a large saucepan of salted water to the boil, add the pasta and cook according to the packet instructions until *al dente*.

4 Pour the wine over the chicken livers in the pan and let it sizzle, then lower the heat and simmer gently for 5 minutes.

5 Add the remaining butter to the pan. As soon as it has melted, add the tomatoes, toss to mix, then add the remaining sage and the parsley. Stir well. Taste and add salt if needed.

6 Drain the pasta and turn it into a warmed bowl. Pour the sauce over and toss well. Serve immediately.

Penne with Chicken & Cheese

Broccoli, garlic and Gorgonzola cheese form a great partnership with strips of chicken.

Serves 4

225g/8oz broccoli, divided into small florets
50g/2oz/4 tbsp butter
2 chicken breast fillets, skinned and cut into thin strips
2 garlic cloves, crushed
350g/12oz penne
120ml/4fl oz/½ cup dry white wine
200ml/7fl oz/scant 1 cup double cream
90g/3½ oz Gorgonzola cheese, rind removed and finely diced
salt and freshly ground black pepper
grated Parmesan cheese, to serve

1 Plunge the broccoli into a saucepan of boiling salted water. Bring back to a boil and boil for 2 minutes, then drain in a colander and refresh under cold running water.

2 Melt the butter in a large frying pan or saucepan, add the chicken and garlic, with salt and pepper to taste, and stir well. Fry over a medium heat for 3 minutes.

3 Meanwhile, bring a large saucepan of salted water to the boil, add the pasta and cook according to the packet instructions until *al dente*.

4 Pour the wine and cream over the chicken mixture in the pan, stir to mix, then simmer, stirring occasionally, for about 5 minutes until the sauce has reduced and thickened. Add the broccoli, increase the heat, toss to heat it through and mix it with the chicken. Taste and adjust the seasoning as necessary. Drain the pasta and add it to the sauce. Stir in the Gorgonzola and toss well. Serve with grated Parmesan.

Variation
Use leeks instead of broccoli if you prefer. Fry them with the chicken.

Pappardelle with Chicken & Mushrooms

Rich and creamy, this is a good supper party dish.

Serves 4

15g/½oz dried porcini mushrooms
175ml/6fl oz/¾ cup warm water
30ml/2 tbsp butter
1 garlic clove, crushed
1 small handful fresh flat leaf parsley, coarsely chopped
1 small leek, chopped
120ml/4fl oz/½ cup dry white wine
250ml/8fl oz/1 cup Chicken Stock
350g/12oz pappardelle
2 chicken breast fillets, skinned and cut into thin strips
105ml/7 tbsp mascarpone cheese
salt and freshly ground black pepper
fresh basil leaves, to garnish

1 Put the dried mushrooms in a bowl. Pour in the warm water and allow to soak for 15–20 minutes. Turn into a fine sieve set over a bowl and squeeze the mushrooms with your hands to release as much liquid as possible. Chop the mushrooms finely and set aside the strained soaking liquid until required.

2 Melt the butter in a medium frying pan, add the mushrooms, garlic, parsley and leek, with salt and pepper to taste. Cook over a low heat, stirring frequently, for about 5 minutes, then pour in the wine and stock, and bring to the boil. Lower the heat and simmer for about 5 minutes or until reduced and thickened.

3 Meanwhile, bring a large saucepan of salted water to the boil, adding the reserved soaking liquid. Add the pasta and cook according to the packet instructions until *al dente*.

4 Add the chicken to the sauce and simmer for 5 minutes or until just tender. Add the mascarpone a spoonful at a time, stirring well after each addition, then add one or two spoonfuls of the water used for cooking the pasta.

5 Drain the pasta and turn it into a warmed large bowl. Add the chicken and sauce, and toss well. Serve immediately, topped with the basil leaves.

Farfalle with Chicken & Cherry Tomatoes

Quick to prepare and easy to cook, this colourful dish is full of flavour.

Serves 4

350g/12oz chicken breast fillets, skinned and cut into bite-size pieces
60ml/4 tbsp Italian dry vermouth
10ml/2 tsp chopped fresh rosemary
15ml/1 tbsp olive oil
1 onion, finely chopped
90g/3½oz piece Italian salami, diced
350g/12oz farfalle
15ml/1 tbsp balsamic vinegar
400g/14oz cherry tomatoes
good pinch of crushed dried red chillies
salt and freshly ground black pepper
fresh rosemary sprigs, to garnish

1 Put the pieces of chicken in a large bowl, pour in the dry vermouth and sprinkle with half the chopped rosemary, and salt and pepper to taste. Stir well and set aside.

2 Heat the oil in a large frying pan or saucepan, add the onion and salami, and fry over a medium heat for about 5 minutes, stirring frequently.

3 Meanwhile, bring a large saucepan of salted water to the boil, add the pasta and cook according to the packet instructions until *al dente*.

4 Add the chicken and vermouth to the onion and salami, increase the heat to high and fry for 3 minutes or until the chicken is white on all sides. Sprinkle in the balsamic vinegar. Add the cherry tomatoes and crushed dried red chillies. Stir well and simmer for a few minutes more. Taste and adjust the seasoning as necessary.

5 Drain the pasta and turn it into the sauce. Add the remaining chopped rosemary, and toss to mix the pasta and sauce together. Serve immediately in warmed bowls, garnished with the rosemary sprigs.

Tagliatelle with Chicken & Herb Sauce

A rich, creamy dish made with vermouth and fromage frais, this just needs a simple green salad accompaniment.

Serves 4

30ml/2 tbsp olive oil
1 red onion, cut into wedges
350g/12oz tagliatelle
1 garlic clove, chopped
350g/12oz chicken, diced
300ml/ ½ pint/1 ¼ cups dry vermouth
45ml/3 tbsp chopped fresh mixed herbs
150ml/ ¼ pint/ ⅔ cup fromage frais
salt and freshly ground black pepper
shredded fresh mint, to garnish

1 Heat the oil in a large frying pan and fry the onion for about 5–7 minutes until softened and the layers separate.

2 Bring a large saucepan of salted water to the boil, add the tagliatelle and cook according to the packet instructions.

3 Add the garlic and chicken to the frying pan and fry for 10 minutes, stirring occasionally, until the chicken is browned all over and cooked through.

4 Pour the vermouth over the chicken, bring to the boil and boil rapidly until reduced by about half.

5 Stir in the mixed herbs, fromage frais and seasoning, and heat through gently, but do not boil.

6 Drain the pasta thoroughly and toss it with the sauce to coat. Serve immediately, garnished with shredded fresh mint.

Cook's Tip
If you don't want to use vermouth, use dry white wine instead. Orvieto and frascati are two Italian wines that are ideal to use in this sauce.

Penne with Chicken & Ham Sauce

A meal in itself, this colourful pasta sauce is perfect for a midweek lunch or dinner.

Serves 4

350g/12oz penne
25g/1oz/2 tbsp butter
1 onion, chopped
1 garlic clove, chopped
1 bay leaf
450ml/ ¾ pint/scant 2 cups dry white wine
150ml/ ¼ pint/ ⅔ cup crème fraîche
225g/8oz/1 ½ cups cooked chicken, skinned, boned and diced
115g/4oz/ ⅔ cup cooked lean ham, diced
115g/4oz/1 cup Gouda cheese, grated
15ml/1 tbsp chopped fresh mint
salt and freshly ground black pepper
finely shredded fresh mint, to garnish

1 Bring a large saucepan of salted water to the boil, add the pasta and cook according to the instructions on the packet until *al dente*.

2 Heat the butter in a large frying pan and gently fry the onion for 10 minutes until softened.

3 Add the garlic, bay leaf and wine, and bring to the boil. Boil rapidly until reduced by half. Remove the bay leaf, then stir in the crème fraîche and return to the boil.

4 Add the chicken, ham and cheese, and simmer for 5 minutes, stirring occasionally until heated through. Add the chopped mint and seasoning to taste.

5 Drain the pasta thoroughly and turn it into a large warmed serving bowl. Add the sauce, toss to coat well, then serve, garnished with shredded mint.

Pasta Spirals with Chicken & Tomato Sauce

A recipe for a speedy supper – serve this dish with a mixed bean salad.

Serves 4

15ml/1 tbsp olive oil
1 onion, chopped
1 carrot, chopped
1 garlic clove, chopped
400g/14oz can chopped tomatoes
15ml/1 tbsp tomato purée
150ml/ ¼ pint/ ⅔ cup Chicken Stock
350g/12oz pasta spirals (fusilli)
50g/2oz sun-dried tomatoes in olive oil, drained weight
225g/8oz boneless chicken, diagonally sliced
salt and freshly ground black pepper
fresh mint sprigs, to garnish

1 Heat the oil in a large frying pan, and fry the onion and carrot for 5 minutes, stirring occasionally.

2 Stir the garlic, canned chopped tomatoes, tomato purée and stock into the onion and carrot, and bring to the boil. Simmer for 10 minutes, stirring occasionally.

3 Bring a large saucepan of salted water to the boil, add the pasta spirals and cook according to the packet instructions until *al dente*.

4 Pour the sauce into a food processor or blender and process until smooth. Return the sauce to the pan.

5 Chop the sun-dried tomatoes and stir into the sauce along with the chicken. Bring back to the boil, then simmer for 10 minutes until the chicken is cooked. Season to taste.

6 Drain the pasta thoroughly and toss it in the sauce. Serve immediately, garnished with fresh mint.

Pasta with Chicken & Sausage Sauce

A lovely meaty sauce with a strong tomato flavour coating farfalle (small bow-shaped pasta).

Serves 4

45ml/3 tbsp olive oil
450g/1lb chicken breast fillets, skinned and cut into 1cm/ ½in pieces
3 small spicy cooked sausages, cut diagonally into 1cm/ ½in slices
6 spring onions, cut diagonally into 5mm/ ¼in lengths
10 sun-dried tomatoes in oil, drained and chopped
250ml/8fl oz/1 cup canned chopped tomatoes
1 medium courgette, cut diagonally into 5mm/ ¼in slices
350g/12oz farfalle
salt and freshly ground black pepper

1 Heat the olive oil in a frying pan. Add the chicken and sausage pieces with a little salt and pepper, and cook for about 10 minutes until browned. Using a slotted spoon, remove the chicken and sausage from the pan, and drain on kitchen paper.

2 Add the spring onions and sun-dried tomatoes to the pan, and cook for about 5 minutes until softened.

3 Stir in the canned tomatoes and cook for about 5 minutes until thickened, stirring from time to time.

4 Add the courgette, and return the chicken and sausage to the pan. Cook for 5 minutes longer until the courgette is just tender and the meat is heated through. Taste and adjust the seasoning as necessary.

5 Bring a large saucepan of salted water to the boil, add the farfalle and cook according to the packet instructions until *al dente*. Drain the pasta thoroughly, and toss with the chicken and sausage sauce. Serve immediately.

Italian Chicken

The chicken is finished in a sauce of tomatoes, black olives, garlic and herbs, with added zing from some ready-made red pesto, and served on a bed of noodles.

Serves 4

30ml/2 tbsp plain flour
4 chicken portions (legs, breasts or quarters)
30ml/2 tbsp olive oil
1 onion, chopped
2 garlic cloves, chopped
1 red pepper, seeded and chopped
400g/14oz can chopped tomatoes
30ml/2 tbsp red pesto sauce
4 sun-dried tomatoes in oil, drained and chopped
150ml/ ¼ pint/ ⅔ cup Chicken Stock
5ml/1 tsp dried oregano
8 black olives, stoned
salt and freshly ground black pepper
chopped fresh basil and whole basil leaves, to garnish
cooked tagliatelle, to serve

1 Place the flour and seasoning in a plastic bag. Add the chicken pieces and shake well until coated. Heat the oil in a flameproof casserole, add the chicken and brown quickly. Remove using a slotted spoon and set aside.

2 Lower the heat and add the onion, garlic and red pepper, and cook for 5 minutes. Stir in the canned chopped tomatoes, red pesto sauce, sun-dried tomatoes, stock and oregano, and bring to the boil.

3 Return the sautéed chicken portions to the casserole, season lightly, cover and simmer for 30–35 minutes or until the chicken is cooked.

4 Add the olives and simmer for a further 5 minutes. Transfer to a warmed serving dish, sprinkle with the chopped basil and garnish with whole basil leaves. Serve hot with tagliatelle.

Chicken with Mushrooms

Serve on a dish surrounded with nutty brown rice or tagliatelle verde. White wine or brandy may be used to deglaze the pan in place of dry sherry.

Serves 4

4 large chicken breast fillets, skinned
45ml/3 tbsp olive oil
1 onion, thinly sliced
1 garlic clove, crushed
225g/8oz/3 cups button mushrooms, quartered
30ml/2 tbsp dry sherry
15ml/1 tbsp lemon juice
150ml/ ¼ pint/ ⅔ cup single cream
salt and freshly ground black pepper
fresh parsley, to garnish

1 Divide each chicken breast into two natural fillets. Place the fillets between two sheets of clear film and flatten to a thickness of 5mm/ ¼in with a rolling pin. Cut into 2.5cm/1in diagonal strips.

2 Heat 30ml/2 tbsp of the oil in a large frying pan and cook the onion and garlic gently until tender.

3 Add the mushrooms and cook for a further 5 minutes. Remove the vegetables from the pan and keep warm.

4 Increase the heat. Add the remaining oil and fry the chicken very quickly, in small batches, for 3–4 minutes until lightly coloured. Season each batch with a little salt and pepper. Remove and keep warm while frying the rest of the chicken.

5 Add the sherry and lemon juice to the pan and quickly return the chicken, onions, garlic and mushrooms, stirring well to coat.

6 Stir in the cream and bring to just below boiling point. Adjust the seasoning to taste. Serve immediately, garnished with parsley.

Cannelloni al Forno

A lighter alternative to the usual beef-filled, béchamel-coated version, this recipe uses chicken breast.

Serves 4–6

450g/1lb/generous 3 cups chopped cooked chicken breast
225g/8oz/3 cups mushrooms
2 garlic cloves, crushed
30ml/2 tbsp chopped fresh flat leaf parsley
15ml/1 tbsp chopped fresh tarragon
1 egg, beaten
fresh lemon juice
12–18 cannelloni tubes
butter, for greasing
450ml/¾ pint/scant 2 cups Fresh Tomato Sauce
50g/2oz/⅔ cup grated Parmesan cheese
1 fresh flat leaf parsley sprig, to garnish
salt and freshly ground black pepper

1 Preheat the oven to 200°C/400°F/Gas 6. Place the cooked chicken in a food processor and process until finely minced. Transfer to a bowl.

2 Place the mushrooms, garlic, parsley and tarragon in the food processor, and process until finely minced.

3 Beat the mushroom mixture into the chicken with the egg. Stir in salt, pepper and lemon juice to taste.

4 Bring a large saucepan of salted water to the boil, add the cannelloni and cook according to the packet instructions.

5 Place the chicken mixture in a piping bag fitted with a large plain nozzle. Use this to fill each tube of cannelloni.

6 Lay the filled cannelloni tightly together in a single layer in a buttered, shallow, ovenproof dish. Spoon over the tomato sauce and sprinkle with Parmesan cheese. Bake in the oven for 30 minutes or until brown and bubbling. Serve garnished with a sprig of parsley.

Chicken Lasagne

Based on the Italian beef lasagne, this dish will be popular with all the family.

Serves 8

30ml/2 tbsp olive oil
900g/2lb minced raw chicken
225g/8oz rindless streaky bacon rashers, chopped
2 garlic cloves, crushed
450g/1lb leeks, sliced
225g/8oz carrots, diced
30ml/2 tbsp tomato purée
450ml/¾ pint/scant 2 cups Chicken Stock
12 sheets (no need to precook) lasagne verde
salt and freshly ground black pepper
green salad, to serve

For the cheese sauce

50g/2oz/4 tbsp butter
50g/2oz/½ cup plain flour
600ml/1 pint/2½ cups milk
115g/4oz/1 cup grated mature Cheddar cheese
1.5ml/¼ tsp dry English mustard

1 Heat the oil in a large, flameproof casserole and brown the minced chicken and bacon briskly, separating the pieces with a wooden spoon. Add the garlic, leeks and carrots, and cook for 5 minutes until softened. Add the tomato purée, stock and seasoning. Bring to the boil, cover and simmer for 30 minutes.

2 To make the sauce, melt the butter in a saucepan, add the flour and gradually blend in the milk, stirring until smooth. Bring to the boil, stirring all the time until thickened, and simmer for 3 minutes. Add half the cheese, the mustard and season to taste.

3 Preheat the oven to 190°C/375°F/Gas 5. Layer the chicken mixture, lasagne and half the cheese sauce in a 2.5 litre/5 pint/12½ cup ovenproof dish, starting and finishing with a layer of chicken.

4 Pour the remaining half of the cheese sauce over the top to cover, sprinkle with the remaining grated cheese and bake in the oven for 1 hour or until bubbling and lightly browned on top. Serve with green salad.

Smoked Chicken, Yellow Pepper & Sun-dried Tomato Pizzettes

Smoked chicken is now widely available in supermarkets and makes a special topping for these small pizzas.

Serves 4

30ml/2 tbsp olive oil, plus extra for greasing
4 ready-made 10–13cm/4–5in pizza bases
2 yellow peppers, seeded and cut into thin strips
60ml/4 tbsp sun-dried tomato purée
175g/6oz sliced smoked chicken or turkey, chopped
150g/6oz mozzarella cheese, cubed
30ml/2 tbsp chopped fresh basil
salt and freshly ground black pepper

1 Preheat the oven to 220°C/425°F/Gas 7. Grease two baking sheets and place two pizza bases on each one, spaced well apart.

2 Heat half of the oil in a frying pan and stir-fry the peppers for 3–4 minutes.

3 Brush the pizza bases generously with the sun-dried tomato purée. Arrange the smoked chicken or turkey and yellow peppers evenly on top.

4 Scatter over the mozzarella cheese and basil. Season with salt and pepper.

5 Drizzle over the remaining oil and bake for 15–20 minutes until crisp and golden. Serve immediately.

Variation
For a vegetarian pizza with a similar smoky taste, omit the chicken, roast or grill the yellow peppers and remove the skins before using, and replace the mozzarella with Bavarian smoked cheese.

Chicken, Shiitake Mushroom & Coriander Pizza

The addition of shiitake mushrooms adds an earthy flavour to this colourful pizza, while fresh red chilli adds a hint of spiciness.

Serves 3–4

60ml/4 tbsp olive oil
350g/12oz chicken breast fillets, skinned and cut into thin strips
1 bunch spring onions, sliced
1 fresh red chilli, seeded and chopped
1 red pepper, seeded and cut into thin strips
75g/3oz fresh shiitake mushrooms, wiped and sliced
45–60ml/3–4 tbsp chopped fresh coriander
1 ready-made 25–30cm/10–12in pizza base
150g/5oz mozzarella cheese
salt and freshly ground black pepper

1 Preheat the oven to 220°C/425°F/Gas 7. Heat 30ml/2 tbsp of the olive oil in a wok or large frying pan. Add the chicken, spring onions, chilli, red pepper and mushrooms, and stir-fry over a high heat for 2–3 minutes until the chicken is firm but still slightly pink inside. Season to taste.

2 Pour off any excess oil, then set aside the chicken mixture to cool. Stir the fresh coriander into the cooled chicken mixture.

3 Brush the pizza base with 15ml/1 tbsp of the oil. Spoon over the chicken mixture and drizzle over the remaining olive oil.

4 Grate the mozzarella cheese and sprinkle it evenly over the pizza. Bake on an oiled baking sheet for 15–20 minutes until crisp and golden. Serve immediately.

Variation
Other flavoursome fresh mushrooms, such as chestnut, chanterelle or field mushrooms, could be used instead of the shiitake.

Chicken Liver Kebabs

These may be grilled indoors and served with rice and broccoli or barbecued outdoors and served with salads and baked jacket potatoes.

Serves 4

115g/4oz rindless streaky bacon rashers
350g/12oz chicken livers, trimmed
12 large (no need to presoak) stoned prunes
12 cherry tomatoes
8 button mushrooms
30ml/2 tbsp olive oil
mixed leaf salad, to serve

1 Cut each rasher of bacon into two pieces, wrap a piece around each chicken liver and secure in position with wooden cocktail sticks.

2 Wrap the stoned prunes around the cherry tomatoes.

3 Thread the bacon-wrapped livers on to metal skewers with the prune-wrapped tomatoes and the mushrooms. Brush with oil. Cook under a preheated grill for 5 minutes on each side. Alternatively, cover the tomatoes and prunes with a strip of foil to protect them and cook over a hot barbecue for 5 minutes on each side.

4 Remove the cocktail sticks from the livers. Serve the kebabs immediately on warmed plates, accompanied by a mixed leaf salad.

Cook's Tip

Light the barbecue 30–45 minutes before you intend to cook. The coals will be at the right temperature when they are glowing and covered with a thin layer of greyish white ash.

Chicken, Bacon & Corn Kebabs

Don't wait for barbecue weather to have kebabs. If you are serving them to children, remember to remove the skewers first.

Serves 4

2 sweetcorn cobs
8 thick back bacon rashers
8 brown cap mushrooms, halved
2 small chicken breast fillets
30ml/2 tbsp sunflower oil
15ml/1 tbsp lemon juice
15ml/1 tbsp maple syrup
salt and freshly ground black pepper
green or mixed leaf salad, to serve

1 Cook the corn in boiling water until tender, then drain and cool. Stretch the bacon rashers with the back of a heavy knife and cut each in half. Wrap a piece of bacon around each half mushroom.

2 Cut both the corn and chicken into eight equal pieces. Mix together the oil, lemon juice, maple syrup and seasoning, and brush liberally over the chicken.

3 Thread the corn, bacon-wrapped mushrooms and chicken pieces alternately on metal skewers and brush all over with the lemon dressing.

4 Grill the kebabs under a preheated grill for 8–10 minutes, turning them once and basting occasionally with any extra dressing. Serve hot with either a crisp green or mixed leaf salad.

Cook's Tip

Made from the sap of a North American tree, pure maple syrup is expensive, but its flavour is vastly superior to blended varieties.

Sweet-&-sour Kebabs

This marinade contains sugar and will burn very easily, so grill the kebabs slowly, turning often. Serve with harlequin rice.

Serves 2
2 chicken breast fillets, skinned
8 pickling onions or 2 medium onions, peeled
4 rindless streaky bacon rashers
3 firm bananas
1 red pepper, seeded and diced
flat leaf parsley sprig, to garnish

For the marinade
30ml/2 tbsp soft brown sugar
15ml/1 tbsp Worcestershire sauce
30ml/2 tbsp lemon juice
salt and freshly ground black pepper

1 To make the marinade, mix together ingredients in a bowl. Cut each chicken breast into four pieces, add to the marinade, cover and leave for at least 4 hours or preferably overnight.

2 Blanch the onions in boiling water for 5 minutes and drain. If using medium onions, quarter them after blanching.

3 Cut each rasher of bacon in half. Peel the bananas and cut each into three pieces. Wrap a rasher of bacon around each piece of banana.

4 Thread the bacon-wrapped banana pieces on to metal skewers with the chicken pieces, onions and pepper pieces. Brush with the marinade.

5 Barbecue over low coals or cook under a low preheated grill for 15 minutes, turning and basting frequently with the marinade. Garnish with parsley and serve.

Cook's Tip
Pour boiling water over the small onions and then drain, to make peeling easier.

Citrus Kebabs

A piquant orange, lemon and mint marinade with a hint of cumin makes these kebabs special.

Serves 4
4 chicken breast fillets, skinned
fresh mint sprigs and orange, lemon or lime slices, to garnish
salad leaves, to serve

For the marinade
finely grated rind and juice of ½ orange
finely grated rind and juice of ½ small lemon or lime
30ml/2 tbsp olive oil
30ml/2 tbsp clear honey
30ml/2 tbsp chopped fresh mint
1.5ml/¼ tsp ground cumin
salt and freshly ground black pepper

1 Cut the chicken into 2.5cm/1in cubes. To make the marinade, mix the ingredients together in a bowl. Add the chicken cubes and leave to marinate for at least 2 hours.

2 Thread the chicken pieces on to metal skewers and barbecue over low coals or grill under a low preheated grill for 15 minutes, basting with the marinade and turning frequently.

3 Serve the kebabs on a bed of salad leaves, garnished with mint sprigs and orange, lemon or lime slices.

Harlequin Rice

This is a delicious and colourful accompaniment to kebabs.

Serves 4
30ml/2 tbsp olive oil
225g/8oz/generous 1 cup cooked rice
115g/4oz/1 cup cooked peas
1 small red pepper, diced
salt and freshly ground black pepper

1 Heat the oil in a frying pan and add the rice, peas and diced red pepper.
2 Season to taste with salt and pepper. Stir until heated through, then serve immediately.

Chicken, Banana & Pineapple Kebabs

Here, fruit and a sweet-sharp marinade help keep the chicken wonderfully moist during cooking.

Serves 4

4 boned chicken thighs, skinned and cubed
½ small fresh pineapple
2 firm bananas
fresh orange segments and bay leaves, to garnish
cooked rice, to serve

For the marinade

45ml/3 tbsp sunflower oil
15ml/1 tbsp clear honey
5ml/1 tsp wholegrain mustard
5ml/1 tsp crushed coriander seeds
grated rind and juice of 1 orange
4 cardamom pods

1 To make the marinade, combine the oil, honey, mustard, coriander seeds and orange rind and juice in a shallow dish. Crush the cardamom pods and stir in the seeds.

2 Add the prepared chicken cubes to the dish and turn to coat them all over with the marinade. Then cover the dish and leave to marinate in the fridge for at least 2 hours.

3 Just before cooking, core the pineapple and cut it into neat wedges, leaving the skin on. Peel and slice the bananas. Add the pineapple wedges and banana slices to the marinade and turn them over to coat them thoroughly.

4 Drain the chicken, pineapple and banana, reserving the marinade. Thread alternately on to eight metal skewers.

5 Grill the kebabs on a rack under a preheated moderate grill, turning occasionally and brushing them with the reserved marinade, for about 15 minutes until the chicken is golden and cooked through. Serve the kebabs on a bed of rice, garnished with fresh orange segments and bay leaves.

Chicken with Herb & Ricotta Stuffing

These little chicken drumsticks are full of flavour and the stuffing and bacon helps to keep them moist and tender.

Serves 4

60ml/4 tbsp ricotta cheese
1 garlic clove, crushed
45ml/3 tbsp mixed chopped fresh herbs, e.g. chives, flat leaf parsley and mint
30ml/2 tbsp fresh brown breadcrumbs
8 chicken drumsticks
8 smoked streaky bacon rashers
5ml/1 tsp wholegrain mustard
15ml/1 tbsp sunflower oil
salt and freshly ground black pepper

1 Mix together the ricotta cheese, garlic, herbs and breadcrumbs. Season well with salt and pepper.

2 Carefully loosen the skin of each drumstick and spoon a little of the herb stuffing underneath, smoothing the skin back over firmly, but gently.

3 Wrap a bacon rasher around the wide end of each drumstick, to hold the skin in place over the stuffing while it is cooking.

4 Mix together the mustard and oil, and brush over the chicken. Cook on a medium-hot barbecue, or under a preheated grill, for about 25 minutes, turning occasionally, until the juices run clear and not pink when the flesh is pierced with the point of a knife. Serve immediately.

Cook's Tip

Ricotta is a creamy white whey cheese from Italy, widely available from supermarkets and delicatessens.

Grilled Poussins with Citrus Glaze

This recipe is suitable for many kinds of small birds, including pigeons, snipe and partridges, provided they are young and tender.

Serves 4

2 poussins, about 675g/1½lb each
50g/2oz/4 tbsp butter, softened
30ml/2 tbsp olive oil
2 garlic cloves, crushed
2.5ml/½ tsp dried thyme
1.5ml/¼ tsp cayenne pepper
grated rind and juice of 1 lemon
grated rind and juice of 1 lime
30ml/2 tbsp clear honey
salt and freshly ground black pepper
fresh dill, to garnish
tomato salad, to serve

1 Using kitchen scissors or poultry shears, cut along both sides of the backbone of each bird; remove and discard. Cut the birds in half along the breast bone, then use a rolling pin to flatten them.

2 Beat the butter in a small bowl, then beat in 15ml/1 tbsp of the olive oil, the garlic, thyme, cayenne, salt and pepper, half the lemon and lime rind and 15ml/1 tbsp each of the lemon and lime juice.

3 Using your fingertips, carefully loosen the skin of each poussin breast. Using a round-bladed knife or small palette knife, spread the butter mixture evenly between the skin and breast meat.

4 Preheat the grill and line a grill pan with foil. In a small bowl, mix together the remaining olive oil, lemon and lime juices, and rind and the honey. Place the bird halves, skin side up, in the grill pan and brush with the juice mixture.

5 Grill for 10–12 minutes, basting once or twice with the juices. Turn over and grill for 7–10 minutes, basting once, or until the juices run clear when the thigh is pierced with a knife. Serve with tomato salad, garnished with dill.

Grilled Spatchcocked Poussins

These little, herb-marinated chickens can be cooked under the grill, but taste best if they are cooked over charcoal.

Serves 4

2 large or 4 small poussins
fresh herbs, to garnish
mixed salad leaves, to serve

For the marinade

150ml/¼ pint/⅔ cup olive oil
1 onion, grated
1 garlic clove, crushed
15ml/1 tbsp chopped fresh mint
15ml/1 tbsp chopped fresh flat leaf parsley
15ml/1 tbsp chopped fresh coriander
5–10ml/1–2 tsp ground cumin
5ml/1 tsp paprika
pinch of cayenne pepper

1 Tuck the wings of each poussin under the body and remove the wishbone. Turn the birds over and cut along each side of the backbone using kitchen scissors or poultry shears, then remove and discard.

2 Push down on each bird to break the breast bone. Keeping the bird flat, push a skewer through the wings and breast. Push another skewer through the thighs.

3 To make the marinade, blend together all the ingredients in a bowl. Spread the marinade over both sides of the poussins. Place in a large, shallow dish, cover with clear film and marinate for at least 4 hours or overnight.

4 Prepare a barbecue or preheat the grill. Barbecue the poussins for about 25–35 minutes, turning occasionally and brushing with the marinade. If grilling, cook under a medium grill about 7.5cm/3in from the heat for 25–35 minutes or until cooked through, turning and basting occasionally.

5 When the birds are cooked, cut them in half. Garnish with herbs and serve at once with salad leaves.

Chicken Wings Teriyaki-style

This simple, oriental glaze can be used with any cut of chicken or with fish.

Serves 4

1 garlic clove, crushed
45ml/3 tbsp soy sauce
30ml/2 tbsp dry sherry
10ml/2 tsp clear honey
10ml/2 tsp grated fresh root ginger
5ml/1 tsp sesame oil
12 chicken wings
15ml/1 tbsp sesame seeds, toasted

1 Place the garlic, soy sauce, sherry, honey, ginger and sesame oil in a large bowl and beat with a fork to mix evenly. Add the chicken wings and toss thoroughly to coat in the marinade. Cover and leave in the fridge for 30 minutes or longer.

2 Cook the wings on a fairly hot barbecue for 20–25 minutes, turning occasionally and brushing with the remaining marinade. Sprinkle with the toasted sesame seeds and serve hot.

Sticky Ginger Chicken

A quick, tasty way of cooking chicken drumsticks.

Serves 4

30ml/2 tbsp lemon juice
30ml/2 tbsp light muscovado sugar
5ml/1 tsp grated fresh ginger root
10ml/2 tsp soy sauce
8 chicken drumsticks, skinned
freshly ground black pepper

1 Mix together the juice, sugar, ginger, soy sauce and pepper. Slash the chicken drumsticks, then toss the chicken in the glaze.

2 Cook under a hot grill, turning occasionally and brushing with the glaze, until the chicken is golden and the juices run clear, not pink, when it is pierced.

Spanish Chicken

A colourful, one-pot dish, ideal for a weekday supper when you are craving something a little unusual.

Serves 8

30ml/2 tbsp plain flour
10ml/2 tsp ground paprika
2.5ml/½ tsp salt
16 chicken drumsticks
60ml/4 tbsp olive oil
about 1.2 litres/2 pints/5 cups Chicken Stock
1 onion, finely chopped
2 garlic cloves, crushed
450g/1lb/2¼ cups long-grain rice
2 bay leaves
225g/8oz/1½ cups diced cooked ham
115g/4oz/1 cup pimento-stuffed green olives
1 green pepper, seeded and diced
2 × 400g/14oz cans chopped tomatoes, with their juice
fresh flat leaf parsley, to garnish

1 Preheat the oven to 180°C/350°F/Gas 4. Shake together the flour, paprika and salt in a plastic bag, add the chicken drumsticks and toss to coat.

2 Heat the oil in a large frying pan and, working in batches, brown the chicken slowly on both sides. Remove from the pan, drain on kitchen paper and keep warm.

3 Meanwhile, in a large saucepan, bring the stock to the boil and add the onion, garlic, rice and bay leaves. Lower the heat and simmer for 10 minutes.

4 Remove the pan from the heat and add the ham, olives, green pepper and canned tomatoes with their juice. Transfer to a shallow, ovenproof dish.

5 Arrange the chicken on top, cover and bake for 30–40 minutes or until the chicken and rice are tender. Add a little more stock during the cooking time if necessary to prevent the dish from drying out.

6 Remove and discard the bay leaves. Taste and adjust the seasoning as necessary. Serve the drumsticks on top of the rice, garnished with flat leaf parsley.

Crispy Chicken with Garlicky Rice

Chicken wings cooked until they are really tender have a surprising amount of meat on them, and make a very economical supper for a crowd of youngsters. Provide lots of kitchen paper or napkins for the sticky fingers.

Serves 4

1 large onion, chopped
2 garlic cloves, crushed
30ml/2 tbsp sunflower oil
175g/6oz/scant 1 cup patna or basmati rice
350ml/12fl oz/1½ cups hot Chicken Stock
10ml/2 tsp finely grated lemon rind
30ml/2 tbsp chopped fresh mixed herbs
8–12 chicken wings
50g/2oz/½ cup plain flour
salt and freshly ground black pepper
Fresh Tomato Sauce, to serve

1 Preheat the oven to 200°C/400°F/Gas 6. Fry the onion and garlic in the oil in a large, ovenproof casserole until golden. Add the rice and toss until well coated in oil.

2 Stir in the stock, lemon rind and herbs, and bring to the boil. Cover and cook in the middle of the oven for 40–50 minutes. Stir the rice once or twice during cooking.

3 Meanwhile, dry the chicken wings with kitchen paper. Season the flour with salt and pepper, and use to coat the wings thoroughly, dusting off any excess.

4 Place the chicken wings in a small roasting tin and cook in the top of the oven for 30–40 minutes, turning once, until crisp and golden brown all over.

5 Serve the rice and the chicken wings together with fresh tomato sauce.

Jambalaya

A popular classic from the Southern States of the USA, this is a wonderful mix of flavours. Everything is cooked together in the same pan, so you save on washing up as well as enjoying a great meal.

Serves 6

30ml/2 tbsp vegetable oil
4 chicken breast fillets, skinned and cut into chunks
450g/1lb cooked spicy sausage, sliced
175g/6oz/1 cup cubed smoked ham
1 large onion, chopped
2 celery sticks, chopped
2 green peppers, seeded and chopped
3 garlic cloves, crushed
250ml/8fl oz/1 cup canned chopped tomatoes
475ml/16fl oz/2 cups Chicken Stock
5ml/1 tsp cayenne pepper
1 fresh thyme sprig, chopped, or 1.5ml/¼ tsp dried thyme
2 flat leaf parsley sprigs
1 bay leaf
275g/10oz/1⅔ cups rice
salt and freshly ground black pepper
4 spring onions, finely chopped

1 Heat the oil in a large, heavy-based frying pan. Add the chicken chunks and sausage slices, and cook for about 5 minutes until well browned. Stir in the ham cubes and cook for 5 minutes more.

2 Add the onion, celery, peppers, crushed garlic, tomatoes, chicken stock, cayenne pepper, fresh or dried thyme, parsley and bay leaf to the frying pan. Bring to the boil, stirring constantly.

3 Stir in the rice, and salt and pepper to taste. When the liquid returns to the boil, reduce the heat and cover the pan tightly. Simmer for 10 minutes.

4 Remove the pan from the heat and, without removing the lid, set aside for 20 minutes to let the rice finish cooking.

5 Discard the bay leaf. Scatter the chopped spring onions on top of the jambalaya just before serving.

Yogurt Chicken & Rice

An unusual Middle Eastern dish in which marinated chicken is layered between flavoured and plain rice.

Serves 6

40g/1½ oz/3 tbsp butter
1.5kg/3–3½ lb chicken
1 large onion, chopped
250ml/8fl oz/1 cup Chicken Stock
2 eggs
475ml/16fl oz/2 cups plain yogurt
2–3 saffron strands, dissolved in 15ml/1 tbsp boiling water
5ml/1 tsp ground cinnamon
450g/1lb/2¼ cups basmati rice
75g/3oz zereshk or dried cranberries
salt and freshly ground black pepper
herb salad, to serve

1 Melt 25g/1oz/2 tbsp of the butter, and fry the chicken and onion for 4–5 minutes until the onion is softened and the chicken browned. Add the stock, salt and pepper, and bring to the boil. Reduce the heat and simmer for about 45 minutes or until the chicken is cooked and the stock reduced by half.

2 Skin and bone the chicken. Cut the flesh into large pieces and place in a large bowl. Reserve the stock.

3 In a bowl, beat the eggs and blend with the yogurt. Add the saffron water and cinnamon, and season with salt and pepper. Pour over the chicken and leave to marinate for up to 2 hours.

4 Cook the rice in a large saucepan of boiling salted water for 5 minutes, then reduce the heat and simmer very gently for 10 minutes until half cooked. Drain, rinse in lukewarm water and drain again.

5 Transfer the chicken from the yogurt mixture to another bowl and mix half the rice into the yogurt mixture.

6 Preheat the oven to 160°C/325°F/Gas 3 and grease a large 10cm/4in deep ovenproof dish.

7 Place the rice and yogurt mixture in the bottom of the dish, arrange the chicken pieces in a layer on top and then add the plain rice. Sprinkle with the zereshk or cranberries.

8 Mix the remaining butter with the reserved chicken stock and pour over the rice. Cover tightly with foil and cook in the oven for 35–45 minutes.

9 Leave the dish to cool for a few minutes. Place on a cold, damp cloth, which will help lift the rice from the bottom of the dish, then run a knife around the edges of the dish. Place a large flat plate over the dish, invert and turn out. You should have a rice "cake" which can be cut into wedges. Serve hot with a herb salad.

Cook's Tip
Zereshk is a small sour berry that grows on trees by the water in the warmer part of Iran. It is traditionally served with Persian rice dishes.

Risotto with Chicken

Smooth, mild and almost creamy – few dishes can equal a good risotto when it is made with the best ingredients in the traditional Italian way.

Serves 4

30ml/2 tbsp olive oil
25g/8oz chicken breast fillets, skinned and cut into 2.5cm/1in cubes
1 onion, finely chopped
1 garlic clove, finely chopped
1.5ml/¼ tsp saffron strands, soaked in a little hot water
50g/2oz Parma ham, cut into thin strips
450g/1lb/2¼ cups risotto rice, preferably arborio
120ml/4fl oz/½ cup dry white wine
1.75 litres/3 pints/7½ cups simmering chicken stock
25g/1oz/2 tbsp butter (optional)
25g/1oz/⅓ cup grated Parmesan cheese, plus extra to serve
salt and freshly ground black pepper
fresh flat leaf parsley, to garnish

1 Heat the oil in a wide, heavy-based pan over moderately high heat. Add the chicken cubes and cook, stirring, until they start to turn white.

2 Reduce the heat to low and add the finely chopped onion, garlic, saffron and its soaking water and Parma ham. Cook, stirring, until the onion is soft. Stir in the rice. Sauté for 1–2 minutes, stirring constantly.

3 Add the wine and bring to the boil. Simmer gently until almost all the wine is absorbed.

4 Add the simmering stock, a ladleful at a time, and cook, stirring continuously, until the rice is just tender and the risotto creamy. Allow each ladleful of stock to be almost completely absorbed before you add the next.

5 Add the butter, if using, and Parmesan cheese, and stir in well. Season with salt and pepper to taste. Serve the risotto hot, sprinkled with a little more Parmesan and garnished with flat leaf parsley.

Seville Chicken

This Spanish dish incorporates oranges and almonds, favourite ingredients around Seville, where the orange and almond trees are a familiar and wonderful sight.

Serves 4

1 orange
plain flour, for dusting
8 chicken thighs
45ml/3 tbsp olive oil
1 large Spanish onion, roughly chopped
2 garlic cloves, crushed
1 red pepper, seeded and sliced
1 yellow pepper, seeded and sliced
115g/4oz chorizo sausage, sliced
50g/2oz/½ cup flaked almonds
225g/8oz/generous 1 cup brown basmati rice
about 600ml/1 pint/2½ cups Chicken Stock
400g/14oz can chopped tomatoes
175ml/6fl oz/¾ cup white wine
generous pinch of dried thyme
salt and freshly ground black pepper
fresh thyme sprigs, to garnish

1 Pare a thin strip of rind from the orange and set it aside. Peel the orange, then cut it into segments, working over a bowl to catch the juice.

2 Place some flour in a plastic bag and season with salt and pepper. Put the chicken thighs into the bag and shake to coat well. Dust off any excess.

3 Heat the oil in a large frying pan and fry the chicken pieces on both sides until nicely browned. Transfer to a plate. Add the onion and garlic to the pan and fry for 4–5 minutes until the onion begins to brown. Add the red and yellow peppers, and fry, stirring occasionally, until slightly softened.

4 Add the chorizo, stir-fry for a few minutes, then sprinkle over the almonds and rice. Cook, stirring, for 1–2 minutes.

5 Pour in the chicken stock, tomatoes and wine, and add the reserved strip of orange rind and the thyme. Season well. Bring to simmering point, stirring, then return the chicken pieces to the pan.

6 Cover tightly and cook over a very low heat for 1–1¼ hours until the rice and chicken are tender. Just before serving, add the orange segments and allow to heat through briefly. Garnish with fresh thyme and serve.

Cook's Tip

Cooking times for this dish will depend largely on the heat. If the rice seems to be drying out too quickly, add a little more stock or wine and reduce the heat. If, after 40 minutes or so, the rice is still barely cooked, increase the heat a little. Make sure the rice is kept below the liquid (the chicken can lie on the surface) and stir occasionally if it seems to be cooking unevenly.

Chicken Pilaff

The French marmite pot is ideal for this recipe. The tall sides slant inwards, reducing evaporation and ensuring that the rice cooks slowly without becoming dry.

Serves 3–4

15–20 dried chanterelle mushrooms
15–30ml/1–2 tbsp olive oil
15g/½oz/1 tbsp butter
4 thin rindless smoked streaky bacon rashers, chopped
3 chicken breast fillets, skinned and cut into thin slices
4 spring onions, sliced
225g/8oz/generous 1 cup basmati rice
450ml/¾ pint/scant 2 cups hot Chicken Stock
salt and freshly ground black pepper

1 Preheat the oven to 180°C/350°F/Gas 4. Soak the mushrooms for 10 minutes in warm water. Drain, reserving the liquid. Slice the mushrooms, discarding the stalks.

2 Heat the olive oil and butter in a frying pan. Fry the bacon for 2–3 minutes. Add the chicken and stir-fry until the pieces are golden brown all over. Transfer the chicken and bacon mixture to a bowl using a slotted spoon.

3 Briefly fry the mushrooms and spring onions in the fat remaining in the pan, then add them to the chicken pieces.

4 Add the rice to the pan, with a little more olive oil if necessary. Stir-fry for 2–3 minutes. Spoon the rice into an earthenware marmite pot or casserole.

5 Pour the hot chicken stock and reserved mushroom liquid over the rice in the marmite pot or casserole. Stir in the reserved chicken and mushroom mixture, and season.

6 Cover with a double piece of foil and secure with a lid. Cook the pilaff in the oven for 30–35 minutes until the rice is tender. Serve hot.

Caribbean Peanut Chicken

Peanut butter adds a richness to this dish as well as a delicious depth of flavour all of its own.

Serves 4

4 boneless chicken breast fillets, skinned and cut into thin strips
225g/8oz/generous 1 cup white long-grain rice
15g/½oz/1 tbsp butter, plus extra for greasing
30ml/2 tbsp groundnut oil
1 onion, finely chopped
2 tomatoes, peeled, seeded and chopped
1 fresh green chilli, seeded and sliced
60ml/4 tbsp smooth peanut butter
450ml/¾ pint/scant 2 cups Chicken Stock
lemon juice, to taste
salt and freshly ground black pepper
lime wedges and fresh flat leaf parsley sprigs, to garnish

For the marinade

15ml/1 tbsp sunflower oil
1–2 garlic cloves, crushed
5ml/1 tsp chopped fresh thyme
25ml/5 tsp medium curry powder
juice of ½ lemon

1 To make the marinade, mix all the ingredients together in a large bowl. Stir in the chicken and cover loosely with clear film. Set aside in a cool place for 2–3 hours.

2 Meanwhile, cook the rice in a large saucepan of boiling salted water until tender. Drain well and turn into a generously buttered casserole.

3 Preheat the oven to 180°C/350°F/Gas 4. Heat 15ml/1 tbsp of the oil and the butter in a flameproof casserole, and fry the chicken pieces for 4–5 minutes until evenly browned. Add more oil if necessary.

4 Transfer the chicken to a plate. Add the onion to the flameproof casserole and fry for 5–6 minutes until lightly browned, adding more oil if necessary. Stir in the chopped tomatoes and chilli. Cook over a gentle heat for 3–4 minutes, stirring occasionally. Remove from the heat.

5 Mix the peanut butter with the chicken stock. Stir into the tomato and onion mixture, then return the chicken. Add the lemon juice and seasoning to taste, and spoon the mixture over the rice in the other casserole.

6 Cover and cook in the oven for 15–20 minutes or until piping hot. Use a large spoon to toss the rice with the chicken mixture. Serve at once, garnished with lime wedges and fresh parsley sprigs.

Cook's Tip

If the casserole is not large enough to allow you to toss the rice with the chicken mixture before serving, invert a large, deep plate over the casserole, turn both over and toss the mixture on the plate.

Joloff Chicken & Rice

A famous West African dish.

Serves 4

1kg/2¼lb chicken, cut into 4–6 pieces
2 garlic cloves, crushed
5ml/1 tsp dried thyme
30ml/2 tbsp palm or vegetable oil
400g/14oz can chopped tomatoes
15ml/1 tbsp tomato purée
1 onion, chopped
450ml/¾ pint/scant 2 cups Chicken Stock or water
30ml/2 tbsp dried shrimps, ground
1 fresh green chilli, seeded and finely chopped
350g/12oz/1¾ cups long-grain rice

1 Rub the chicken with the garlic and thyme, and set aside. Heat the oil in a large saucepan until hazy and then add the chopped tomatoes, tomato purée and onion. Cook over a moderately high heat for about 15 minutes until the tomatoes are well reduced, stirring frequently.

2 Reduce the heat a little, add the chicken pieces and stir well to coat. Cook for 10 minutes, stirring, then add the stock or water, the ground dried shrimps and the chilli. Bring to the boil and simmer for 5 minutes, stirring occasionally.

3 Put the rice in a separate saucepan. Scoop 300ml/½ pint/1¼ cups of the sauce into a measuring jug, dilute to 450ml/¾ pint/scant 2 cups and stir into the rice. Cook, covered, until the liquid is absorbed, place a piece of foil on top of the rice, cover the pan with a lid and cook over a low heat for 20 minutes until the rice is cooked; add more water if necessary.

4 Transfer the chicken pieces to a warmed serving plate. Simmer the sauce until reduced by half. Pour over the chicken and serve with the rice.

Cook's Tip

Dried shrimps are available from specialist African, Caribbean and Asian food stores.

Chicken & Vegetable Tagine

This lightly spiced Moroccan stew is traditionally served with couscous, but rice alone makes an equally delicious accompaniment if couscous is not available.

Serves 4

30ml/2 tbsp groundnut oil
4 chicken breast fillets, skinned and cut into large pieces
1 large onion, chopped
2 garlic cloves, crushed
1 small parsnip, cut into 2.5cm/1in pieces
1 small turnip, cut into 2cm/¾in pieces
3 carrots, cut into 4cm/1½in pieces
4 tomatoes, chopped
1 cinnamon stick
4 cloves
5ml/1 tsp ground ginger
1 bay leaf
1.5–2.5ml/¼–½ tsp cayenne pepper
350ml/12fl oz/1½ cups Chicken Stock
400g/14oz can chick-peas, drained
1 red pepper, seeded and sliced
150g/5oz green beans, halved
1 piece preserved lemon peel, thinly sliced
20–30 stoned brown or green olives
salt

For the rice and couscous

750ml/1¼ pints/3 cups Chicken Stock
225g/8oz/generous 1 cup long-grain rice
115g/4oz/⅔ cup couscous
45ml/3 tbsp chopped fresh coriander

1 Heat half of the oil in a large, flameproof casserole and fry the chicken pieces for a few minutes until evenly browned. Transfer to a plate.

2 Heat the remaining oil and fry the onion, garlic, parsnip, turnip and carrots together over a medium heat for 4–5 minutes until the vegetables are lightly flecked with brown, stirring frequently. Lower the heat, cover and sweat the vegetables for 5 minutes more, stirring occasionally.

3 Add the tomatoes, cook for a few minutes, then add the cinnamon stick, cloves, ginger, bay leaf and cayenne. Cook for 1–2 minutes. Pour in the chicken stock and add the chick-peas. Return the browned chicken pieces to the casserole and season with salt. Cover and simmer for 25 minutes.

4 Meanwhile, to make the rice and couscous accompaniment, bring the chicken stock to the boil in a large saucepan. Add the rice and simmer for about 5 minutes until almost tender. Remove the pan from the heat, stir in the couscous, cover tightly and leave for about 5 minutes.

5 When the vegetables in the tagine are almost tender, stir in the red pepper slices and green beans, and simmer for 10 minutes. Add the preserved lemon peel and olives, stir well and cook for 5 minutes more or until the vegetables are perfectly tender.

6 Stir the chopped coriander into the rice and couscous mixture, and pile it on to a plate. Serve the chicken tagine in the traditional dish, if you have one, or in the casserole.

Chicken Paella

There are many variations of this basic recipe. Any seasonal vegetables can be added, as can mussels and other seafood. Serve straight from the pan.

Serves 4

4 chicken legs (thighs and drumsticks)
60ml/4 tbsp olive oil
1 large onion, finely chopped
1 garlic clove, crushed
5ml/1 tsp ground turmeric
115g/4oz chorizo sausage
225g/8oz/generous 1 cup long-grain rice
600ml/1 pint/2½ cups Chicken Stock
4 tomatoes, peeled, seeded and chopped
1 red pepper, seeded and sliced
115g/4oz/1 cup frozen peas
salt and freshly ground black pepper

1 Preheat the oven to 180°C/350°F/Gas 4. Cut the chicken legs in half through the joint.

2 Heat the oil in a 30cm/12in paella pan or large, flameproof casserole and brown the chicken pieces on both sides. Add the onion and garlic, and stir in the turmeric. Cook for 2 minutes.

3 Slice the sausage and add to the pan, with the rice and stock. Bring to the boil and season to taste. Cover and bake in the oven for 15 minutes.

4 Remove the pan from the oven and add the chopped tomatoes, sliced red pepper and frozen peas. Return to the oven and cook for a further 10–15 minutes or until the chicken is tender and the rice has absorbed the stock. Serve hot.

Cook's Tip

There are many varieties of chorizo, a well-known Spanish sausage. They are all made from pork and incorporate paprika, which gives them their typical colouring. They are all quite spicy, and some are very hot.

Chicken Stroganov

This is based on the classic Russian dish, usually made with fillet of beef. Serve with rice to which chopped celery, spring onions and parsley have been added.

Serves 4

4 chicken breast fillets, skinned
45ml/3 tbsp olive oil
1 large onion, thinly sliced
225g/8oz/3 cups mushrooms, sliced
300ml/½ pint/1¼ cups soured cream
salt and freshly ground black pepper
15ml/1 tbsp chopped fresh parsley, to garnish
cooked rice, chopped celery, spring onions and parsley, to serve

1 Divide each chicken breast into two natural fillets, place between two sheets of clear film and flatten each to a thickness of 5mm/¼in with a rolling pin. Slice on the diagonal into 2.5cm/1in strips.

2 Heat 30ml/2 tbsp of the oil in a large frying pan and cook the onion slowly until soft but not coloured.

3 Add the mushrooms and cook until golden brown. Remove the vegetables from the pan and keep warm.

4 Increase the heat, add the remaining oil to the pan and fry the chicken very quickly, in small batches, for 3–4 minutes until lightly coloured. Remove each batch and keep warm while frying the rest of the chicken.

5 Return all the chicken, onion and mushrooms to the pan, and season with salt and pepper to taste. Stir in the soured cream and bring to the boil. Sprinkle with chopped parsley and serve immediately.

Cook's Tip

If soured cream is not available, fresh double cream may be used, "soured" with the juice of ½ lemon.

Chicken Piri-piri

A classic Portuguese dish based on a hot sauce made from Angolan chillies, this is popular wherever there are Portuguese communities, and is often served in southern Africa.

Serves 4

4 chicken breasts
30–45ml/2–3 tbsp olive oil
1 large onion, finely sliced
2 carrots, cut into thin strips
1 large or 2 small parsnip(s), cut into thin strips
1 red pepper, seeded and sliced
1 yellow pepper, seeded and sliced
1 litre/1¾ pints/4 cups Chicken Stock
3 tomatoes, peeled, seeded and chopped
generous dash of piri-piri sauce
15ml/1 tbsp tomato purée
½ cinnamon stick
1 fresh thyme sprig, plus extra to garnish
1 bay leaf
275g/10oz/1½ cups white long-grain rice
15ml/1 tbsp lime or lemon juice
salt and freshly ground black pepper

1 Preheat the oven to 180°C/350°F/Gas 4. Rub the chicken skin with a little salt and pepper. Heat 30ml/2 tbsp of the oil in a large frying pan and brown the chicken portions on all sides. Transfer to a plate.

2 Add some more oil to the pan, if necessary, and fry the onion for 2–3 minutes until slightly softened. Add the carrots, parsnip(s) and red and yellow peppers, stir-fry for a few minutes then cover and sweat for 4–5 minutes until quite soft.

3 Pour in the chicken stock and add the tomatoes, piri-piri sauce, tomato purée and cinnamon stick. Stir in the thyme and bay leaf. Season to taste and bring to the boil. Using a ladle, spoon off 300ml/½ pint/1¼ cups of the liquid and set aside in a small pan.

4 Put the rice in the bottom of a casserole. Using a slotted spoon, scoop the vegetables out of the frying pan and spread them over the rice. Arrange the chicken pieces on top. Pour over the spicy chicken stock from the frying pan, cover the casserole tightly and cook in the oven for about 45 minutes until both the rice and chicken are completely tender.

5 Meanwhile, heat the reserved chicken stock, adding a few more drops of piri-piri sauce and the lime or lemon juice.

6 To serve, spoon the chicken and rice on to warmed serving plates and garnish with thyme. Serve the sauce separately or poured over the chicken.

Cook's Tip

Piri-piri sauce can be obtained from speciality food stores, or use Tabasco sauce as an alternative.

Chicken & Bean Risotto

Brown rice, red kidney beans, sweetcorn and broccoli make this a filling and nutritious meal-in-a-pot using only a small quantity of chicken.

Serves 4–6

1 onion, chopped
2 garlic cloves, crushed
1 fresh red chilli, seeded and finely chopped
175g/5oz/2½ cups mushrooms, sliced
2 celery sticks, chopped
225g/8oz/generous 1 cup long-grain brown rice
450ml/¾ pint/scant 2 cups Chicken Stock
150ml/¼ pint/⅔ cup white wine
400g/14oz can red kidney beans
225g/8oz chicken breast fillet, skinned and diced
200g/7oz can sweetcorn kernels
115g/4oz/¾ cup sultanas
175g/6oz small broccoli florets
30–45ml/2–3 tbsp chopped fresh mixed herbs
salt and freshly ground black pepper

1 Put the onion, garlic, chilli, mushrooms, celery, rice, stock and wine in a saucepan. Cover, bring to the boil, lower the heat and simmer for 15 minutes.

2 Rinse and drain the kidney beans. Stir the chicken, kidney beans, sweetcorn and sultanas into the pan. Cook for a further 20 minutes until almost all the liquid has been absorbed.

3 Cook the broccoli in a separate saucepan of boiling salted water for 5 minutes, then drain.

4 Stir the broccoli and chopped herbs into the risotto, season to taste and serve immediately.

Variation
Replace the kidney beans with another type of canned beans, such as black-eyed or cannellini.

Chicken Korma with Saffron Rice

Mild and fragrant, this dish is, quite understandably, an old favourite.

Serves 4

75g/3oz/¾ cup flaked almonds
15ml/1 tbsp ghee or butter
about 15ml/1 tbsp sunflower oil
675g/1½lb chicken breast fillets, skinned and cut into bite-size pieces
1 onion, chopped
4 green cardamom pods
2 garlic cloves, crushed
10ml/2 tsp ground cumin
5ml/1 tsp ground coriander
1 cinnamon stick
good pinch of chilli powder
300ml/½ pint/1¼ cups canned coconut milk
175ml/6fl oz/¾ cup Chicken Stock
5ml/1 tsp tomato purée (optional)
75ml/5 tbsp single cream
15–30ml/1–2 tbsp fresh lime or lemon juice
10ml/2 tsp grated lime or lemon rind
5ml/1 tsp garam masala
salt and freshly ground black pepper

For the saffron rice

275g/10oz/1½ cups basmati rice
750ml/1¼ pints/3 cups Chicken Stock
generous pinch of saffron threads, crushed, then soaked in hot water

1 Dry fry the flaked almonds in a small frying pan until pale golden. Transfer about two thirds of the almonds to a plate and continue to dry fry the remainder until they are slightly deeper in colour. Transfer the darker almonds to a separate plate and set them aside for the garnish. Let the paler almonds cool, then grind them in a spice mill or coffee grinder.

2 Heat the ghee or butter and oil in a wok or large frying pan and fry the chicken pieces, in batches if necessary, until evenly browned. Transfer to a plate.

3 Add a little more oil to the pan if necessary and fry the onion for 2 minutes, then stir in the cardamom pods and garlic, and fry for 3–4 minutes more until the onion is lightly flecked with brown. Stir in the ground almonds, the cumin, coriander, cinnamon stick and chilli powder, and fry for 1 minute. Stir in the coconut milk, chicken stock and tomato purée, if using.

4 Bring to simmering point, then return the chicken to the pan and season. Cover and cook over a gentle heat for 10 minutes until the chicken is tender. Set aside, covered.

5 Place the rice in a saucepan with the stock and saffron water. Bring to the boil over a medium heat, then cover tightly and cook over a low heat for 10 minutes or according to the instructions on the packet until the rice is just tender.

6 Just before the rice is ready, reheat the korma until it is simmering gently. Stir in the cream, the citrus juice and rind, and the garam masala. Taste and season as necessary. Pile the rice into a warmed serving dish and spoon the korma into a separate dish. Garnish with the reserved browned almonds. Serve immediately.

Chicken in a Cashew Nut Sauce

This chicken dish has a deliciously thick and nutty sauce, and it is best served with plain boiled rice.

Serves 4

2 medium onions
30ml/2 tbsp tomato purée
50g/2oz/ ½ cup cashew nuts
7.5ml/1½ tsp garam masala
5ml/1 tsp crushed garlic
5ml/1 tsp chilli powder
15ml/1 tbsp lemon juice
1.5ml/ ¼ tsp ground turmeric
5ml/1 tsp salt
15ml/1 tbsp plain low-fat yogurt
15ml/1 tbsp corn oil
30ml/2 tbsp chopped fresh coriander
15ml/1 tbsp sultanas
450g/1lb skinless boneless chicken, cubed
175g/6oz/2½ cups button mushrooms
300ml/ ½ pint/1¼ cups water

1 Cut the onions into quarters, place in a food processor or blender and process for about 1 minute.

2 Add the tomato purée, cashew nuts, garam masala, garlic, chilli powder, lemon juice, turmeric, salt and yogurt to the onions. Process for a further 1–1½ minutes.

3 In a heavy-based saucepan, heat the oil, lower the heat to medium and pour in the spice mixture from the food processor. Fry for about 2 minutes, lowering the heat if necessary.

4 Add half the chopped coriander, the sultanas and chicken, and continue to stir-fry for a further 1 minute.

5 Add the mushrooms, pour in the water and bring to a simmer. Cover the saucepan and cook over a low heat for about 10 minutes.

6 After this time, check to see that the chicken is cooked through and the sauce is thick. Cook for a little longer if necessary. Serve, garnished with the remaining chopped fresh coriander.

Fragrant Chicken Curry

In this dish, the mildly spiced sauce is thickened using lentils rather than the traditional onions fried in ghee.

Serves 4

75g/3oz/ ⅓ cup red lentils
30ml/2 tbsp mild curry powder
10ml/2 tsp ground coriander
5ml/1 tsp cumin seeds
475ml/16fl oz/2 cups vegetable stock
8 chicken thighs, skinned
225g/8oz fresh spinach, shredded or frozen spinach, thawed and well drained
15ml/1 tbsp chopped fresh coriander
salt and freshly ground black pepper
fresh coriander, to garnish
boiled white or brown basmati rice and grilled poppadums, to serve

1 Rinse the lentils under cold running water. Put into a large, heavy-based saucepan with the curry powder, ground coriander, cumin seeds and stock.

2 Bring to the boil, then lower the heat. Cover and simmer gently for 10 minutes.

3 Add the chicken and spinach to the lentils. Re-cover and simmer gently for a further 40 minutes or until the chicken has cooked.

4 Stir in the chopped fresh coriander and season to taste. Serve, garnished with fresh coriander sprigs, accompanied by rice and grilled poppadums.

Chicken in Green Almond Sauce

The sauce in this Mexican dish, deliciously thickened with ground almonds, is given its beautiful colour by fresh coriander, green pepper and tomatillos.

Serves 6

1.5kg/3–3½lb chicken, cut into serving portions
475ml/16fl oz/2 cups Chicken Stock
1 onion, chopped
1 garlic clove, chopped
115g/4oz/2 cups fresh coriander, coarsely chopped
1 green pepper, seeded and chopped
1 jalapeño chilli, seeded and chopped
275g/10oz can tomatillos
115g/4oz/1 cup ground almonds
30ml/2 tbsp corn oil
salt
fresh coriander, to garnish
cooked rice, to serve

1 Put the chicken into a flameproof casserole or pan. Pour in the stock, bring to a simmer, cover and cook for 45 minutes until tender. Drain the stock into a measuring jug and set aside.

2 Put the onion, garlic, coriander, green pepper, chilli, tomatillos with their juice and the almonds in a food processor. Purée fairly coarsely.

3 Heat the oil in a frying pan, add the almond mixture and cook over a low heat, stirring, for 3–4 minutes. Scrape the mixture into the casserole or pan with the chicken.

4 Make the stock up to 475ml/16fl oz/2 cups with water, if necessary. Stir it into the casserole or pan. Mix gently and simmer just long enough to blend the flavours and heat the chicken pieces through. Add salt to taste. Serve at once, garnished with coriander and accompanied by rice.

Cook's Tip
If the colour of the sauce seems a little pale, add 2–3 outer leaves of dark green cos lettuce. Cut out the central veins, chop the leaves and add to the food processor.

Moroccan Chicken Couscous

The spicy chicken dish is served on a fragrant bed of couscous.

Serves 4
For the chicken

15ml/1 tbsp butter
15ml/1 tbsp sunflower oil
4 chicken portions
2 onions, finely chopped
2 garlic cloves, crushed
2.5ml/½ tsp ground cinnamon
1.5ml/¼ tsp ground ginger
1.5ml/¼ tsp ground turmeric
30ml/2 tbsp orange juice
10ml/2 tsp clear honey
salt
fresh mint sprigs, to garnish

For the couscous

350g/12oz/2 cups couscous
10ml/2 tsp caster sugar
30ml/2 tbsp sunflower oil
2.5ml/½ tsp ground cinnamon
pinch of grated nutmeg
15ml/1 tbsp orange blossom water
30ml/2 tbsp sultanas
50g/2oz/½ cup chopped blanched almonds
45ml/3 tbsp chopped pistachio nuts

1 Heat the butter and oil in a large pan and add the chicken portions, skin side down. Fry for 3–4 minutes until the skin is golden, then turn over. Add the onions, garlic, spices and a pinch of salt. Pour over the orange juice and 300ml/½ pint/1¼ cups water. Cover and bring to the boil, then reduce the heat and simmer for about 30 minutes.

2 Meanwhile, place the couscous with 5ml/1 tsp salt in a bowl and cover with 350ml/12fl oz/1½ cups water. Stir once and leave to stand for 5 minutes. Stir in the sugar, 15ml/1 tbsp of the oil, the cinnamon, nutmeg, orange blossom water and sultanas.

3 Heat the remaining oil in a pan and lightly fry the almonds until golden. Stir into the couscous with the pistachio nuts. Line a steamer with greaseproof paper and spoon in the couscous. Steam over the chicken for 10 minutes.

4 Remove the steamer. Stir the honey into the chicken liquid and boil for 3–4 minutes. Spoon the couscous on to a warmed serving platter. Top with the chicken and sauce. Garnish and serve.

Chicken & Rice Omelette

These quickly cooked omelettes are a great favourite with children, topped with a splash of tomato ketchup.

Serves 4

115g/4oz boneless chicken thigh, skinned and diced
35ml/7 tsp butter
1 small onion, chopped
30g/1¼oz/¼ cup chopped carrot
2 shiitake mushrooms, stems removed and chopped
15ml/1 tbsp finely chopped fresh parsley
375g/13oz/2¼ cups freshly boiled rice
30ml/2 tbsp fresh tomato ketchup
6 large eggs
60ml/4 tbsp milk
salt and freshly ground black or white pepper
fresh tomato ketchup and fresh parsley sprigs, to garnish

1 Season the chicken. Melt 7.5ml/1½ tsp of the butter in a frying pan. Fry the chopped onion for 1 minute, then add the chicken and fry until it is white and cooked. Add the carrot pieces and mushrooms, stir-fry until soft over a moderate heat, then add the chopped parsley. Set aside and clean the frying pan.

2 Melt another 7.5ml/1½ tsp of the butter in the frying pan, add the rice and stir well. Mix in the fried ingredients and tomato ketchup, adding salt and pepper to taste. Keep warm.

3 Beat the eggs lightly in a bowl, add the milk, 2.5ml/½ tsp salt and pepper to taste. Melt 5ml/1 tsp of the butter in an omelette pan over a moderate heat. Pour in a quarter of the egg mixture and stir it briefly with a fork, then leave to set for 1 minute. Top with a quarter of the rice mixture. Fold the omelette over the rice and slide it to the edge of the pan to shape it into a cylinder. Do not cook the omelette too much.

4 Invert the omelette on to a warmed plate, cover with a sheet of kitchen paper and press neatly into a rectangular shape. Cook another three omelettes from the remaining ingredients. Serve with tomato ketchup on top, garnished with parsley.

Chicken Cakes with Teriyaki Sauce

These little chicken cakes, about the size of small meatballs, are cooked with a glaze and garnished with spring onions.

Serves 4

400g/14oz minced chicken
1 small egg
60ml/4 tbsp grated onion
7.5ml/1½ tsp sugar
7.5ml/1½ tsp soy sauce
cornflour, for coating
½ bunch spring onions, finely shredded
15ml/1 tbsp oil

For the teriyaki sauce

30ml/2 tbsp sake or dry white wine
30ml/2 tbsp sugar
30ml/2 tbsp mirin
30ml/2 tbsp soy sauce

1 Mix the minced chicken with the egg, grated onion, sugar and soy sauce until the ingredients are thoroughly combined and well bound together. This process takes about 3 minutes, until the mixture is quite sticky, which gives a good texture. Shape the mixture into 12 small, flat, round cakes and dust them lightly all over with cornflour.

2 Soak the shredded spring onions in cold water for 5 minutes and drain well.

3 Heat the oil in a frying pan. Place the chicken cakes in the pan in a single layer, and cook over a moderate heat for 3 minutes. Turn the chicken cakes and cook for 3 minutes on the second side.

4 To make the teriyaki sauce, mix all the ingredients together in a bowl. Pour the sauce into the frying pan and turn the chicken cakes until they are evenly glazed. Move or gently shake the pan constantly to prevent the sauce from burning.

5 Arrange the chicken cakes on a warmed serving plate and top with the spring onion shreds. Serve immediately.

Chicken Lollipops

These tasty stuffed wings can be served hot or cold. They can be prepared and frozen in advance.

Makes 12
12 large chicken wings
225g/8oz/3 cups dried breadcrumbs
30ml/2 tbsp sesame seeds
2 eggs, beaten
oil, for deep frying

For the filling
5ml/1 tsp cornflour
1.5ml/¼ tsp salt
2.5ml/½ tsp fresh thyme leaves
pinch of freshly ground black pepper

1 Remove the wing tips and discard or use them for making stock. Skin the second joint sections, removing the two small bones, and reserve the meat for the filling.

2 To make the filling, place all the ingredients in a bowl and add the reserved chicken meat. Mix well.

3 Holding the large end of the bone on the third section of the wing and using a sharp knife, cut the skin and flesh away from the bone, scraping down and pulling the meat over the small end, forming a pocket. Repeat this process with the remaining wing sections.

4 Fill the tiny pockets with the filling. Mix the breadcrumbs and the sesame seeds together. Place the breadcrumb mixture and the beaten eggs in separate dishes.

5 Brush the meat with beaten egg and roll in the breadcrumb mixture to cover. Chill and repeat to give a second layer, forming a thick coating. Chill until ready to fry.

6 Preheat the oven to 180°C/350°F/Gas 4. Heat 5cm/2in oil in a heavy-based pan until hot, but not smoking or the breadcrumbs will burn. Gently fry two or three lollipops at a time until golden brown, remove and drain on kitchen paper. Complete the cooking in the oven for 15–20 minutes or until tender. Serve hot or cold.

Pan-fried Honey Chicken Drumsticks

Flavoured with a sweet marinade before frying, these drumsticks are served with a wine sauce.

Serves 4
120ml/4fl oz/ ½ cup clear honey
juice of 1 lemon
30ml/2 tbsp soy sauce
15ml/1 tbsp sesame seeds
2.5ml/½ tsp fresh or dried thyme leaves
12 chicken drumsticks
75g/3oz/ ¾ cup plain flour
40g/1½oz/3 tbsp butter or margarine
45ml/3 tbsp vegetable oil
120ml/4fl oz/ ½ cup white wine
120ml/4fl oz/ ½ cup Chicken Stock
salt and freshly ground black pepper
fresh flat leaf parsley, to garnish

1 In a large bowl, combine the honey, lemon juice, soy sauce, sesame seeds and thyme. Add the chicken drumsticks and mix to coat them well. Leave to marinate in a cool place for 2 hours or more, turning occasionally.

2 Mix 2.5ml/ ½ tsp each of salt and pepper with the flour in a shallow bowl. Drain the drumsticks, reserving the marinade. Roll them in the seasoned flour to coat all over.

3 Heat the butter or margarine with the oil in a large, heavy-based frying pan. When hot and sizzling, add the drumsticks and brown on all sides. Reduce the heat to medium-low and cook for 12–15 minutes until the chicken is done.

4 Check that the chicken is cooked through by piercing the thickest part with a fork: the juices should run clear. Remove the drumsticks from the pan, place on a serving platter and keep hot.

5 Pour off most of the fat from the pan. Add the white wine, chicken stock and reserved marinade, and stir well to mix in the cooking juices on the bottom of the pan. Bring to the boil and simmer until reduced by half. Season to taste, then spoon the sauce over the drumsticks and serve, garnished with flat leaf parsley.

Chicken with Sweet Potatoes

Sweet potatoes are still an undervalued vegetable. A dish like this, in which they are baked with chicken and finished with an orange and ginger glaze, shows them at their best.

Serves 6

grated rind and juice of 1 large navel orange
75ml/3fl oz soy sauce
2.5cm/1in piece fresh root ginger, peeled and finely grated
1.5ml/¼ tsp pepper
1.2kg/2½lb chicken portions
50g/2oz/½ cup plain flour
45ml/3 tbsp corn oil
25g/1oz/2 tbsp butter or margarine
900g/2lb sweet potatoes, peeled and cut into 2.5cm/1in pieces
45ml/3 tbsp light brown sugar
steamed broccoli, to serve

1 In a polythene bag, combine the orange rind and juice, soy sauce, ginger and pepper. Add the chicken pieces. Put the bag in a mixing bowl (this will keep the chicken immersed in the marinade) and seal. Leave to marinate in the fridge overnight.

2 Preheat the oven to 220°C/425°F/Gas 7. Drain the chicken, reserving the marinade. Coat the chicken with flour, shaking off any excess.

3 Heat 30ml/2 tbsp of the oil in a frying pan. Add the chicken pieces and brown on all sides. Remove from the pan and drain.

4 Put the remaining oil and the butter or margarine in a 30 × 23cm/12 × 9in ovenproof dish. Briefly heat in the oven.

5 Put the potato pieces in the bottom of the dish, tossing well to coat with the butter and oil. Arrange the chicken portions in a single layer on top of the potatoes. Cover with foil and bake for 40 minutes.

6 Mix the reserved marinade with the brown sugar. Remove the foil from the baking dish and pour the marinade mixture over the chicken and potatoes. Bake, uncovered, for about 20 minutes until the chicken and potatoes are cooked through and tender. Serve with steamed broccoli.

Golden Chicken

One of those rare dishes that is better cooked in advance and reheated. The chicken (preferably an old boiling fowl and not a young roaster) cooks in its own rich gravy. Leaving it to cool helps in the removal of any fat and improves the flavour.

Serves 5–6

15–30ml/1–2 tbsp oil
2.5kg/5½lb chicken
30ml/2 tbsp plain flour
2.5ml/½ tsp paprika
600ml/1 pint/2½ cups boiling water
salt and freshly ground black pepper
cooked rice and broccoli, to serve

1 Preheat the oven to 160°C/325°F/Gas 3. Heat the oil in a large, flameproof casserole and sauté the chicken slowly on all sides until the skin is brown. A boiling fowl is fatter, so you should prick the skin with a fork on the back and legs to release the fat as the chicken cooks.

2 Transfer the chicken to a plate and sprinkle the flour into the oil remaining in the casserole, adding a little more if necessary, to make a paste. Add the paprika and seasoning, and gradually pour in the boiling water, stirring all the time to make a thick sauce. When the sauce is simmering, replace the chicken, spoon some of the sauce over the top and cover tightly with a sheet of foil and then the lid.

3 Cook in the centre of the oven for about 1 hour and then turn the chicken over. Continue cooking for about 2 hours or until the chicken is tender (a roaster will cook far quicker than a boiler). Add a little extra boiling water if the sauce appears to be drying up.

4 When the meat on the legs is tender, the chicken is done. Leave to cool, then pour the gravy into a bowl. When it is cold, chill in the fridge until the fat solidifies into a pale layer on the top. Remove with a spoon.

5 Joint the chicken, place in a clean pan and pour over the cold gravy. Reheat thoroughly and serve with rice and broccoli.

Pan-fried Chicken with Pesto

Pan-fried chicken, served with warm pesto, makes a deliciously quick main course. Serve with rice noodles and braised mixed vegetables.

Serves 4
15ml/1 tbsp olive oil
4 chicken breast fillets, skinned
fresh basil leaves, to garnish
braised baby carrots and celery, to serve

For the pesto
90ml/6 tbsp olive oil
50g/2oz/½ cup pine nuts
50g/2oz/⅔ cup grated Parmesan cheese
50g/2oz/1 cup fresh basil leaves
15g/½oz/¼ cup fresh parsley
2 garlic cloves, crushed
salt and freshly ground black pepper

1 Heat the 15ml/1 tbsp oil in a frying pan. Add the chicken fillets and cook gently for 15–20 minutes, turning several times, until tender, lightly browned and thoroughly cooked.

2 Meanwhile, to make the pesto, place the olive oil, pine nuts, Parmesan cheese, basil, parsley, garlic and salt and pepper to taste in a blender or food processor, and process until smooth and well mixed.

3 Remove the chicken from the pan, cover and keep hot. Reduce the heat slightly, then add the pesto to the pan and cook gently, stirring constantly, for a few minutes until the pesto has warmed through.

4 Pour the warm pesto over the chicken, then garnish with basil leaves and serve with braised baby carrots and celery.

Succulent Fried Chicken

Crisp-coated deep-fried chicken, tender and succulent within, is justifiably popular.

Serves 4
250ml/8fl oz/1 cup milk
1 egg, beaten
150g/5oz/1¼ cups plain flour
5ml/1 tsp paprika
8 chicken portions
oil, for deep frying
salt and freshly ground black pepper
lemon wedges and fresh flat leaf parsley, to garnish

1 Mix the milk with the beaten egg in a shallow dish. On a sheet of greaseproof paper, combine the flour, paprika, salt and pepper.

2 One at a time, dip the chicken portions in the egg mixture and turn them to coat all over. Then dip them in the flour and shake off any excess.

3 Deep fry in hot oil for 25–30 minutes, turning the pieces so they brown and cook evenly. Drain well on kitchen paper and serve very hot, garnished with lemon wedges and parsley.

Chicken Bitki

A Polish dish, in which finely chopped chicken and mushrooms are formed into small sausage shapes and fried. You could use guinea fowl to mimic the game flavour of Polish chicken.

Makes 12
15g/½oz/1 tbsp butter, melted
115g/4oz/1½ cups flat mushrooms, finely chopped
50g/2oz/1 cup fresh white breadcrumbs
350g/12oz chicken breast fillets, skinned and finely chopped
2 eggs, separated
1.5ml/¼ tsp grated nutmeg
30ml/2 tbsp plain flour
45ml/3 tbsp oil
salt and freshly ground black pepper
green salad and grated pickled beetroot, to serve

1 Melt the butter in a pan and fry the mushrooms for 5 minutes until soft and all the juices have evaporated. Set aside to cool.

2 Mix the breadcrumbs, chicken, egg yolks, nutmeg, salt and pepper and mushrooms together in a bowl.

3 In a clean bowl, whisk the egg whites until stiff. Stir half into the chicken mixture, then fold in the remainder.

4 Shape the mixture into 12 even sausages, about 7.5cm/3in long and 2.5cm/1in wide. Roll in the flour to coat.

5 Heat the oil in a frying pan and fry the bitki for 10 minutes, turning until evenly golden brown and cooked through. Serve hot with a green salad and pickled beetroot.

Cook's Tip
It is always better to use freshly grated nutmeg rather than ready ground because the essential oils that give it its flavour are very volatile.

Layered Chicken & Mushroom Potato Bake

A delicious and moist combination of chicken, vegetables and gravy in a simple, one-dish meal topped with crunchy slices of potato.

Serves 4–6

15ml/1 tbsp olive oil
4 large chicken breast fillets, cut into chunks
1 leek, finely sliced into rings
50g/2oz/4 tbsp butter
25g/1oz/¼ cup plain flour
475ml/16fl oz/2 cups milk
5ml/1 tsp wholegrain mustard
1 carrot, very finely diced
225g/8oz/3 cups button mushrooms, finely sliced
900g/2lb main-crop potatoes, finely sliced
salt and freshly ground black pepper

1 Preheat the oven to 180°C/350°F/Gas 4. Heat the oil in a large saucepan and fry the chicken for 5 minutes until browned. Add the leek and fry for a further 5 minutes.

2 Add half the butter to the pan and allow it to melt. Then sprinkle the flour over and stir in the milk. Cook over a low heat until thickened, then stir in the mustard. Add the carrots with the mushrooms. Season with salt and pepper.

3 Line the base of a 1.75 litre/3 pint/7½ cup ovenproof dish with potato slices. Spoon one third of the chicken mixture over. Cover with another layer of potatoes. Repeat the layering, finishing with a layer of potatoes. Top with the remaining butter in knobs.

4 Bake in the oven for 1½ hours, covering with foil after 30 minutes' cooking time. Serve hot.

Cook's Tip
The liquid from the mushrooms keeps the chicken moist and the potatoes help to mop up any excess juices.

Chicken with Potato Dumplings

Poached chicken breast in a creamy sauce topped with light herb and potato dumplings makes a delicate yet hearty meal.

Serves 6

1 onion, chopped
300ml/½ pint/1¼ cups vegetable stock
120ml/4fl oz/½ cup white wine
4 large chicken breasts
300ml/½ pint/1¼ cups single cream
15ml/1 tbsp chopped fresh tarragon
salt and freshly ground black pepper

For the dumplings
225g/8oz main-crop potatoes, boiled and mashed
175g/6oz/1¼ cups suet
115g/4oz/1 cup self-raising flour
30ml/2 tbsp chopped mixed fresh herbs
50ml/2fl oz/¼ cup water

1 Place the onion, stock and wine in a deep-sided frying pan. Add the chicken and simmer for 20 minutes, covered. Remove the chicken from the stock, cut into chunks and reserve.

2 Strain the stock and discard the onion. Reduce the stock by one third over a high heat. Stir in the cream and tarragon, and simmer until just thickened. Stir in the chicken and season. Spoon the mixture into a 900ml/1½ pint/3¾ cup ovenproof dish. Preheat the oven to 190°C/375°F/Gas 5.

3 To make the dumplings, mix together the ingredients in a bowl with salt and pepper, and stir in the water to make a soft dough. Divide into six and shape into balls with floured hands.

4 Place on top of the chicken mixture and bake uncovered for 30 minutes until the dumplings are browned and cooked through. Serve immediately.

Cook's Tip
Do not reduce the sauce too much before it is cooked in the oven as the dumplings absorb quite a lot of the liquid.

Persian Chicken

A sauce flavoured with cinnamon, saffron and lemon juice makes this simple dish quite special.

Serves 4

15ml/1 tbsp oil
4 chicken portions
1 large onion, chopped
3 garlic cloves, finely chopped
5ml/1 tsp ground cinnamon
2–3 saffron strands, soaked in 15ml/1 tbsp boiling water
30ml/2 tbsp lemon juice
475ml/16fl oz/2 cups water
salt and freshly ground black pepper
cooked rice, yogurt and salad, to serve

1 Heat the oil in a large saucepan or flameproof casserole and sauté the chicken portions until golden. Remove from the pan and set aside.

2 Add the onion to the pan and fry gently over a moderate heat for about 5 minutes, stirring frequently, until softened and golden, then add the garlic and fry briefly.

3 Stir in the cinnamon, saffron, lemon juice and seasoning. Return the chicken to the pan, add the water and bring to the boil over a medium heat.

4 Reduce the heat, cover and simmer for 30–45 minutes until the chicken is cooked and the sauce reduced to 120ml/4fl oz/½ cup. Serve with rice, yogurt and salad.

Cook's Tip

Cinnamon is the dried rolled bark of a tropical tree. It is available in sticks, which are difficult to grind, and ready ground.

Chicken with Cajun Sauce

Real Cajun sauce, from the American deep South, must start with a Cajun roux.

Serves 4

115g/4oz/1 cup plain flour
1.5kg/3½ lb chicken, cut into 8 portions
250ml/8fl oz/1 cup buttermilk
vegetable oil, for frying
salt and freshly ground black pepper
fresh parsley sprigs, to garnish

For the sauce

115g/4oz/½ cup lard or vegetable oil
65g/2½ oz/generous ½ cup plain flour
2 onions, chopped
2–3 celery sticks, chopped
1 large green pepper, seeded and chopped
2 garlic cloves, finely chopped
250ml/8fl oz/1 cup passata
450ml/¾ pint/scant 2 cups red wine or Chicken Stock
225g/8oz tomatoes, peeled and chopped
2 bay leaves
15ml/1 tbsp soft brown sugar
5ml/1 tsp grated orange rind
2.5ml/½ tsp cayenne pepper

1 To make the sauce, melt the lard and stir in the flour. Cook over a low heat, stirring, for 15–20 minutes or until golden brown.

2 Add the onions, celery, green pepper and garlic and cook, stirring, until softened. Stir in the remaining sauce ingredients and season. Bring to the boil, then simmer for 1 hour or until the sauce is rich and thick. Stir from time to time.

3 Meanwhile, prepare the chicken. Put the flour in a polythene bag and season. Dip each piece of chicken in buttermilk, then dredge in the flour. Set aside for 20 minutes.

4 Heat 2.5cm/1in oil in a frying pan. Fry the chicken pieces, turning once, for 30 minutes until deep golden and cooked. Drain on kitchen paper. Add them to the sauce, garnish and serve.

Thyme & Lime Chicken

Spring onion-stuffed chicken thighs are coated in butter infused with lime juice, thyme and garlic.

Serves 4

8 chicken thighs
30ml/2 tbsp chopped spring onion
5ml/1 tsp dried or chopped fresh thyme
2 garlic cloves, crushed
juice of 1 lime
90ml/6 tbsp melted butter
salt and freshly ground black pepper
lime slices, chopped spring onions and fresh coriander sprigs, to garnish
cooked rice, to serve

1 Put the chicken thighs in an ovenproof dish skin side down and, using a sharp knife, make a slit lengthways along each thigh bone. Mix the spring onion with a little salt and pepper, and press the mixture into the slits.

2 Mix together the thyme, garlic, lime juice and all but 30ml/2 tbsp of the melted butter in a small bowl, and spoon a little over each chicken thigh.

3 Spoon the remaining melted butter over the top. Cover the chicken loosely with clear film and leave to marinate in a cool place for several hours or overnight in the fridge.

4 Preheat the oven to 190°C/375°F/Gas 5. Remove the clear film from the chicken and cover the dish with foil. Bake the chicken for 1 hour, then remove the foil and cook for a few more minutes to brown. Serve hot, garnished with lime, spring onions and coriander, and accompanied by rice.

Cook's Tip

You may need to use two limes, depending on their size and juiciness. Or, for a less sharp flavour, use lemons instead.

Palava Chicken

A variation of a popular Ghanaian dish, which was originally made from fish. In Sierra Leone, peanut butter is often added.

Serves 4

675g/1½ lb chicken breast fillets, skinned
2 garlic cloves, crushed
30ml/2 tbsp butter or margarine
30ml/2 tbsp palm or vegetable oil
1 onion, finely chopped
4 tomatoes, peeled and chopped
30ml/2 tbsp peanut butter
600ml/1 pint/2½ cups Chicken Stock or water
1 fresh thyme sprig or 5ml/1 tsp dried thyme
225g/8oz frozen leaf spinach, thawed and chopped
1 fresh chilli, seeded and chopped
salt and freshly ground black pepper
boiled yams, to serve

1 Cut the chicken fillets into thin slices, place in a bowl and stir in the garlic and a little salt and pepper. Melt the butter or margarine in a large frying pan and fry the chicken over a moderate heat, turning once or twice to brown evenly. Transfer to a plate, using a slotted spoon, and set aside.

2 Heat the oil in a large saucepan, and fry the onion and tomatoes over a high heat for 5 minutes until soft. Reduce the heat, add the peanut butter and half of the stock or water, and blend together well.

3 Cook for 4–5 minutes, stirring all the time to prevent the peanut butter from burning, then add the remaining stock or water, the thyme, spinach, chilli and seasoning. Stir in the chicken slices and cook over a moderate heat for about 10–15 minutes until the chicken is cooked through. Pour into a warmed serving dish and serve with boiled yams.

Cook's Tip

If you have time fresh spinach adds a fresher flavour. Egusi – ground melon seed – can be used instead of peanut butter.

Hunter's Chicken

This traditional Italian dish sometimes has strips of green pepper in the sauce for extra colour and flavour instead of mushrooms.

Serves 4

15g/½oz/¼ cup dried porcini mushrooms
30ml/2 tbsp olive oil
15g/½oz/1 tbsp butter
4 chicken portions, on the bone, skinned
1 large onion, thinly sliced
400g/14oz can chopped tomatoes
150ml/¼ pint/⅔ cup red wine
1 garlic clove, crushed
leaves of 1 fresh rosemary sprig, finely chopped
115g/4oz/1½ cups fresh field mushrooms, thinly sliced
salt and freshly ground black pepper
fresh rosemary sprigs, to garnish
creamed potato or polenta, to serve

1 Put the porcini in a bowl, add 250ml/8fl oz/1 cup warm water and leave to soak for 20–30 minutes. Remove from the liquid and squeeze the porcini over the bowl. Strain the liquid and reserve. Finely chop the porcini.

2 Heat the oil and butter in a large, flameproof casserole until foaming. Add the chicken and sauté over a medium heat for 5 minutes or until golden. Drain on kitchen paper.

3 Add the onion and porcini to the pan. Cook gently, stirring frequently, for 3 minutes until the onion has softened but not browned. Stir in the chopped tomatoes, wine and reserved mushroom soaking liquid, then add the crushed garlic and chopped rosemary, with salt and pepper to taste. Bring to the boil, stirring all the time.

4 Return the chicken to the casserole and turn to coat with the sauce. Cover and simmer gently for 30 minutes.

5 Add the fresh mushrooms and stir well to mix into the sauce. Continue simmering gently for 10 minutes or until the chicken is tender. Taste and adjust the seasoning as necessary. Transfer to a warmed serving dish and garnish with rosemary. Serve hot, with creamed potato or polenta, if you like.

Pan-fried Chicken

The essence of this dish is to cook it quickly over a fierce heat, and it therefore works best with small quantities. To serve four people, double the quantities and either cook in batches or use two pans.

Serves 2

2 chicken breast fillets, skinned
1 small fresh red or green chilli, seeded and finely sliced
2 garlic cloves, finely sliced
3 spring onions, sliced
4–5 thin slices fresh root ginger
2.5ml/ ½ tsp ground coriander
2.5ml/ ½ tsp ground cumin
30ml/2 tbsp olive oil
25ml/1 ½ tsp lemon juice
30ml/2 tbsp pine nuts
15ml/1 tbsp raisins (optional)
oil, for frying
15ml/1 tbsp chopped fresh coriander
15ml/1 tbsp chopped fresh mint
salt and freshly ground black pepper
sprigs of fresh mint and lemon wedges, to garnish
cooked rice or couscous, to serve

1 Cut the chicken fillets lengthways into three or four thin slices. Place in a shallow bowl. Blend together the chilli, garlic, spring onions, spices, olive oil, lemon juice, pine nuts and raisins, if using. Season, then pour over the chicken pieces, stirring to coat. Cover with clear film and leave in a cool place for 1–2 hours.

2 Lift the chicken out of the dish, reserving the marinade. Brush a heavy-based frying pan with oil, and heat. Add the chicken slices and stir-fry over a fairly high heat for 3–4 minutes until the chicken is browned on all sides. Add the reserved marinade and continue to cook over a high heat for 6–8 minutes until the chicken is cooked through.

3 Reduce the heat, stir in the herbs, cook for 1 minute, then garnish and serve.

Country Chicken Sauté

Chicken portions in a bacon, mushroom and wine sauce.

Serves 4

175g/6oz/1 cup chopped bacon
10ml/2 tsp oil
1.75kg/3½lb chicken, cut into 8 portions
seasoned flour, for coating
225g/8oz/3 cups mushrooms, quartered
butter
45ml/3 tbsp dry white wine
250ml/8fl oz/1 cup Chicken Stock

1 Cook the bacon in the oil until lightly coloured. Remove and reserve.

2 Dredge the chicken in seasoned flour and fry until evenly browned. Remove and set aside.

3 Add the mushrooms and butter to the pan, and sauté until softened. Return the bacon and chicken, and add the wine and stock. Bring to the boil, cover and cook over a low heat for 20–25 minutes or until the chicken is tender.

Stoved Chicken

"Stoved" is derived from the French étouffer – to cook in a covered pot – and originates from the Franco/Scottish "Alliance" of the 17th century.

Serves 4

900g/2lb potatoes, cut into 5mm/¼in slices
2 large onions, thinly sliced
15ml/1 tbsp chopped fresh thyme
25g/1oz/2 tbsp butter
15ml/1 tbsp oil
2 large bacon rashers, rinded and chopped
4 large chicken portions, halved
1 bay leaf, plus extra to garnish
600ml/1 pint/2½ cups Chicken Stock
salt and freshly ground black pepper

1 Preheat the oven to 150°C/300°F/Gas 2. Make a layer of half the potato slices in the base of a casserole. Cover with half the onions. Sprinkle with half the thyme and season well.

2 Heat the butter and oil in a large frying pan, add the bacon and chicken, and fry until browned. Transfer the chicken and bacon to the casserole. Reserve the fat in the pan.

3 Sprinkle the remaining thyme and some seasoning over the chicken, and add the bay leaf. Cover with the remaining onion, followed by a final layer of potato. Sprinkle with seasoning.

4 Pour the stock into the casserole, brush the potatoes with the reserved fat, then cover tightly and cook in the oven for about 2 hours until the chicken is tender.

5 Preheat the grill. Uncover the casserole, place under the grill and cook until the slices of potato are beginning to brown and crisp. Serve hot, garnished with bay leaves.

Cook's Tip
Instead of buying large chicken joints and cutting them in half, choose either chicken thighs or drumsticks – or use a mixture of the two.

Chicken with Mushrooms & Tomatoes

Quickly cooked on top of the stove, this dish lends itself to endless variation and reheats well.

Serves 4

40g/1½oz/¼ cup plain flour
1kg/2¼lb chicken portions
15ml/1 tbsp olive oil
3 small onions or large shallots, sliced
175g/6oz/1½ cups mushrooms, quartered
1 garlic clove, crushed
60ml/4 tbsp dry white wine
120ml/4fl oz/½ cup Chicken Stock
350g/12oz tomatoes, peeled, seeded and chopped, or 250ml/8fl oz/1 cup canned chopped tomatoes
salt and freshly ground black pepper
fresh flat leaf parsley sprig, to garnish

1 Put the flour into a polythene bag, and season with salt and pepper. One at a time, drop the chicken portions into the bag and shake to coat with flour. Tap off the excess.

2 Heat the oil in a heavy, flameproof casserole. Fry the chicken over a medium-high heat until golden brown, turning once. Transfer to a plate and keep warm.

3 Pour off all but 15ml/1 tbsp of fat from the casserole. Add the onions or shallots, mushrooms and garlic. Cook until golden, stirring frequently.

4 Return the chicken to the casserole with any juices. Add the wine and bring to the boil, then stir in the stock and tomatoes. Bring back to the boil, reduce the heat, cover and simmer over a low heat for about 20 minutes until the chicken is tender and the juices run clear when the thickest part of the meat is pierced with a knife.

5 Tilt the pan and skim off any fat that has risen to the surface. Taste the sauce and adjust the seasoning as necessary. Serve, garnished with flat leaf parsley.

Burgundy Chicken

There are many versions of this traditional French dish, but this one is especially delicious. Serve it with warm French bread.

Serves 4

30ml/2 tbsp olive oil
25g/1oz/1 tbsp butter
1.75kg/3½ lb chicken, cut into 8 portions
115g/4oz gammon, cut into 5mm/¼in strips
115g/4oz button onions, peeled
115g/4oz/1½ cups button mushrooms
2 garlic cloves, crushed
30ml/2 tbsp brandy
250ml/8fl oz/1 cup red wine
300ml/½ pint/1¼ cups Chicken Stock
1 bouquet garni
25g/1oz/1 tbsp butter, blended with 30ml/2 tbsp flour
salt and freshly ground black pepper
fresh parsley, to garnish
French bread, to serve

1 Preheat the oven to 160°C/325°F/Gas 3. Heat the oil and butter in a large flameproof casserole and brown the chicken portions on both sides.

2 Add the gammon strips, peeled onions, mushrooms and garlic, and stir to mix.

3 Pour over the brandy and set it alight. Add the red wine, stock, bouquet garni and seasoning. Cover and cook in the oven for about 1 hour.

4 Remove the chicken from the casserole and keep warm. Add the butter and flour mixture to the sauce and heat, stirring, on top of the stove until thickened. Taste and adjust the seasoning as necessary.

5 Return the chicken to the casserole and continue cooking for several minutes. Serve, garnished with parsley and accompanied by French bread.

Yassa Chicken

A speciality of Senegal, where instead of frying the chicken, they often grill it before adding it to the sauce. For a less tangy flavour, you can reduce the lemon juice.

Serves 4

150ml/¼ pint/⅔ cup lemon juice
60ml/4 tbsp malt vinegar
3 onions, sliced
60ml/4 tbsp groundnut or vegetable oil
1kg/2¼ lb chicken portions
1 fresh thyme sprig
1 fresh green chilli, seeded and finely chopped
2 bay leaves
450ml/ ¾ pint/scant 2 cups Chicken Stock

1 Mix the lemon juice, vinegar, onions and 30ml/2 tbsp of the oil together in a bowl. Place the chicken in a shallow dish and pour over the lemon mixture. Cover with clear film and leave to marinate for 3 hours.

2 Heat the remaining oil in a large frying pan and fry the chicken pieces for 4–5 minutes until browned.

3 Add the marinated onions. Fry for 3 minutes, then add the marinade, thyme, chilli, bay leaves and half the stock.

4 Cover the pan and simmer gently over a moderate heat for about 35 minutes until the chicken is cooked through, adding the remaining stock as the sauce evaporates. Serve hot.

Chicken with Ham & Cheese

This tasty combination comes from the Emilia-Romagna region of Italy, where it is also prepared with veal.

Serves 4

4 small chicken breast fillets, skinned
seasoned flour
50g/2oz/4 tbsp butter
3–4 fresh sage leaves, plus extra to garnish
4 thin slices prosciutto crudo or cooked ham, cut in half
50g/2oz/⅔ cup grated Parmesan cheese

1 Cut each chicken fillet in half lengthways. Coat in the seasoned flour.

2 Heat the butter in a frying pan with the sage. Add the chicken and cook for 15 minutes over a low heat until golden, turning as necessary.

3 Transfer to a flameproof dish or grill pan. Place one piece of ham on each chicken fillet, and top with the Parmesan. Grill for 3–4 minutes or until the cheese has melted. Serve, garnished with sage.

Chicken Pancakes

A good way of using up leftover cooked chicken, these make a very quick and tasty lunch or supper dish if prepared with bought pancakes.

Serves 4

225g/8oz cooked, boned chicken
25g/1oz/2 tbsp butter
1 small onion, finely chopped
50g/2oz/¾ cup mushrooms, finely chopped
30ml/2 tbsp plain flour
150ml/¼ pint/⅔ cup Chicken Stock or milk
15ml/1 tbsp chopped fresh parsley
8 small or 4 large cooked pancakes
oil, for brushing
30ml/2 tbsp grated cheese
salt and freshly ground black pepper
watercress, to garnish

1 Remove the skin from the chicken and cut the meat into cubes. Set aside.

2 Heat the butter in a saucepan and gently cook the onion until tender. Add the mushrooms. Cook with the lid on for a further 3–4 minutes.

3 Add the flour and then the stock or milk, stirring continuously. Boil to thicken and simmer for 2 minutes. Season with salt and pepper. Add the chicken and parsley.

4 Divide the filling equally between the pancakes, roll them up and arrange in a greased ovenproof dish. Preheat the grill.

5 Brush the pancakes with a little oil and sprinkle with the cheese. Grill until browned. Serve garnished with watercress.

Cook's Tip
Home-made pancakes can be frozen, interleaved with greaseproof paper, in freezer bags. They thaw in minutes.

Chicken Crisp

Potato crisps and grated cheese make a different – and super-quick – topping for this dish.

Serves 4

115g/4oz/1 cup pasta shapes
175g/6oz broccoli, cut into florets
50g/2oz/4 tbsp butter
1 red onion, thinly sliced
4 streaky bacon rashers, chopped
225g/8oz chicken breast fillets, skinned and cut into chunks
60ml/4 tbsp plain flour
450ml/¾ pint/scant 2 cups milk
3 small packets plain potato crisps
75g/3oz/¾ cup cheese, grated
salt and freshly ground black pepper

1 Bring a large saucepan of salted water to the boil, add the pasta and cook according to the instructions on the packet until *al dente*. Add the broccoli for the last 5 minutes of the cooking time. Drain well.

2 Meanwhile, melt the butter in a heavy-based saucepan and fry the sliced onion until it begins to soften. Add the bacon and chicken, and fry gently until browned all over. Add the flour and mix well.

3 Remove the pan from the heat and gradually mix in the milk. Season, return to the heat and bring to the boil, stirring all the time. Stir in the drained pasta and broccoli. Tip the mixture into a shallow, heatproof dish.

4 Preheat the grill. Cover the top of the mixture with the crisps and sprinkle with the cheese. Put under the hot grill for a few minutes until the cheese has melted and is golden brown. Serve immediately.

Variation
If preferred, substitute flavoured crisps, such as cheese and onion or cheese and chives, for the plain.

Chicken with Olives

Chicken breast fillets may be flattened for quick and even cooking. Here they are prepared with black olives and tomatoes.

Serves 4

4 chicken breast fillets, about 150–175g/5–6oz each, skinned
1.5ml/¼ tsp cayenne pepper
75–105ml/5–7 tbsp extra virgin olive oil
1 garlic clove, finely chopped
16–24 stoned black olives
6 ripe plum tomatoes, quartered
small handful of fresh basil leaves
salt

1 Place each chicken breast between two sheets of clear film and pound with the flat side of a meat mallet or roll out with a rolling pin to flatten to about 1cm/½in thick. Season with salt and the cayenne pepper.

2 Heat 45–60ml/3–4 tbsp of the olive oil in a large, heavy-based frying pan over a medium-high heat. Add the chicken and cook for 4–5 minutes until golden brown and just cooked, turning once. Transfer the chicken to warmed serving plates and keep warm.

3 Wipe out the frying pan and return to the heat. Add the remaining oil and fry the garlic for 1 minute until golden and fragrant. Stir in the olives, cook for a further 1 minute, then stir in the tomatoes.

4 Shred the basil leaves and stir into the olive and tomato mixture, then spoon it over the chicken and serve at once.

Cook's Tip
If the tomato skins are at all tough, remove them. Score the base of each tomato with a knife, then plunge them into boiling water for 45 seconds. Cool quickly in cold water. The skin should then peel off easily.

Chicken, Carrot & Leek Parcels

These intriguing parcels may sound a bit fiddly for every-day cooking, but they take very little time and you can freeze them – ready to cook gently from frozen.

Serves 4

oil, for greasing
2 small leeks, sliced
4 chicken breast fillets
2 carrots, grated
4 stoned black olives, chopped
1 garlic clove, crushed
15–30ml/1–2 tbsp olive oil
8 canned anchovy fillets, drained
salt and freshly ground black pepper
black olives and fresh herb sprigs, to garnish

1 Preheat the oven to 200°C/400°F/Gas 6. Prepare four sheets of greaseproof paper about 23cm/9in square and grease them.

2 Divide the leeks equally among the sheets of greaseproof paper, placing them near the edge. Season the chicken fillets well on both sides and place one on each pile of leeks.

3 Mix the carrots, olives, garlic and oil together. Season lightly and place on top of the chicken portions. Top each with two of the anchovy fillets, then carefully wrap up each parcel, making sure the paper folds are secure and positioned underneath and the carrot mixture on top.

4 Bake for 20 minutes and serve hot, in the paper, garnished with black olives and fresh herb sprigs.

Cook's Tip
You can also wrap the chicken and vegetables in foil, but remove the foil before serving.

Mediterranean Chicken

This is the perfect after-work supper-party dish: it is quick to prepare and full of sunshine flavours.

Serves 4

4 chicken breast portions, about 675g/1½ lb total weight
115g/4oz/1 cup soft cheese with garlic and herbs
450g/1lb courgettes
2 red peppers, seeded
450g/1lb plum tomatoes
4 celery sticks
about 45ml/3 tbsp olive oil
275g/10oz onions, roughly chopped
3 garlic cloves, crushed
8 sun-dried tomatoes, roughly chopped
5ml/1 tsp dried oregano
30ml/2 tbsp balsamic vinegar
5ml/1 tsp paprika
salt and freshly ground black pepper
olive ciabatta or crusty bread, to serve

1 Preheat the oven to 190°C/375°F/Gas 5. Loosen the skin of each chicken portion, without removing it, to make a pocket. Divide the cheese into four and push one quarter underneath the skin of each chicken portion in an even layer.

2 Cut the courgettes and peppers into similar-size chunky pieces. Quarter the tomatoes and slice the celery sticks.

3 Heat 30ml/2 tbsp of the oil in a large, shallow, flameproof casserole. Cook the onions and garlic for 4 minutes until they are soft and golden, stirring frequently.

4 Add the courgettes, peppers and celery to the casserole, and cook for a further 5 minutes.

5 Stir in the tomatoes, sun-dried tomatoes, oregano and balsamic vinegar. Season well.

6 Place the chicken on top of the vegetables, drizzle over a little more olive oil, and season with salt and the paprika. Bake in the oven for 35–40 minutes or until the chicken is golden and cooked through. Serve with plenty of olive ciabatta or crusty bread to mop up the juices.

Stuffed Chicken Breasts

This dish consists of large chicken breasts filled with a herby spinach mixture, then topped with butter and baked until mouth-wateringly tender.

Serves 6

115g/4oz floury main-crop potatoes, diced
115g/4oz spinach leaves, finely chopped
1 egg, beaten
30ml/2 tbsp chopped fresh coriander
4 large chicken breasts
50g/2oz/4 tbsp butter
salt and freshly ground black pepper
fresh coriander sprigs, to garnish
fried mushrooms, to serve

For the sauce

400g/14oz can chopped tomatoes
1 garlic clove, crushed
150ml/¼ pint/⅔ cup Chicken Stock
30ml/2 tbsp chopped fresh coriander

1 Preheat the oven to 180°C/350°F/Gas 4. Boil the potatoes in a large saucepan of boiling water for 15 minutes or until tender. Drain, place in a large bowl and roughly mash.

2 Stir the spinach into the potato with the egg and coriander. Season with salt and pepper to taste.

3 Cut almost all the way through the chicken breasts and open out to form a pocket in each. Spoon the filling into the centre and fold the chicken back over again. Secure with cocktail sticks and place in a roasting tin. Dot with butter and cover with foil. Bake for 25 minutes. Remove the foil and cook for a further 10 minutes until the chicken is golden.

4 Meanwhile, to make the sauce, heat the tomatoes, garlic and stock in a saucepan. Boil rapidly for 10 minutes. Season and stir in the coriander.

5 Remove the chicken from the oven and place on warmed serving plates with fried mushrooms. Pour the sauce over, garnish with coriander and serve.

Koftas in Tomato Sauce

Delicious, lightly spiced chicken meatballs in a rich tomato sauce.

Serves 4

675g/1½lb chicken
1 onion, grated
1 garlic clove, crushed
15ml/1 tbsp chopped fresh parsley
2.5ml/ ½ tsp ground cumin
2.5ml/ ½ tsp ground coriander
1 egg, beaten
seasoned flour, for coating
60ml/4 tbsp olive oil
salt and freshly ground black pepper
chopped fresh parsley, to garnish
cooked pasta and grated Parmesan cheese, to serve

For the tomato sauce

15g/ ½oz/1 tbsp butter
15g/ ½oz/1 tbsp plain flour
200ml/7fl oz/scant 1 cup Chicken Stock
425g/15oz can chopped tomatoes, with their juice
5ml/1 tsp caster sugar
1.5ml/¼ tsp dried mixed herbs

1 Preheat the oven to 180°C/350°F/Gas 4. Remove any skin and bone from the chicken, and mince or chop the meat finely.

2 Put the chicken into a bowl together with the onion, garlic, parsley, spices, seasoning and beaten egg. Mix together thoroughly and shape into 24 × 4cm/1½in balls. Roll lightly in seasoned flour to coat.

3 Heat the oil in a frying pan and brown the balls in small batches. Remove and drain on kitchen paper.

4 To make the tomato sauce, melt the butter in a large saucepan. Add the flour, and then blend in the stock and tomatoes along with their juice. Add the sugar and herbs. Bring to the boil, cover and simmer for 10–15 minutes.

5 Place the chicken balls in a shallow, ovenproof dish and pour over the sauce. Cover and bake for 30–40 minutes.

6 Serve the koftas and sauce, garnished with parsley, accompanied by pasta plus grated Parmesan cheese.

Pasta with Turkey & Tomatoes

The flavour of the tomatoes is intensified by roasting and gives an extra boost to the dish, so it is worth taking the trouble to do this.

Serves 4

675g/1½lb ripe but firm plum tomatoes, peeled and quartered
90ml/6 tbsp olive oil
5ml/1 tsp dried oregano
350g/12oz broccoli florets
1 small onion, sliced
5ml/1 tsp dried thyme
450g/1lb turkey breast fillet, cubed
3 garlic cloves, finely chopped
15ml/1 tbsp lemon juice
350g/12oz/3 cups dried pasta twists
salt and freshly ground black pepper

1 Preheat the oven to 200°C/400°F/Gas 6. Place the tomatoes in an ovenproof dish. Drizzle over 15ml/1 tbsp of the oil, scatter over the oregano and season with salt. Bake for 30–40 minutes until the tomatoes are just browned.

2 Meanwhile, bring a large pan of salted water to the boil. Add the broccoli and cook for about 5 minutes until just tender. Drain and set aside.

3 Heat a further 30ml/2 tbsp of the oil in a large, non-stick frying pan. Add the onion, thyme, turkey and salt to taste. Cook over a high heat for 5–7 minutes, stirring frequently, until the meat is cooked and beginning to brown. Add the garlic and cook for a further 1 minute, stirring frequently.

4 Remove from the heat. Stir in the lemon juice and season with pepper. Set aside and keep warm.

5 Bring another large pan of salted water to the boil. Add the pasta and cook according to the packet instructions until *al dente*. Drain and place in a large serving bowl. Toss the pasta with the remaining oil.

6 Add the broccoli to the turkey mixture and toss into the pasta. Stir the tomatoes gently into the pasta mixture. Serve immediately.

Spaghetti & Turkey in Cheese Sauce

An Italian-American recipe, this makes an excellent family meal. Serve it with a tossed green salad.

Serves 4–6

75g/3oz/6 tbsp butter
350g/12oz turkey breast fillet, cut into thin strips
2 pieces bottled roasted pepper, drained, rinsed, dried and cut into thin strips
175g/6oz spaghetti
50g/2oz/½ cup plain flour
900ml/1½ pints/3¾ cups hot milk
115g/4oz/1⅓ cups grated Parmesan cheese
1.5–2.5ml/¼–½ tsp mustard powder
salt and freshly ground black pepper
salad leaves, to garnish

1 Melt about a third of the butter in a saucepan, add the turkey and sprinkle with a little salt and plenty of pepper. Toss the turkey over a medium heat for about 5 minutes until the meat turns white, then add the roasted pepper strips and toss to mix. Remove from the pan using a slotted spoon and set aside.

2 Preheat the oven to 180°C/350°F/Gas 4. Bring a large saucepan of salted water to the boil, add the pasta and cook according to the packet instructions until *al dente*.

3 Meanwhile, melt the remaining butter over low heat in the pan in which the turkey was cooked. Sprinkle in the flour and cook, stirring, for 1–2 minutes. Increase the heat to medium.

4 Add the milk a little at a time, whisking vigorously. Bring to the boil and cook, stirring, until the sauce is smooth. Add two thirds of the grated Parmesan, then whisk in mustard, salt and pepper to taste. Remove from the heat.

5 Drain the pasta and return it to the clean pan. Mix in half the cheese sauce, then spoon the mixture around the edge of an ovenproof dish. Stir the turkey mixture into the remaining cheese sauce and spoon into the dish. Sprinkle the remaining Parmesan over the top and bake for 15–20 minutes until the topping is just crisp. Serve hot with salad leaves.

Turkey with Yellow Pepper Sauce

Escalopes of turkey are wrapped around a garlicky cream-cheese filling and served with pepper purée.

Serves 4

30ml/2 tbsp olive oil
2 large yellow peppers, seeded and chopped
1 small onion, chopped
15ml/1 tbsp freshly squeezed orange juice
300ml/½ pint/1¼ cups Chicken Stock
4 turkey escalopes
75g/3oz/6 tbsp cream cheese with garlic
12 fresh basil leaves
25g/1oz/2 tbsp butter
salt and freshly ground black pepper
cooked pasta and black olives, to serve

1 Heat half the oil in a frying pan and gently fry the peppers and onion until beginning to soften. Add the orange juice and stock, and cook until very soft.

2 Meanwhile, lay the turkey escalopes between two sheets of clear film and beat with the side of a rolling pin to flatten.

3 Spread the escalopes with the cream cheese. Chop half the basil and sprinkle on top, then roll up, tucking in the ends like an envelope, and secure neatly with half a cocktail stick.

4 Heat the remaining oil and the butter in a frying pan and fry the turkey parcels for 7–8 minutes, turning them frequently, until golden and cooked.

5 Meanwhile, press the pepper mixture through a sieve, or blend until smooth, then strain back into the pan. Season to taste and warm through, or serve cold, with the turkey, accompanied by pasta, black olives and garnished with the remaining basil leaves.

Variation
Chicken breast fillets and plain cream cheese could be used in place of the turkey, if you prefer.

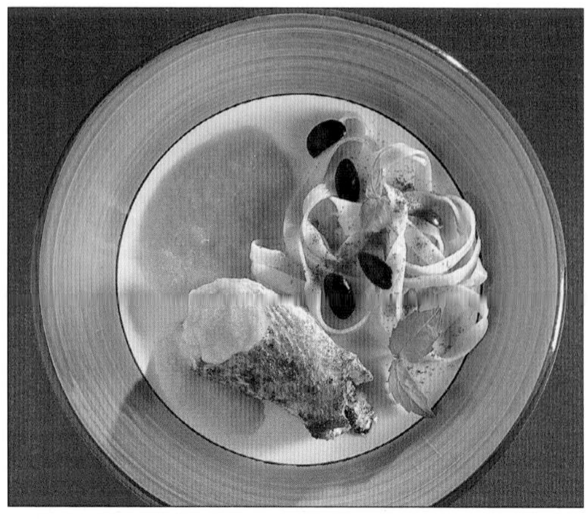

Stir-fried Turkey with Broccoli & Mushrooms

This is a really easy, tasty supper dish which works well with chicken too.

Serves 4

115g/4oz broccoli florets
4 spring onions
5ml/1 tsp cornflour
45ml/3 tbsp oyster sauce
15ml/1 tbsp dark soy sauce
120ml/4fl oz/½ cup Chicken Stock
10ml/2 tsp lemon juice
45ml/3 tbsp groundnut oil
450g/1lb turkey steaks, cut into strips about 5mm × 5cm/¼ × 2in
1 small onion, chopped
2 garlic cloves, crushed
10ml/2 tsp grated fresh root ginger
115g/4oz fresh shiitake mushrooms, sliced
75g/3oz/⅓ cup baby sweetcorn, halved lengthways
15ml/1 tbsp sesame oil
salt and freshly ground black pepper
egg noodles, to serve

1 Divide the broccoli florets into smaller sprigs and cut the stalks into thin diagonal slices. Finely chop the white parts of the spring onions and slice the green parts into thin shreds. In a bowl, blend together the cornflour, oyster sauce, soy sauce, stock and lemon juice. Set aside.

2 Heat a wok until hot, add 30ml/2 tbsp of the groundnut oil and swirl it around. Add the turkey and stir-fry for about 2 minutes until golden and crispy at the edges. Remove the turkey from the wok and keep warm.

3 Add the remaining oil and stir-fry the onion, garlic and ginger for about 1 minute. Increase the heat, add the broccoli, mushrooms and sweetcorn, and stir-fry for 2 minutes.

4 Return the turkey to the wok, then add the sauce with the chopped spring onion whites and seasoning. Cook, stirring, for about 1 minute until the sauce has thickened. Stir in the sesame oil. Serve immediately on a bed of egg noodles with the finely shredded spring onion greens scattered on top.

Turkey Rolls with Gazpacho Sauce

This Spanish-style recipe uses quick-cooking turkey steaks which are served with a refreshing sauce made from crunchy raw mixed vegetables.

Serves 4

4 turkey breast steaks
15ml/1 tbsp red pesto or tomato purée
4 chorizo sausages

For the gazpacho sauce
1 green pepper, seeded and chopped
1 red pepper, seeded and chopped
7.5cm/3in piece cucumber
1 medium-size tomato
1 garlic clove
45ml/3 tbsp olive oil
15ml/1 tbsp red wine vinegar
salt and freshly ground black pepper

1 To make the gazpacho sauce, place the peppers, cucumber, tomato, garlic, 30ml/2 tbsp of the oil and the vinegar in a food processor, and process until almost smooth. Season to taste with salt and pepper, and set aside.

2 If the turkey breast steaks are quite thick, place them between two sheets of clear film and beat them with the side of a rolling pin, to flatten them slightly.

3 Spread the pesto or tomato purée over the turkey and then place a chorizo on each piece and roll up firmly.

4 Slice the rolls thickly and thread them on to skewers, piercing them through the spiral. Grill on a medium-hot barbecue or under a preheated grill for 10–12 minutes, brushing with remaining oil and turning once. Serve with the gazpacho sauce.

Cook's Tip

If using wooden skewers, soak them in cold water for 30 minutes to prevent them from charring.

Turkey Scaloppine with Lemon & Sage

For this Italian-inspired dish, turkey is marinated in fresh lemon juice with sage, then coated in breadcrumbs and fried in double-quick time.

Serves 4

4 turkey breast steaks, about 175g/6oz each
15ml/1 tbsp grated lemon rind
15ml/1 tbsp chopped fresh or 5ml/1 tsp dried sage
50ml/2fl oz/¼ cup lemon juice
90ml/6 tbsp vegetable oil
65g/2½oz/1 cup fine dry breadcrumbs
salt and freshly ground black pepper
fresh sage leaves and lemon slices, to garnish
steamed new potatoes and courgettes, to serve

1 Place each turkey steak between two sheets of clear film and beat with the side of a rolling pin until about 5mm/¼in thick. Sprinkle with salt and pepper.

2 In a small bowl, combine the lemon rind, sage, lemon juice and 30ml/2 tbsp of the oil. Stir well to mix.

3 Arrange the turkey scaloppine, in one layer, in one or two shallow dish(es). Divide the lemon mixture between the scaloppine and rub in well. Leave to marinate for 20 minutes.

4 Heat the remaining oil in a frying pan. Dredge the turkey scaloppine in the breadcrumbs, shaking off the excess. Fry for about 2 minutes on each side until golden brown.

5 Garnish with sage leaves and lemon slices, and serve with new potatoes and courgettes.

Variation

For a delicious alternative, substitute fresh tarragon leaves for the sage.

Turkey Meat Loaf

Bursting with the Mediterranean flavours of green pepper, onion, garlic, sun-dried tomatoes, pine nuts and herbs, this makes an especially good midweek supper.

Serves 4

15ml/1 tbsp olive oil
1 onion, chopped
1 green pepper, seeded and finely chopped
1 garlic clove, finely chopped
450g/1lb minced turkey
50g/2oz/1 cup fresh white breadcrumbs
1 egg, beaten
50g/2oz/½ cup pine nuts
12 sun-dried tomatoes in oil, drained and chopped
85ml/3fl oz/⅓ cup milk
10ml/2 tsp chopped fresh or 2.5ml/½ tsp dried rosemary
5ml/1 tsp fennel seeds
2.5ml/½ tsp dried oregano
salt and freshly ground black pepper
salad, to serve

1 Preheat the oven to 190°C/375°F/Gas 5. Heat the oil in a frying pan. Add the onion, green pepper and garlic, and cook over a low heat for 8–10 minutes, stirring frequently, until the vegetables are just softened. Remove from the heat and leave to cool.

2 Place the minced turkey in a large bowl. Add the onion mixture and all the remaining ingredients and mix together until thoroughly combined.

3 Transfer to a 21 × 12cm/8½ × 4½in loaf tin, packing down firmly. Bake for about 1 hour, until golden brown. Serve with salad.

Turkey Spirals

These little spirals are very simple to make and an excellent way to pep up plain turkey.

Serves 4

4 thinly sliced turkey breast steaks, about 90g/3½oz each
20ml/4 tsp tomato purée
15g/½oz/½ cup large basil leaves
1 garlic clove, crushed
15ml/1 tbsp milk
30ml/2 tbsp wholemeal flour
salt and freshly ground black pepper
passata or Fresh Tomato Sauce and pasta with fresh basil, to serve

1 Place the turkey steaks between two sheets of clear film and flatten slightly with a rolling pin. Spread each steak with tomato purée, then top with a few basil leaves, a little crushed garlic, and salt and pepper. Roll up firmly around the filling and secure with a cocktail stick. Brush with milk and sprinkle with flour to coat lightly.

2 Cook under a medium-hot grill for 15–20 minutes, turning occasionally. Serve hot, sliced, with passata or fresh tomato sauce and pasta, sprinkled with fresh basil leaves.

Pancake Parcels

These quick and easy pancakes are filled with a turkey and apple mixture.

Serves 4

For the filling

30ml/2 tbsp oil
450g/1lb minced turkey
30ml/2 tbsp snipped fresh chives
2 green eating apples, cored and diced
25g/1oz/¼ cup flour
175ml/6fl oz/¾ cup Chicken Stock
salt and freshly ground black pepper

For the pancakes

115g/4oz/1 cup plain flour
pinch of salt
1 egg, beaten
300ml/½ pint/1¼ cups milk
oil, for frying
lightly cooked mangetouts, to serve

For the sauce

60ml/4 tbsp cranberry sauce
50ml/2fl oz/¼ cup Chicken Stock
15ml/1 tbsp clear honey
15g/½oz/1 tbsp cornflour

1 To make the filling, heat the oil and fry the turkey for 5 minutes. Add the chives and apples, and then the flour. Stir in the stock and seasoning. Bring to the boil, stirring, lower the heat and simmer for 20 minutes, stirring occasionally.

2 To make the pancakes, sift the flour into a bowl with the salt. Make a well in the centre and drop in the egg. Beat it in gradually with the milk to form a smooth batter.

3 Heat the oil in a 15cm/5in omelette pan. Pour off the oil and add one quarter of the batter and cook for 2–3 minutes. Turn the pancake over and cook for a further 2 minutes. Make three more in the same way, adding more oil to the pan.

4 To make the sauce, heat the cranberry sauce, stock and honey in a pan. Mix the cornflour with 20ml/4 tsp water, stir it into the sauce and bring to the boil, stirring until clear.

5 Lay the pancakes on a chopping board, spoon the filling into the centre and fold over around the filling. Place on a plate and spoon on the sauce. Serve with mangetouts.

Turkey Breasts with Tomato Salsa

Turkey can lack flavour, but this is a great way of turning it into a tasty meal with the minimum of fat or fuss.

Serves 4

4 turkey breast fillets, about 175g/6oz each, skinned
30ml/2 tbsp lemon juice
30ml/2 tbsp olive oil
2.5ml/½ tsp ground cumin
2.5ml/½ tsp dried oregano
salt and freshly ground black pepper
salad leaves, to serve

For the salsa

1 fresh green chilli
450g/1lb tomatoes, seeded and chopped
200g/7oz can sweetcorn kernels, drained
3 spring onions, chopped
15ml/1 tbsp finely chopped fresh parsley
30ml/2 tbsp finely chopped fresh coriander
30ml/2 tbsp lemon juice
45ml/3 tbsp olive oil

1 Place the turkey fillets between two sheets of clear film and beat with a meat mallet or the side of a rolling pin until thin. Blend the lemon juice, oil, cumin, oregano and pepper in a shallow dish. Add the turkey and turn to coat. Cover and leave to stand for at least 2 hours, or chill overnight.

2 To make the salsa, roast the chilli over a gas flame, holding it with tongs, until charred on all sides. (Alternatively, char the skin under the grill.) Leave to cool for 5 minutes. Wearing rubber gloves, carefully rub off the charred skin. For a less fiery salsa, discard the seeds. Chop the chilli finely and place in a bowl. Add all the remaining salsa ingredients to the chilli, plus salt to taste, and stir well until mixed thoroughly. Set aside.

3 Remove the turkey breast fillets from the marinade. Season lightly on both sides with salt to taste.

4 Heat a heavy-based ridged frying pan. When hot, add the turkey breasts and cook for about 3 minutes until browned. Turn and cook the meat on the other side for a further 3–4 minutes until cooked through. Serve immediately with the salsa and salad leaves.

Turkey Surprise Packages

Let diners open their own parcels and savour the aroma to the full.

Serves 4

30ml/2 tbsp chopped fresh parsley
4 turkey breast steaks, about 150–175g/5–6oz each
8 streaky bacon rashers
2 spring onions, cut into thin strips
50g/2oz fennel, cut into thin strips
1 carrot, cut into thin strips
1 small celery stick, cut into thin strips
grated rind and juice of 1 lemon
salt and freshly ground black pepper
lemon wedges, to serve

1 Sprinkle parsley over each turkey breast steak and pat it into the meat using your hands. Wrap 2 rashers of bacon round each one.

2 Preheat the oven to 190°C/375°F/Gas 5. Cut four 30cm/12in circles out of baking parchment or greaseproof paper and put a turkey breast just off centre on each one.

3 Arrange the vegetable strips on top of the steaks, sprinkle the lemon rind and juice over, and season well with salt and pepper.

4 Fold the paper over the turkey and vegetables and, starting at one side, twist and fold the paper edges together. Work your way round the semi-circle, to seal the edges of the parcel together neatly.

5 Place the parcels in a roasting tin and cook for 35–45 minutes or until the turkey is cooked and tender. Serve the packages with lemon wedges for squeezing.

Cook's Tip

The cut surfaces of fennel will turn brown very quickly when exposed to the air. If you have to cut the fennel in advance of using, drop it in a bowl of water acidulated with a little lemon juice.

Turkey Croquettes

A crisp patty of flavoursome smoked turkey mixed with mashed potato and spring onions and rolled in breadcrumbs, served with a tangy tomato sauce.

Serves 4

450g/1lb main-crop potatoes, diced
3 eggs
30ml/2 tbsp milk
175g/6oz smoked turkey rashers, finely chopped
2 spring onions, thinly sliced
115g/4oz/2 cups fresh white breadcrumbs
vegetable oil, for deep frying
salt and freshly ground black pepper

For the sauce

15ml/1 tbsp olive oil
1 onion, finely chopped
400g/14oz can tomatoes, drained
30ml/2 tbsp tomato purée
15ml/1 tbsp chopped fresh parsley

1 Boil the potatoes in salted water for 20 minutes or until tender. Drain and return the pan to a low heat to make sure all the excess water evaporates.

2 Mash the potatoes with 2 of the eggs and the milk. Season well with salt and pepper. Stir in the turkey and spring onions. Chill for 1 hour.

3 Meanwhile, to make the sauce, heat the oil in a frying pan and fry the onion for 5 minutes until softened. Add the tomatoes and tomato purée, stir and simmer for 10 minutes. Stir in the parsley, season with salt and pepper, and keep the sauce warm until needed.

4 Beat the remaining egg and place in a dish. Place the breadcrumbs in a separate dish. Divide the potato mixture into eight portions. Shape each one into a sausage shape and dip into the beaten egg and then into the breadcrumbs, shaking off any excess.

5 Heat the vegetable oil in a deep-fat fryer to 165°C/330°F and deep fry the croquettes for 5 minutes or until golden and crisp. Drain on kitchen paper. Serve with the sauce.

Duck Breasts with Pineapple & Ginger

For this Chinese dish, use the boneless duck breasts that are widely available or alternatively do as the Chinese and use a whole bird, saving the legs for another meal and using the carcass to make stock.

Serves 2–3

4 spring onions, chopped
2 duck breast fillets, skinned
15ml/1 tbsp light soy sauce
225g/8oz can pineapple rings
75ml/5 tbsp water
4 pieces drained Chinese stem ginger in syrup, plus 45ml/3 tbsp syrup from the jar
30ml/2 tbsp cornflour, mixed to a thin paste with a little water
¼ each red and green pepper, seeded and cut into thin strips
salt and freshly ground black pepper
cooked thin egg noodles, baby spinach and green beans, to serve

1 Select a shallow bowl that will fit into your steamer and that will accommodate the duck breasts side by side. Spread out the chopped spring onions in the bowl, arrange the duck breasts on top and cover with non-stick baking paper. Set the steamer over boiling water and cook the duck for about 1 hour or until tender. Remove the duck from the steamer and leave to cool.

2 Cut the duck into thin slices. Place on a plate and moisten with a little of the cooking juices from the steaming bowl. Strain the remaining juices into a small saucepan and set aside. Cover the duck slices with the baking paper or foil and keep warm.

3 Drain the pineapple rings, reserving 75ml/5 tbsp of the juice. Add this to the reserved cooking juices, with the measured water. Stir in the ginger syrup, soy sauce, then stir in the cornflour paste and cook, stirring, until thickened. Season to taste.

4 Cut the pineapple and ginger into attractive shapes. Put the cooked noodles, baby spinach and green beans on a plate, add slices of duck and top with the pineapple, ginger and pepper strips. Pour over the sauce and serve.

Duck Breasts with Orange Sauce

A simple variation on the classic dish using a whole roast duck – and much quicker to prepare.

Serves 4

4 duck breasts
15ml/1 tbsp sunflower oil
2 oranges
150ml/¼ pint/⅔ cup orange juice
15ml/1 tbsp port
30ml/2 tbsp Seville orange marmalade
15g/½oz/1 tbsp butter
5ml/1 tsp cornflour
salt and freshly ground black pepper
sautéed potatoes and steamed green beans, to serve

1 Season the duck breast skin. Heat the oil in a frying pan over a moderate heat and add the duck breasts, skin side down. Cover and cook for 3–4 minutes until lightly browned. Turn the breasts over, lower the heat slightly and cook uncovered for 5–6 minutes.

2 Peel the skin and pith from the oranges. Working over a bowl to catch any juice, slice either side of the membranes to release the orange segments, then set aside with the juice.

3 Remove the duck breasts from the pan using a slotted spoon, drain on kitchen paper and keep warm in the oven while making the sauce. Drain off the fat from the pan.

4 Add the segmented oranges, all but 30ml/2 tbsp of the orange juice, the port and the orange marmalade to the pan. Bring to the boil and then reduce the heat slightly. Whisk small knobs of the butter into the sauce and season to taste.

5 Blend the cornflour with the reserved orange juice, pour into the pan and stir until slightly thickened. Add the duck breasts and cook gently for about 3 minutes. Arrange the sliced breasts on warmed plates and pour over the sauce. Serve with sautéed potatoes and steamed green beans.

Duck & Ginger Chop Suey

Chicken can also be used in this recipe, but duck gives a richer contrast of flavours.

Serves 4

2 duck breasts, about 175g/6oz each
45ml/3 tbsp sunflower oil
1 small egg, lightly beaten
1 garlic clove
175g/6oz/¾ cup beansprouts
2 slices fresh root ginger, cut into matchsticks
10ml/2 tsp oyster sauce
2 spring onions, cut into matchsticks
salt and freshly ground black pepper

For the marinade

15ml/1 tbsp clear honey
10ml/2 tsp rice wine
10ml/2 tsp light soy sauce
10ml/2 tsp dark soy sauce

1 Remove the skin and fat from the duck, cut the breasts into thin strips and place in a bowl. To make the marinade, mix all the ingredients together in a bowl. Pour the marinade over the duck, cover, chill and leave overnight.

2 Next day, make the omelette. Heat a small frying pan and add 15ml/1 tbsp of the oil. When the oil is hot, pour in the egg and swirl it around into an even layer. When the omelette is cooked, remove it from the pan, leave it to cool, then cut into strips. Drain the duck and discard the marinade.

3 Bruise the garlic with the flat side of a knife blade. Heat a wok or large frying pan, then add 10ml/2 tsp of the oil. When the oil is hot, add the garlic and fry for 30 seconds, pressing it to release the flavour. Discard. Add the beansprouts with seasoning and stir-fry for 30 seconds. Transfer to a heated dish, draining off any liquid.

4 Heat the wok again and add the remaining oil. When the oil is hot, stir-fry the duck for 3 minutes until cooked. Add the ginger and oyster sauce, and stir-fry for a further 2 minutes. Add the beansprouts, egg strips and spring onions, stir-fry briefly and serve immediately.

Stir-fried Crispy Duck

This stir-fry would be delicious wrapped in flour tortillas or steamed Chinese pancakes, served with a little extra warm plum sauce.

Serves 2

275–350g/10–12oz duck breast fillets
30ml/2 tbsp plain flour
60ml/4 tbsp oil
1 bunch spring onions, halved lengthways and cut into 5cm/2in strips
275g/10oz/2½ cups green cabbage, finely shredded
225g/8oz can water chestnuts, drained and sliced
50g/2oz/½ cup unsalted cashew nuts
115g/4oz cucumber, cut into strips
45ml/3 tbsp plum sauce
15ml/1 tbsp light soy sauce
salt and freshly ground black pepper
sliced spring onions, to garnish

1 Trim the skin and a little of the fat from the duck and thinly slice the meat. Season the flour well and use it to coat each piece of duck.

2 Heat the oil in a wok or large frying pan and cook the duck over a high heat until golden and crisp. Keep stirring to prevent the duck from sticking. Remove using a slotted spoon and drain on kitchen paper. You may need to cook the duck in batches.

3 Add the spring onions to the pan and cook for 2 minutes. Stir in the shredded cabbage and cook for 5 minutes or until softened and golden.

4 Return the duck to the pan with the water chestnuts, cashews and cucumber. Stir-fry for 2 minutes.

5 Add the plum sauce and soy sauce with plenty of seasoning, and heat for 2 minutes. Serve piping hot, garnished with sliced spring onions.

Chicken & Curry Mayonnaise Sandwich

A very useful and appetizing way of using leftover pieces of chicken.

Makes 2
4 slices Granary bread
25g/1oz/2 tbsp softened butter
115g/4oz cooked chicken, sliced
1 bunch watercress, trimmed

For the curry mayonnaise
120ml/4fl oz/½ cup ready-made mayonnaise
10ml/2 tsp concentrated curry paste
2.5ml/ ½ tsp lemon juice
10ml/2 tsp sieved apricot jam

1 To make the curry mayonnaise, put all the ingredients in a bowl and mix thoroughly. Chill until required.

2 Spread the bread with butter and arrange the chicken over two of the slices. Spread curry mayonnaise over the chicken slices.

3 Arrange sprigs of watercress on top, cover with the remaining bread and press lightly together. Cut in half and serve.

Variation

For an alternative spicy mayonnaise, add 5ml/1 tsp English mustard, 5ml/1 tsp Worcestershire sauce and a dash of Tabasco sauce to the ready-made mayonnaise.

Oriental Chicken Sandwich

This filling is also good served in warmed pitta bread, in which case cut the chicken into small cubes before brushing with the soy mixture, grill on skewers and serve warm.

Makes 2
175g/6oz chicken breast fillet, skinned
15ml/1 tbsp soy sauce
5ml/1 tsp clear honey
5ml/1 tsp sesame oil
1 garlic clove, crushed
4 slices white bread
60ml/4 tbsp peanut sauce
25g/1oz beansprouts
25g/1oz red pepper, seeded and finely sliced

1 Place the chicken breast in a heatproof dish or roasting tin. Mix together the soy sauce, honey, sesame oil and garlic. Brush over the chicken breast.

2 Grill the chicken for 3–4 minutes on each side until cooked through, then slice thinly.

3 Spread two slices of the white bread with some of the peanut sauce.

4 Lay the chicken on the sauce-covered bread.

5 Spread a little more sauce over the chicken.

6 Sprinkle over the beansprouts and red pepper, and sandwich together with the remaining slices of bread. Serve.

Cook's Tip

For home-made peanut sauce, stir together 1 seeded and ground fresh red chilli, 30ml/2 tbsp coconut milk and 115g/4oz crunchy peanut butter over a low heat until thick and smooth. Stir in 5ml/1 tsp brown sugar, 5ml/1 tsp lemon juice and salt to taste. Set aside to cool.

Chicken & Pesto Jackets

Although it is usually served with pasta, pesto can also give a wonderful lift to many other dishes. Here it is combined with chicken and yogurt to make a tasty topping for jacket potatoes.

Serves 4

4 baking potatoes, pricked
2 chicken breast fillets
250ml/8fl oz/1 cup plain yogurt
15ml/1 tbsp pesto sauce
fresh basil sprigs, to garnish

1 Preheat the oven to 200°C/400°F/Gas 6. Bake the potatoes for about 1¼ hours or until they are soft on the inside when tested with a skewer.

2 About 20 minutes before the potatoes are ready, cook the chicken breasts, leaving the skin on so that the flesh remains moist. Either bake the breasts in a dish alongside the potatoes in the oven or cook them on a rack under a moderately hot preheated grill.

3 Stir together the yogurt and pesto in a small bowl. Skin the chicken breasts and cut them into slices.

4 When the potatoes are cooked through, cut them open. Fill the potatoes with the chicken slices, top with the yogurt sauce, garnish with basil and serve.

Variation
This filling would work equally well with sweet potatoes. Bake them in the same way until soft on the inside.

Fried Chicken

This is Japanese-style fried chicken, flavoured with ginger. It may be cooked with or without its skin, according to individual personal preference.

Serves 4

8 boneless chicken thighs
oil, for deep frying
about 90g/3½oz/scant ½ cup cornflour, for coating
salad leaves, to serve

For the marinade
50g/2oz piece fresh root ginger
60ml/4 tbsp sake or dry white wine
60ml/4 tbsp soy sauce

1 To make the marinade, peel and grate the ginger, and squeeze it over a bowl to extract its juice. Add the sake or white wine and the soy sauce.

2 Cut the chicken thighs into four chunks and add to the marinade, rubbing it in well with your hands. Set aside in a cool place for 30 minutes.

3 Heat the oil slowly to 165–170°C/330–340°F. Lift the chicken out of the marinade and pat dry on kitchen paper. Dust generously with cornflour. When the oil is hot, lower in the chicken pieces. To maintain the oil temperature, do not add too many chicken pieces at once. Deep fry the chicken pieces for 4–5 minutes until crisp, golden and cooked through. Remove the chicken from the pan.

4 Halve one chicken piece to make sure it is cooked inside. Drain the rest of the chicken on kitchen paper, then serve hot or cold, with salad.

Cook's Tip
Use Japanese rather than Chinese soy sauce for a more authentic flavour.

Hot Turkey Sandwich

A generous open sandwich that can be made with leftover roast turkey breast, served with a delicious hot mushroom gravy.

Serves 4

50g/2oz/4 tbsp butter or margarine
½ small onion, finely chopped
225g/8oz/3 cups button mushrooms, quartered
500g/1¼lb roast turkey breast
475ml/16fl oz/2 cups thick turkey gravy
4 thick slices wholewheat bread
fresh parsley sprigs, to garnish

1 Melt half the butter or margarine in a frying pan. Add the onion and cook for 5 minutes, until softened.

2 Add the mushrooms and cook for about 5 minutes, stirring occasionally, until the moisture they render has evaporated.

3 Meanwhile, skin the turkey breast and carve the meat into four thick slices.

4 In a saucepan, heat up the turkey gravy. Stir in the onion and mushroom mixture.

5 Spread the slices of bread with the remaining butter or margarine. Set a slice on each of four plates and top with the turkey slices. Pour the mushroom gravy over the turkey and serve hot, garnished with parsley.

Variation
If preferred, the sandwich bread may be toasted and buttered.

Chinese Duck in Pitta

This recipe is based on Chinese crispy duck, but uses duck breast instead of whole duck. After 15 minutes' cooking, the duck breast will still have a pinkish tinge. If you like it well cooked, leave it in the oven for a further 5 minutes.

Makes 2

1 duck breast, about 175g/6oz
3 spring onions
7.5cm/3in piece cucumber
2 round pitta breads
30ml/2 tbsp hoisin sauce
radish chrysanthemum and spring-onion tassel, to garnish

1 Preheat the oven to 220°C/425°F/Gas 7. Skin the duck breast, place the skin and breast separately on a rack in a roasting tin and cook in the oven for 10 minutes.

2 Remove the skin from the oven, cut into pieces and return to the oven with the breast for a further 5 minutes.

3 Meanwhile, cut the spring onions and cucumber into fine shreds about 4cm/1½in long.

4 Heat each pitta bread in the oven for a few minutes until puffed up, then split in half to make a pocket. Slice the duck breast thinly.

5 Stuff the duck breast into the pitta bread with a little spring onion, cucumber, crispy duck skin and some hoisin sauce. Serve, garnished with a radish chrysanthemum and spring-onion tassel.

Variation
Use Chinese chives instead of spring onions and plum sauce instead of hoisin.

Traditional Roast Chicken

Serve with bacon rolls, chipolata sausages, gravy and stuffing balls or Bread Sauce.

Serves 4
1.5kg/3½lb chicken
4 streaky bacon rashers
25g/1oz/2 tbsp butter
salt and freshly ground black pepper

For the prune and nut stuffing
25g/1oz/2 tbsp butter
50g/2oz/½ cup chopped stoned prunes
50g/2oz/½ cup chopped walnuts
50g/2oz/1 cup fresh breadcrumbs
1 egg, beaten
15ml/1 tbsp chopped fresh parsley
15ml/1 tbsp snipped fresh chives
30ml/2 tbsp sherry or port

For the gravy
30ml/2 tbsp plain flour
300ml/½ pint/1¼ cups Chicken Stock or vegetable cooking water

1 Preheat the oven to 190°C/375°F/Gas 5. To make the stuffing, mix all the ingredients together in a bowl and season well. Stuff the neck end of the chicken quite loosely, allowing room for the breadcrumbs to swell during cooking. (Any remaining stuffing can be shaped into small balls and fried.) Tuck the neck skin under the bird to secure the stuffing and hold in place with the wing tips or sew with thread or fine strips.

2 Place in a roasting tin and cover with the bacon rashers. Spread with the butter, cover loosely with foil and roast for about 1½ hours until the juices run clear when the thickest part of the thigh is pierced with a knife or skewer. Baste with the juices in the roasting tin three or four times during cooking.

3 Remove any trussing string and transfer to a serving plate. Cover with the foil and leave to rest while making the gravy. Carefully spoon off the fat from the juices in the roasting tin. Blend the flour into the juices and cook gently until golden brown. Add the stock or vegetable water and bring to the boil, stirring until thickened. Adjust the seasoning to taste, then strain the gravy into a jug or gravy boat. Serve with the chicken.

Honey Roast Chicken

A delicious variation on the classic roast, this is filled with a bacon and mushroom stuffing and basted with honey and brandy.

Serves 4
1.5kg/3½lb chicken
30ml/2 tbsp clear honey
15ml/1 tbsp brandy
25ml/5 tsp flour
175ml/6fl oz/⅔ cup Chicken Stock
French beans, to serve

For the stuffing
2 shallots, chopped
4 bacon rashers, rinded and chopped
50g/2oz/¾ cup button mushrooms, quartered
15g/½oz/1 tbsp butter or margarine
2 thick slices white bread, diced
15ml/1 tbsp chopped fresh parsley
salt and freshly ground black pepper

1 To make the stuffing, gently fry the shallots, bacon and mushrooms in a frying pan for 5 minutes, then transfer to a bowl. Pour off all but 30ml/2 tbsp of bacon fat from the pan. Add the butter or margarine to the pan and fry the bread until golden brown. Add the bread to the bacon mixture. Stir in the parsley, and salt and pepper to taste. Leave to cool.

2 Preheat the oven to 180°C/350°F/Gas 4. Pack the stuffing into the neck end of the chicken and truss with string. Transfer the chicken to a roasting tin that just holds it.

3 Mix the honey with the brandy. Brush half of the mixture over the chicken. Roast for about 1 hour 20 minutes until the juices run clear when the thickest part of the thigh is pierced with a skewer or knife. Baste the chicken frequently with the remaining honey mixture during roasting.

4 Transfer the chicken to a warmed serving platter. Cover with foil and set aside. Strain the cooking juices into a degreasing jug. Set aside to let the fat rise, then pour off the fat. Stir the flour into the sediment in the roasting pan. Add the cooking juices and the chicken stock. Boil rapidly until the gravy has thickened, stirring constantly to prevent lumps from forming. Pour into a gravy boat and serve with the chicken and French beans.

Roasted Chicken with Fresh Herbs & Garlic

A smaller chicken can also be roasted in this way.

Serves 4
1.75kg/4lb chicken or 4 small poussins
finely grated rind and juice of 1 lemon
1 garlic clove, crushed
30ml/2 tbsp olive oil
2 fresh thyme sprigs
2 fresh sage sprigs
75g/3oz/6 tbsp unsalted butter, softened
salt and freshly ground black pepper

1 Season the chicken or poussins well with salt and pepper. Mix the lemon rind and juice, garlic and olive oil together and pour them over the chicken. Leave to marinate for at least 2 hours in a non-metallic dish.

2 When the chicken has marinated, preheat the oven to 230°C/450°F/Gas 8. Place the herbs in the cavity of the bird and smear the butter over the skin. Season well.

3 Roast the chicken for 10 minutes, then turn the oven down to 190°C/375°F/Gas 5. Baste the chicken well and then roast for a further 1½ hours until the juices run clear when the thickest part of the thigh is pierced with a skewer or knife. Leave to rest for 10–15 minutes before carving to serve.

Bread Sauce

Smooth and surprisingly delicate, this old-fashioned sauce is traditionally served with roast chicken, turkey and various game birds.

Serves 6
1 small onion
4 cloves
1 bay leaf
300ml/ ½ pint/1¼ cups milk
115g/4oz/2 cups fresh white breadcrumbs
15g/ ½oz/1 tbsp butter
15ml/1 tbsp single cream
salt and freshly ground black pepper

1 Peel the onion and stick the cloves into it. Put it into a saucepan with the bay leaf and milk. Bring to the boil, then remove from the heat and set aside to stand for 15–20 minutes.

2 Remove the bay leaf and onion. Return to the heat and stir in the breadcrumbs. Simmer for 4–5 minutes or until thick and creamy. Stir in the butter and cream, then season to taste.

Roast Chicken with Lemon & Herbs

For this French roasting method, a well-flavoured chicken is essential – use a free-range or corn-fed bird if possible.

Serves 4
1.3kg/3lb chicken
1 unwaxed lemon, halved
small bunch of fresh thyme sprigs
1 bay leaf
15g/ ½oz/1 tbsp butter, softened
60–90ml/4–6 tbsp Chicken Stock or water
salt and freshly ground black pepper

1 Preheat the oven to 200°C/400°F/Gas 6. Season the chicken inside and out with salt and pepper.

2 Squeeze the juice of one lemon half and then place the juice, the squeezed lemon half, the thyme and bay leaf in the chicken cavity. Tie the legs with string and rub the breast with butter.

3 Place the chicken on a rack in a roasting tin. Squeeze over the juice of the other lemon half. Roast the chicken for 1 hour, basting two or three times, until the juices run clear when the thickest part of the thigh is pierced with a knife or skewer.

4 Pour the juices from the cavity into the roasting tin and transfer the chicken to a carving board. Cover loosely with foil and leave to rest for 10–15 minutes before carving.

5 Skim off the fat from the cooking juices. Add the stock or water and boil over a medium heat, scraping the base of the tin, until slightly reduced. Strain and serve with the chicken.

Cook's Tip
Be sure to save the carcasses of roast poultry for stock. Freeze them until you have several, then simmer with aromatic vegetables, herbs and water.

Olive Oil Roasted Chicken with Mediterranean Vegetables

Aubergine, red pepper, fennel, garlic and potatoes are roasted in the chicken juices until they are meltingly tender.

Serves 4

1.75kg/4lb chicken
150ml/ ¼ pint/ ⅔ cup extra virgin olive oil
½ lemon
few sprigs of fresh thyme
450g/1lb small new potatoes
1 aubergine, cut into 2.5cm/1in cubes
1 red pepper, seeded and quartered
1 fennel bulb, trimmed and quartered
8 large garlic cloves, unpeeled
coarse salt and freshly ground black pepper

1 Preheat the oven to 200°C//400°F/Gas 6. Rub the chicken all over with some of the olive oil and season with pepper. Place the lemon half inside the bird, with a sprig or two of thyme. Put the chicken, breast side down, in a large roasting tin. Roast for about 30 minutes.

2 Remove the chicken from the oven and season with salt. Turn the chicken right side up and baste with the juices from the tin. Surround the bird with the potatoes, roll them in the juices and return the tin to the oven to continue roasting.

3 After 30 minutes add the aubergine, red pepper, fennel and garlic. Drizzle with the remaining oil and season. Add any remaining thyme. Return to the oven and cook for 30–50 minutes more, turning the vegetables occasionally.

4 To find out if the chicken is cooked, push the tip of a sharp knife or skewer into the thickest part of the thigh: if the juices run clear, it is done. The vegetables should be tender and just beginning to brown.

5 Serve the chicken and vegetables from the pan, or transfer the vegetables to a serving dish, joint the chicken and place it on top. Serve the skimmed juices in a gravy boat.

Roast Chicken Stuffed with Forest Mushrooms

Use a free-range bird for this dish and let its flavour mingle with the aroma of woodland mushrooms.

Serves 4

25g/1oz/2 tbsp unsalted butter, plus extra for basting and to finish the gravy
1 shallot, chopped
225g/8oz wild mushrooms, e.g. chanterelles, ceps, bay boletus, oyster, trimmed and chopped
40g/1½oz/ ¾ cup fresh white breadcrumbs
2 egg yolks
1.75kg/4lb chicken
½ celery stick, chopped
½ small carrot, chopped
75g/3oz potato, peeled and chopped
250ml/8fl oz/1 cup Chicken Stock, plus extra if required
10ml/2 tsp wine vinegar
salt and freshly ground black pepper
fresh parsley sprigs, to garnish
roast potatoes and carrots, to serve

1 Preheat the oven to 220°C/425°F/Gas 7. Melt the butter in a saucepan and gently fry the shallot. Add half of the mushrooms and cook for 2–3 minutes until the juices run. Remove from the heat and stir in the breadcrumbs, seasoning and egg yolks. Spoon the stuffing into the neck of the chicken, enclose and fasten the skin on the underside with a skewer.

2 Rub the chicken with some butter and season. Put the celery, carrot, potato and remaining mushrooms in a roasting tin. Place the chicken on top, add the stock and roast for 1¼ hours or until the juices run clear when the thickest part of the thigh is pierced with a knife or skewer.

3 Transfer the chicken to a carving board, then process the vegetables and mushrooms. Pour the mixture back into the tin and heat gently, adjusting the consistency with chicken stock if necessary. Taste and adjust the seasoning, then add the vinegar and a knob of butter, and stir briskly. Pour the sauce into a jug or gravy boat. Serve the chicken with roast potatoes and carrots, garnished with parsley and accompanied by the sauce.

Roast Chicken with Celeriac

Celeriac mixed with chopped bacon, onion and herbs makes a moist and tasty stuffing.

Serves 4

1.5kg/3½lb chicken
15g/½oz/1 tbsp butter
celery leaves and parsley, to garnish

For the stuffing

450g/1lb celeriac, chopped
25g/1oz/2 tbsp butter
3 bacon rashers, rinded and chopped
1 onion, finely chopped
leaves from 1 fresh thyme sprig, chopped
leaves from 1 small fresh tarragon sprig, chopped
30ml/2 tbsp chopped fresh parsley
75g/3oz/1½ cups fresh brown breadcrumbs
dash of Worcestershire sauce
1 egg, beaten
salt and freshly ground black pepper

1 To make the stuffing, cook the celeriac in boiling water until tender. Drain well and chop finely.

2 Heat the butter in a saucepan, and gently cook the bacon and onion until the onion is soft. Stir in the celeriac and herbs, and cook, stirring occasionally, for 2–3 minutes. Meanwhile, preheat the oven to 200°C/400°F/Gas 6.

3 Remove the pan from the heat and stir in the breadcrumbs, Worcestershire sauce, seasoning and sufficient egg to bind. Use to stuff the neck end of the chicken. Season the bird's skin, then rub with the butter.

4 Roast the chicken, basting occasionally with the juices, for 1¼–1½ hours until the juices run clear when the thickest part of the thigh is pierced with a skewer or knife.

5 Turn off the oven, prop the door open slightly and allow the chicken to rest for 10–15 minutes before carving and serving, garnished with celery leaves and parsley.

Roast Chicken with Herb & Orange Bread Stuffing

Tender roast chicken scented with orange and herbs, served with gravy.

Serves 4–6

2 onions
25g/1oz/2 tbsp butter, plus extra
150g/5oz/2½ cups soft white breadcrumbs
30ml/2 tbsp chopped fresh mixed herbs
grated rind of 1 orange
1.5kg/3½lb chicken with giblets
1 carrot, sliced
1 bay leaf
1 fresh thyme sprig
900ml/1½ pints/3¾ cups water
15ml/1 tbsp tomato purée
10ml/2 tsp cornflour, mixed to a thin paste with 15ml/1 tbsp cold water
salt and freshly ground black pepper
chopped fresh thyme, to garnish

1 Preheat the oven to 200°C/400°F/Gas 6. Finely chop one of the onions. Melt the butter in a pan and add the chopped onion. Cook for 3–4 minutes until soft. Stir in the breadcrumbs, chopped mixed herbs and orange rind. Season well.

2 Remove the giblets and put aside. Wash the neck end of the chicken and dry with kitchen paper. Spoon in the stuffing, then rub a little butter into the breast and season it well. Put the chicken into a roasting tin and cook in the oven for 20 minutes, then reduce the heat to 180°C/350°F/Gas 4 and cook for a further 1 hour or until the juices run clear when the thickest part of the thigh is pierced with a knife or skewer.

3 Put the giblets, the remaining onion, the carrot, bay leaf, thyme and water into a large saucepan. Bring to the boil, then simmer while the chicken is roasting.

4 Place the chicken on a warmed serving platter and leave to rest. Skim the fat off the cooking juices, strain the juices and stock into a pan, and discard the giblets and vegetables. Simmer for about 5 minutes. Whisk in the tomato purée. Whisk the cornflour paste into the gravy and cook for 1 minute. Season and serve with the chicken, garnished with chopped thyme.

Stuffed Roast Masala Chicken

At one time this dish was cooked only in Indian palaces.

Serves 4–6

1 sachet saffron powder
2.5ml/ ½ tsp grated nutmeg
15ml/1 tbsp warm milk
1.3kg/3lb chicken
90ml/6 tbsp ghee or melted butter
50g/2oz/ ½ cup desiccated coconut, toasted
steamed carrots, to serve

For the stuffing

3 medium onions, finely chopped
2 fresh green chillies, chopped
50g/2oz/scant ½ cup sultanas
50g/2oz/ ½ cup ground almonds
50g/2oz/ ½ cup dried apricots, soaked in water until soft
3 hard-boiled eggs, coarsely chopped
salt

For the masala

4 spring onions, chopped
2 garlic cloves, crushed
5ml/1 tsp five-spice powder
4–6 green cardamom pods
2.5ml/ ½ tsp ground turmeric
5ml/1 tsp freshly ground black pepper
30ml/2 tbsp plain yogurt
75ml/5 tbsp hot water

1 Preheat the oven to 180°C/350°F/Gas 4. Mix the saffron, nutmeg and milk. Brush the inside of the chicken with the mixture and spread some under the skin.

2 Heat 60ml/4 tbsp of the ghee or butter in a frying pan and fry the chicken all over. Remove from the pan and keep warm.

3 To make the stuffing, fry the onions, chillies and sultanas for 2–3 minutes in the same ghee or butter. Remove from the heat, allow to cool, then mix in the ground almonds, apricots, chopped eggs and salt, and use to stuff the chicken.

4 To make the masala, heat the remaining ghee or butter in a pan and gently fry all the ingredients except the water for 2–3 minutes. Add to the water in a roasting tin.

5 Place the chicken on the masala, and roast in the oven for 1 hour. Remove the chicken, set aside and keep warm. Return the masala to the pan and cook until reduced. Pour over the chicken. Sprinkle with toasted coconut and serve with carrots.

Roast Chicken with Almonds

In this Moroccan dish the chicken is stuffed with a mixture of couscous, nuts and fruit.

Serves 4

1.5kg/3½lb chicken
pinch of ground ginger
pinch of ground cinnamon
pinch of saffron, dissolved in 30ml/2 tbsp boiling water
2 onions, chopped
300ml/ ½ pint/1¼ cups Chicken Stock
45ml/3 tbsp flaked almonds
15ml/1 tbsp plain flour
salt and freshly ground black pepper
lemon wedges and fresh coriander, to garnish

For the stuffing

50g/2oz/ ⅓ cup couscous
120ml/4fl oz/ ½ cup Chicken Stock
20g/¾oz/1½ tbsp butter
1 shallot, finely chopped
½ small cooking apple, peeled, cored and chopped
25ml/5 tsp flaked almonds
30ml/2 tbsp ground almonds
30ml/2 tbsp chopped fresh coriander
good pinch of paprika
pinch of cayenne pepper

1 Preheat the oven to 180°C/350°F/Gas 4. To make the stuffing, place the couscous in a bowl, bring the chicken stock to the boil and pour it over the couscous. Stir with a fork and set aside for 10 minutes for the couscous to swell.

2 Meanwhile, melt the butter in a small frying pan and fry the shallot for 2–3 minutes until soft. Fluff up the couscous, and stir in the shallot and all the butter from the pan. Add the remaining stuffing ingredients, season and stir well.

3 Loosely push the couscous mixture into the neck end of the chicken and truss the bird neatly.

4 Blend the ginger and cinnamon with the saffron water. Rub the chicken with salt and pepper, and then pour over the saffron water.

5 Place the chicken in a small roasting tin or dish so that it fits snugly. Spoon the chopped onions and stock around the edge, and then cover the dish with foil, pinching the foil around the edges of the dish firmly so that the chicken sits in a foil "tent".

6 Cook in the oven for 1¼ hours, then increase the temperature to 200°C/400°F/Gas 6. Transfer the chicken to a plate and strain the cooking liquid into a jug, reserving the chopped onions. Place the chicken back in the roasting tin with the onions, baste with a little of the cooking liquid and scatter with the flaked almonds.

7 Return to the oven and cook for about 30 minutes until the chicken is golden brown and the juices run clear when the thickest part of the thigh is pierced with a knife or skewer.

8 Pour off the fat from the reserved cooking juices and pour into a small saucepan. Blend the flour with 30ml/2 tbsp cold water, stir into the pan with the cooking juices and heat gently, stirring to make a smooth sauce. Garnish the chicken with lemon wedges and coriander, and serve with the sauce.

Sunday Roast Chicken

As you might expect, rum features in the glaze for this Caribbean-style roast.

Serves 6

1.5kg/3½lb chicken
5ml/1 tsp paprika
5ml/1 tsp dried thyme
2.5ml/½ tsp dried tarragon
5ml/1 tsp garlic granules
15ml/1 tbsp lemon juice
30ml/2 tbsp clear honey
45ml/3 tbsp dark rum
melted butter, for basting
300ml/½ pint/1¼ cups Chicken Stock
salt and freshly ground black pepper
lime quarters and herbs, to garnish

1 Place the chicken in a roasting tin and sprinkle with the paprika, thyme, tarragon, garlic granules and salt and pepper. Rub the mixture all over the chicken, lifting the skin and spreading the seasoning underneath it too. Cover the chicken loosely with clear film and leave to marinate in a cool place for at least 2 hours or preferably overnight in the fridge.

2 Preheat the oven to 190°C/375°F/Gas 5. Blend together the lemon juice, honey and rum, and pour over and under the skin of the chicken, rubbing it in well.

3 Spoon the melted butter over the chicken, then roast for 1½–2 hours or until the juices run clear when the thickest part of the thigh is pierced with a skewer or knife.

4 Transfer the chicken to a warmed serving platter and leave to rest while you make the gravy. Pour the juices from the roasting tin into a small saucepan. Add the stock and simmer over a low heat for 10 minutes or until reduced. Adjust the seasoning and pour into a jug. Serve with the chicken, garnished with lime quarters and herbs.

Cook's Tip
Extra herbs and rum can be used to make a richer, tastier gravy, if you like.

Harissa-spiced Roast Chicken

The spices and fruit in the stuffing give this chicken an unusual flavour.

Serves 4–5

1.5kg/3½lb chicken
30–60ml/2–4 tbsp garlic and spice aromatic oil
a few bay leaves
10ml/2 tsp clear honey
10ml/2 tsp tomato purée
60ml/4 tbsp lemon juice
150ml/¼ pint/⅔ cup Chicken Stock
2.5–5ml/½–1 tsp harissa

For the stuffing
25g/1oz/2 tbsp butter
1 onion, chopped
1 garlic clove, crushed
7.5ml/1½ tsp ground cinnamon
2.5ml/½ tsp ground cumin
225g/8oz/1⅓ cups dried fruit, soaked for several hours or overnight in water to cover
25g/1oz/¼ cup blanched almonds, finely chopped
salt and freshly ground black pepper

1 To make the stuffing, melt the butter in a saucepan. Add the onion and garlic, and cook gently for 5 minutes until soft. Add the cinnamon and cumin and cook, stirring, for 2 minutes. Drain the dried fruit, chop it roughly and add to the stuffing with the almonds. Season with salt and pepper, and cook for 2 minutes more. Tip into a bowl and leave to cool.

2 Preheat the oven to 200°C/400°F/Gas 6. Stuff the neck of the chicken with the fruit mixture, reserving any excess. Brush the garlic and spice oil over the chicken. Place the chicken in a roasting tin, tuck in the bay leaves and roast for 1–1¼ hours, basting occasionally, until the juices run clear when the thickest part of the thigh is pierced with a knife or skewer.

3 Transfer the chicken to a carving board. Pour off any excess fat from the roasting tin. Stir the honey, tomato purée, lemon juice, stock and harissa into the juices in the roasting tin. Add salt to taste. Bring to the boil, lower the heat and simmer for 2 minutes, stirring frequently.

4 Reheat any excess stuffing. Carve the chicken, pour the sauce into a small bowl and serve with the stuffing and chicken.

East African Roast Chicken

Smothered in a generous layer of butter combined with spices, herbs and coconut milk, this chicken is left to stand overnight to allow the flavours to mingle.

Serves 6

1.75kg/4lb chicken
30ml/2 tbsp softened butter, plus extra for basting
3 garlic cloves, crushed
5ml/1 tsp freshly ground black pepper
5ml/1 tsp ground turmeric
2.5ml/½ tsp ground cumin
5ml/1 tsp dried thyme
15ml/1 tbsp finely chopped fresh coriander
60ml/4 tbsp thick coconut milk
60ml/4 tbsp medium-dry sherry
5ml/1 tsp tomato purée
salt and chilli powder
fresh coriander leaves, to garnish

1 Remove the giblets from the chicken, if necessary, rinse out the cavity and pat the skin dry.

2 Put the butter and all the remaining ingredients in a bowl and mix together well to form a thick paste.

3 Gently ease the skin of the chicken away from the flesh and rub the flesh generously with the herb and butter mixture. Rub more of the mixture over the skin, legs and wings of the chicken and into the neck cavity.

4 Place the chicken in a roasting tin, cover loosely with foil and leave to marinate overnight in the fridge.

5 Preheat the oven to 190°C/375°F/Gas 5. Cover the chicken with clean foil and roast for 1 hour, then turn the chicken over and baste with the pan juices. Cover again with foil and cook for 30 minutes.

6 Remove the foil and place the chicken breast side up. Rub with a little extra butter and roast for a further 10–15 minutes until the juices run clear when the thickest part of the thigh is pierced with a skewer or knife and the skin is golden brown. Allow the chicken to rest for 10–15 minutes in a warm place before serving, garnished with coriander leaves.

Spicy Roast Chicken

Roasting chicken like this in an oven that has not been preheated produces a particularly crispy skin.

Serves 4

1.5kg/3½lb chicken
juice of 1 lemon
4 garlic cloves, finely chopped
15ml/1 tbsp each cayenne pepper, paprika and dried oregano
10ml/2 tsp olive oil
salt and freshly ground black pepper
fresh coriander sprigs, to garnish
sliced mixed peppers, to serve

1 Using a sharp knife or poultry shears, remove the backbone from the chicken. Turn it breast side up. With the heel of your hand, press down firmly to break the breastbone and open the chicken out flat like a book. Insert a skewer through the chicken, at the thighs, to keep it flat during cooking.

2 Place the chicken in a shallow dish and pour over the lemon juice. Place the garlic, cayenne, paprika, oregano, black pepper and oil in a small bowl and mix well. Rub evenly over the surface of the chicken.

3 Cover the chicken and leave to marinate for 2–3 hours at room temperature, or chill the chicken overnight and then return to room temperature before roasting.

4 Season both sides of the chicken with salt and place it, skin side up, in a shallow roasting tin.

5 Put the tin in a cold oven and set the temperature to 200°C/400°F/Gas 6. Roast for about 1 hour until the chicken is done, basting with the juices in the tin. To test whether the chicken is cooked, prick the thickest part of the flesh with a skewer or knife: the juices that run out should be clear. Serve the chicken hot, garnished with coriander sprigs and accompanied by mixed peppers.

Moroccan Roast Chicken

Ideally this chicken should be cooked whole, Moroccan-style, on a spit over hot charcoal. However, it is still excellent roasted in a hot conventional oven and can be cooked whole, halved or in quarters.

Serves 4–6

1.75kg/4lb chicken
2 small shallots
1 garlic clove
1 fresh parsley sprig
1 fresh coriander sprig
5ml/1 tsp salt
7.5ml/1½ tsp paprika
pinch of cayenne pepper
5–7.5ml/1–1½ tsp ground cumin
about 40g/1½oz/3 tbsp butter
½–1 lemon (optional)
sprigs of fresh parsley or coriander, to garnish

1 Remove the chicken giblets if necessary and rinse out the cavity with cold running water. Pat dry with kitchen paper. Unless cooking it whole, cut the chicken in half or into quarters using poultry shears or a sharp knife.

2 Place the shallots, garlic, herbs, salt and spices in a food processor or blender and process until the shallots are finely chopped. Add the butter and process to make a smooth paste.

3 Thoroughly rub the paste over the skin of the chicken and then allow it to stand for 1–2 hours.

4 Preheat the oven to 200°C/400°F/Gas 6 and place the chicken in a roasting tin. If using, quarter the lemon and place one or two quarters around the chicken pieces (or in the body cavity if the chicken is whole) and squeeze a little juice over the skin. Roast in the oven for 1–1¼ hours (2–2¼ hours for a whole bird) until the juices run clear when the thickest part of the thigh is pierced with a skewer or knife. Baste occasionally during cooking with the juices in the roasting tin. If the skin starts to brown too quickly, cover the chicken loosely with foil or greaseproof paper.

5 Allow the chicken to stand for 10–15 minutes, covered in foil, before carving. Serve, garnished with parsley or coriander.

Chicken with 40 Cloves of Garlic

This recipe is not as alarming as it sounds. Long, slow cooking makes the garlic soft, fragrant and sweet, and the delicious flavour permeates the chicken meat.

Serves 4–6

½ lemon
fresh rosemary sprigs
1.5–1.75kg/3½–4lb chicken
4 or 5 whole garlic bulbs
60ml/4 tbsp olive oil
salt and freshly ground black pepper
steamed broad beans and spring onions, to serve

1 Preheat the oven to 190°C/375°F/Gas 5. Place the lemon half and the rosemary sprigs in the chicken. Separate three or four of the garlic bulbs into cloves and remove the papery husks, but do not peel. Slice the top off the remaining garlic bulb.

2 Heat the oil in a large, flameproof casserole. Add the chicken, turning it in the hot oil to coat the skin completely. Season with salt and pepper, and add all the garlic.

3 Cover the casserole with a sheet of foil, then the lid, to seal in the steam and the flavour. Cook for 1–1¼ hours until the chicken juices run clear when the thickest part of the thigh is pierced with a skewer or knife.

4 Serve the chicken with the garlic, accompanied by steamed broad beans and spring onions.

Cook's Tip

Make sure that each guest receives an equal portion of garlic. The idea is to mash the garlic into the pan juices to make an aromatic sauce.

Chicken Breasts with Burnt Almond Stuffing

Breadcrumbs are often the basis of stuffings, but this Jewish dish uses crunchy vegetables and matzo meal.

Serves 4

4 fat spring onions
2 carrots
2 celery sticks
30ml/2 tbsp oil
60ml/4 tbsp flaked almonds
300ml/ 1/2 pint/1 1/4 cups Chicken Stock
90ml/6 tbsp medium-ground matzo meal
4 chicken breasts with skin
salt and freshly ground black pepper
fresh dill sprigs, to garnish
mixed salad, to serve

1 Preheat the oven to 190°C/375°F/Gas 5. Slice the onions and chop the carrots and celery. Heat the oil in a frying pan and sauté the almonds until they are light brown. Remove with a slotted spoon and set aside. Add the chopped vegetables to the pan and sauté over a medium heat for a few minutes.

2 Add the seasoning and pour in half of the stock. Cook over a high heat until the liquid is slightly reduced and the vegetables are just moist. Mix in the matzo meal and the sautéed almonds.

3 Ease the skin off the chicken breasts on one side and press some of the stuffing underneath each one. Press the skin back over the stuffing and slash the skin to stop it curling up. Arrange the breasts in a roasting tin.

4 Roast the chicken breasts, skin side up, for about 20–30 minutes or until the meat is tender and white. The skin should be crisp and brown.

5 Keep the chicken warm while you make the gravy. Pour the remaining stock into the roasting tin and, over a medium heat, stir in any chicken juices or remaining bits of stuffing. Bring to the boil and then strain into a jug. Serve with a mixed salad and garnish with fresh dill sprigs.

Chicken Roulé

Relatively simple to prepare, this recipe uses mince as a filling. It is rolled in chicken meat spread with a creamy garlic cheese that just melts in the mouth.

Serves 4

4 chicken breast fillets, about 115g/4oz each
115g/4oz minced beef
30ml/2 tbsp chopped fresh chives
225g/8oz/1 cup roulé cream cheese with garlic
30ml/2 tbsp clear honey
salt and freshly ground black pepper
cooked green beans and mushrooms, to serve

1 Preheat the oven to 190°C/375°F/Gas 5. Place the chicken breasts between two pieces of clear film and beat with a meat mallet or rolling pin until 5mm/¼in thick and joined together.

2 Place the minced beef in a large saucepan. Fry for 3 minutes, stirring constantly to break up the clumps, then add the fresh chives and seasoning. Remove from the heat and leave to cool.

3 Place the chicken on a board and spread with the roulé. Top with the mince mixture. Carefully roll up the chicken to form a sausage shape.

4 Brush with honey and place in a roasting tin. Cook for 1 hour in the oven. Remove from the tin and slice thinly. Serve with freshly cooked green beans and mushrooms.

Cook's Tip

Chives are one of the classic four fines herbes and have a subtle oniony flavour. They are often better snipped with kitchen scissors, rather than chopped – and this is an easier method of preparing them too. The attractive, round pink flowers are also edible and make an interesting garnish.

Chicken in a Tomato Coat

This roasted chicken keeps deliciously moist as it cooks in its red "jacket".

Serves 4–6

1.5–1.75kg/3½–4lb chicken
1 small onion
knob of butter
75ml/5 tbsp Fresh Tomato Sauce
30ml/2 tbsp chopped mixed fresh herbs, e.g. parsley, tarragon, sage, basil and marjoram, or 10ml/2 tsp dried mixed herbs
small glass of dry white wine
2–3 small tomatoes, sliced
olive oil
a little cornflour (optional)
salt and freshly ground black pepper

1 Preheat the oven to 190°C/375°F/Gas 5. Wash and wipe dry the chicken, and place in a roasting tin. Place the onion, the knob of butter and some seasoning inside the chicken.

2 Spread most of the tomato sauce over the chicken, and sprinkle with half the herbs and some seasoning. Pour the wine into the roasting tin.

3 Cover with foil, then roast for 1½ hours, basting occasionally. Remove the foil, spread with the remaining sauce and the sliced tomatoes, and drizzle with oil. Continue cooking for a further 20–30 minutes until the chicken juices run clear when the thickest part of the thigh is pierced with a skewer or knife.

4 Remove the chicken from the oven and leave to rest for 10–15 minutes. Sprinkle with the remaining herbs, then carve into portions. Serve with the juices from the roasting tin, thickened with a little cornflour, if you wish.

Cook's Tip

Whenever possible, buy sun-ripened tomatoes, which have a sweeter and more concentrated flavour than those grown under glass. Plum tomatoes are ideal for cooking, as they are much less watery than standard varieties.

Cold Sliced Roast Chicken

Cooking the chestnut stuffing under the skin keeps the breast meat succulent and creates an attractive striped effect when the chicken is carved. An excellent dish for a buffet.

Serves 6–8

2 onions, cut in half
30–45ml/2–3 tbsp vegetable oil
65g/2½oz/1¼ cups fresh white breadcrumbs
200g/7oz/¾ cup unsweetened chestnut purée
2kg/4½lb chicken
salt and freshly ground black pepper
fresh flat leaf parsley, to garnish
lettuce leaves and potato salad, to serve

1 Chop 1 of the onions finely. Heat half of the vegetable oil in a small frying pan and sauté the chopped onion until golden. Stir in 120ml/4fl oz/½ cup boiling water, take the pan off the heat and leave to stand for 5 minutes to allow some of the liquid to be absorbed.

2 Mix the breadcrumbs and chestnut purée with the onion and any liquid in the pan. Season well. Leave to cool completely.

3 Preheat the oven to 220°C/425°F/Gas 7. Wipe the chicken well with kitchen paper, inside and out, and carefully slide your hand under the skin on the breast to ease it away from the meat. Press the stuffing underneath the skin all over the breast.

4 Brush a roasting tin with the remaining oil and put in the chicken, breast side down, with the remaining onion. Roast for 1 hour, basting occasionally and pouring away any excess.

5 Turn the chicken over and continue to roast for a further 15 minutes or until the juices run clear when the thickest part of the thigh is pierced with a skewer or knife. Cover the top with a strip of foil if it looks too brown.

6 When the chicken is cooked, leave it to cool before cutting downwards into slices. Garnish with flat leaf parsley, and serve with lettuce leaves and potato salad.

Crispy Roasted Spring Chickens

These small birds, roasted with a honey glaze, are delicious either hot or cold. One bird is sufficient for two servings.

Serves 4

2 x 900g/2lb chickens
30ml/2 tbsp clear honey
30ml/2 tbsp sherry
15ml/1 tbsp vinegar
salt and freshly ground black pepper
salad leaves and lime wedges, to garnish

1 Preheat the oven to 180°C/350°F/Gas 4. Tie the birds into shape and place on a wire rack over the sink. Pour over boiling water to plump the flesh, then pat dry with kitchen paper.

2 To make the honey glaze, mix the honey, sherry and vinegar together in a small bowl, and brush over the birds. Season well.

3 Place the rack in a roasting tin and cook for 45–55 minutes, basting with the glaze until crisp and golden brown. Garnish with salad leaves and lime wedges, and serve hot or cold.

Basic Herb Stuffing

This simple herb stuffing is suitable for all poultry.

1 small onion, finely chopped
15g/½oz/1 tbsp butter
115g/4oz/2 cups fresh white breadcrumbs
15ml/1 tbsp chopped fresh parsley
5ml/1 tsp dried mixed herbs
1 egg, beaten
salt and freshly ground black pepper

1 Fry the onion in the butter until tender. Set aside to cool.
2 Add to the remaining ingredients and mix thoroughly. Season well with salt and pepper.

Middle Eastern Spring Chickens

This dish is widely enjoyed in the Lebanon and Syria. The stuffing is a delicious blend of meat, nuts and rice.

Serves 6–8

2 x 1kg/2¼lb chickens
about 15g/½oz/1 tbsp butter
plain yogurt and salad, to serve

For the stuffing

45ml/3 tbsp oil
1 onion, chopped
450g/1lb minced lamb
75g/3oz/¾ cup almonds, chopped
75g/3oz/¾ cup pine nuts
350g/12oz/1½ cups cooked rice
salt and freshly ground black pepper

1 Preheat the oven to 180°C/350°F/Gas 4. To make the stuffing, heat the oil in a large frying pan and sauté the onion over a low heat until slightly softened. Add the minced lamb and cook over a moderate heat for 4–8 minutes until well browned, stirring frequently. Set aside.

2 Heat a small, heavy-based pan over a moderate heat and dry-fry the almonds and pine nuts for 2–3 minutes until golden, shaking the pan frequently.

3 Combine the meat mixture, almonds, pine nuts and cooked rice. Season to taste with salt and pepper. Spoon the stuffing mixture into the body cavities of the chickens. (Cook any leftover stuffing separately in a greased ovenproof dish.) Rub the chickens all over with the butter.

4 Place the chickens in a large roasting tin, cover with foil and bake in the oven for 45–60 minutes. After about 30 minutes, remove the foil and baste the chickens with the cooking juices.

5 Continue roasting without the foil until the chickens are cooked through: the juices will run clear when the thickest part of the thigh is pierced with a skewer or knife. Serve the chickens, cut into portions, with yogurt and a salad.

French-style Pot-roast Poussins

Small, young chickens are cooked with tender baby vegetables in a wine-enriched stock – the perfect early summer meal.

Serves 4

15ml/1 tbsp olive oil
1 onion, sliced
1 large garlic clove, sliced
50g/2oz/⅓ cup diced lightly smoked bacon
2 poussins, just under 450g/1lb each
30ml/2 tbsp melted butter
2 baby celery hearts, quartered
8 baby carrots
2 small courgettes, cut into chunks
8 small new potatoes
600ml/1 pint/2½ cups Chicken Stock
150ml/¼ pint/⅔ cup dry white wine
1 bay leaf
2 fresh thyme sprigs
2 fresh rosemary sprigs
15g/½oz/1 tbsp butter, softened
15ml/1 tbsp plain flour
salt and freshly ground black pepper
fresh herbs, to garnish

1 Preheat the oven to 190°C/375°F/Gas 5. Heat the oil in a large, flameproof casserole and add the onion, garlic and bacon. Sauté for 5–6 minutes until the onions have softened. Brush the poussins with a little of the melted butter and season well. Place on top of the onion mixture and arrange the prepared vegetables around them. Pour the chicken stock and wine around the birds, and add the herbs.

2 Cover, cook in the oven for 20 minutes, then remove the lid and brush the birds with the remaining melted butter. Cook for a further 25–30 minutes until golden.

3 Transfer the poussins to a warmed serving platter and cut each in half. Remove the vegetables with a draining spoon and arrange them round the birds. Cover with foil and keep warm.

4 Discard the herbs from the cooking juices. In a bowl, mix the softened butter and flour to form a paste. Bring the cooking liquid to the boil and then whisk in spoonfuls of the paste until thickened. Season the sauce, and serve with the poussins and vegetables, garnished with herbs.

Baby Chickens with Cranberry Sauce

Fresh cranberries make a delicious sauce for these simply roasted poussins.

Serves 4

4 poussins, with giblets (optional), about 450g/1lb each
40g/1½oz/3 tbsp butter or margarine
1 onion, quartered
50ml/2fl oz/¼ cup port
175ml/6fl oz/¾ cup Chicken Stock
30ml/2 tbsp clear honey
150g/5oz/1¼ cups cranberries
salt and freshly ground black pepper
cooked new potatoes and broccoli, to serve

1 Preheat the oven to 230°C/450°F/Gas 8. Smear the poussins on all sides with 25g/1oz/2 tbsp of the butter or margarine. Arrange them, on their sides, in a roasting tin in which they will fit comfortably. Sprinkle them with salt and pepper. Add the onion quarters to the tin. Chop the giblets and livers, if using, and arrange them around the poussins.

2 Roast for 20 minutes, basting frequently. Turn the poussins on to their other sides and roast for 20 minutes more, basting often. Turn them breast up and continue roasting for about 15 minutes until they are cooked through. Transfer to a warmed serving dish. Cover with foil and set aside.

3 Skim any fat off the juices in the roasting tin. Put the tin over a medium heat and bring the juices to the boil. Add the port and bring back to the boil, stirring well to dislodge any particles sticking to the bottom of the tin.

4 Strain the sauce into a small saucepan. Add the chicken stock, return to the boil and boil until reduced by half. Stir in the honey and cranberries. Simmer for about 3 minutes until the cranberries pop.

5 Remove the pan from the heat and swirl in the remaining butter or margarine. Season to taste, pour the sauce into a jug or gravy boat and serve with the poussins, accompanied by new potatoes and broccoli.

Poussins with Bulgur Wheat & Vermouth

These young birds are filled with a bulgur wheat and nut stuffing laced with vermouth, and served with a medley of roast vegetables finished with a vermouth glaze.

Serves 4

50g/2oz/ ⅓ cup bulgur wheat
150ml/ ¼ pint/ ⅔ cup dry white vermouth
60ml/4 tbsp olive oil
1 large onion, finely chopped
2 carrots, finely chopped
75g/3oz/ ¾ cup pine nuts, chopped
5ml/1 tsp celery seeds
4 poussins
3 red onions, quartered
4 baby aubergines, halved
4 patty pan squashes
12 baby carrots
45ml/3 tbsp corn syrup
salt and freshly ground black pepper

1 Preheat the oven to 200°C/400°F/Gas 6. Put the bulgur wheat in a heatproof bowl, pour over half the vermouth and cover with boiling water. Set aside.

2 Heat half the oil in a large, shallow frying pan. Add the onion and carrots, and fry for 10 minutes, then remove the pan from the heat and stir in the pine nuts, celery seeds and the well-drained bulgur wheat.

3 Stuff the poussins with the bulgur wheat mixture. Place them in a roasting tin, brush with oil and sprinkle with salt and pepper. Roast for 45–55 minutes until the juices run clear when the thickest part of the thigh is pierced with a skewer or knife.

4 Meanwhile, spread out the red onions, aubergines, patty pans and baby carrots in a single layer on a baking sheet.

5 Mix the corn syrup with the remaining vermouth and oil in a small bowl. Season with salt and pepper to taste. Brush the corn syrup mixture over the vegetables and roast for 35–45 minutes until golden. Cut each poussin in half and serve immediately with the roasted vegetables.

Poussins with Raisin-walnut Stuffing

This easy-to-prepare traditional American dish offers something different for a midweek supper.

Serves 4

250ml/8fl oz/1 cup port
90g/3½oz/ ⅔ cup raisins
15ml/1 tbsp walnut oil
75g/3oz/1 cup mushrooms, finely chopped
1 large celery stick, finely chopped
1 small onion, chopped
50g/2oz/1 cup fresh breadcrumbs
50g/2oz/ ½ cup chopped walnuts
15ml/1 tbsp each chopped fresh basil and parsley or 30ml/2 tbsp chopped fresh parsley
2.5ml/ ½ tsp dried thyme
75g/3oz/6 tbsp butter, melted
4 poussins
salt and freshly ground black pepper
salad and vegetables, to serve

1 Preheat the oven to 180°C/350°F/Gas 4. In a small bowl, combine the port and raisins, and leave to soak for 20 minutes.

2 Meanwhile, heat the oil in a non-stick frying pan. Add the mushrooms, celery and onion, and cook over a low heat for 8–10 minutes until softened. Allow to cool slightly.

3 Drain the raisins, reserving the port. Combine the raisins, breadcrumbs, walnuts, basil (if using), parsley and thyme in a bowl. Stir in the onion mixture and 60ml/4 tbsp of the melted butter. Add salt and pepper to taste.

4 Fill the cavity of each bird with the stuffing mixture. Do not pack too tightly. Tie the legs together, looping the tail with string to enclose the stuffing securely.

5 Brush the birds with the remaining butter and place in a roasting tin just large enough to hold them comfortably. Pour over the reserved port. Roast, basting occasionally, for about 1 hour or until the juices run clear when the thickest part of the thigh is pierced with a skewer or knife. Serve immediately, pouring some of the pan juices over each bird. Accompany with salad and vegetables.

Baked Poussins

The important factor in this recipe is a good, long marinating time before cooking, which allows the spicy yogurt mixture to penetrate and the flavours to permeate the birds.

Serves 4

475ml/16fl oz/2 cups plain yogurt
60ml/4 tbsp olive oil
1 large onion, grated
2 garlic cloves, crushed
2.5ml/½ tsp paprika
2–3 saffron strands, soaked in 15ml/1 tbsp boiling water
juice of 1 lemon
4 poussins, halved
oil, for greasing
salt and freshly ground black pepper
cos lettuce salad, to serve

1 In a bowl, blend together the plain yogurt, olive oil, grated onion, crushed garlic, paprika, saffron strands with their soaking water and lemon juice, and season to taste with salt and freshly ground black pepper.

2 Place the poussin halves in a shallow dish and pour over the yogurt mixture, ensuring that they are well coated, spreading with the back of a spoon or your fingers. Cover and leave to marinate overnight in a cool place or for at least 4 hours in the fridge.

3 Preheat the oven to 180°C/350°F/Gas 4. Arrange the poussins in a greased ovenproof dish and bake in the oven for 30–45 minutes, basting frequently until cooked. Serve with a cos lettuce salad.

Cook's Tip

The poussins can also be barbecued, which makes them, if anything, even more delicious.

Parmesan Chicken Bake

The tomato sauce may be made the day before and left to cool. Serve with crusty bread and salad.

Serves 4

4 chicken breast fillets, skinned
60ml/4 tbsp plain flour
45ml/3 tbsp olive oil
salt and freshly ground black pepper

For the tomato sauce

15ml/1 tbsp olive oil
1 onion, finely chopped
1 celery stick, finely chopped
1 red pepper, seeded and diced
1 garlic clove, crushed
400g/14oz can chopped tomatoes, with their juice
150ml/¼ pint/⅔ cup Chicken Stock
15ml/1 tbsp tomato purée
10ml/2 tsp caster sugar
15ml/1 tbsp chopped fresh basil
15ml/1 tbsp chopped fresh parsley

To assemble

225g/8oz mozzarella cheese, sliced
60ml/4 tbsp grated Parmesan cheese
30ml/2 tbsp fresh breadcrumbs

1 To make the tomato sauce, heat the oil in a frying pan. Add the onion, celery, red pepper and garlic, and cook gently until tender. Add the tomatoes with their juice, the stock, tomato purée, sugar and herbs. Season and bring to the boil. Simmer for 30 minutes until thick, stirring occasionally.

2 Divide each chicken fillet into two natural pieces, place between sheets of clear film and flatten to a thickness of 5mm/¼in with a rolling pin or meat mallet. Season the flour with salt and pepper. Toss the chicken breasts in the flour to coat, shaking to remove the excess.

3 Preheat the oven to 180°C/350°F/Gas 4. Heat the oil in a large frying pan and cook the chicken quickly in batches for 3–4 minutes until coloured.

4 To assemble, layer the chicken pieces in an ovenproof dish with the cheeses and thick tomato sauce, finishing with a layer of cheese and breadcrumbs on top. Bake, uncovered, for 20–30 minutes or until golden brown. Serve immediately.

Crunchy Stuffed Chicken Breasts

These can be prepared ahead of time as long as the stuffing is quite cold before it is spooned into the "pockets". It is an ideal dish for entertaining.

Serves 4

4 chicken breast fillets
25g/1oz/2 tbsp butter
1 garlic clove, crushed
15ml/1 tbsp Dijon mustard
cooked vegetables, to serve

For the stuffing

15g/½oz/1 tbsp butter
1 bunch spring onions, sliced
10g/3 tbsp fresh breadcrumbs
25g/1oz/2 tbsp pine nuts
1 egg yolk
15ml/1 tbsp chopped fresh parsley
salt and freshly ground black pepper
60ml/4 tbsp grated cheese

For the topping

2 bacon rashers, rinded and finely chopped
50g/2oz/1 cup fresh breadcrumbs
15ml/1 tbsp grated Parmesan cheese
15ml/1 tbsp chopped fresh parsley

1 Preheat the oven to 200°C/400°F/Gas 6. First, make the stuffing. Heat the butter in a heavy-based frying pan and cook the spring onions, stirring occasionally, until soft. Remove from the heat and allow to cool for a few minutes. Add the remaining ingredients and mix thoroughly.

2 To make the topping, fry the chopped bacon until crisp, then drain well on kitchen paper. Place the breadcrumbs, grated Parmesan cheese and parsley in a bowl, and add the bacon. Mix thoroughly to combine.

3 Carefully cut a pocket in each chicken breast, using a sharp knife. Divide the stuffing into four and use to fill the pockets. Transfer the chicken breasts to a buttered ovenproof dish.

4 Melt the remaining butter, mix it with the crushed garlic and mustard, and brush liberally over the chicken. Press on the topping and bake, uncovered, for about 30–40 minutes or until tender. Serve with vegetables.

Oven-fried Chicken

An easy way of cooking "fried" chicken with a crisp breadcrumb coating – once it is in the oven, you can turn your attention to preparing the rest of the meal without any worries.

Serves 4

4 large chicken portions
50g/2oz/½ cup plain flour
2.5ml/½ tsp salt
1.5ml/¼ tsp black pepper
1 egg
30ml/2 tbsp water
30ml/2 tbsp finely chopped mixed fresh herbs, e.g. parsley, basil and thyme
50g/2oz/1 cup fresh breadcrumbs
115g/4oz/¾ cup grated Parmesan cheese
oil, for greasing
lemon wedges, to serve

1 Preheat the oven to 200°C/400°F/Gas 6. Rinse the chicken portions and pat dry with kitchen paper.

2 Combine the flour, salt and pepper on a large plate and stir with a fork to mix. Coat the chicken portions on all sides with the seasoned flour and shake off the excess.

3 Sprinkle a little water on to the chicken portions and coat again lightly with the seasoned flour.

4 Beat the egg with 30ml/2 tbsp water in a shallow dish and stir in the herbs. Combine the breadcrumbs and grated Parmesan cheese on a plate.

5 Dip the chicken portions into the egg mixture, turning to coat them evenly, then roll in the breadcrumbs, patting them on with your fingertips to help them stick.

6 Place the chicken portions in a greased shallow roasting tin or ovenproof dish large enough to hold them in one layer. Bake for 20–30 minutes until thoroughly cooked and golden brown. Serve at once, with lemon wedges for squeezing.

Chicken Baked in a Salt Crust

This unusual dish is extremely simple to make. Once it is cooked, you just break away the salt crust to reveal the wonderfully tender, golden-brown chicken within.

Serves 4
bunch of mixed fresh herbs, e.g. rosemary, thyme, marjoram and parsley
1.5kg/3½lb corn-fed chicken
about 1.5kg/3½lb/7 cups coarse sea salt
1 egg white
1–2 whole garlic bulbs, baked for 1 hour, to serve

1 Preheat the oven to 190°C/375°F/Gas 5. Stuff the herbs into the chicken cavity, then truss the chicken.

2 Mix together the sea salt and egg white until all the salt crystals are moistened. Select a roasting tin into which the chicken will fit neatly, then line it with a large double layer of foil. Spread a thick layer of moistened salt in the foil-lined tin and place the chicken on top. Cover with the remaining salt and press into a neat shape, over and around the chicken, making sure it is completely enclosed.

3 Bring the foil edges up and over the chicken to enclose it and bake in the oven for 1½ hours. Remove from the oven and leave to rest for 10 minutes.

4 Carefully lift the foil package from the container and open it. Break the salt crust to reveal the chicken inside. Brush any traces of salt from the bird, then serve with baked whole garlic bulbs. Each clove can be slipped from its skin and eaten with a bite of chicken.

Cook's Tip
Sea salt is available in the form of whole crystals and coarsely or finely ground. Coarsely ground salt works best here.

Roast Turkey

A classic roast, served with stuffing balls, chipolata sausages and gravy. Roast potatoes and Brussels sprouts are the traditional accompaniments.

Serves 8
4.5kg/10lb turkey, with giblets (thawed overnight if frozen)
1 large onion, peeled and stuck with 6 whole cloves
50g/2oz/4 tbsp butter, softened
10 chipolata sausages
salt and freshly ground black pepper

For the stuffing
225g/8oz rindless streaky bacon, chopped
1 large onion, finely chopped
450g/1lb pork sausagemeat
25g/1oz/⅓ cup rolled oats
30ml/2 tbsp chopped fresh parsley
10ml/2 tsp dried mixed herbs
1 large egg, beaten
115g/4oz/½ cup dried apricots, finely chopped

For the gravy
25g/1oz/2 tbsp plain flour
450ml/¾ pint/scant 2 cups giblet stock

1 Preheat the oven to 200°C/400°F/Gas 6. To make the stuffing, cook the bacon and onion gently in a pan until the bacon is crisp and the onion tender. Transfer to a large bowl and mix in all the remaining stuffing ingredients. Season to taste.

2 Stuff the neck end of the turkey, tuck the flap of skin under and secure it with a small skewer or stitch it with thread. Reserve any remaining stuffing.

3 Put the whole onion, studded with cloves, in the body cavity of the turkey and tie the legs together. Weigh the stuffed bird and calculate the cooking time; allow 15 minutes per 450g/1lb plus 15 minutes over. Place the turkey in a large roasting tin.

4 Spread the turkey with the butter and season it with salt and pepper. Cover it loosely with foil and cook it for 30 minutes. Baste the turkey with the pan juices. Then lower the oven temperature to 180°C/350°F/Gas 4 and cook for the remainder of the calculated time (about 3½ hours for a 4.5kg/10lb bird). Baste it every 30 minutes or so. Remove the foil from the turkey for the last hour of cooking and baste it.

5 Using wet hands, shape the remaining stuffing into small balls or pack it into a greased ovenproof dish. Cook in the oven for 20 minutes or until golden brown and crisp.

6 About 20 minutes before the end of cooking, place the chipolatas in an ovenproof dish and put them into the oven.

7 The turkey is cooked if the juices run clear when the thickest part of the thigh is pierced with a skewer or knife. Transfer it to a serving plate, cover with foil and let it stand for 10–15 minutes before carving. To make the gravy, spoon off the fat from the roasting tin, leaving the meat juices. Blend in the flour and cook for 2 minutes. Gradually stir in the stock and bring to the boil. Check the seasoning and pour into a jug or gravy boat. Remove the skewer or thread from the bird and pour any juices into the gravy. To serve, surround the turkey with the chipolata sausages and stuffing balls.

Roast Duckling with Honey

A sweet-and-sour orange sauce is the perfect foil for this rich-tasting Polish duck recipe, and frying the orange rind intensifies the flavour.

Serves 4

2.25kg/5lb duckling
2.5ml/ ½ tsp ground allspice
1 orange
15ml/1 tbsp sunflower oil
30ml/2 tbsp plain flour
150ml/ ¼ pint/ ⅔ cup duck or Chicken Stock
10ml/2 tsp red wine vinegar
15ml/1 tbsp clear honey
salt and freshly ground black pepper
watercress and thinly pared orange rind, to garnish

1 Preheat the oven to 220°C/425°F/Gas 7. Using a fork, pierce the duckling all over, except the breast, so that the fat runs out during cooking.

2 Rub all over the skin of the duckling with ground allspice and sprinkle with salt and pepper to season, pressing into the surface of the bird.

3 Put the duckling on a rack over a roasting tin and cook for about 20 minutes. Then reduce the oven temperature to 190°C/375°F/Gas 5 and cook for a further 2 hours.

4 Meanwhile, thinly pare the rind from the orange and cut into very fine strips. Heat the oil in a pan and gently fry the orange rind for 2–3 minutes. Squeeze the juice from the orange and set aside.

5 Transfer the duckling to a warmed serving dish and keep warm. Drain off all but 30ml/2 tbsp fat from the tin, sprinkle in the flour and stir well.

6 Stir in the stock, vinegar, honey, orange juice and rind. Bring to the boil, stirring all the time. Simmer for 2–3 minutes and season to taste. Pour into a serving bowl or jug.

7 Serve the duckling, garnished with watercress and thinly pared orange rind and accompanied by the sauce.

Roast Wild Duck with Juniper

Wild duck should be served slightly underdone or the meat will be very tough.

Serves 2

15ml/1 tbsp juniper berries, fresh if possible
1 wild duck (preferably a mallard)
25g/1oz/2 tbsp butter, softened
45ml/3 tbsp gin
120ml/4fl oz/ ½ cup duck or Chicken Stock
120ml/4fl oz/ ½ cup whipping cream
salt and freshly ground black pepper
watercress, to garnish

1 Preheat the oven to 230°C/450°F/Gas 8. Reserve a few juniper berries for garnishing and put the remainder in a heavy polythene bag. Crush coarsely with a rolling pin.

2 Wipe the duck with damp kitchen paper. Tie the legs with string, then spread the butter over the duck. Season and press the crushed juniper berries on to the skin.

3 Place the duck in a roasting tin and roast for 20–25 minutes, basting occasionally; it is ready if the juices run clear when the thickest part of the thigh is pierced with a knife. Pour the juices from the cavity into the roasting tin and transfer the duck to a carving board. Cover loosely with foil and leave to stand for 10–15 minutes.

4 Skim off as much fat as possible from the roasting tin, leaving as much of the juniper as possible, and place the tin over a medium-high heat. Add the gin and stir, scraping the sediment from the base and bring to the boil. Cook until the liquid has almost evaporated, then add the stock and boil to reduce by half. Add the cream and boil for 2 minutes or until the sauce thickens slightly. Strain into a small saucepan and keep warm.

5 Carve the legs from the duck and separate the thighs from the drumsticks. Remove the breasts and arrange the duck in a warmed serving dish. Pour a little sauce over, sprinkle with the reserved juniper berries and garnish with watercress. Hand the rest of the sauce separately in a jug or gravy boat.

Wild Duck Roasted with Morels & Madeira

Wild duck has a rich, autumnal flavour that combines well with stronger-tasting mushrooms.

Serves 4

2 x 1kg/2¼lb mallards (dressed and barded weight)
50g/2oz/4 tbsp unsalted butter
75ml/5 tbsp Madeira or sherry
1 medium onion, halved and sliced
½ celery stick, chopped
1 small carrot, chopped
10 large dried morel mushrooms
225g/8oz/3 cups blewits, parasol and field mushrooms, trimmed and sliced
600ml/1 pint/2½ cups Chicken Stock, boiling
1 fresh thyme sprig
10ml/2 tsp wine vinegar
salt and freshly ground black pepper
fresh parsley sprigs and carrot juliennes, to garnish
game chips, to serve

1 Preheat the oven to 190°C/375°F/Gas 5 and season the ducks with salt and pepper. Melt half of the butter in a heavy-based frying pan. Add the ducks and brown the birds evenly. Transfer them to a shallow dish.

2 Heat the sediment in the pan, pour in the Madeira or sherry and bring to the boil, stirring constantly and scraping the base to deglaze the pan. Pour this liquid over the birds and set the dish aside.

3 Heat the remaining butter in a large, flameproof casserole and add the onion, celery and carrot. Place the birds on top (reserve the Madeira or sherry) and cook in the oven for 40 minutes.

4 Tie all the mushrooms in a 45cm/18in square of muslin. Add the stock, the Madeira or sherry from the frying pan, the thyme and the muslin bag to the casserole. Cover and return to the oven for 40 minutes.

5 Transfer the birds to a warmed serving platter, remove and discard the thyme and set the mushrooms aside. Process the braising liquid in a food processor or blender and pour it back into the casserole. Break open the muslin bag and stir the mushrooms into the sauce. Add the vinegar, season to taste and heat through gently.

6 Garnish the ducks with parsley and carrot. Serve with game chips and hand the Madeira or sherry sauce separately in a jug or gravy boat.

Cook's Tip
Mallard is the most popular wild duck, although widgeon and teal are good substitutes. A widgeon will serve two, but allow one teal per person.

Duckling Jubilee

This East European dish partners roast duck with a lightly spiced apricot sauce.

Serves 4

2kg/4½lb duckling
60ml/4 tbsp chopped fresh parsley
1 lemon, quartered
3 carrots, sliced
2 celery sticks, sliced
1 onion, roughly chopped
salt and freshly ground black pepper
apricots and sage flowers, to garnish

For the sauce

425g/15oz can apricots in syrup
50g/2oz/¼ cup granulated sugar
10ml/2 tsp English mustard
60ml/4 tbsp apricot jam
15ml/1 tbsp lemon juice
10ml/2 tsp grated lemon rind
50ml/2fl oz/¼ cup orange juice
1.5ml/¼ tsp each ground ginger and ground coriander
60–75ml/4–5 tbsp brandy

1 Preheat the oven to 220°C/425°F/Gas 7. Clean the duck well and pat dry with kitchen paper. Season the skin liberally. Mix together the parsley, lemon, carrots, celery and onion in a bowl, then spoon this mixture into the cavity of the duck.

2 Cook the duck for 45 minutes on a rack set over a roasting tin. Baste the duck occasionally with its juices. Remove the duck from the oven and prick the skin well. Return it to the oven, reduce the temperature to 180°C/350°F/Gas 4 and cook for a further 1–1½ hours or until golden brown, tender and crisp.

3 Meanwhile, to make the sauce, put the apricots and their syrup, the sugar and mustard in a food processor or blender. Add the jam and process until smooth.

4 Pour the apricot mixture into a pan and stir in the lemon juice and rind, orange juice and spices. Bring to the boil, add the brandy and cook for a further 1–2 minutes. Remove from the heat and adjust the seasoning. Pour into a jug or gravy boat.

5 Discard the fruit, vegetables and herbs from inside the duck and arrange the bird on a serving platter. Garnish with fresh apricots and sage flowers. Serve the sauce separately.

Roast Goose with Apples

The apples are filled with a hazelnut, raisin and orange stuffing and roasted around the bird.

Serves 6

115g/4oz/scant 1 cup raisins
grated rind and juice of 1 orange
25g/1oz/2 tbsp butter
1 onion, finely chopped
75g/3oz/¾ cup hazelnuts, chopped
175g/6oz/3 cups fresh white breadcrumbs
15ml/1 tbsp clear honey
15ml/1 tbsp chopped fresh marjoram
30ml/2 tbsp chopped fresh parsley
6 red eating apples
15ml/1 tbsp lemon juice
4.5–5kg/10–11lb young goose
salt and freshly ground black pepper
fresh herbs, to garnish
orange wedges, red cabbage and green beans, to serve

1 Preheat the oven to 220°C/425°F/Gas 7. Put the raisins in a bowl and pour over the orange juice. Melt the butter in a frying pan and fry the onions for 5 minutes. Add the nuts and cook for 4–5 minutes or until beginning to brown. Add the onion and nuts to the raisins with 50g/2oz/1 cup of the breadcrumbs, the orange rind, honey, herbs and seasoning. Mix well.

2 Remove the apple cores to leave a 2cm/¾in hole. Make a shallow cut horizontally around the middle of each apple. Brush the cut and the cavity with the lemon juice. Pack the centre of each apple with nut and raisin stuffing, reserving the remainder.

3 Mix the remaining breadcrumbs into the leftover stuffing and place in the bird's cavity. Close with a small skewer. Place the goose in a roasting tin and prick the skin with a skewer. Roast for 30 minutes, then reduce the temperature to 180°C/350°F/Gas 4 and cook for a further 3 hours or until the juices run clear when the thickest part of the thigh is pierced with a skewer or knife. Pour off the excess fat from time to time.

4 Bake the apples around the goose for the last 30–40 minutes of its cooking time. Rest the goose for 10–15 minutes before carving. Garnish with fresh herbs and serve with the stuffed apples, orange wedges, red cabbage and green beans.

Roast Goose with Caramelized Apples & Port & Orange Gravy

Choose a young goose with a pliable breast bone.

Serves 8

4.5–5.5kg/10–12lb goose, with giblets
salt and freshly ground black pepper

For the apple and nut stuffing

225g/8oz/1 cup prunes
150ml/¼ pint/⅔ cup port
675g/1½lb cooking apples, peeled, cored and cubed
1 large onion, chopped
4 celery sticks, sliced
15ml/1 tbsp dried mixed herbs
finely grated rind of 1 orange
1 goose liver, chopped
450g/1lb pork sausagemeat
115g/4oz/1 cup chopped pecans or walnuts
2 eggs

For the caramelized apples

50g/2oz/4 tbsp butter
60ml/4 tbsp redcurrant jelly
30ml/2 tbsp red wine vinegar
8 small dessert apples, peeled and cored

For the gravy

30ml/2 tbsp plain flour
600ml/1 pint/2½ cups giblet stock
juice of 1 orange

1 To make the stuffing, soak the prunes in the port the day before serving. Then stone and cut each into four pieces, reserving the port. Mix with all the remaining stuffing ingredients and season. Moisten with half the reserved port.

2 Preheat the oven to 200°C/400°F/Gas 6. Stuff the neck end of the goose, tucking the flap of skin under and securing it with a small skewer. Remove the excess fat from the cavity and pack it with the stuffing. Tie the legs together to hold them in place.

3 Weigh the stuffed goose and calculate the cooking time: allow 15 minutes per 450g/1lb. Put the bird on a rack in a roasting tin and rub the skin with salt. Prick the skin all over.

4 Roast the goose for 30 minutes, then reduce the oven temperature to 180°C/350°F/Gas 4 and roast for the remaining cooking time. Pour off any fat produced during cooking into a bowl. The goose is cooked if the juices run clear when the thickest part of the thigh is pierced with a skewer or knife. Pour a little cold water over the breast to crisp the skin.

5 Meanwhile, to make the caramelized apples, melt the butter with the redcurrant jelly and vinegar in a small roasting tin or shallow ovenproof dish. Put in the apples, baste them well and cook in the oven for 15–20 minutes. Baste halfway through the cooking time. Do not overcook them or they will collapse.

6 Lift the goose on to a serving dish and let it stand for 10–15 minutes before carving. Pour off the excess fat from the roasting tin, leaving any sediment in the bottom. To make the gravy, stir the flour into the sediment and cook gently until golden brown, then blend in the stock. Bring to the boil, add the remaining reserved port, the orange juice and seasoning. Simmer for 2–3 minutes. Strain into a jug or gravy boat. Surround the goose with the caramelized apples, spoon over the redcurrant glaze and serve with the gravy.

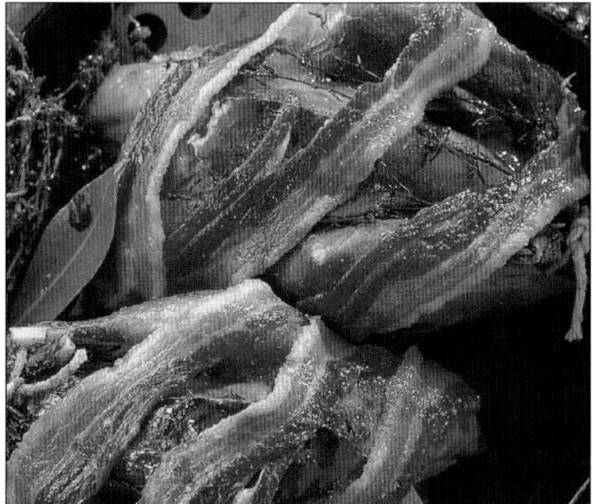

Roast Pheasant with Port

Roasting young pheasant in foil keeps the flesh particularly tender and moist.

Serves 4

oil, for brushing
2 hen pheasants, about 675g/1½lb each
50g/2oz/4 tbsp unsalted butter, softened
8 fresh thyme sprigs
2 bay leaves
6 streaky bacon rashers
15ml/1 tbsp plain flour
175ml/6fl oz/¾ cup game or Chicken Stock, plus more if needed
15ml/1 tbsp redcurrant jelly
45–60ml/3–4 tbsp port
freshly ground black pepper

1 Preheat the oven to 230°C/450°F/Gas 8. Line a large roasting tin with a sheet of strong foil large enough to enclose the pheasants. Lightly brush the foil with oil.

2 Wipe the pheasants with damp kitchen paper and remove any extra fat or skin. Using your fingertips, carefully loosen the skin of the breasts. Spread the butter between the skin and breast meat of each bird. Tie the legs securely with string then lay the thyme sprigs and a bay leaf over the breast of each bird. Lay bacon rashers over the breasts, place the birds in the foil-lined tin and season with pepper. Bring together the long ends of the foil, fold over securely to enclose, then seal the ends.

3 Roast the birds for 20 minutes, then reduce the oven temperature to 190°C/375°F/Gas 5 and cook for a further 40 minutes. Uncover the birds and roast for 10–15 minutes more or until they are browned and the juices run clear when the thickest part of the thigh is pierced with a knife or skewer. Transfer the birds to a board and leave to stand, covered with clean foil, for 10–15 minutes before carving.

4 Pour the juices from the foil into the roasting tin and skim off any fat. Sprinkle in the flour and cook over a medium heat, stirring, until smooth. Whisk in the stock and redcurrant jelly, and bring to the boil. Simmer until the sauce thickens slightly, adding more stock if needed, then stir in the port and adjust the seasoning to taste. Strain and serve with the pheasants.

Pheasant in Green Pipian Sauce

An unusual and delicious way of cooking pheasant, Mexican-style, that keeps it wonderfully moist.

Serves 4

2 pheasants
30ml/2 tbsp corn oil
175g/6oz/generous 1 cup pepitas (Mexican pumpkin seeds)
15ml/1 tbsp achiote (annatto) seeds
1 onion, finely chopped
2 garlic cloves, chopped
275g/10oz can tomatillos (Mexican green tomatoes)
475ml/16fl oz/2 cups Chicken Stock
salt and freshly ground black pepper
fresh coriander, to garnish

1 Preheat the oven to 180°C/350°F/Gas 4. Using a large, sharp knife or poultry shears, cut the pheasants in half lengthways and season well with salt and pepper. Heat the oil in a large frying pan and sauté the pheasant pieces until lightly browned on all sides. Lift out of the pan, drain and arrange, skin side up, in a single layer in a roasting tin. Set aside.

2 Grind the pepitas finely in a nut grinder or a food processor. Shake through a sieve into a bowl. Grind the achiote seeds, add them to the bowl and set to one side.

3 Place the onion, garlic, tomatillos and their juice into a food processor and purée. Pour into a saucepan. Add the pepita mixture, stir in the stock and simmer over a very low heat for 10 minutes. Do not let the mixture boil as it will separate. Remove from the heat and leave to cool.

4 Pour the sauce over the pheasant halves. Bake for 40 minutes or until tender, basting from time to time with the sauce. Garnish with coriander and serve.

Cook's Tip
Achiote is a typical ingredient in Yucatán. There is no substitute. Look for it in Caribbean and tropical markets.

Chicken, Barley & Apple Casserole

Barley is underrated as a casserole ingredient these days: it is nutritious and makes a really tasty and filling meal.

Serves 4

15ml/1 tbsp sunflower oil
1 large onion, sliced
1 garlic clove, crushed
3 carrots, cut into chunky sticks
2 celery sticks, thickly sliced
115g/4oz/⅔ cup pot or pearl barley
4 chicken breast fillets, skinned
750ml/1¼ pint/3 cups Chicken Stock
1 bay leaf
few sprigs each of fresh thyme and marjoram, plus extra to garnish
3 dessert apples

1 Heat the oil in a flameproof casserole and sauté the onion for about 5 minutes until soft. Stir in the garlic, carrots and celery, and continue to cook over a gentle heat for a further 5 minutes.

2 Stir in the pot or pearl barley, then add the chicken breast fillets, stock and herbs. Bring to the boil, lower the heat, cover the casserole and cook gently for 1 hour.

3 Core the apples and slice them thickly. Add to the casserole, replace the lid and cook for 15 minutes more or until the apples are just tender but not mushy.

4 Divide the barley, vegetables and cooking juices among four warmed plates and arrange the chicken on top. Garnish with fresh herbs and serve.

Cook's Tip

You can also cook the casserole in a preheated 190°C/375°F/Gas 5 oven. The timings are the same. Chicken thighs can be substituted for breast fillets – they are not as "meaty" but are good value for money.

Country Cider Hot-pot

Root vegetables, chopped bacon and prunes all bring flavour to the wonderful cider gravy in this filling chicken dish.

Serves 4

30ml/2 tbsp plain flour
4 boneless chicken portions
25g/1oz/2 tbsp butter
15ml/1 tbsp vegetable oil
15 baby onions
4 streaky bacon rashers, rinded and chopped
10ml/2 tsp Dijon mustard
450ml/¾ pint/scant 2 cups dry cider
3 carrots, chopped
2 parsnips, chopped
12 ready-to-eat prunes, stoned
1 fresh rosemary sprig
1 bay leaf
salt and freshly ground black pepper
mashed potatoes, to serve

1 Preheat the oven to 160°C/325°F/Gas 3. Place the flour and seasoning in a polythene bag, add the chicken portions and shake until coated. Set aside.

2 Heat the butter and oil in a flameproof casserole. Add the onions and bacon, and fry over a moderate heat for 4 minutes until the onions have softened. Remove from the pan with a slotted spoon and set aside.

3 Add the floured chicken portions to the oil in the casserole and fry until they are browned all over, then spread a little of the mustard over the top of each portion.

4 Return the onions and bacon to the casserole. Pour in the cider and add the carrots, parsnips, prunes, rosemary and bay leaf. Season well. Bring to the boil, then cover and transfer to the oven. Cook for about 1½ hours until the chicken is tender.

5 Remove the rosemary sprig and bay leaf, and serve the chicken hot with creamy mashed potatoes.

Chicken in Creamed Horseradish

The piquant flavour of the horseradish sauce gives this quick dish a sophisticated and unusual taste. If you are using fresh horseradish, halve the quantity.

Serves 4

30ml/2 tbsp olive oil
4 chicken portions
25g/1oz/2 tbsp butter
25g/1oz/2 tbsp plain flour
450ml/¾ pint/scant 2 cups Chicken Stock
30ml/2 tbsp creamed horseradish sauce
15ml/1 tbsp chopped fresh parsley
salt and freshly ground black pepper
mashed potatoes and lightly cooked French beans, to serve

1 Heat the oil in a large, flameproof casserole and gently brown the chicken portions on both sides over a medium heat. Remove the chicken from the casserole and keep warm.

2 Wipe out the casserole, then add the butter and allow to melt. Stir in the flour and gradually blend in the stock. Bring to the boil, stirring all the time.

3 Add the horseradish sauce and season with salt and pepper. Return the chicken to the casserole, cover and simmer for 30–40 minutes or until tender.

4 Transfer to a serving dish and sprinkle with the chopped parsley. Serve with mashed potatoes and French beans.

Cook's Tip

Fresh horseradish requires very careful handling, as the volatile mustard oils given off when it is peeled and grated irritate the mucous membranes and the eyes, causing them to water. Dried flaked horseradish root is a safer substitute.

Chicken with Tomatoes & Honey

An easy-to-make Moroccan-style dish served with a sprinkling of toasted almonds and sesame seeds.

Serves 4

30ml/2 tbsp sunflower oil
25g/1oz/2 tbsp butter
4 chicken quarters or 1 whole chicken, quartered
1 onion, grated or very finely chopped
1 garlic clove, crushed
5ml/1 tsp ground cinnamon
good pinch of ground ginger
1.5kg/3½lb tomatoes, peeled, seeded and roughly chopped
30ml/2 tbsp clear honey
50g/2oz/½ cup blanched almonds
15ml/1 tbsp sesame seeds
salt and freshly ground black pepper
Moroccan corn bread, to serve

1 Heat the oil and butter in a large, flameproof casserole. Add the chicken pieces and cook over a medium heat for about 3 minutes until the chicken is lightly browned.

2 Add the onion, garlic, cinnamon, ginger, tomatoes and seasoning. Heat gently until the tomatoes begin to bubble.

3 Lower the heat, cover and simmer very gently for 1 hour, stirring and turning the chicken occasionally, until it is completely cooked through. Transfer the chicken pieces to a plate and set aside.

4 Increase the heat and cook the tomatoes until the sauce is reduced to a thick purée, stirring frequently. Stir in the honey, cook for a minute, then return the chicken to the pan and cook for 2–3 minutes to heat through. Dry-fry the almonds and sesame seeds or toast under the grill until golden.

5 Transfer the chicken and sauce to a warmed serving dish, and sprinkle with the almonds and sesame seeds. Serve with Moroccan corn bread.

Chicken Kdra with Chick-peas & Almonds

A kdra is a type of Moroccan tagine. The almonds in this recipe are precooked until soft, adding an interesting texture and flavour to the chicken.

Serves 4

75g/3oz/ ¾ cup blanched almonds
75g/3oz/scant ½ cup chick-peas, soaked in water overnight
4 part-boned chicken breasts, skinned
50g/2oz/4 tbsp butter
2.5ml/ ½ tsp saffron
2 Spanish onions, thinly sliced
900ml/1½ pints/3¾ cups Chicken Stock
1 small cinnamon stick
60ml/4 tbsp chopped fresh flat leaf parsley, plus extra to garnish
lemon juice, to taste
salt and freshly ground black pepper

1 Place the almonds in a saucepan of water and simmer for 1½–2 hours until fairly soft. Drain and set aside.

2 Cook the chick-peas for 1–1½ hours until soft. Drain, then place in a bowl of cold water and rub with your fingers to remove the skins. Discard the skins and drain.

3 Place the chicken breasts in a flameproof casserole together with the butter, half of the saffron, salt and plenty of black pepper. Heat gently, stirring, until the butter has melted.

4 Add the onions and stock, bring to the boil and then add the chick-peas and cinnamon stick. Cover and cook very gently for 45–60 minutes until the chicken is completely tender.

5 Transfer the chicken to a serving plate and keep warm. Bring the sauce to the boil and simmer until well reduced, stirring frequently. Remove and discard the cinnamon stick. Add the cooked almonds, the parsley and remaining saffron to the sauce, and cook for a further 2–3 minutes. Sharpen the sauce with a little lemon juice, then pour over the chicken and serve, garnished with extra parsley.

Chicken with Preserved Lemon & Olives

This is one of the most famous Moroccan dishes. You must use preserved lemon, as fresh lemon simply doesn't have the mellow flavour required.

Serves 4

30ml/2 tbsp olive oil
1 Spanish onion, chopped
3 garlic cloves
1cm/ ½in piece fresh root ginger, grated, or 2.5ml/ ½ tsp ground ginger
2.5–5ml/ ½–1 tsp ground cinnamon
pinch of saffron
4 chicken quarters, preferably breasts, halved if liked
750ml/1¼ pints/3 cups Chicken Stock
30ml/2 tbsp chopped fresh coriander
30ml/2 tbsp chopped fresh parsley
1 preserved lemon
115g/4oz/ ⅔ cup Moroccan tan olives
salt and freshly ground black pepper
lemon wedges and fresh coriander sprigs, to garnish

1 Heat the oil in a large, flameproof casserole and fry the onion for 6–8 minutes over a moderate heat until lightly golden, stirring occasionally.

2 Crush the garlic and blend with the ginger, cinnamon, saffron and seasoning. Stir into the pan and fry for 1 minute. Add the chicken pieces and fry over a moderate heat for 2–3 minutes until lightly browned. Add the stock, coriander and parsley, bring to the boil, then cover and simmer very gently for 45 minutes.

3 Rinse the preserved lemon under cold water, discard the flesh and cut the peel into small pieces. Stir into the pan with the olives and simmer for a further 15 minutes until the chicken is very tender.

4 Transfer the chicken to a plate and keep warm. Bring the sauce to the boil and cook for 3–4 minutes until reduced and fairly thick. Pour over the chicken and serve, garnished with lemon wedges and coriander sprigs.

Chicken Fricassée Forestier

The term fricassée is used to describe a light stew, usually of chicken that is first sautéed in butter. The accompanying sauce can vary, but here wild mushrooms and bacon provide a rich flavour.

Serves 4

3 chicken breasts, sliced
50g/2oz/4 tbsp unsalted butter
15ml/1 tbsp vegetable oil
115g/4oz rindless streaky bacon, cut into pieces
75ml/5 tbsp dry sherry or white wine
1 medium onion, chopped
350g/12oz/4½ cups assorted wild mushrooms, such as chanterelles, ceps, bay boletus, horn of plenty, chicken of the woods, hedgehog fungus, saffron milk-caps, closed field mushrooms and cauliflower fungus, trimmed and sliced
40g/1½oz/3 tbsp plain flour
550ml/18fl oz/2½ cups Chicken Stock
10ml/2 tsp lemon juice
60ml/4 tbsp chopped fresh parsley
salt and freshly ground black pepper
boiled rice, carrots and baby sweetcorn, to serve

1 Season the chicken with pepper. Heat half of the butter with the oil in a large, heavy-based frying pan or flameproof casserole, and brown the chicken and bacon pieces. Transfer to a shallow dish and pour off any excess fat.

2 Return the pan to the heat and brown the sediment. Pour in the sherry or wine and stir to deglaze the pan. Pour the sherry or wine liquid over the chicken and wipe the pan clean.

3 Fry the onion in the remaining butter until golden brown. Add the mushrooms and cook, stirring frequently, for 6–8 minutes until their juices begin to run. Stir in the flour, then remove from the heat. Gradually add the chicken stock and stir well until the flour is completely absorbed.

4 Add the reserved chicken and bacon with the sherry or wine juices, return to the heat and stir to thicken. Simmer for about 10–15 minutes and then add the lemon juice, parsley and seasoning. Serve with boiled rice, carrots and baby sweetcorn.

Coq au Vin

This classic French dish was originally made with an old rooster, marinated then slowly braised until tender.

Serves 4

1.5–1.75kg/3½–4lb chicken, cut into portions
25ml/1½ tbsp olive oil
225g/8oz baby onions
15g/½oz/1 tbsp butter
225g/8oz/3 cups mushrooms, quartered if large
30ml/2 tbsp plain flour
750ml/1¼ pints/3 cups dry red wine
250ml/8fl oz/1 cup Chicken Stock, or more to cover
1 bouquet garni
salt and freshly ground black pepper

1 Pat the chicken pieces dry and season with salt and pepper. Place in a large, heavy-based frying pan, skin side down, and cook over a medium-high heat for 10–12 minutes or until golden brown. Transfer to a plate.

2 Meanwhile, heat the oil in a large, flameproof casserole over a medium-low heat, add the onions and cook, covered, until evenly browned, stirring frequently.

3 Wipe the frying pan clean and melt the butter in it over a medium heat. Add the mushrooms and sauté, stirring, until golden brown.

4 Sprinkle the onions in the casserole with flour and cook for 2 minutes, stirring frequently, then add the wine and boil for 1 minute, stirring. Add the chicken, mushrooms, stock and bouquet garni. Bring to the boil, reduce the heat to very low and simmer, covered, for 45–50 minutes until the chicken is tender and the juices run clear when the thickest part of the meat is pierced with a skewer or knife.

5 Transfer the chicken pieces and vegetables to a plate. Strain the cooking liquid, skim off the fat and return the liquid to the pan. Boil to reduce by one third, then return the chicken and vegetables to the casserole and simmer for 3–4 minutes to heat through. Serve immediately.

Chicken with Chianti

Together the robust, full-flavoured Italian red wine and red pesto give this sauce a rich colour and almost spicy flavour, while the grapes add a delicious touch of sweetness.

Serves 4

45ml/3 tbsp olive oil
4 part-boned chicken breasts, skinned
1 medium red onion
30ml/2 tbsp red pesto
300ml/ ½ pint/1¼ cups Chianti
300ml/ ½ pint/1¼ cups water
115g/4oz red grapes, halved lengthways and seeded if necessary
salt and freshly ground black pepper
fresh parsley leaves, to garnish
rocket salad, to serve

1 Heat 30ml/2 tbsp of the oil in a large frying pan, add the chicken breasts and sauté over a medium heat for about 5 minutes until they have changed colour on all sides. Remove using a slotted spoon and drain on kitchen paper.

2 Cut the onion in half, through the root. Trim off the root, then slice the onion halves lengthways to create thin wedges.

3 Heat the remaining oil in the pan, add the onion wedges and red pesto, and cook gently, stirring constantly, for about 3 minutes until the onion is softened, but not browned.

4 Add the Chianti and water to the pan, and bring to the boil, stirring. Return the chicken to the pan and season with salt and pepper to taste.

5 Reduce the heat, then cover the pan and simmer gently for about 20 minutes or until the chicken is tender and cooked through, stirring occasionally.

6 Add the grapes to the pan and cook over a low to medium heat until heated through. Taste the sauce and adjust the seasoning as necessary. Serve the chicken hot, garnished with parsley and accompanied by the rocket salad.

Chicken Casserole with Spiced Figs

A Spanish recipe which, rather unusually, combines chicken with succulent figs.

Serves 4

150g/5oz/ ⅔ cup granulated sugar
120ml/4fl oz/ ½ cup white wine vinegar
1 lemon slice
1 cinnamon stick
450g/1lb fresh figs
120ml/4fl oz/ ½ cup medium sweet white wine
pared rind of ½ lemon
1.5kg/3½lb chicken, cut into eight portions
50g/2oz lardons, or thick streaky bacon cut into strips
15ml/1 tbsp olive oil
50ml/2fl oz/ ¼ cup Chicken Stock
salt and freshly ground black pepper

1 Put the sugar, vinegar, lemon slice and cinnamon stick in a pan with 120ml/4fl oz/ ½ cup water. Bring to the boil, then simmer for 5 minutes. Add the figs, cover and simmer for 10 minutes. Remove from the heat, cover and leave to stand for 3 hours.

2 Preheat the oven to 180°C/350°F/Gas 4. Drain the figs and place in a bowl. Add the wine and lemon rind. Season the chicken with salt and pepper.

3 In a large frying pan, cook the lardons or streaky bacon strips until the fat melts and they turn golden. Transfer to a shallow, ovenproof dish, leaving any fat in the pan. Add the oil to the pan and brown the chicken pieces all over.

4 Drain the figs, adding the wine to the chicken in the frying pan. Boil until the sauce has reduced and is syrupy. Transfer the contents of the frying pan to the ovenproof dish and cook in the oven, uncovered, for about 20 minutes.

5 Add the figs and chicken stock, cover and return to the oven for a further 10 minutes. Taste and adjust the seasoning as necessary. Serve hot.

Chicken with Lemons & Olives

A real Mediterranean chicken dish, enhanced with two ingredients particularly associated with the region.

Serves 4

2.5ml/½ tsp ground cinnamon
2.5ml/½ tsp ground turmeric
1.5kg/3½lb chicken
30ml/2 tbsp olive oil
1 large onion, thinly sliced
5cm/2in piece fresh root ginger, peeled and grated
600ml/1 pint/2½ cups Chicken Stock
2 preserved lemons or limes, cut into wedges
75g/3oz/¾ cup stoned brown olives
15ml/1 tbsp clear honey
60ml/4 tbsp chopped fresh coriander
salt and freshly ground black pepper
fresh coriander sprigs, to garnish

1 Preheat the oven to 190°C/375°F/Gas 5. Mix the ground cinnamon and turmeric in a bowl with a little salt and pepper, and rub all over the chicken skin to give an even coating.

2 Heat the oil in a shallow frying pan and fry the chicken on all sides until golden. Transfer the chicken to an ovenproof dish.

3 Add the onion to the pan and fry for 3 minutes. Stir in the ginger and stock, and bring just to the boil. Pour over the chicken, cover with a lid and bake in the oven for 30 minutes.

4 Remove the chicken from the oven and add the preserved lemons or limes, brown olives and honey. Bake, uncovered, for a further 45 minutes until the chicken is tender.

5 Stir in the chopped coriander and season to taste. Garnish with coriander sprigs and serve at once.

Cook's Tip
Preserved lemons (or limes) will provide the most authentic flavour to this dish, but if they are unavailable, you can substitute fresh ones.

Chicken with Chorizo

The addition of chorizo sausage and sherry gives a warm, interesting flavour to this simple Spanish casserole. Serve with rice or boiled potatoes.

Serves 4

1 medium chicken, jointed, or 4 chicken legs, halved
10ml/2 tsp ground paprika
60ml/4 tbsp olive oil
2 small onions, sliced
6 garlic cloves, thinly sliced
150g/5oz chorizo sausage, sliced
400g/14oz can chopped tomatoes
12–16 bay leaves
75ml/5 tbsp medium sherry
salt and freshly ground black pepper
boiled rice or potatoes, to serve

1 Preheat the oven to 190°C/375°F/Gas 5. Coat the chicken pieces in the paprika, making sure that they are evenly covered, then season with salt. Heat the olive oil in a frying pan and fry the chicken until brown.

2 Transfer to an ovenproof dish. Add the onions to the pan and fry quickly. Add the garlic and sliced chorizo, and fry for about 2 minutes.

3 Add the tomatoes, 2 of the bay leaves and the sherry, and bring to the boil. Pour over the chicken and cover with a lid. Bake for 45 minutes.

4 Remove the lid and season to taste. Cook for a further 20 minutes until the chicken is tender and golden. Serve with rice or potatoes, garnished with bay leaves.

Variation
For a Portuguese version of this dish, substitute linguica for the chorizo and white port for the sherry.

Chicken, Leek & Bacon Casserole

A moist whole chicken, braised on a bed of leeks and bacon, and topped with a creamy tarragon sauce.

Serves 4–6

15ml/1 tbsp vegetable oil
25g/1oz/2 tbsp butter
1.5kg/3½lb chicken
225g/8oz streaky bacon
450g/1lb leeks
250ml/8fl oz/1 cup Chicken Stock
250ml/8fl oz/1 cup double cream
15ml/1 tbsp chopped fresh tarragon
salt and freshly ground black pepper

1 Preheat the oven to 180°C/350°F/Gas 4. Heat the oil and melt the butter in a large, flameproof casserole. Add the chicken and cook it, breast side down, for 5 minutes until golden. Remove from the casserole and set aside.

2 Dice the bacon and add to the casserole. Cook for 4–5 minutes until golden. Top and tail the leeks, cut them into 2.5cm/1in pieces and add to the bacon. Cook for 5 minutes until the leeks begin to brown.

3 Return the chicken to the casserole, placing it on top of the bacon and leeks. Cover and put into the oven. Cook for 1½ hours or until the juices run clear when the thickest part of the thigh is pierced with a skewer or knife.

4 Remove the chicken, bacon and leeks from the casserole and keep warm. Skim the fat from the juices. Pour in the stock and cream, and bring to the boil. Cook for 4–5 minutes until slightly reduced and thickened.

5 Stir in the tarragon and seasoning to taste. Carve the chicken and serve with the bacon, leeks and a little sauce.

Chicken with Red Cabbage

Cooked together like this with red wine, both chicken and cabbage are melt-in-the-mouth tender.

Serves 4

50g/2oz/4 tbsp butter
4 large chicken portions, halved
1 onion, chopped
500g/1¼lb red cabbage, finely shredded
4 juniper berries, crushed
12 cooked chestnuts
120ml/4fl oz/½ cup red wine
salt and freshly ground black pepper
sprigs of fresh thyme, to garnish

1 Heat the butter in a heavy, flameproof casserole, add the chicken pieces and cook over a medium heat until lightly browned. Transfer to a plate.

2 Add the onion to the casserole and fry gently until soft and light golden brown. Stir the cabbage and juniper berries into the casserole, season and cook over a moderate heat for 6–7 minutes, stirring once or twice.

3 Stir in the chestnuts, then tuck the chicken pieces under the cabbage so that they are on the bottom of the casserole. Pour in the red wine.

4 Cover and cook gently for about 40 minutes until the chicken juices run clear when the thickest part of a portion is pierced with a skewer or knife and the cabbage is very tender. Adjust the seasoning to taste and serve garnished with thyme.

Variation

You could substitute pheasant or partridge for the chicken in this recipe. Even older birds will remain pleasantly moist, and red cabbage is a traditional accompaniment to game.

Chicken Thighs with Lemon & Garlic

Versions of this classic dish can be found in Spain and Italy, although this particular recipe is of French origin.

Serves 4

600ml/1 pint/2½ cups Chicken Stock
20 large garlic cloves
25g/1oz/2 tbsp butter
15ml/1 tbsp olive oil
8 chicken thighs
1 lemon, peeled, pith removed and thinly sliced
30ml/2 tbsp plain flour
150ml/¼ pint/⅔ cup dry white wine
salt and freshly ground black pepper
chopped fresh parsley or basil, to garnish
boiled new potatoes or rice, to serve

1 Put the stock into a pan and bring to the boil. Add the garlic cloves, cover and simmer gently for 40 minutes. Strain the stock, reserving the garlic, and set aside.

2 Heat the butter and oil in a sauté or frying pan, add the chicken thighs and cook gently on all sides until golden. Transfer them to an ovenproof dish. Preheat the oven to 190°C/375°F/Gas 5.

3 Distribute the reserved garlic and the lemon slices among the chicken pieces. Add the flour to the fat in the pan in which the chicken was browned and cook, stirring, for 1 minute. Add the wine, stirring constantly and scraping the bottom of the pan, then add the stock. Cook, stirring, until the sauce has thickened and is smooth. Season with salt and pepper to taste.

4 Pour the sauce over the chicken, cover and cook in the oven for 40–45 minutes. If a thicker sauce is required, lift out the chicken pieces and reduce the sauce by boiling rapidly until it reaches the desired consistency.

5 Scatter the chopped parsley or basil over the chicken and serve with boiled new potatoes or rice.

Mediterranean Chicken with Turnips

Turnips are popular in all parts of the Mediterranean, and teamed with poultry in a casserole they make a substantial meal.

Serves 4

30ml/2 tbsp sunflower oil
8 chicken thighs or 4 chicken portions
4 small turnips
2 onions, chopped
2 garlic cloves, crushed
6 tomatoes, peeled and chopped
250ml/8fl oz/1 cup tomato juice
250ml/8fl oz/1 cup Chicken Stock
120ml/4fl oz/½ cup white wine
5ml/1 tsp paprika
good pinch of cayenne pepper
20 black olives, stoned
½ lemon, cut into wedges
salt and freshly ground black pepper
couscous, to serve

1 Preheat the oven to 160°C/325°F/Gas 3. Heat 15ml/1 tbsp of the oil in a large frying pan and fry the chicken until lightly browned. Peel the turnips and cut into julienne strips.

2 Transfer the chicken to a large casserole. Add the remaining oil to the frying pan and fry the onions and garlic for 4–5 minutes until lightly golden brown, stirring occasionally.

3 Add the turnips and stir-fry for about 2–3 minutes. Add the tomatoes, tomato juice, stock, wine, paprika, cayenne and seasoning. Bring to the boil. Pour over the chicken. Stir in the olives and lemon wedges.

4 Cover tightly and cook in the oven for 1–1¼ hours until the chicken is tender. Adjust the seasoning to taste. Serve on a bed of couscous.

Cook's Tip

This dish is especially tasty made with navets *or French turnips, which have a very delicate flavour. Young* navets *do not require peeling, and their pale purple and white skins will enhance the appearance of the dish.*

Chicken, Pepper & Bean Stew

This colourful and filling one-pot meal needs only crusty bread to serve.

Serves 4–6

1.75kg/4lb chicken, cut into portions
paprika
30ml/2 tbsp olive oil
25g/1oz/2 tbsp butter
2 onions, chopped
½ each green and yellow pepper, seeded and chopped
450g/1lb/2 cups peeled, chopped, fresh or canned plum tomatoes
250ml/8fl oz/1 cup white wine
475ml/16fl oz/2 cups Chicken Stock or water
45ml/3 tbsp chopped fresh parsley
2.5ml/ ½ tsp Tabasco sauce
15ml/1 tbsp Worcestershire sauce
2 x 200g/7oz cans sweetcorn kernels
115g/4oz broad beans (fresh or frozen)
45ml/3 tbsp plain flour
salt and freshly ground black pepper
fresh parsley sprigs, to garnish

1 Rinse the chicken and pat dry. Sprinkle lightly with salt and a little paprika. Heat the oil with the butter in a flameproof casserole over a medium-high heat. Add the chicken pieces and fry until golden brown on all sides (cook in batches, if necessary). Remove from the pan and set aside.

2 Reduce the heat and cook the onions and peppers for 8–10 minutes until softened. Increase the heat, then add the tomatoes and their juice, the wine, stock or water, parsley, Tabasco and Worcestershire sauces. Stir and bring to the boil.

3 Return the chicken to the pan, pushing it into the sauce. Cover and simmer for 30 minutes, stirring occasionally. Stir in the sweetcorn and beans, partly cover and cook for 30 minutes.

4 Tilt the pan and skim off the surface fat. Mix the flour with a little water in a small bowl to make a paste. Stir in about 175ml/6fl oz/¾ cup of the hot sauce from the pan into the flour mixture and then stir into the stew and mix well. Cook for 5–8 minutes more, stirring occasionally. Taste the stew and adjust the seasoning as necessary. Serve in shallow soup dishes or large bowls, garnished with parsley sprigs.

Chicken & Aubergine Khoresh

This Persian dish is often served on festive occasions in its country of origin and is believed to have been a favourite of kings.

Serves 4

about 60ml/4 tbsp oil
1 whole chicken or 4 large chicken portions
1 large onion, chopped
2 garlic cloves, crushed
400g/14oz can chopped tomatoes
250ml/8fl oz/1 cup water
3 aubergines, sliced
3 peppers, preferably red, green and yellow, seeded and sliced
30ml/2 tbsp lemon juice
15ml/1 tbsp ground cinnamon
salt and freshly ground black pepper
cooked rice, to serve

1 Heat 15ml/1 tbsp of the oil in a large saucepan or flameproof casserole and fry the chicken or chicken portions for about 10 minutes, turning to brown on all sides. Add the onion and fry for a further 4–5 minutes until the onion is golden brown.

2 Add the garlic, the chopped tomatoes and their liquid, water and seasoning. Bring to the boil, then reduce the heat, cover the pan and simmer gently for 10 minutes.

3 Meanwhile, heat the remaining oil and fry the aubergines, in batches, until lightly golden. Transfer to a plate with a slotted spoon. Add the peppers to the pan and fry for a few minutes until slightly softened.

4 Place the aubergines over the chicken or chicken portions and then add the peppers. Sprinkle over the lemon juice and cinnamon, then cover and continue cooking over a low heat for about 45 minutes or until the chicken is cooked (the juices should run clear when the thickest part of the thigh is pierced with a skewer or knife).

5 Transfer the chicken to a serving plate, and spoon the aubergines and peppers around the edge. Reheat the sauce if necessary, adjust the seasoning and pour over the chicken. Serve with rice.

Chicken with Herbs & Lentils

Parsley, marjoram and thyme lend their flavours to this dish, which is served topped with delicious garlic butter.

Serves 4

115g/4oz piece thick bacon or belly pork, rinded and chopped
1 large onion, sliced
4 chicken portions
450ml/¾ pint/scant 2 cups Chicken Stock
1 bay leaf
2 sprigs fresh parsley
2 sprigs fresh marjoram
2 sprigs fresh thyme
225g/8oz/1 cup green or brown lentils
salt and freshly ground black pepper
25–50g/1–2oz/2–4 tbsp garlic butter, to serve

1 Fry the bacon or pork gently in a large, heavy-based flameproof casserole until all the fat runs out and the meat begins to brown. Add the onion and fry for another 2 minutes. Remove the bacon or pork and onion from the casserole using a slotted spoon and set aside.

2 Preheat the oven to 190°C/375°F/Gas 5. Add the chicken portions to the fat remaining in the casserole and fry for about 10 minutes until lightly brown all over. Remove from the casserole and set aside.

3 Return the bacon or pork and onions to the casserole. Stir in the stock, bay leaf, the stalks and some of the leafy parts of the parsley, marjoram and thyme (keep some herb sprigs for the garnish), and the lentils. Season to taste.

4 Place the browned chicken portions on top of the lentils. Sprinkle with seasoning and some of the herbs. Cover the casserole and cook in the oven for about 40 minutes.

5 Serve with a knob of garlic butter on each portion of chicken and a few of the remaining herb sprigs scattered over.

Winter Chicken with Root Vegetables

A casserole of wonderfully tender chicken, root vegetables and lentils, finished with crème fraîche, mustard and tarragon.

Serves 4

350g/12oz onions
350g/12oz trimmed leeks
225g/8oz carrots
450g/1lb swede
30ml/2 tbsp oil
4 chicken portions, about 900g/2lb total weight
115g/4oz/½ cup green lentils
475ml/16fl oz/2 cups Chicken Stock
300ml/½ pint/1¼ cups apple juice
10ml/2 tsp cornflour
45ml/3 tbsp crème fraîche
10ml/2 tsp wholegrain mustard
30ml/2 tbsp chopped fresh tarragon
salt and freshly ground black pepper
fresh tarragon sprigs, to garnish

1 Preheat the oven to 190°C/375°F/Gas 5. Roughly chop the onions, leeks, carrots and swede into similar-size pieces.

2 Heat the oil in a large, flameproof casserole. Season the chicken portions with salt and pepper, and fry them until golden. Drain on kitchen paper.

3 Add the onions to the casserole and cook for 5 minutes, stirring, until they begin to soften and colour. Add the leeks, carrots, swede and lentils, and stir over a medium heat for 2 minutes.

4 Return the chicken to the casserole. Add the stock, apple juice and seasoning. Bring to the boil and cover. Cook in the oven for 50 minutes to 1 hour or until the chicken is tender.

5 Place the casserole over a medium heat. Blend the cornflour with 30ml/2 tbsp water and add to the casserole with the crème fraîche, mustard and tarragon. Adjust the seasoning. Simmer gently for about 2 minutes, stirring. Serve, garnished with tarragon sprigs.

Chicken with Shallots

Shallots are cooked whole in this casserole, which makes the most of their superb, mild onion flavour.

Serves 4

1.3kg/3lb chicken or 4 chicken portions
seasoned flour, for coating
30ml/2 tbsp sunflower oil
25g/1oz/2 tbsp butter
115g/4oz/⅔ cup unsmoked streaky bacon, rinded and chopped
2 garlic cloves
450ml/¾ pint/scant 2 cups red wine
1 bay leaf
2 fresh thyme sprigs
250g/9oz shallots
115g/4oz/1½ cups button mushrooms, halved if large
10ml/2 tsp plain flour
salt and freshly ground black pepper

1 Preheat the oven to 180°C/350°F/Gas 4. If using a whole chicken, cut into four or eight pieces. Place the seasoned flour in a polythene bag, add the chicken pieces and shake to coat.

2 Heat half the oil and half the butter in a flameproof casserole and fry the bacon and garlic for 3–4 minutes. Add the chicken and fry until lightly browned. Add the wine, bay leaf and thyme, and bring to the boil. Cover and cook in the oven for 1 hour.

3 Boil the shallots in salted water for 10 minutes. Heat the remaining oil in a small frying pan and fry the shallots for 3–4 minutes until beginning to brown. Add the mushrooms and fry for a further 2–3 minutes.

4 Stir the shallots and mushrooms into the chicken casserole, and cook for a further 8–10 minutes. Using a fork, blend the flour with the remaining butter to make a thick paste.

5 Transfer the chicken, shallots and mushrooms to a serving dish and keep warm. Bring the liquid to the boil, then add small pieces of the flour paste, stirring vigorously after each addition. When the sauce is thick, either pour it over the chicken pieces or return the chicken to the casserole, and serve.

Old-fashioned Chicken Fricassée

A fricassée is a classic dish in which poultry is first seared in fat, then braised with liquid until cooked. This recipe is finished with a little cream, but you can leave it out if you wish.

Serves 4–6

1.2–1.3kg/2½–3lb chicken, cut into portions
50g/2oz/4 tbsp butter
30ml/2 tbsp vegetable oil
25g/1oz/¼ cup plain flour
250ml/8fl oz/1 cup dry white wine
750ml/1¼ pints/3 cups Chicken Stock
1 bouquet garni
1.5ml/¼ tsp white pepper
225g/8oz/3 cups button mushrooms, trimmed
5ml/1 tsp lemon juice
16–24 small white onions, peeled
120ml/4fl oz/½ cup water
5ml/1 tsp sugar
90ml/6 tbsp whipping cream
salt
30ml/2 tbsp chopped fresh parsley, to garnish

1 Wash the chicken pieces, then pat dry with kitchen paper. Melt half the butter with the oil in a large, heavy-based flameproof casserole over a medium heat. Add half the chicken pieces and cook for 10 minutes, turning occasionally, or until just golden in colour. Transfer to a plate, then cook the remaining pieces in the same way.

2 Return the seared chicken pieces to the casserole. Sprinkle with the flour, turning the pieces to coat. Cook over a low heat for about 4 minutes, turning occasionally.

3 Pour in the wine, bring to the boil and add the stock. Push the chicken pieces to one side and scrape the base of the casserole, stirring until well blended.

4 Bring the liquid to the boil, add the bouquet garni and season with a pinch of salt and the white pepper. Cover and simmer over a medium heat for 25–30 minutes until the chicken is tender and the juices run clear when the thickest part of the thigh is pierced with a knife or skewer.

5 Meanwhile, in a frying pan, heat the remaining butter over a medium-high heat. Add the mushrooms and lemon juice, and cook for 3–4 minutes until the mushrooms are golden, stirring.

6 Add the onions, water and sugar to the pan, swirling to dissolve the sugar. Simmer for about 10 minutes, until just tender. Tip the onions and any juices into a bowl with the mushrooms and set aside.

7 When the chicken is cooked, transfer the pieces to a deep serving dish and cover with foil to keep warm. Discard the bouquet garni. Add any cooking juices from the vegetables to the casserole. Bring to the boil and cook, stirring frequently, until the sauce is reduced by half.

8 Whisk the cream into the sauce and cook for 2 minutes. Add the mushrooms and onions, and cook for a further 2 minutes. Adjust the seasoning, then pour the sauce over the chicken, sprinkle with parsley and serve.

Country Chicken Casserole

Succulent chicken joints oven-cooked in a wine-enriched vegetable sauce are excellent with rice.

Serves 4

2 chicken breasts, skinned
2 chicken legs, skinned
30ml/2 tbsp plain wholemeal flour
15ml/1 tbsp sunflower oil
300ml/ ½ pint/1¼ cups Chicken Stock
300ml ½ pint/1¼ cups white wine
30ml/2 tbsp passata
15ml/1 tbsp tomato purée
4 rashers lean smoked back bacon, chopped
1 large onion, sliced
1 garlic clove, crushed
1 green pepper, seeded and sliced
225g/8oz/3 cups button mushrooms
225g/8oz carrots, sliced
1 bouquet garni
225g/8oz frozen Brussels sprouts
175g/6oz/1½ cups frozen petits pois
salt and freshly ground black pepper
chopped fresh parsley, to garnish
cooked rice, to serve

1 Preheat the oven to 180°C/350°F/Gas 4. Coat the chicken joints with seasoned flour. Heat the oil in a large, flameproof casserole, add the chicken and cook until browned all over. Remove and keep warm.

2 Add any remaining flour to the pan and cook for 1 minute. Gradually stir in the stock and wine, then add the passata and tomato purée. Bring to the boil, stirring, then return the chicken to the casserole. Add the bacon, onion, garlic, green pepper, mushrooms, carrots and bouquet garni, and stir. Cover and bake for 1½ hours, stirring once or twice. Stir in the Brussels sprouts and petits pois, cover and cook for a further 30 minutes.

3 Discard the bouquet garni. Season the casserole to taste. Garnish with parsley and serve immediately with rice.

Cook's Tip
Use fresh Brussels sprouts and peas if available, and use red wine in place of white for a change.

Chicken Stew with Blackberries & Lemon Balm

This unusual stew combines some wonderful flavours, and the inclusion of red wine and blackberries gives it a dramatic appearance.

Serves 4

4 chicken breasts, partly boned
25g/1oz/2 tbsp butter
15ml/1 tbsp sunflower oil
25g/1oz/ ¼ cup flour
150ml/ ¼ pint/ ⅔ cup red wine
150ml/ ¼ pint/ ⅔ cup Chicken Stock
grated rind of ½ orange
15ml/1 tbsp orange juice
3 sprigs fresh lemon balm, finely chopped, plus 1 sprig to garnish
150ml/ ¼ pint/ ⅔ cup double cream
1 egg yolk
115g/4oz/ ⅔ cup blackberries, plus 50g/2oz/ ⅓ cup, to garnish
salt and freshly ground black pepper

1 Preheat the oven to 180°C/350°F/Gas 4. Remove any skin from the chicken and season the meat with salt and pepper. Heat the butter and oil in a frying pan, add the chicken and fry to seal it all over, then transfer to a casserole.

2 Stir the flour into the frying pan, then gradually add the wine and stock, and bring to the boil, stirring constantly. Add the orange rind and juice, together with the chopped lemon balm. Pour over the chicken in the casserole. Cover and cook in the oven for about 40 minutes.

3 In a bowl, blend the cream with the egg yolk, add a little of the liquid from the casserole and mix well. Stir the mixture back into the casserole with the blackberries. Cover and cook for another 10–15 minutes.

4 Taste the casserole and adjust the seasoning as necessary. Serve, garnished with blackberries and lemon balm.

Chicken Ghiveci

A hearty Romanian stew of chicken with colourful vegetables and herbs.

Serves 6

60ml/4 tbsp vegetable oil or melted lard
1 mild onion, thinly sliced
2 garlic cloves, crushed
2 red peppers, seeded and sliced
1.5kg/3½lb chicken
90ml/6 tbsp tomato purée
3 potatoes, diced
5ml/1 tsp chopped fresh rosemary
5ml/1 tsp chopped fresh marjoram
5ml/1 tsp chopped fresh thyme
3 carrots, cut into chunks
½ small celeriac, cut into chunks
120ml/4fl oz/½ cup dry white wine
2 courgettes, sliced
salt and freshly ground black pepper
chopped fresh rosemary and marjoram, to garnish
dark rye bread, to serve

1 Heat the oil or lard in a large, heavy-based flameproof casserole. Add the onion and garlic, and cook for 1–2 minutes until soft. Add the red peppers.

2 Joint the chicken into six portions, place in the casserole and brown gently on all sides for about 15 minutes.

3 Add the tomato purée, potatoes, herbs, carrots, celeriac and white wine. Season to taste with salt and pepper. Cook over a gentle heat, covered, for a further 40–50 minutes.

4 Add the courgette slices 5 minutes before the end of the cooking time. Adjust the seasoning to taste. Garnish with the herbs and serve with dark rye bread.

Cook's Tip
If fresh herbs are unavailable, replace each with 2.5ml/½ tsp dried herbs.

Cassoulet

Based on the traditional French dish, this recipe is full of delicious flavours and makes a welcoming and warming meal.

Serves 6

450g/1lb chicken or duck breast fillets
225g/8oz thick-cut streaky pork or unsmoked streaky bacon rashers
450g/1lb Toulouse or garlic sausages
45ml/3 tbsp oil
450g/1lb onions, chopped
2 garlic cloves, crushed
2 x 425g/15oz cans cannellini beans, rinsed and drained
225g/8oz carrots, roughly chopped
400g/14oz can chopped tomatoes
15ml/1 tbsp tomato purée
1 bouquet garni
30ml/2 tbsp chopped fresh thyme
about 475ml/16fl oz/2 cups Chicken Stock
115g/4oz/2 cups fresh white breadcrumbs
salt and freshly ground black pepper
fresh thyme sprigs, to garnish (optional)

1 Preheat the oven to 160°C/325°F/Gas 3. Cut the chicken or duck breast and pork or bacon rashers into large pieces. Twist the sausages and cut into short lengths.

2 Heat the oil in a large flameproof casserole. Add the meat and cook in batches until well browned. Remove from the pan using a slotted spoon and drain on kitchen paper.

3 Add the onions and garlic to the pan and cook for 3–4 minutes or until beginning to soften, stirring frequently. Stir in the beans, carrots, tomatoes, tomato purée, bouquet garni, thyme and seasoning. Return the meat to the casserole and mix until well combined with the vegetables. Add enough of the stock just to cover the meat and beans. Bring to the boil. Cover tightly and cook in the oven for 1 hour.

4 Remove the cassoulet from the oven, add a little more stock or water if necessary and remove the bouquet garni. Sprinkle over the breadcrumbs and return to the oven, uncovered, for a further 40 minutes. Garnish with fresh thyme sprigs, if using.

Chicken with Melting Onions & Beans

This substantial Bulgarian casserole is bursting with flavour, texture and colour.

Serves 4–6

275g/10oz/1½ cups dried kidney or other beans, soaked in water overnight
8–12 chicken portions, such as thighs and drumsticks
12 bacon rashers, rinded
2 large onions, thinly sliced
250ml/8fl oz/1 cup dry white wine
2.5ml/½ tsp chopped fresh sage or oregano
2.5ml/½ tsp chopped fresh rosemary
generous pinch of grated nutmeg
150ml/¼ pint/⅔ cup soured cream
15ml/1 tbsp chilli powder or paprika
salt and freshly ground black pepper
fresh rosemary sprigs and lemon wedges, to garnish

1 Preheat the oven to 180°C/350°F/Gas 4. Drain the beans, place in a saucepan and cover with fresh cold water. Bring to the boil and boil rapidly for 20 minutes. Rinse and drain well. Trim the chicken pieces, and season with salt and pepper.

2 Arrange the bacon around the sides and base of an ovenproof dish. Sprinkle over half of the onion and then half the beans, followed by the remaining onion and then the remaining beans.

3 In a bowl, mix together the wine with the fresh sage or oregano, the rosemary and nutmeg. Pour the mixture over the onion and beans.

4 In another bowl, mix together the soured cream and the chilli powder or paprika. Toss the chicken in the soured cream mixture and place on top of the beans.

5 Cover the dish with foil and bake for 1¼–1½ hours, removing the foil for the last 15 minutes of the cooking time. Serve, garnished with rosemary sprigs and lemon wedges.

Chicken-in-a-pot

A traditional Bulgarian way of cooking chicken slowly and evenly in its own juices.

Serves 6–8

8 chicken portions
6–8 firm ripe tomatoes, chopped
2 garlic cloves, crushed
3 onions, chopped
60ml/4 tbsp oil or melted lard
250ml/8fl oz/1 cup Chicken Stock
2 bay leaves
10ml/2 tsp paprika
10 white peppercorns, bruised
handful of parsley, stalks reserved and leaves finely chopped
salt

1 Put the chicken, tomatoes and garlic in a flameproof casserole. Cover and cook gently for 10–15 minutes.

2 Add the remaining ingredients, except the parsley leaves, and stir well. Cover tightly and cook over a very low heat, stirring occasionally, for about 1¾–2 hours or until the chicken is tender. Five minutes before the end of the cooking time, stir in the parsley. Adjust the seasoning as necessary. Serve hot.

Chicken with Apricots

A deliciously fruity combination that is quick and easy.

Serves 4

4 chicken portions
seasoned flour
45ml/3 tbsp olive oil
350 g/12oz dried apricots, soaked overnight
salt and freshly ground black pepper

1 Coat the chicken in the seasoned flour. Heat the oil and fry the chicken until browned on all sides. Remove from the pan.

2 Add any remaining flour to the pan and cook, stirring for 1 minute. Gradually stir in the apricot soaking water and bring to the boil, stirring constantly. Return the chicken to the pan and add the apricots. Season to taste, cover and simmer for 45–50 minutes. Serve hot.

Individual Noodle Casseroles

Traditionally, in Japan, these individual chicken, leek and spinach casseroles are cooked in earthenware pots.

Serves 4

115g/4oz boneless chicken thigh
2.5ml/½ tsp salt
2.5ml/½ tsp sake or dry white wine
2.5ml/½ tsp soy sauce
1 leek
115g/4oz spinach, trimmed
300g/11oz dried udon noodles or 500g/1¼lb fresh noodles
4 shiitake mushrooms, stems removed
4 small eggs
seven flavour spice, to serve

For the soup

1.4 litres/2⅓ pints/6 cups instant dashi
22.5ml/4½ tsp soy sauce
5ml/1 tsp salt
15ml/1 tbsp mirin

1 Cut the chicken into small chunks and sprinkle with the salt, sake or wine and soy sauce. Cut the leek diagonally into 4.5cm/1¾in slices. Cook the spinach in a little water for 1–2 minutes, then drain and soak in cold water for 1 minute. Drain, squeeze lightly, then cut into 4cm/1½in lengths.

2 Cook the noodles. Boil dried udon noodles according to the packet instructions, allowing 3 minutes less than the suggested cooking time. If using fresh udon noodles, place them in boiling water, disentangle them and then drain.

3 Bring the ingredients for the soup to the boil in a saucepan and add the chicken and leek. Skim, then cook for 5 minutes. Divide the udon noodles among four individual flameproof casseroles. Divide the soup, chicken and leeks among them. Place over a moderate heat, then divide the shiitake mushrooms among the casseroles.

4 Gently break an egg into each casserole. Cover and simmer for 2 minutes. Divide the spinach among the casseroles and simmer for 1 minute.

5 Serve immediately, standing the hot casseroles on plates or table mats. Sprinkle seven flavour spice over the casseroles.

Filipino Chicken Pot

This nourishing dish is one of many taken to the Philippines by the Spanish in the 16th century.

Serves 4–6

3 chicken legs
15ml/1 tbsp vegetable oil
350g/12oz lean pork, diced
1 chorizo sausage, sliced (optional)
1 small carrot, roughly chopped
1 medium onion, roughly chopped
175g/6oz/1 cup dried haricot beans, soaked in water overnight
1.75 litres/3 pints/7½ cups water
1 garlic clove, crushed
30ml/2 tbsp tomato purée
1 bay leaf
2 chicken stock cubes
350g/12oz sweet potatoes or new potatoes, peeled
10ml/2 tsp chilli sauce
30ml/2 tbsp white wine vinegar
3 firm tomatoes, peeled, seeded and chopped
225g/8oz Chinese leaves, shredded
salt and freshly ground black pepper
3 spring onions, shredded, to garnish
boiled rice, to serve

1 Divide the chicken drumsticks from the thighs. Chop off the narrow end of each drumstick and discard.

2 Heat the oil in a wok or large saucepan, add the chicken, pork, chorizo, if using, the carrot and onion, then brown evenly.

3 Drain and rinse the haricot beans; drain again. Add to the chicken with the water, garlic, tomato purée and bay leaf. Bring to the boil and simmer for 2 hours.

4 Crumble in the chicken stock cubes, add the sweet or new potatoes and the chilli sauce, then simmer for 15–20 minutes until the potatoes are cooked.

5 Add the vinegar, tomatoes and Chinese leaves, and simmer for 1–2 minutes. Season to taste with salt and pepper. The dish is intended to provide enough liquid to be served as a first-course broth. This is followed by a main course of the meat and vegetables, scattered with the shredded spring onions. Serve with rice as an accompaniment.

Chicken with Lentils & Coconut

This delicious, tangy chicken stew comes from Kenya. The amount of lemon juice can be reduced, if you prefer a less sharp sauce.

Serves 4–6

6 chicken thighs or portions
2.5–3.5ml/ ½–¾ tsp ground ginger
50g/2oz/ ¼ cup mung beans
60ml/4 tbsp corn oil
2 onions, finely chopped
2 garlic cloves, crushed
5 tomatoes, peeled and chopped
1 fresh green chilli, seeded and finely chopped
30ml/2 tbsp lemon juice
300ml/ ½ pint/1 ¼ cups coconut milk
300ml/ ½ pint/1 ¼ cups water
15ml/1 tbsp chopped fresh coriander
salt and freshly ground black pepper
cooked green vegetable and rice or chapatis, to serve

1 Season the chicken pieces with the ginger and a little salt and freshly ground pepper, and set aside in a cool place to allow the spices to penetrate the meat. Meanwhile, boil the mung beans in plenty of water for 35 minutes until soft, then mash well.

2 Heat the oil in a large saucepan over a moderate heat and fry the chicken pieces, in batches if necessary, until evenly browned. Transfer to a plate and set aside, reserving the oil and chicken juices in the pan.

3 In the same pan, fry the onions and garlic for 5 minutes, then add the tomatoes and chilli, and cook for a further 1–2 minutes, stirring well.

4 Add the mashed mung beans, lemon juice and coconut milk to the pan. Simmer for 5 minutes, then add the chicken pieces and a little water if the sauce is too thick. Stir in the chopped coriander and simmer for about 35 minutes until the chicken is cooked through.

5 Taste and adjust the seasoning as necessary. Serve with a green vegetable and rice or chapatis.

Chicken with Pimientos

In this Mediterranean Jewish recipe, chicken is cooked in the oven with sweet red peppers, or pimientos.

Serves 6

2kg/4½lb chicken
3 ripe tomatoes
2 large red peppers (pimientos)
60–90ml/4–6 tbsp olive oil
1 large onion, sliced
2 garlic cloves, crushed
15ml/1 tbsp sugar
salt and freshly ground black pepper
fresh flat leaf parsley, to garnish
boiled rice and black olives, to serve

1 Preheat the oven to 190°C/375°F/Gas 5. Joint the chicken and cut into six pieces; set aside. Peel and chop the tomatoes, and seed and slice the red peppers.

2 Heat half of the oil in a large, heavy-based frying pan and sauté the onion, garlic and red peppers for 3 minutes. Transfer to an ovenproof dish.

3 Add the chicken pieces to the frying pan, with a little more oil if necessary, and fry until browned all over. Add to the vegetables in the dish.

4 Fry the tomatoes in the remaining oil for a few minutes. Add the sugar, seasoning and 15ml/1 tbsp water, then spoon the mixture over the chicken.

5 Cook, uncovered, in the oven for about 1 hour. Cover if the chicken is getting too brown. Halfway through, pour the juices into a jug and leave to stand.

6 Serve the chicken with boiled rice and black olives, garnished with flat leaf parsley. Pour the fat off the juices in the jug, reheat and hand round as extra gravy.

Leftover Turkey Casserole

A different way of using up cooked turkey – crisply coated and set in a golden baked batter.

Serves 6

120ml/4fl oz/ ½ cup corn oil
4 eggs
475ml/16fl oz/2 cups milk
115g/4oz/1 cup flour
675g/1½lb boneless cooked turkey, cubed
120ml/4fl oz/ ½ cup thick plain yogurt
275g/10oz/3 cups cornflakes, crushed
salt and freshly ground black pepper
steamed broccoli, carrots and celeriac, to serve

1 Preheat the oven to 220°C/425°F/Gas 7. Pour the oil into a 33 x 23cm/13 x 9in ovenproof dish and heat in the oven for about 10 minutes.

2 Meanwhile, beat the eggs in a mixing bowl. Add the milk. Sift in the flour, and add a little salt and pepper. Mix until the batter is smooth. Set aside.

3 Coat the turkey cubes in the yogurt, then roll in the crushed cornflakes to coat all over.

4 Remove the dish from the oven and pour in the prepared batter. Arrange the turkey pieces on top. Return to the oven and bake for 35–40 minutes until the batter is set and golden. Serve hot with steamed broccoli, carrots and celeriac.

Cook's Tip

There are many different types of yogurt available. Greek yogurt, which may be made either from cow's or ewe's milk, is rich and creamy and is, therefore, ideally suited to this dish. Low-fat yogurt is less suitable, but natural, plain yogurt is perfectly satisfactory.

Turkey with Apples, Bay & Madeira

This casserole will win you many compliments without the worry of a complicated menu. The unusual and tasty apple garnish looks especially attractive.

Serves 4

675g/1½lb turkey breast fillets, cut into 2cm/ ¾in slices
50g/2oz/4 tbsp butter
2 tart apples, peeled, cored and sliced
60ml/4 tbsp Madeira
150ml/ ¼ pint/ ⅔ cup Chicken Stock
3 bay leaves, plus extra, to garnish
10ml/2 tsp cornflour
150ml/ ¼ pint/ ⅔ cup double cream
salt and freshly ground black pepper
steamed patty pan squashes, to serve

For the apple garnish

15g/ ½oz/1 tbsp butter
2 tart apples, peeled, cored and sliced
30ml/2 tbsp Madeira

1 Preheat the oven to 180°C/350°F/Gas 4. Season the turkey. Melt 25g/1oz/2 tbsp of the butter in a frying pan and fry the meat to seal it. Transfer to a casserole.

2 Add the remaining butter to the pan with the sliced apples and cook over a low heat for 1–2 minutes. Add the Madeira, stock and bay leaves to the pan and stir in. Simmer for another couple of minutes.

3 Pour the contents of the frying pan around the chicken in the casserole. Cover and bake in the oven for about 40 minutes.

4 Blend the cornflour with a little of the cream to a smooth paste, then add the rest of the cream. Add this mixture to the casserole and cook in the oven for a further 10 minutes to allow the sauce to thicken.

5 To make the apple garnish, melt the butter in a pan and fry the apple slices over a low heat. Add the Madeira and set it alight. Once the flames have died down, continue to fry the apples until they are lightly browned. Garnish the casserole with the apples and bay leaves and serve with the patty pan squashes.

Duck & Chestnut Casserole

Serve this casserole with a mixture of mashed potatoes and celeriac, to soak up the rich duck juices.

Serves 4–6

2kg/4½lb duck
45ml/3 tbsp olive oil
175g/6oz small onions
50g/2oz field mushrooms, sliced
50g/2oz/1 cup shiitake mushrooms, sliced
300ml/ ½ pint/1¼ cups red wine
300ml/ ½ pint/1¼ cups beef stock
225g/8oz canned, peeled, unsweetened chestnuts, drained
salt and freshly ground black pepper
mashed potatoes and celeriac, to serve
fresh parsley, to garnish

1 Joint the duck into 8 pieces. Heat the oil in a large frying pan and brown the duck pieces. Remove from the frying pan using a slotted spoon and set aside.

2 Add the onions to the pan and cook for about 10 minutes until well browned.

3 Add the mushrooms and cook for a few minutes more. Deglaze the pan with the red wine and boil to reduce the volume by half. Meanwhile, preheat the oven to 180°C/350°F/ Gas 4.

4 Pour the contents of the frying pan into a casserole and stir in the stock. Add the browned duck and the chestnuts, season well and cook in the oven for 1½ hours. Serve with mashed potatoes and celeriac, garnished with parsley.

Cook's Tip
Unlike some poultry, duck freezes well because its high fat content ensures that it retains its flavour and moisture when it is thawed. However, the flesh can easily be damaged, so check the packaging carefully before buying. Fresh duck is also available all year round.

Duck Stew with Olives

In this Provençal recipe, the sweetness of the onions counterbalances the saltiness of the olives.

Serves 6–8

2 × 1.3kg/3lb ducks, quartered, or 8 duck leg quarters
225g/8oz small onions
30ml/2 tbsp plain flour
350ml/12fl oz/1½ cups dry red wine
475ml/16fl oz/2 cups duck or Chicken Stock
1 bouquet garni
115g/4oz/1 cup stoned green or black olives, or a combination
salt, if needed, and freshly ground black pepper

1 Put the duck pieces, skin side down, in a large frying pan over a medium heat and cook for 10–12 minutes until well browned, turning to colour evenly and cooking in batches if necessary. Pour off the fat from the pan.

2 Heat 15ml/1 tbsp of the duck fat in a large, flameproof casserole. Add the onions and cook, covered, over a medium-low heat until evenly browned, stirring frequently. Sprinkle with the flour and continue cooking, uncovered, for 2 minutes, stirring frequently.

3 Stir in the wine and bring to the boil, then add the duck pieces, stock and bouquet garni. Bring back to the boil, then reduce the heat to very low and simmer, covered, for about 40 minutes, stirring occasionally.

4 Rinse the olives in several changes of cold water. If they are very salty, put them into a saucepan, cover with water and bring to the boil, then drain and rinse. Add the olives to the casserole and continue cooking for a further 20 minutes until the duck is very tender.

5 Transfer the duck pieces, onions and olives to a plate. Strain the cooking liquid, skim off the fat and return the liquid to the pan. Boil to reduce by about one third, then adjust the seasoning and return the duck and vegetables to the casserole. Simmer gently to heat through before serving.

Traditional Chicken Pie

Chicken, vegetables and herbs in a creamy white sauce with a top crust of rich pastry: a perennial family favourite.

Serves 6

50g/2oz/4 tbsp butter or margarine
1 medium onion, chopped
3 carrots, cut into 1cm/½in dice
1 parsnip, cut into 1cm/½in dice
45ml/3 tbsp plain flour
350ml/12fl oz/1½ cups Chicken Stock
90ml/6 tbsp medium sherry
90ml/6 tbsp dry white wine
175ml/6fl oz/¾ cup whipping cream
115g/4oz/1 cup frozen peas, thawed
350g/12oz cooked chicken meat, in chunks
5ml/1 tsp dried thyme
15ml/1 tbsp finely chopped fresh parsley
salt and freshly ground black pepper

For the pastry
165g/5½oz/1⅓ cups plain flour, plus extra for dusting
2.5ml/½ tsp salt
115g/4oz/½ cup lard or vegetable fat
30–45ml/2–3 tbsp iced water
1 egg
30ml/2 tbsp milk

1 To make the pastry, sift the flour and salt into a mixing bowl. Using a pastry blender, cut in the fat until the mixture resembles coarse breadcrumbs. Sprinkle in the water, 15ml/1 tbsp at a time, tossing lightly with a fork until the dough forms a ball. Dust with flour, wrap and chill until required.

2 Preheat the oven to 200°C/400°F/Gas 6. Heat half of the butter or margarine in a saucepan. Add the onion, carrots and parsnip, and cook for about 10 minutes until softened. Remove the vegetables from the pan using a slotted spoon.

3 Melt the remaining butter or margarine in the saucepan. Add the flour and cook for 5 minutes, stirring constantly. Stir in the stock, sherry and wine. Bring the sauce to the boil and continue boiling for 1 minute, stirring continuously.

4 Add the cream, peas, chicken, thyme and parsley to the sauce. Season to taste with salt and pepper. Simmer for 1 minute, stirring. Transfer to a 2 litre/3½ pint/8¾ cup ovenproof dish.

5 On a lightly floured surface, roll out the pastry to 1cm/½in thickness. Lay the pastry over the dish and trim off the excess. Dampen the rim of the dish. Using a fork, press the pastry to the rim to seal.

6 Lightly whisk the egg with the milk. Brush the pastry all over with the egg glaze. Cut decorative shapes from the pastry trimmings and arrange on top of the pie. Brush again with the egg glaze. Make one or two holes in the crust so that steam can escape during baking.

7 Bake the pie for about 35 minutes until the pastry is golden brown. Serve hot.

Old-fashioned Chicken Pie

The chicken can be roasted and the sauce prepared a day in advance.

Serves 4

1.75kg/4lb chicken
1 onion, quartered
1 fresh tarragon or rosemary sprig
25g/1oz/2 tbsp butter
115g/4oz/1½ cups button mushrooms
30ml/2 tbsp plain flour
300ml/½ pint/1¼ cups Chicken Stock
115g/4oz/¾ cup cooked ham, diced
30ml/2 tbsp chopped fresh parsley
450g/1lb ready-made puff or flaky pastry
1 egg, beaten
salt and freshly ground black pepper

1 Preheat the oven to 200°C/400°F/Gas 6. Put the chicken into a casserole with the onion and herbs. Add 300ml/½ pint/1¼ cups water and season. Cover with a lid and cook in the oven for about 1¼ hours or until tender.

2 Remove the chicken from the casserole and strain the cooking liquid into a measuring jug. Allow to cool and remove any fat. Make up to 300ml/½ pint/1¼ cups with water.

3 Remove bones and skin from the chicken and cut the meat into cubes. Melt the butter in a pan and cook the mushrooms for 2–3 minutes. Sprinkle in the flour and blend in the stock. Bring to the boil, season and add the ham, chicken and parsley. Turn into a pie dish and cool before covering with pastry.

4 Roll out the pastry to 5cm/2in larger than the pie dish. Cut a narrow strip to place around the edge. Dampen with a little water and stick to the rim. Brush with beaten egg. Lay the pastry loosely over the pie and press firmly on to the rim. Trim away the excess and knock up the sides. Crimp the edge and cut a hole in the centre to allow steam to escape. Decorate with pastry leaves cut from the trimmings.

5 Brush the top of the pie with beaten egg and bake in the oven for about 35 minutes or until the pastry is golden brown.

Chicken Pie with Mushrooms

The filling in this pie has an intense mushroom flavour, using chicken stock rather than the more usual milk and butter.

Serves 4–6

900g/2lb cooked roast or boiled chicken
45ml/3 tbsp olive oil, plus extra for greasing
275g/10oz mixed dark mushrooms, e.g. flat, oyster and chestnut
25ml/5 tsp flour
300ml/½ pint/1¼ cups Chicken Stock
15ml/1 tbsp soy sauce
1 egg white
salt and freshly ground black pepper

For the pastry

150g/5oz/generous ½ cup margarine, chilled
225g/8oz/2 cups plain flour
1 egg yolk
60ml/4 tbsp cold water

1 To make the pastry, cut the margarine into small pieces and rub it into the flour until the mixture resembles breadcrumbs. Mix the egg yolk with the water and stir it into the mixture. Form the dough into a ball, cover and chill for 30 minutes.

2 Preheat the oven to 220°C/425°F/Gas 7. Cut the cooked chicken into pieces and put them in a greased pie dish of about 1.75 litres/3 pints/7½ cups capacity.

3 Heat half the oil in a frying pan. Slice the mushrooms thickly and sauté them over a high heat for about 3 minutes. Add the rest of the oil and stir in the flour. Season with pepper and gradually add the stock, stirring to make a thick sauce.

4 Stir in the soy sauce and adjust the seasoning. Pour the mushroom sauce over the chicken. Roll out the pastry and cut one piece slightly larger than the size of the dish. Also cut some long strips about 2cm/¾in wide. Place the strips round the rim of the pie dish, then lift the pastry lid on to the top, pressing it down on top of the strips. Knock up the edges with a knife.

5 Lightly whisk the egg white and brush it over the pie. Bake in the oven for about 30–35 minutes or until golden brown.

Chicken & Leek Pie

Crisp, light pastry made with fresh herbs tops a tarragon-flavoured chicken and leek sauce to make this tempting savoury pie.

Serves 4

175g/6oz/1½ cups plain flour, plus extra
pinch of salt
90g/3½oz/7 tbsp margarine
15ml/1 tbsp chopped fresh mixed herbs
3 leeks, sliced
45ml/3 tbsp cornflour
400ml/14fl oz/1⅔ cups milk
15–30ml/1–2 tbsp chopped fresh tarragon
350g/12oz cooked, skinless, boneless chicken breast, diced
200g/7oz can sweetcorn kernels, drained
salt and freshly ground black pepper
fresh herb sprigs and salt flakes, to garnish

1 To make the pastry, place the flour and salt in a bowl and rub in 75g/3oz/6 tbsp of the margarine until the mixture resembles breadcrumbs. Stir in the mixed herbs and add a little cold water to make smooth, firm dough. Wrap the pastry in a polythene bag and chill for 30 minutes.

2 Preheat the oven to 190°C/375°F/Gas 5. Steam the leeks for about 10 minutes until just tender. Drain and keep warm.

3 Meanwhile, blend the cornflour with 75ml/5 tbsp of the milk. Heat the remaining milk in a saucepan to boiling point, then pour it on to the cornflour mixture, stirring constantly. Return the mixture to the pan and heat gently until the sauce comes to the boil and thickens, stirring constantly. Simmer gently for about 2 minutes, stirring. Add the remaining margarine to the pan with the chopped tarragon, leeks, chicken and sweetcorn. Season to taste with salt and pepper, and mix together well.

4 Spoon the mixture into a 1.2 litre/2 pint/5 cup pie dish. Roll out the pastry on a lightly floured surface to a shape slightly larger than the pie dish. Trim, decorate the top with the pastry trimmings, if liked, and make a slit in the centre to allow steam to escape. Bake for 35–40 minutes until the pastry is golden brown. Serve at once, sprinkled with herbs and salt flakes.

Chicken Bouchée

A spectacular centrepiece, this light pastry case contains a delicious chicken and mushroom filling.

Serves 4

450g/1lb ready-made puff pastry
1 egg, beaten

For the filling

15ml/1 tbsp oil
450g/1lb minced chicken
25g/1oz/¼ cup plain flour
150ml/¼ pint/⅔ cup milk
150ml/¼ pint/⅔ cup Chicken Stock
4 spring onions, chopped
25g/1oz/¼ cup redcurrants
75g/3oz/generous 1 cup button mushrooms, sliced
15ml/1 tbsp chopped fresh tarragon
salt and freshly ground black pepper

1 Preheat the oven to 200°C/400°F/Gas 6. Roll out half the pastry on a lightly floured surface to a 25cm/10in oval. Roll out the remainder to an oval of the same size and draw a smaller 20cm/8in oval in the centre.

2 Brush the edge of the first pastry shape with the beaten egg and place the smaller oval on top. Place on a dampened baking sheet and cook for 30 minutes in the oven.

3 To make the filling, heat the oil in a large pan. Fry the minced chicken for 5 minutes, stirring frequently to break up any lumps. Add the flour and cook for a further 1 minute. Stir in the milk and stock, and bring to the boil. Add the spring onions, redcurrants and mushrooms. Cook for 20 minutes. Stir in the tarragon and season to taste.

4 Place the pastry bouchée on a serving plate, remove the oval centre and spoon in the filling. Replace the pastry oval to form a lid. Serve immediately.

Variation
You can also use shortcrust pastry for this dish and cook as a traditional chicken pie.

Kotopitta

This is based on a Greek chicken pie. Serve hot or cold with a Greek salad made from tomatoes, cucumber and cubes of feta cheese.

Serves 4

275g/10oz filo pastry, thawed if frozen
30ml/2 tbsp olive oil
75g/3oz/¾ cup chopped toasted almonds
30ml/2 tbsp milk
Greek salad, to serve

For the filling

15ml/1 tbsp olive oil
1 medium onion, finely chopped
1 garlic clove, crushed
45g/1lb boneless cooked chicken
50g/2oz feta cheese, crumbled
2 eggs, beaten
15ml/1 tbsp chopped fresh parsley
15ml/1 tbsp chopped fresh coriander
15ml/1 tbsp chopped fresh mint
salt and freshly ground black pepper

1 To make the filling, heat the oil in a large frying pan and cook the onion gently until soft. Add the garlic and cook for a further 2 minutes. Transfer to a bowl.

2 Remove the skin from the chicken and mince or chop the meat finely. Add to the onion with the rest of the filling ingredients. Mix together thoroughly and season to taste with salt and pepper.

3 Preheat the oven to 190°C/375°F/Gas 5. Have a damp dish towel ready to keep the filo pastry covered. Unravel the pastry and cut the whole batch into a 30cm/12in square. Taking half the sheets (cover the remainder), brush one sheet with a little olive oil, lay it on a well-greased 1.5 litre/2½ pint/6¼ cup ovenproof dish and sprinkle with a few chopped, toasted almonds. Repeat with the other (uncovered) sheets of filo, overlapping them alternately into the dish. Spoon in the filling and cover the pie in the same way with the rest of the pastry.

4 Fold in the overlapping edges and mark a diamond pattern on the surface of the pie with a sharp knife. Brush with milk and sprinkle on any remaining almonds. Bake for 20–30 minutes or until golden brown on top. Serve with Greek salad.

Chicken & Ham Pie

This domed double-crust pie is suitable for a cold buffet and for picnics.

Serves 8

400g/14oz ready-made shortcrust pastry
800g/1¾lb chicken breast fillets, skinned
350g/12oz uncooked gammon
about 60ml/4 tbsp double cream
6 spring onions, finely chopped
15ml/1 tbsp chopped fresh tarragon
10ml/2 tsp chopped fresh thyme
grated rind and juice of ½ large lemon
5ml/1 tsp ground mace
salt and freshly ground black pepper
beaten egg or milk, to glaze
salad, to serve

1 Preheat the oven to 190°C/375°F/Gas 5. Roll out one third of the pastry and use it to line a 20cm/8in pie tin 5cm/2in deep. Place on a baking sheet.

2 Mince 115g/4oz of the chicken with the gammon, then mix with the cream, spring onions, herbs, lemon rind, 15ml/1 tbsp of the lemon juice and the seasoning to make a soft mixture; add more cream if necessary. Cut the remaining chicken into 1cm/½in pieces and mix with the remaining lemon juice, the mace and seasoning.

3 Make a layer of one third of the gammon mixture in the pastry base, cover with half the chopped chicken, then add another layer of one third of the gammon. Add all the remaining chicken followed by the remaining gammon. Dampen the edges of the pastry base. Roll out the remaining pastry to make a lid for the pie and place in position. Trim neatly and crimp the edges.

4 Use the pastry trimmings to make a lattice decoration on the pie lid. Make a small hole in the centre of the lid, brush all over with beaten egg or milk, then bake for about 20 minutes. Reduce the oven temperature to 160°C/325°F/Gas 3 and bake for a further 1–1¼ hours; cover the top with foil if the pastry becomes too brown. Transfer the pie to a wire rack and leave to cool before serving, accompanied by salad.

Chicken Charter Pie

Since this dish comes from Cornwall, cream is typically used in the filling.

Serves 4

50g/2oz/4 tbsp butter
4 chicken legs
1 onion, finely chopped
150ml/¼ pint/⅔ cup milk
150ml/¼ pint/⅔ cup soured cream
4 spring onions, quartered
20g/¾oz finely chopped fresh parsley
225g/8oz ready-made puff pastry
2 eggs, beaten, plus extra for glazing
120ml/4fl oz/½ cup double cream
salt and freshly ground black pepper
lightly cooked carrots, to serve

1 Melt the butter in a heavy-based pan and brown the chicken legs. Transfer to a plate. Add the onion to the pan and cook until soft. Add the milk, soured cream, spring onions, parsley and seasoning, bring to the boil, then simmer for 2 minutes.

2 Return the chicken to the pan with any juices, cover and cook very gently for 30 minutes. Transfer the chicken and sauce mixture to a 1.2 litre/2 pint/5 cup pie dish and leave to cool.

3 Meanwhile, roll out the pastry until about 2cm/¾in larger all round than the top of the pie dish. Leave the pastry to relax while the chicken is cooling.

4 Preheat the oven to 220°C/425°F/Gas 7. Cut off a narrow strip around the edge of the puff pastry and place it on the edge of the pie dish. Moisten the strip with cold water, then cover the dish with the pastry. Press the edges together. Make a hole in the centre of the pastry and insert a small funnel of foil. Brush the pastry with a little beaten egg, then bake for 15–20 minutes.

5 Reduce the oven temperature to 180°C/350°F/Gas 4. Mix the eggs and cream, and pour into the pie through the funnel. Shake gently, then return to the oven for 5–10 minutes. Remove from the oven and leave for 5–10 minutes before serving hot with carrots.

Chicken Pasties

These individual chicken and Stilton pies are wrapped in a crisp shortcrust pastry and shaped into pasties. They can be served hot or cold.

Makes 4

350g/12oz/3 cups self-raising flour, plus extra
2.5ml/½ tsp salt
75g/3oz/6 tbsp lard, plus extra for greasing
75g/3oz/6 tbsp butter
60–75ml/4–5 tbsp cold water
beaten egg, to glaze
salad, to serve

For the filling

450g/1lb boned and skinned chicken thighs
25g/1oz/¼ cup chopped walnuts
25g/1oz spring onions, sliced
50g/2oz/½ cup Stilton, crumbled
25g/1oz celery, finely chopped
2.5ml/½ tsp dried thyme
salt and freshly ground black pepper

1 Preheat the oven to 200°C/400°F/Gas 6. Mix the flour and salt in a bowl. Rub in the lard and butter with your fingers until the mixture resembles fine breadcrumbs. Using a knife to cut and stir, mix in the cold water to form a stiff, pliable dough.

2 Turn out on to a lightly floured surface and knead gently until smooth. Divide into 4 equal pieces and roll out each piece to a thickness of 5mm/¼in, keeping a good round shape. Cut each one into a 20cm/8in circle, using a plate as a guide.

3 Remove any fat from the chicken thighs and cut the meat into small cubes. Mix the chicken with the walnuts, spring onions, Stilton, celery, thyme and seasoning, and divide among the four pastry circles.

4 Brush the edge of the pastry with beaten egg and fold over, pinching and crimping the edges together well. Place on a greased baking sheet and bake in the oven for about 45 minutes or until golden brown. Serve hot or cold, with salad.

Chicken Parcels with Herb Butter

These crisp, light, little filo pastry packets, dusted with Parmesan cheese, enclose chicken breast moistened with a herb-flavoured butter.

Serves 4

4 chicken breast fillets, skinned
150g/5oz/10 tbsp butter, softened, plus extra for greasing
90ml/6 tbsp chopped fresh mixed herbs, e.g. thyme, parsley, oregano and rosemary
5ml/1 tsp lemon juice
5 large sheets filo pastry, thawed if frozen
1 egg, beaten
30ml/2 tbsp grated Parmesan cheese
salt and freshly ground black pepper
salad leaves, to serve

1 Season the chicken fillets and fry in 25g/1oz/2 tbsp of the butter to seal and brown lightly. Allow to cool.

2 Preheat the oven to 190°C/375°F/Gas 5. Put the remaining butter, the herbs, lemon juice and seasoning in a food processor and process until smooth. Melt half the herb butter.

3 Take one sheet of filo pastry and brush with a little melted herb butter. Fold the filo pastry sheet in half and brush again with butter. Place a chicken fillet about 2.5cm/1in from the top end.

4 Dot the chicken with a quarter of the remaining unmelted herb butter. Fold in the sides of the pastry, then roll up to enclose it completely. Place, seam side down, on a lightly greased baking sheet. Repeat with the other chicken fillets.

5 Brush the filo parcels with beaten egg. Cut the last sheet of filo into strips, then scrunch and arrange on top. Brush the parcels once again with the egg glaze, then sprinkle with Parmesan. Bake for about 35–40 minutes until golden brown. Serve hot, accompanied by salad leaves.

Chicken en Croûte

Chicken breasts layered with herbs and orange-flavoured stuffing and wrapped in a light puff pastry make an impressive dinner-party dish.

Serves 8

450g/1lb ready-made puff pastry
4 large chicken breast fillets, skinned
1 egg, beaten
lightly cooked vegetables, to serve

For the stuffing

115g/4oz leeks, thinly sliced
50g/2oz/⅓ cup streaky bacon, chopped
25g/1oz/2 tbsp butter
115g/4oz/2 cups fresh white breadcrumbs
30ml/2 tbsp chopped fresh herbs, e.g. parsley, thyme, marjoram and chives
grated rind of 1 large orange
1 egg, beaten
salt and freshly ground black pepper

1 To make the stuffing, cook the leeks and bacon in the butter until soft. Put the breadcrumbs, herbs and seasoning in a bowl. Add the leeks and butter with the orange rind and bind with beaten egg. If the mixture is too dry, add a little orange juice.

2 Preheat the oven to 200°C/400°F/Gas 6. Roll out the pastry to a large rectangle 30 x 40cm/12 x 16in. Trim the edges and reserve the trimmings for the decoration.

3 Place the chicken breasts between two pieces of clear film and flatten to a thickness of 5mm/¼in with a rolling pin or meat mallet. Spread one-third of the stuffing over the centre of the pastry. Lay two chicken breasts, side by side, over the stuffing. Cover with another third of the stuffing, then repeat with two more chicken breasts and the rest of the stuffing.

4 Cut diagonally from each corner of the pastry to the chicken. Brush with beaten egg. Bring up the sides and overlap them slightly. Trim away any excess and fold the ends over like a parcel. Turn over on to a greased baking sheet. Using a sharp knife, lightly criss-cross the pastry into a diamond pattern. Brush with beaten egg and cut leaves from the trimmings to decorate the top. Bake for 50–60 minutes. Serve hot with vegetables.

Chicken & Apricot Filo Pie

The filling for this pie has a Middle Eastern flavour – minced chicken combined with apricots, bulgur wheat, nuts and spices.

Serves 6

75g/3oz/½ cup bulgur wheat
75g/3oz/6 tbsp butter
1 onion, chopped
450g/1lb minced chicken
50g/2oz/¼ cup ready-to-eat dried apricots, finely chopped
25g/1oz/¼ cup blanched almonds, chopped
5ml/1 tsp ground cinnamon
2.5ml/½ tsp ground allspice
50ml/2fl oz/¼ cup Greek yogurt
15ml/1 tbsp snipped fresh chives
30ml/2 tbsp chopped fresh parsley
6 large sheets filo pastry, thawed if frozen
salt and freshly ground black pepper
fresh whole chives, to garnish

1 Preheat the oven to 200°C/400°F/Gas 6. Put the bulgur wheat in a bowl with 120ml/4fl oz/½ cup boiling water. Soak for 5–10 minutes until the water is absorbed.

2 Heat 25g/1oz/2 tbsp of the butter in a pan and gently fry the onion and chicken until pale golden, stirring frequently. Add the apricots, almonds and bulgur wheat, and cook for a further 2 minutes. Remove from the heat and stir in the cinnamon, allspice, yogurt, chives and parsley. Season to taste.

3 Melt the remaining butter. Unroll the filo pastry and cut into 25cm/10in rounds. Keep the pastry rounds covered with a clean, damp dish towel to prevent them from drying out.

4 Line a 23cm/9in loose-based flan tin with three of the pastry rounds, brushing each one with melted butter as you layer them. Spoon in the chicken mixture and cover with three more pastry rounds, brushed with melted butter as before.

5 Crumple the remaining pastry rounds and place them on top of the pie, then brush over any remaining melted butter. Bake the pie for about 30 minutes until the pastry is golden brown and crisp. Serve hot or cold, cut into wedges and garnished with whole chives.

Tandoori Chicken Kebabs

Before it is cooked, the chicken is marinated in a mixture of yogurt and lemon juice, flavoured with tandoori paste, garlic and fresh coriander.

Serves 4

4 chicken breast fillets, about 175g/6oz each, skinned
15ml/1 tbsp lemon juice
45ml/3 tbsp tandoori paste
45ml/3 tbsp plain yogurt
1 garlic clove, crushed
30ml/2 tbsp chopped fresh coriander
1 small onion, cut into wedges and separated into layers
a little oil, for brushing
salt and freshly ground black pepper
fresh coriander sprigs, to garnish
pilau rice and naan bread, to serve

1 Cut the chicken breasts into 2.5cm/1in cubes, place in a bowl and add the lemon juice, tandoori paste, yogurt, garlic, coriander and seasoning. Cover and leave to marinate in the fridge for 2–3 hours.

2 Preheat the grill to high. Thread alternate pieces of marinated chicken and onion on to four skewers.

3 Brush the onions with a little oil, lay on a grill rack and cook under the preheated grill for 10–12 minutes, turning once.

4 Garnish the kebabs with fresh coriander and serve at once with pilau rice and naan bread.

Cook's Tip
Use chopped, boned and skinned chicken thighs, or turkey breasts, for a cheaper alternative. Tandoori paste is available from specialist Indian foodstores and many supermarkets.

Devilled Chicken

This spicy barbecued chicken dish from southern Italy uses a marinade of dried red chillies, which are a colourful speciality of the Abruzzi region.

Serves 4

120ml/4fl oz/½ cup olive oil
finely grated rind and juice of 1 large lemon
2 garlic cloves, finely chopped
10ml/2 tsp finely chopped or crumbled dried red chillies
12 skinless, boneless chicken thighs, each cut into 3 or 4 pieces
salt and freshly ground black pepper
flat leaf parsley, to garnish
lemon wedges and green salad, to serve

1 Make a marinade by mixing the oil, lemon rind and juice, garlic and chillies in a large, shallow non-metallic dish. Add salt and pepper to taste, and whisk well.

2 Add the chicken pieces to the dish, turning to coat with the marinade. Cover and place in the fridge for at least 4 hours, or preferably overnight.

3 When ready to cook, prepare a barbecue or preheat the grill and thread the chicken pieces on to eight oiled metal skewers. Cook on the barbecue or under a hot grill for 6–8 minutes, turning frequently, until tender.

4 Serve hot, garnished with flat leaf parsley and accompanied by lemon wedges for squeezing and a green salad.

Cook's Tip
Thread the chicken pieces zig-zag fashion on to the skewers so that they do not fall off during cooking.

Chicken Satay with Peanut Sauce

Marinated chicken kebabs served with a peanut sauce.

Serves 4–6

4 chicken breast fillets
15ml/1 tbsp coriander seeds
10ml/2 tsp fennel seeds
2 garlic cloves, crushed
5cm/2in piece lemon grass, shredded
2.5ml/½ tsp ground turmeric
10ml/2 tsp sugar
2.5ml/½ tsp salt
30ml/2 tbsp soy sauce
15ml/1 tbsp sesame oil
juice of ½ lime
mint leaves, lime wedges and cucumber batons, to garnish
lettuce, to serve

For the peanut sauce

150g/5oz/1¼ cups raw peanuts
15ml/1 tbsp vegetable oil, plus extra
2 shallots, finely chopped
1 garlic clove, crushed
1–2 small fresh chillies, seeded and finely chopped
1cm/½in cube shrimp paste
30ml/2 tbsp tamarind sauce
120ml/4fl oz/½ cup coconut milk
15ml/1 tbsp clear honey

1 Cut the chicken into thin strips and thread, zig-zag fashion, on to 12 bamboo skewers. Arrange on a flat plate and set aside.

2 Dry-fry the coriander and fennel seeds in a wok. Grind with a pestle and mortar or food processor, then return to the wok and add the garlic, lemon grass, turmeric, sugar, salt, soy sauce, sesame oil and lime juice. Allow the mixture to cool. Spread it over the chicken and leave in a cool place for up to 8 hours.

3 For the sauce, stir-fry the peanuts with a little oil. Turn out on to a cloth and rub with your hands to remove the skins. Process in a food processor for 2 minutes. Heat the oil in a wok and fry the shallots, garlic and chillies until softened. Add the shrimp paste, tamarind sauce, coconut milk and honey. Simmer briefly, add to the peanuts and process to a thick sauce. Pour into a serving bowl.

4 Brush the chicken with a little vegetable oil and cook under a preheated grill for 6–8 minutes. Serve on a bed of lettuce, garnished with mint leaves, lime wedges and cucumber batons and accompanied by the peanut sauce.

Chicken Tikka Masala

Tender chicken pieces cooked in a creamy, spicy sauce with a hint of tomato and served on naan bread.

Serves 4

675g/1½ lb chicken breast fillets, skinned
90ml/6 tbsp tikka paste
60ml/4 tbsp plain yogurt
30ml/2 tbsp oil
1 onion, chopped
1 garlic clove, crushed
1 fresh green chilli, seeded and chopped
2.5cm/1in piece fresh root ginger, grated
15ml/1 tbsp tomato purée
15ml/1 tbsp ground almonds
250ml/8fl oz/1 cup water
45ml/3 tbsp butter, melted
50ml/2fl oz/¼ cup double cream
15ml/1 tbsp lemon juice
fresh coriander sprigs, plain yogurt and toasted cumin seeds, to garnish
naan bread, to serve

1 Cut the chicken into 2.5cm/1in cubes. Put 45ml/3 tbsp of the tikka paste and all of the yogurt into a bowl. Add the chicken, turn to coat well and leave to marinate for 20 minutes.

2 For the tikka sauce, heat the oil in a pan and fry the onion, garlic, chilli and ginger for 5 minutes. Add the remaining tikka paste and fry for 2 minutes. Add the tomato purée, ground almonds and water, and simmer for 15 minutes.

3 Meanwhile, thread the chicken on to wooden kebab skewers. Preheat the grill.

4 Brush the chicken pieces with the melted butter and grill under a medium heat for 15 minutes, turning occasionally.

5 Put the tikka sauce into a food processor or blender and process until smooth. Return to the pan and stir in the cream and lemon juice.

6 Remove the chicken pieces from the skewers and add to the tikka sauce, then simmer for 5 minutes. Serve on naan bread and garnish with coriander, yogurt and toasted cumin seeds.

Blackened Cajun Chicken & Corn

A classic method of cooking poultry in a spiced coating, from the deep South of the United States. Traditionally, the coating should begin to char and blacken slightly at the edges.

Serves 4

8 chicken joints, e.g. drumsticks, thighs or wings
2 whole sweetcorn cobs
10ml/2 tsp garlic salt
10ml/2 tsp freshly ground black pepper
7.5ml/1½ tsp ground cumin
7.5ml/1½ tsp paprika
5ml/1 tsp cayenne pepper
45ml/3 tbsp melted butter
chopped fresh parsley, to garnish

1 Cut any excess fat from the chicken, but leave the skin on. Slash the deepest parts with a knife to allow the flavours to penetrate the flesh.

2 Pull the husks and silks off the corn cobs and discard. Cut the cobs into thick slices.

3 In a small bowl, mix together all the spices. Put the chicken and corn in a large bowl and brush with melted butter. Sprinkle the spices over them and toss well to coat evenly.

4 Cook the chicken pieces on a medium-hot barbecue or under a preheated grill for about 25 minutes, turning occasionally. Add the corn after 15 minutes of the cooking time and cook, turning often, until golden brown. Serve hot, garnished with chopped parsley.

Cook's Tip
The natural sugar which gives sweetcorn its characteristic flavour starts to turn to starch immediately after picking. When buying, look for plump kernels and always use the cobs on the day of purchase.

Barbecued Jerk Chicken

Jerk refers to the blend of herb and spice seasoning rubbed into meat before it is roasted over charcoal, usually sprinkled with pimiento berries, to make this tasty Caribbean dish.

Serves 4

8 chicken portions
oil, for brushing
salt and freshly ground black pepper
salad leaves, to serve

For the marinade

5ml/1 tsp ground allspice
5ml/1 tsp ground cinnamon
5ml/1 tsp dried thyme
1.5ml/¼ tsp grated nutmeg
10ml/2 tsp demerara sugar
2 garlic cloves, crushed
15ml/1 tbsp finely chopped onion
15ml/1 tbsp chopped spring onion
15ml/1 tbsp vinegar
30ml/2 tbsp oil
15ml/1 tbsp lime juice
1 hot fresh chilli, chopped

1 To make the marinade, combine all the ingredients in a small bowl and mash them together well to form a thick paste.

2 Lay the chicken portions on a plate or board and make several lengthways slits in the flesh. Rub the seasoning all over the chicken and into the slits.

3 Place the chicken portions in a dish, cover with clear film and marinate for several hours, or preferably overnight, in the fridge.

4 Preheat the grill or prepare the barbecue. Shake off any excess seasoning from the chicken. Brush with oil and place either on a baking sheet or on a barbecue grill. Cook under the grill for 45 minutes, turning often, or over hot coals for 30 minutes, turning often. Serve hot with salad leaves.

Cook's Tip
The flavour is best if you marinate the chicken overnight. Sprinkle the charcoal with aromatic herbs, such as bay leaves, for even more flavour when barbecueing.

Spicy Barbecued Chicken

A very easy dish that can be cooked either on the barbecue or in the oven. The sauce has all the hot, sharp and sweet flavours that you would expect.

Serves 4

45ml/3 tbsp vegetable oil
1 large onion, chopped
175ml/6fl oz/ 3/4 cup tomato ketchup
175ml/6fl oz/ 3/4 cup water
40ml/2 1/2 tbsp fresh lemon juice
25ml/1 1/2 tbsp grated horseradish
15ml/1 tbsp light brown sugar
15ml/1 tbsp French mustard
1.3kg/3lb chicken portions
cooked rice, to serve

1 Preheat the oven, if using, to 180°C/350°F/Gas 4. Heat 15ml/1 tbsp of the oil in a saucepan. Add the onion and cook for about 5 minutes until softened. Stir in the tomato ketchup, water, lemon juice, horseradish, sugar and mustard, and bring to the boil. Reduce the heat and simmer the sauce for 10 minutes, stirring occasionally.

2 Meanwhile, heat the remaining oil in a heavy-based frying pan. Add the chicken portions and brown on all sides. Remove from the pan and drain on kitchen paper.

3 Place the chicken in a 28 x 23cm/11 x 9in ovenproof dish and pour the sauce over the top.

4 Bake in the oven for about 1¼ hours until the chicken is cooked and tender, basting occasionally. Alternatively, barbecue over a medium heat for 40–50 minutes, turning once and brushing frequently with the sauce. Serve the chicken on a bed of cooked rice.

Cook's Tip
For a hotter flavour, use English mustard.

Barbecued Chicken Thai-style

Barbecued chicken is served almost everywhere in Thailand, from portable roadside stalls to sports stadiums and beaches.

Serves 4–6

1.5kg/3 1/2 lb chicken, cut into 8–10 pieces
lime wedges and finely sliced red chillies, to garnish
cooked rice, to serve

For the marinade
2 lemon grass stalks, chopped
2.5cm/1in piece fresh root ginger
6 garlic cloves
4 shallots
1/2 bunch coriander roots
15ml/1 tbsp palm sugar
120ml/4fl oz/ 1/2 cup coconut milk
30ml/2 tbsp fish sauce
30ml/2 tbsp soy sauce

1 To make the marinade, put all the ingredients into a food processor and process until smooth.

2 Put the chicken pieces in a wide, shallow dish and pour over the marinade. Leave to marinate in the fridge for at least 4 hours or overnight.

3 Prepare the barbecue or preheat the oven to 200°C/400°F/Gas 6. Barbecue the chicken over glowing coals, or place on a rack over a roasting tin and bake in the oven for about 20–30 minutes or until the chicken is cooked and golden brown. Turn the pieces occasionally and brush frequently with the marinade.

4 Garnish with lime wedges and finely sliced red chillies, and serve with rice.

Cook's Tip
Made from salted anchovies, fish sauce – also known as nam pla – is widely used in Thai cooking in much the same way as soy sauce is used in Chinese cuisine. It is strongly flavoured and very salty, so use with caution. It is available from Asian foodstores and many supermarkets.

Thai Grilled Chicken

Thai grilled chicken is especially delicious when cooked on the barbecue. It should be served with a dipping sauce.

Serves 4–6

900g/2lb chicken drumsticks or thighs
5ml/1 tsp whole black peppercorns
2.5ml/½ tsp caraway or cumin seeds
20ml/4 tsp sugar
10ml/2 tsp paprika
2cm/¾in piece fresh root ginger, peeled
3 garlic cloves, crushed
15g/½ oz fresh coriander, white root or stem, finely chopped
45ml/3 tbsp vegetable oil
salt
6–8 lettuce leaves, to serve

For the garnish

½ cucumber, cut into strips
4 spring onions, trimmed
2 limes, quartered

1 Chop through the narrow end of each chicken drumstick with a heavy knife. Score the chicken pieces deeply to allow the marinade to penetrate. Set aside in a shallow bowl.

2 Grind the peppercorns, caraway or cumin seeds and sugar using a pestle and mortar or food processor. Add the paprika, ginger, garlic, coriander and oil, and grind to a paste.

3 Spread the marinade over the chicken and place in the fridge for 6 hours.

4 Preheat the grill or prepare the barbecue. Cook the chicken for 20 minutes, turning once. Season with salt to taste. Serve on a bed of lettuce leaves, garnished with cucumber, spring onions and lime quarters.

Cook's Tip

Spices are more flavoursome when freshly ground rather than bought ready ground. You can use a pestle and mortar or a small coffee mill kept especially for this purpose. Custom-made spice grinders are also available.

Grilled Spiced Chicken

The sharpness of fresh lime balances the heat and strength of the spices.

Serves 4

5ml/1 tsp coriander seeds
5ml/1 tsp cumin seeds
2 limes
2 garlic cloves, crushed
60ml/4 tbsp chopped fresh coriander
1 small fresh green chilli, seeded and finely chopped
30ml/2 tbsp light soy sauce
60ml/4 tbsp sunflower oil
4 chicken breast fillets, about 175g/6oz each, skinned
green vegetables, to serve

1 Crush the coriander and cumin seeds using a pestle and mortar or a spice or coffee grinder. Cut the rind from the limes into thin shreds using a zester. Squeeze the juice. Blend the spices, lime rind and juice, garlic, fresh coriander, chilli, soy sauce and oil in a bowl. Add the chicken, turn to coat thoroughly, then cover and marinate in the fridge for 24 hours.

2 Remove the chicken from the marinade. Heat a grill or griddle pan and cook the chicken for about 4–6 minutes on each side or until cooked through. Serve with green vegetables.

Thai Dipping Sauce

This has a fiery strength, so use with caution.

Makes 120ml/4fl oz/½ cup

15ml/1 tbsp vegetable oil
15ml/1tbsp fish sauce
2 garlic cloves, finely chopped
2cm/¾in piece root ginger, peeled and finely chopped
3 fresh red chillies, chopped
15ml/1 tbsp finely chopped fresh coriander root
20ml/4 tsp sugar
45ml/3 tbsp dark soy sauce
juice of ½ lime

1 Heat the oil, fish sauce, garlic, ginger and chillies for 1–2 minutes.
2 Remove from the heat and add the remaining ingredients.

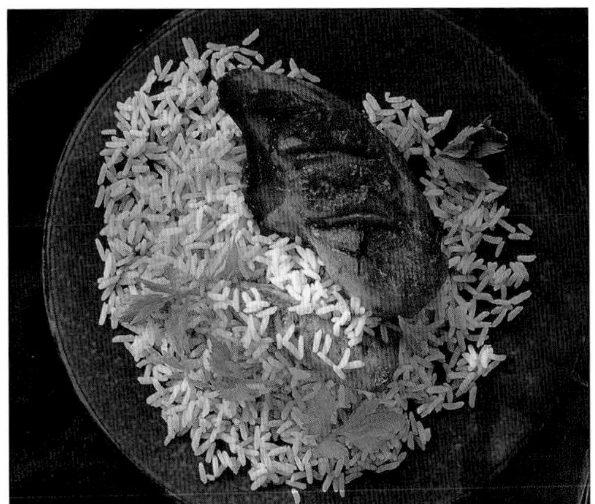

Indonesian Chicken Grill

The flavour of this dish will be more intense if the chicken is marinated for several hours or overnight.

Serves 4

1.5kg/3½ lb chicken
4 garlic cloves, crushed
2 lemon grass stalks, lower 5cm/2in sliced
1cm/½in fresh galangal, peeled and sliced
5ml/1 tsp ground turmeric
about 475ml/16fl oz/2 cups water
3–4 bay leaves
45ml/3 tbsp each dark and light soy sauce
50g/2oz butter or margarine
salt
fresh coriander, to garnish
boiled rice, to serve

1 Cut the chicken into four or eight portions. Slash the fleshy part of each portion twice and set aside.

2 Put the garlic, lemon grass, galangal, turmeric and salt into a food processor and process to a paste or grind using a pestle and mortar. Rub the paste into the chicken pieces and leave for at least 30 minutes. Wear rubber gloves for this, as the turmeric will stain heavily; or wash your hands immediately after using, if you prefer.

3 Transfer the chicken pieces to a wok or heavy-based pan and pour in the water. Add the bay leaves and bring to the boil. Cover and cook gently for 30 minutes, adding a little more water if necessary. Stir from time to time.

4 Preheat the grill or barbecue, or preheat the oven to 200°C/400°F/Gas 6. Just before transferring, add the two soy sauces to the pan together with the butter or margarine. Cook until the chicken is well coated and the sauce has almost been absorbed.

5 Transfer to the grill, barbecue or oven and cook for a further 10–15 minutes, turning the pieces often so that they become golden brown all over. Take care not to let them burn. Baste with the remaining sauce during cooking. Serve with boiled rice, garnished with coriander leaves.

Grilled Cashew Nut Chicken

This dish comes from the beautiful island of Bali where nuts are widely used as a base for sauces and marinades. Serve with a green salad and hot chilli dipping sauce.

Serves 4–6

4 chicken legs
sliced radishes and sliced cucumber, to garnish
Chinese leaves and chilli dipping sauce, to serve

For the marinade

50g/2oz/½ cup raw cashew or macadamia nuts
2 shallots or 1 small onion, finely chopped
2 garlic cloves, crushed
2 small fresh red chillies, chopped
5cm/2in piece lemon grass
15ml/1 tbsp tamarind sauce
30ml/2 tbsp dark soy sauce
15ml/1 tbsp fish sauce (optional)
10ml/2 tsp sugar
2.5ml/½ tsp salt
15ml/1 tbsp rice or white wine vinegar

1 Using a sharp knife, slash the chicken legs several times through to the bone and chop off the knuckle end. Place the chicken in a wide, shallow dish and set aside.

2 To make the marinade, grind the cashew or macadamia nuts in a food processor or using a pestle and mortar.

3 Add the shallots or onion, garlic, chillies and lemon grass, and blend. Add the remaining marinade ingredients.

4 Spread the marinade over the chicken and leave in the fridge for up to 8 hours.

5 Preheat the grill or prepare the barbecue. Grill the chicken under a moderate heat or cook over the barbecue for 15 minutes on each side. Transfer to a serving dish lined with Chinese leaves, garnish with the sliced radishes and cucumber, and serve, accompanied by chilli dipping sauce.

Chicken Breasts Cooked in Spices & Coconut

The chicken is marinated in a highly aromatic, spicy coconut mixture, which doubles as a sauce for the finished dish.

Serves 4

200g/7oz block creamed coconut
300ml/ ½ pint/1¼ cups boiling water
3 garlic cloves, chopped
2 spring onions, chopped
1 fresh green chilli, chopped
5cm/2in piece fresh root ginger, peeled and chopped
5ml/1 tsp fennel seeds
2.5ml/ ½ tsp black peppercorns
seeds from 4 cardamom pods
30ml/2 tbsp ground coriander
5ml/1 tsp ground cumin
5ml/1 tsp ground star anise
5ml/1 tsp grated nutmeg
2.5ml/ ½ tsp ground cloves
2.5ml/ ½ tsp ground turmeric
4 large chicken breast fillets, skinned
onion rings and fresh coriander sprigs, to garnish
naan bread, to serve

1 Break up the coconut and put it in a jug. Pour the boiling water over and set aside until completely dissolved. Place the garlic, spring onions, chilli, ginger and all the spices in a blender or food processor. Add the coconut mixture and process to a smooth paste.

2 Make several diagonal cuts across the chicken fillets. Arrange them in one layer in a shallow dish. Spoon over half the coconut mixture and toss well to coat the chicken evenly. Cover the dish and leave to marinate in the fridge for about 30 minutes, or overnight.

3 Cook the chicken under a preheated grill or on a moderately hot barbecue for 12–15 minutes, turning once, until well browned and thoroughly cooked.

4 Heat the remaining coconut mixture gently until boiling. Serve with the chicken, garnished with onion rings and sprigs of coriander, and accompanied by naan bread.

Drumsticks with Devilish Sauce

Chicken drumsticks marinated with spices, coated with a hot, tomato-based sauce and served on a bed of yellow rice.

Serves 4

8 large chicken drumsticks

For the dry marinade

10ml/2 tsp salt
10ml/2 tsp caster sugar
5ml/1 tsp freshly ground black pepper
5ml/1 tsp ground ginger
5ml/1 tsp dry English mustard powder
5ml/1 tsp paprika
30ml/2 tbsp olive oil

For the sauce

30ml/2 tbsp tomato ketchup
15ml/1 tbsp mushroom ketchup
15ml/1 tbsp chilli sauce
15ml/1 tbsp soy sauce
15ml/1 tbsp fruit sauce

For the yellow rice

25g/1oz/2 tbsp butter
1 medium onion, finely chopped
5ml/1 tsp ground turmeric
225g/8oz/generous 1 cup cooked rice

1 To make the dry marinade, mix all the ingredients together in a bowl. Place the chicken drumsticks in a wide, shallow dish. Rub the marinade into the drumsticks, cover with clear film and leave for at least 1 hour, or preferably overnight.

2 Preheat the grill. Lay the drumsticks on a grill rack and grill slowly under a medium heat for 10 minutes, turning occasionally, until brown and crisp.

3 Meanwhile, to make the sauce, mix all the ingredients together and spoon over the chicken. Continue to cook the chicken for a further 5–7 minutes, basting frequently.

4 To make the yellow rice, heat the butter in a large pan, add the onion and cook until tender. Add the turmeric and cook for a further minute.

5 Add the cooked rice and stir to reheat and colour. Spoon on to a serving plate and arrange the devilled drumsticks on top. Serve immediately.

Grilled Chicken with Pica de Gallo Salsa

This dish originates from Mexico. Its hot, fruity flavours form the essence of Tex-Mex cooking.

Serves 4
4 chicken breasts
pinch each of celery salt and cayenne pepper, combined
30ml/2 tbsp vegetable oil
fresh coriander sprigs, to garnish
corn chips, to serve

For the salsa
275g/10 oz watermelon
175g/6oz canteloupe melon
1 small red onion
1–2 fresh green chillies
30ml/2 tbsp lime juice
60ml/4 tbsp chopped fresh coriander
salt

1 Preheat a moderate grill. Slash the chicken breasts deeply in several places to speed up cooking and to help them absorb the spice flavours.

2 Season the chicken with celery salt and cayenne, brush with oil and grill for about 15 minutes, turning occasionally.

3 To make the salsa, remove the rind and as many seeds as you can from the melons. Finely dice the flesh and put it into a bowl. Finely chop the onion. Split the chillies (discarding the seeds if you do not want a very hot salsa) and chop. Mix the onion and chillies with the melon. Add the lime juice and chopped coriander, and season with a pinch of salt. Turn the salsa into a small bowl.

4 Arrange the grilled chicken on a plate, and serve with the salsa and a handful of corn chips. Garnish with coriander sprigs.

Cook's Tip
To capture the spirit of Tex-Mex food, cook the chicken over a barbecue and eat shaded from the hot summer sun.

Spiced Barbecued Poussins

The coating of ground cumin and coriander on the poussins keeps them moist during grilling as well as giving them a delicious and unusual flavour.

Serves 4
2 garlic cloves, roughly chopped
5ml/1 tsp ground cumin
5ml/1 tsp ground coriander
pinch of cayenne pepper
½ small onion, chopped
60ml/4 tbsp olive oil
2.5ml/ ½ tsp salt
2 poussins
lemon wedges, to garnish

1 Combine the garlic, cumin, coriander, cayenne pepper, onion, olive oil and salt in a blender or food processor. Process to make a paste that will spread smoothly.

2 Cut the poussins in half lengthways. Place them skin side up in a shallow dish and spread with the spice paste. Cover and leave to marinate in a cool place for 2 hours.

3 Barbecue or grill the poussins for 15–20 minutes, turning frequently, until cooked and lightly charred on the outside. Serve immediately, garnished with lemon wedges.

Cook's Tip
Quail can also be cooked in this way. Quail are quite small birds, weighing 115–150g/4–5oz, but with a surprising amount of meat. One bird will usually make a substantial single portion. The meat has quite a delicate flavour and can dry out easily, so this is an especially good way of cooking quail. Wild quail is no longer available, but fresh or frozen Japanese quail is widely available from many supermarkets.

Spiced Honey Chicken Wings

Be prepared to get very sticky when you eat these wings, as the best way to enjoy them is by eating them with your fingers. Provide individual finger bowls for your guests.

Serves 4

1 fresh red chilli, finely chopped
5ml/1 tsp chilli powder
5ml/1 tsp ground ginger
rind of 1 lime, finely grated
12 chicken wings
60ml/4 tbsp sunflower oil
15ml/1 tbsp chopped fresh coriander
30ml/2 tbsp soy sauce
50ml/3½ tbsp clear honey

1 Mix the fresh chilli, chilli powder, ground ginger and lime rind together in a small bowl. Place the chicken wings in a wide, shallow dish. Rub the spice mixture into the chicken skins and leave for at least 2 hours to allow the flavours to penetrate.

2 Heat a wok or heavy-based frying pan and add half the oil. When the oil is hot, add half the wings and stir-fry for 10 minutes, turning regularly until crisp and golden. Drain on kitchen paper. Repeat with the remaining oil and wings.

3 Add the coriander to the hot wok and stir-fry for 30 seconds, then return the wings to the wok and stir-fry for 1 minute.

4 Stir in the soy sauce and honey and stir-fry for 1 minute. Serve the chicken wings hot, with the sauce drizzled over them.

Cook's Tip

These wings are perfect party food, as they are inexpensive, take little time to cook and are easy to nibble. For a more filling meal, use the same flavourings for chicken drumsticks, but cook under the grill for 12–15 minutes, turning frequently, until cooked through and golden.

Cajun-spiced Chicken

These chicken breast fillets are seared in a very hot frying pan which, for best results, should be of heavy cast iron and well seasoned.

Serves 6

6 medium chicken breast fillets, skinned
75g/3oz/6 tbsp butter or margarine
5ml/1 tsp garlic powder
10ml/2 tsp onion powder
5ml/2 tsp cayenne pepper
10ml/2 tsp paprika
7.5ml/1½ tsp salt
2.5ml/½ tsp freshly ground white pepper
5ml/1 tsp freshly ground black pepper
1.5ml/¼ tsp ground cumin
5ml/1 tsp dried thyme
salad leaves and pepper strips, to garnish

1 Slice each chicken breast in half horizontally, making two pieces of about the same thickness. Flatten them slightly with the heel of your hand. Lay them on a large plate or place in a shallow dish.

2 Melt the butter or margarine in a small saucepan over a low heat without letting it colour.

3 Combine all the remaining ingredients, apart from the garnish, in a bowl and stir to blend well. Brush the chicken pieces on both sides with a little of the melted butter or margarine, then sprinkle evenly with the seasoning mixture.

4 Heat a large, heavy-based frying pan over a high heat for about 5–8 minutes, until a drop of water sprinkled on the surface sizzles.

5 Drizzle 5ml/1 tsp melted butter on to each chicken piece. Place them carefully in the frying pan in an even layer, two or three at a time, and cook for 2–3 minutes, until the underside begins to blacken. Turn and cook the other side for 2–3 minutes more. Serve hot, garnished with salad leaves and pepper strips.

Caribbean Fried Chicken

This crispy chicken is superb hot or cold. Served with a salad or vegetables, it makes a delicious lunch and is ideal for picnics and snacks too.

Serves 4–6

4 chicken drumsticks
4 chicken thighs
10ml/2 tsp curry powder
2.5ml/ ½ tsp garlic granules
2.5ml/ ½ tsp freshly ground black pepper
2.5ml/ ½ tsp paprika
about 300ml/ ½ pint/ 1¼ cups milk
oil, for deep frying
50g/2oz/ ½ cup plain flour
salt
mixed salad, to serve

1 Place the chicken pieces in a large bowl and sprinkle with the curry powder, garlic granules, black pepper, paprika and salt to taste. Rub the spices well into the chicken, then cover and leave to marinate in a cool place for at least 2 hours, or overnight in the fridge.

2 Preheat the oven to 180°C/350°F/Gas 4. Pour enough milk into the bowl to cover the chicken and leave to stand for a further 15 minutes.

3 Heat the oil in a large, heavy-based saucepan or deep-fat fryer. Tip the flour on to a plate. Shake off excess milk from the chicken and dip each piece in the flour, turning it to coat well. Fry two or three pieces at a time until golden but not cooked. Continue until all the chicken pieces are fried.

4 Remove the chicken pieces from the oil using a slotted spoon and place on a baking sheet. Bake in the oven for about 30 minutes. Serve hot or cold with mixed salad.

Variation
This recipe would work just as well with turkey breasts, but would require only 15–20 minutes cooking time in the oven.

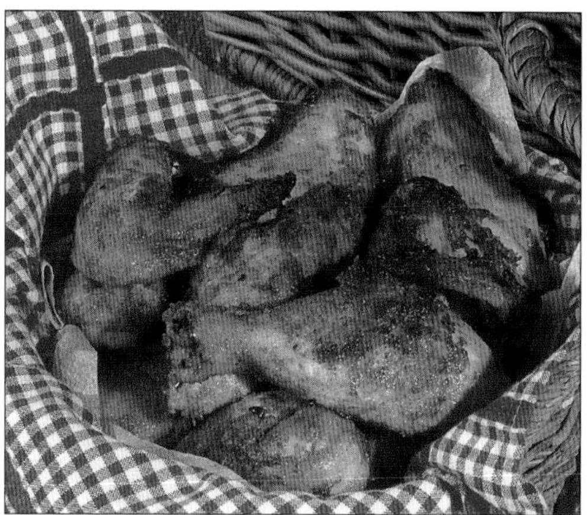

Spicy Fried Chicken

Chicken portions are soaked in buttermilk before they are coated with spiced flour and fried.

Serves 4

120ml/4fl oz/ ½ cup buttermilk
1.3kg/3lb chicken portions
vegetable oil, for frying
50g/2oz/ ½ cup plain flour
15ml/1 tbsp paprika
1.5ml/ ¼ tsp pepper
15ml/1 tbsp water

1 Pour the buttermilk into a large bowl and add the chicken pieces. Stir to coat, then set aside for 5 minutes.

2 Heat 5mm/¼in depth of oil in a large frying pan over a medium-high heat. Do not let the oil overheat.

3 In a bowl or polythene bag, combine the flour, paprika and pepper. One by one, lift the chicken pieces out of the buttermilk and dip into the flour to coat well all over, shaking off any excess.

4 Add the chicken pieces to the hot oil and fry for about 10 minutes until lightly browned, turning them over halfway through the cooking time.

5 Reduce the heat to low and add the water to the frying pan. Cover and cook for 30 minutes, turning the pieces over at 10-minute intervals. Uncover the pan and continue cooking for about 15 minutes until the chicken is very tender and the coating is crisp, turning every 5 minutes. Serve hot.

Cook's Tip
Buttermilk, available from supermarkets, is a by-product of the butter-making process. Nowadays, it is more often cultured skimmed milk produced under controlled conditions, which make it more stable.

Chicken Stir-fry with Five Spices

The chicken is marinated in an aromatic blend of spices and stir-fried with crisp vegetables. If you find it too spicy, serve with a spoonful of soured cream or yogurt.

Serves 4

2.5ml/ ½ tsp each ground turmeric and ground ginger
5ml/1 tsp each salt and freshly ground black pepper
10ml/2 tsp ground cumin
15ml/1 tbsp ground coriander
15ml/1 tbsp caster sugar
450g/1lb chicken breast fillets, skinned
1 bunch spring onions
4 celery sticks
2 red peppers, seeded
1 yellow pepper, seeded
175g/6oz courgettes
175g/6oz mangetouts or sugar snap peas
about 45ml/3 tbsp sunflower oil
15ml/1 tbsp lime juice
15ml/1 tbsp clear honey

1 Mix together the turmeric, ginger, salt, pepper, cumin, coriander and sugar in a bowl until well combined. Cut the chicken into bite-size strips. Add to the spice mixture and stir to coat the chicken pieces thoroughly. Set aside.

2 Prepare the vegetables. Cut the spring onions, celery and peppers into 5cm/2in long, thin strips. Cut the courgettes at a slight angle into thin rounds, and top and tail the mangetouts or sugar snap peas.

3 Heat 30ml/2 tbsp oil in a large, heavy-based frying pan or wok. Stir-fry the chicken in batches until cooked through and golden brown, adding a little more oil if necessary. Remove the chicken from the pan and keep warm.

4 Add a little more oil to the pan and cook the onions, celery, peppers and courgettes over a medium heat for about 8–10 minutes until beginning to soften and turn golden. Add the mangetouts or sugar snap peas and cook for a further 2 minutes.

5 Return the chicken to the pan, with the lime juice and honey. Cook for 2 minutes. Adjust the seasoning and serve.

Spiced Chicken Sauté

A rich tomato sauce coats this chicken, which is first oven-cooked or fried.

Serves 4

1.5kg/3½ lb chicken, cut into 8 pieces
5ml/1 tsp each salt and freshly ground black pepper
2 garlic cloves, crushed
sunflower oil
sliced fresh red chilli and deep-fried onions, to garnish (optional)
boiled rice, to serve

For the sauce

25g/1oz/2 tbsp butter
30ml/2 tbsp sunflower oil
1 onion, sliced
4 garlic cloves, crushed
2 large ripe beefsteak tomatoes, chopped, or 400g/14oz can chopped tomatoes with chilli, drained
600ml/1 pint/2½ cups water
50ml/2fl oz/ ¼ cup dark soy sauce
salt and freshly ground black pepper

1 Preheat the oven to 190°C/375°F/Gas 5. Make two slashes in the fleshy part of each chicken piece. Rub well with the salt, pepper and garlic. Drizzle with a little oil and bake for 30 minutes until brown. Alternatively, shallow fry in hot oil for 12–15 minutes.

2 To make the sauce, heat the butter and oil in a wok or frying pan, and fry the onion and garlic until soft. Add the tomatoes, water, soy sauce and seasoning. Boil briskly for 5 minutes to reduce the sauce and concentrate the flavour.

3 Add the chicken to the sauce in the wok. Turn the chicken pieces over in the sauce to coat them well. Continue cooking slowly for about 20 minutes until the chicken pieces are tender. Stir the mixture occasionally.

4 Arrange the chicken on a warmed serving platter and garnish with the sliced chilli and deep-fried onions, if using. Serve with boiled rice.

Deep-fried Onions

A traditional garnish and accompaniment to many Indonesian dishes. Asian stores sell them ready-prepared, but it is simple to make them at home.

Makes 450g/1lb

450g/1lb onions
oil, for deep frying

1 Peel the onions and slice as evenly and thinly as possible. Spread out on kitchen paper, in an airy place, and set aside to dry for 30 minutes to 2 hours.

2 Heat the oil in a deep-fat fryer or wok to 190°C/375°F and fry the onions in batches until crisp and golden, turning constantly. Drain well on kitchen paper and allow to cool. Store in an airtight container for 2–3 days.

Adobo of Chicken & Pork

Four ingredients are essential in an adobo, one of the best-loved recipes in the Filipino repertoire: vinegar, garlic, peppercorns and bay leaves.

Serves 4

1.3kg/3lb chicken or 4 chicken quarters
350g/12oz pork leg steaks
10ml/2 tsp sugar
60ml/4 tbsp sunflower oil
75ml/5 tbsp wine vinegar or cider vinegar
4 plump garlic cloves, crushed
2.5ml/ ½ tsp black peppercorns, lightly crushed
15ml/1 tbsp light soy sauce
4 bay leaves
2.5ml/ ½ tsp annatto seeds, soaked in 30ml/2 tbsp boiling water, or 2.5ml/ ½ tsp ground turmeric
salt

For the plantain chips

vegetable oil, for deep frying
1–2 large plantains and/or 1 sweet potato

1 Wipe the chicken and cut into eight pieces, or halve the chicken quarters, if using. Cut the pork into neat pieces. Spread the meat out on a board, sprinkle lightly with sugar and set aside.

2 Heat the oil in a wok or large frying pan, and fry the chicken and pork pieces, in batches if necessary, until golden all over.

3 Add the vinegar, garlic, peppercorns, soy sauce and bay leaves and stir well. Strain the annatto seed liquid and stir it into the pan or stir in the turmeric. Add salt to taste. Bring to the boil, cover, lower the heat and simmer for 30–35 minutes. Remove the lid and simmer for 10 minutes more.

4 Meanwhile, to make the plantain chips, heat the oil in a deep-fat fryer to 195°C/383°F. Peel the plantains and/or sweet potato and slice into rounds or chips. Deep fry them, in batches if necessary, until cooked but not brown. Drain on kitchen paper.

5 When ready to serve, reheat the oil and fry the plantains or sweet potato until crisp. Drain. Spoon the adobo into a serving dish and serve with the chips.

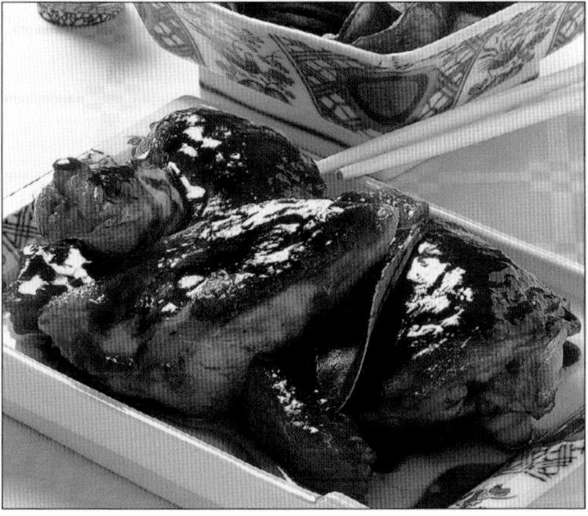

Chicken & Olives

A whole chicken is simmered gently with fresh root ginger, paprika and saffron, and finished with lemon juice and green and black olives.

Serves 4

30ml/2 tbsp olive oil
1.5kg/3½ lb chicken
1 large onion, sliced
15ml/1 tbsp grated fresh root ginger
3 garlic cloves, crushed
5ml/1 tsp paprika
250ml/8fl oz/1 cup Chicken Stock
2–3 saffron strands, soaked in 15ml/1 tbsp boiling water
4–5 spring onions, chopped
15–20 black and green olives, stoned
juice of ½ lemon
salt and freshly ground black pepper
boiled rice and mixed salad, to serve

1 Heat the oil in a large saucepan or flameproof casserole. Add the chicken and sauté until golden on all sides.

2 Add the onion, ginger, garlic and paprika, and season to taste with salt and pepper. Continue to fry over a moderate heat, coating the chicken with the mixture.

3 Add the chicken stock and saffron, and bring to the boil. Cover, lower the heat and simmer gently for 45 minutes.

4 Add the spring onions and cook for a further 15 minutes until the chicken is well cooked and the sauce is reduced to about 120ml/4fl oz/ ½ cup. The chicken juices should run clear when the thickest part of the thigh is pierced with a skewer or the point of a sharp knife. Add the olives and lemon juice, and cook for a further 5 minutes.

5 Transfer the chicken to a large, deep serving plate and pour over the sauce. Serve with rice and a mixed salad.

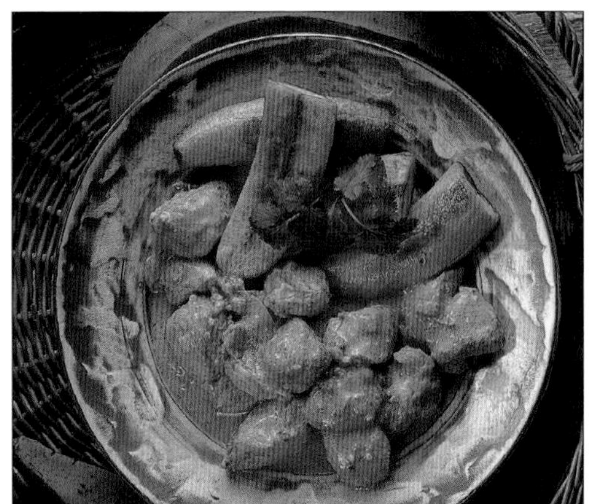

Peanut Chicken

In this Caribbean dish the rich, nutty sauce is best made from smooth peanut butter, though it can also be made with crushed peanuts.

Serves 4

900g/2lb chicken breast fillets, skinned and cut into pieces
2 garlic cloves, crushed
2.5ml/ ½ tsp dried thyme
2.5ml/ ½ tsp freshly ground black pepper
15ml/1 tbsp curry powder
15ml/1 tbsp lemon juice
25g/1oz/2 tbsp butter or margarine
1 onion, chopped
45ml/3 tbsp chopped tomatoes
1 fresh hot chilli, chopped
30ml/2 tbsp smooth peanut butter
about 450ml/ ¾ pint/scant 2 cups warm water
salt
fresh coriander sprigs, to garnish
fried plantain, to serve

1 Place the chicken pieces in a large bowl and stir in the garlic, thyme, pepper, curry powder, lemon juice and a little salt. Cover loosely with clear film and leave to marinate in a cool place for a few hours.

2 Melt the butter or margarine in a large saucepan, add the onion and sauté gently for 5 minutes. Add the seasoned chicken and fry over a medium heat for 10 minutes, turning frequently. Stir in the tomatoes and chilli.

3 Blend the peanut butter with a little of the warm water to a smooth paste and stir into the chicken mixture.

4 Slowly stir in the remaining water, then simmer gently for about 30 minutes, adding a little more water if necessary. Garnish with coriander sprigs and serve with fried plantain.

Variation
You could substitute lime juice for the lemon juice and add 5ml/1 tsp ground allspice with the curry powder.

Chicken Sauce Piquante

Cajun Sauce Piquante is based on the brown Cajun *roux* and has chilli peppers to give it heat: vary the heat by the number you use.

Serves 4

4 chicken legs or 2 legs and 2 breasts
75ml/5 tbsp cooking oil
50g/2oz/ ½ cup plain flour
1 medium onion, chopped
2 celery sticks, sliced
1 green pepper, seeded and diced
2 garlic cloves, crushed
1 bay leaf
2.5ml/ ½ tsp dried thyme
2.5ml/ ½ tsp dried oregano
1–2 fresh red chilli peppers, seeded and finely chopped
400g/14oz can chopped tomatoes, with their juice
300ml/ ½ pint/1 ¼ cups Chicken Stock
salt and freshly ground black pepper
watercress, to garnish
boiled potatoes, to serve

1 Halve the chicken legs through the joint, or the breasts across the middle, to give 8 pieces. In a heavy-based frying pan, fry the chicken pieces in the oil until brown on all sides, lifting them out and setting them aside as they are done.

2 Strain the oil from the pan into a flameproof casserole. Heat it and stir in the flour. Stir constantly over a low heat until the *roux* is the colour of peanut butter. Immediately the *roux* reaches the right stage, tip in the onion, celery and green pepper, and stir over the heat for 2–3 minutes.

3 Add the garlic, bay leaf, thyme, oregano and chilli pepper(s). Stir for 1 minute, then turn down the heat and stir in the tomatoes with their juice.

4 Return the casserole to the heat and gradually stir in the stock. Add the chicken pieces, cover and simmer for 45 minutes until the chicken is tender.

5 If there is too much sauce or it is too runny, remove the lid for the last 10–15 minutes of the cooking time and raise the heat a little. Adjust the seasoning to taste and serve, garnished with watercress and accompanied by boiled potatoes.

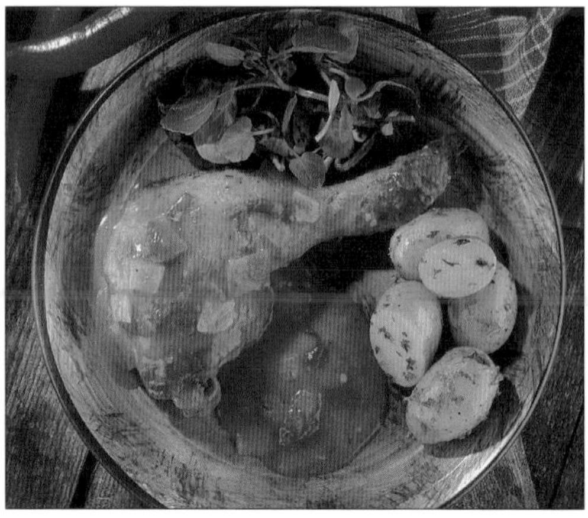

Chicken Bobotie

Perfect for a buffet party, this mild curry dish is set with savoury custard, which makes serving easy.

Serves 8

2 thick slices white bread
450ml/¾ pint/scant 2 cups milk
30ml/2 tbsp olive oil
2 medium onions, finely chopped
40ml/2½ tbsp medium curry powder
1.2kg/2½ lb minced chicken
15ml/1 tbsp apricot jam, chutney or caster sugar
30ml/2 tbsp wine vinegar or lemon juice
3 large eggs, beaten
50g/2oz/⅓ cup raisins or sultanas
butter, for greasing
12 almonds
salt and freshly ground black pepper
boiled rice, to serve

1 Preheat the oven to 180°C/350°F/Gas 4. Soak the bread in 150ml/¼ pint/⅔ cup of the milk.

2 Heat the oil in a frying pan and fry the onions until tender. Add the curry powder and cook for a further 2 minutes.

3 Add the minced chicken and brown all over, stirring to break up any lumps. Remove from the heat, season and add the apricot jam, chutney or caster sugar and vinegar or lemon juice.

4 Mash the bread in the milk and add to the pan together with one of the beaten eggs and the raisins or sultanas.

5 Grease a 1.5 litre/2½ pint/6¼ cup shallow ovenproof dish with butter. Spoon in the chicken mixture and level the top. Cover with buttered foil and bake in the oven for 30 minutes.

6 Meanwhile, beat the remaining eggs with the rest of the milk. Remove the dish from the oven and lower the temperature to 150°C/300°F/Gas 2. Break up the meat using two forks and pour over the beaten egg mixture. Scatter the almonds over the top and return to the oven to bake, uncovered, for 30 minutes until set and golden brown all over. Serve immediately with rice.

Tagine of Chicken

Based on a traditional Moroccan recipe, this spicy chicken stew is served with vegetable couscous.

Serves 8

30ml/2 tbsp olive oil
8 chicken legs, cut in half
1 medium onion, finely chopped
2 garlic cloves, crushed
5ml/1 tsp ground turmeric
2.5ml/½ tsp ground ginger
2.5ml/½ tsp ground cinnamon
450ml/¾ pint/scant 2 cups Chicken Stock
150g/5oz/1¼ cups stoned green olives
1 lemon, sliced
salt and freshly ground black pepper
fresh coriander sprigs, to garnish

For the vegetable couscous

600ml/1 pint/2½ cups Chicken Stock
450g/1lb/2⅔ cups couscous
4 courgettes, thickly sliced
2 carrots, thickly sliced
2 small turnips, cubed
45ml/3 tbsp olive oil
425g/15oz can chick-peas, drained
15ml/1 tbsp chopped fresh coriander

1 Preheat the oven to 180°C/350°F/Gas 4. Heat the oil in a flameproof casserole and brown the chicken all over. Remove from the casserole and keep warm. Add the onion and garlic to the casserole and cook until tender. Add the spices and cook for 1 minute. Pour in the stock and bring to the boil. Return the chicken to the casserole. Cover and bake for 45 minutes.

2 Transfer the chicken to a bowl, cover and keep warm. Skim any fat from the cooking liquid and boil to reduce by one third.

3 Meanwhile, blanch the olives and lemon slices in a pan of boiling water for 2 minutes. Drain and add to the cooking liquid in the casserole. Adjust the seasoning to taste.

4 To make the vegetable couscous, bring the stock to the boil in a large pan and sprinkle in the couscous slowly, stirring. Remove from the heat, cover and set aside for 5 minutes. Cook the vegetables, drain and place in a bowl. Add the couscous, oil and seasoning. Stir the grains and add the remaining ingredients. Garnish, and serve the couscous with the chicken and sauce.

Chicken Thighs Wrapped in Bacon

These tasty chicken "parcels" are first marinated and then baked in a spicy garlic and citrus sauce.

Serves 4

16 bacon rashers, rinded
8 chicken thighs, skinned
cooked rice, to serve

For the marinade

finely grated rind and juice of 1 orange
finely grated rind and juice of 1 lime
5 garlic cloves, finely chopped
15ml/1 tbsp chilli powder
15ml/1 tbsp paprika
5ml/1 tsp ground cumin
2.5ml/½ tsp dried oregano
15ml/1 tbsp olive oil

1 To make the marinade, combine the citrus rind and juice, garlic, chilli powder, paprika, cumin, oregano and olive oil in a small bowl.

2 Wrap 2 rashers of bacon around each chicken thigh in a cross shape. Secure with wooden cocktail sticks. Arrange the wrapped chicken thighs in an ovenproof dish.

3 Pour the marinade over the chicken, cover and leave to stand for 1 hour at room temperature or for several hours in the fridge.

4 Preheat the oven to 190°C/375°F/Gas 5. Place the dish in the oven and bake until the chicken is cooked through and the bacon is crisp: this will take about 40 minutes for small thighs and 1 hour for large thighs. Skim excess fat from the sauce and serve with rice.

Cook's Tip

Chilli powder varies widely in strength, although it is always hot, and some varieties have other spices or herbs added. It is best to buy pure ground chilli powder and add your own flavourings if you want to.

Aromatic Chicken from Madura

An Indonesian dish which is best cooked ahead so that the flavours permeate the chicken flesh, making it even more delicious.

Serves 4

1.5kg/3½lb chicken, cut into quarters, or 4 chicken quarters
5ml/1 tsp sugar
30ml/2 tbsp coriander seeds
10ml/2 tsp cumin seeds
6 whole cloves
2.5ml/½ tsp grated nutmeg
2.5ml/½ tsp ground turmeric
1 small onion
2.5cm/1in piece fresh root ginger, sliced
300ml/½ pint/1¼ cups Chicken Stock or water
salt and freshly ground black pepper
boiled rice and Deep-fried Onions, to serve

1 Cut each chicken quarter in half. Place in a flameproof casserole, sprinkle with sugar and salt, and toss together.

2 Dry-fry the coriander, cumin and whole cloves in a heavy-based frying pan until the spices give off a good aroma. Add the nutmeg and turmeric, and heat briefly. Grind in a food processor or using a pestle and mortar.

3 If using a processor, process the onion and ginger until finely chopped. Otherwise, finely chop the onion and ginger, and pound to a paste using a pestle and mortar. Add the spices and stock or water, and mix well. Season to taste.

4 Pour the mixture over the chicken in the casserole. Cover and cook over a gentle heat for about 45–50 minutes until the chicken pieces are really tender. Serve portions of the chicken, with the sauce, on a bed of boiled rice, scattered with crisp deep-fried onions.

Cook's Tip

Add a large piece of bruised ginger and a small onion to the chicken stock to ensure a good flavour.

Curried Apricot & Chicken Casserole

A mild curried and fruity chicken dish served with almond rice, this makes a good winter meal.

Serves 4

15ml/1 tbsp oil
8 large boned and skinned chicken thighs
1 medium onion, finely chopped
5ml/1 tsp medium curry powder
30ml/2 tbsp plain flour
450ml/ ¾ pint/scant 2 cups Chicken Stock
juice of 1 large orange
8 dried apricots, halved
15ml/1 tbsp sultanas
salt and freshly ground black pepper

For the almond rice

225g/8oz/1 cup cooked rice
15g/½oz/1 tbsp butter
50g/2oz/ ½ cup toasted almonds

1 Preheat the oven to 190°C/375°F/Gas 5. Heat the oil in a large frying pan. Cut the chicken into cubes and brown quickly all over in the oil. Add the onion and cook gently until soft and lightly browned.

2 Transfer to a large, flameproof casserole, sprinkle in the curry powder and cook again for a few minutes. Add the flour, and blend in the stock and orange juice. Bring to the boil and season with salt and pepper.

3 Add the apricots and sultanas, cover and cook in the oven for 1 hour or until tender. Adjust the seasoning to taste.

4 To make the almond rice, reheat the precooked rice with the butter and season to taste. Stir in the toasted almonds. Serve with the chicken.

Variation

This recipe would also work well with diced turkey breast or other boneless turkey meat.

Spiced Chicken & Apricot Pie

This pie is unusually sweet-sour and very moreish. Use boneless turkey instead of chicken if you wish, or even some leftovers from a roast turkey – the dark, moist leg meat is best.

Serves 6

30ml/2 tbsp sunflower oil
1 large onion, chopped
450g/1lb boneless chicken, roughly chopped
15ml/1 tbsp curry paste or powder
30ml/2 tbsp apricot or peach chutney
115g/4oz/ ½ cup ready-to-eat dried apricots, halved
115g/4oz cooked carrots, sliced
5ml/1 tsp dried mixed herbs
60ml/4 tbsp crème fraîche
350g/12oz ready-made shortcrust pastry
a little egg or milk, to glaze
salt and freshly ground black pepper
cooked vegetables, to serve

1 Heat the oil in a large, heavy-based frying pan and fry the onion and chicken until just colouring. Add the curry paste or powder and fry, stirring constantly, for 2 minutes more.

2 Add the chutney, apricots, carrots, herbs and crème fraîche to the pan, and season to taste with salt and pepper. Mix well, then transfer to a deep 900ml–1.2 litre/1½–2 pint/3¾–5 cup pie dish.

3 Preheat the oven to 190°C/375°F/Gas 5. Roll out the pastry to 2.5cm/1in wider than the pie dish. Cut a strip of pastry from the edge. Dampen the rim of the dish, press on the strip, then brush this strip with water and place the sheet of pastry on top. Press to seal and trim to fit.

4 Use the pastry trimmings to decorate the top of the pie if you wish. Brush all over with beaten egg or milk, to glaze, and bake in the oven for 40 minutes until crisp and golden. Serve hot with vegetables.

Chicken with Turmeric

Colourful, aromatic and creamy, this is a perfect dish to serve to guests for an informal supper.

Serves 4

1.5kg/3½lb chicken, cut into 8 pieces, or 4 chicken quarters, each halved
15ml/1 tbsp sugar
3 macadamia nuts or 6 almonds
2 garlic cloves, crushed
1 large onion, quartered
2.5cm/1in piece fresh galangal, peeled and sliced, or 5ml/1 tsp powdered galangal
1–2 lemon grass stalks, lower 5cm/2in sliced, top bruised
1cm/½in cube terasi (fermented shrimp paste)
4cm/1½in piece fresh turmeric, peeled and sliced, or 15ml/1 tbsp ground turmeric
15ml/1 tbsp tamarind pulp, soaked in 150ml/¼ pint/⅔ cup warm water
60–90ml/4–6 tbsp oil
400ml/14fl oz/1⅔ cups coconut milk
salt and freshly ground black pepper
Deep-fried Onions, to garnish

1 Rub the chicken joints with a little sugar and set them aside.

2 Grind the nuts and garlic in a food processor with the onion, galangal, sliced lemon grass, *terasi* and turmeric. Alternatively, pound the ingredients to a paste using a pestle and mortar. Strain the tamarind pulp and reserve the juice. Discard the contents of the strainer.

3 Heat the oil in a wok or heavy-based frying pan and cook the paste, without browning, until it gives off a spicy aroma. Add the pieces of chicken and toss well in the spices. Add the strained tamarind juice.

4 Spoon the coconut cream off the top of the milk and set it to one side. Add the coconut milk to the pan. Cover and cook for 45 minutes or until the chicken is tender.

5 Just before serving, stir in the reserved coconut cream while bringing to the boil. Season to taste with salt and pepper, and serve at once, garnished with deep-fried onions.

Mole Poblano de Guajolote

This is the greatest festive dish of Mexico, served at any special occasion. The traditional accompaniments are rice, beans, tortillas and guacamole.

Serves 6–8

2.75–3.6kg/6–8lb turkey, cut into serving portions
1 onion, chopped
1 garlic clove, chopped
90ml/6 tbsp lard or corn oil
salt
fresh coriander and 30ml/2 tbsp toasted sesame seeds, to garnish

For the sauce

6 dried ancho chillies
4 dried pasilla chillies
4 dried mulato chillies
1 drained canned chipotle chilli, seeded and chopped (optional)
2 onions, chopped
2 garlic cloves, chopped
450g/1lb tomatoes, peeled and chopped
1 stale tortilla, torn into pieces
50g/2oz/⅓ cup seedless raisins
115g/4oz/1 cup ground almonds
45ml/3 tbsp sesame seeds, ground
5ml/1 tsp ground cinnamon
2.5ml/½ tsp ground anise
1.5ml/¼ tsp ground black peppercorns
60ml/4 tbsp lard or corn oil
40g/1½oz unsweetened chocolate, broken into squares
15ml/1 tbsp sugar
salt and freshly ground black pepper

1 Put the turkey pieces into a large flameproof casserole in one layer. Add the onion, garlic and enough cold water to cover. Season with salt, bring to a gentle simmer, cover and cook for about 1 hour or until the turkey is tender.

2 Lift the turkey out of the casserole and pat dry with kitchen paper. Reserve the stock. Heat the lard or oil in a large frying pan and sauté the turkey until lightly browned all over. Transfer to a plate and set aside. Reserve the oil in the pan.

3 Meanwhile, to make the sauce, put the dried chillies in a dry frying pan over a gentle heat and roast them for a few minutes, shaking the pan frequently. Remove the stems and shake out the seeds. Tear the pods into pieces and put these into a small bowl. Add sufficient warm water just to cover and soak, turning from time to time, for 30 minutes until soft.

4 Tip the chillies with their soaking water into a food processor. Add the *chipotle* chilli, if using, with the onions, garlic, tomatoes, tortilla, raisins, ground almonds, ground sesame seeds and spices. Process to a purée. Do this in batches if necessary.

5 Add the lard or oil to the fat remaining in the frying pan used for sautéing the turkey. Heat the mixture, then add the chilli and spice paste. Cook, stirring, for 5 minutes.

6 Transfer the cooked spice mixture to the casserole in which the turkey was originally cooked. Stir in 475ml/16fl oz/2 cups of the reserved turkey stock (make it up with water if necessary). Add the chocolate, and season with salt and pepper. Cook over a low heat until the chocolate has melted. Stir in the sugar. Add the turkey to the casserole and more stock if needed. Cover and simmer very gently for 30 minutes. Serve, garnished with fresh coriander and sprinkled with toasted sesame seeds.

Simple Chicken Curry

Curry powder can be bought in three different strengths – mild, medium and hot. Use the type you prefer to suit your taste.

Serves 4

8 chicken legs (thighs and drumsticks)
30ml/2 tbsp olive oil
1 onion, thinly sliced
1 garlic clove, crushed
15ml/1 tbsp medium curry powder
15ml/1 tbsp plain flour
450ml/ ¾ pint/scant 2 cups Chicken Stock
1 beefsteak tomato
15ml/1 tbsp mango chutney
15ml/1 tbsp lemon juice
salt and freshly ground black pepper
boiled rice, to serve

1 Cut the chicken legs in half. Heat the oil in a large, flameproof casserole and brown the chicken on all sides. Remove from the casserole and keep warm.

2 Add the onion and garlic to the casserole and cook over a fairly low heat until tender. Add the curry powder and cook gently for 2 minutes, stirring.

3 Stir in the flour and gradually blend in the stock. Season to taste with salt and pepper. Bring to the boil, return the chicken pieces to the casserole, cover and simmer for 20–30 minutes or until tender.

4 Peel the tomato by blanching in boiling water for 15 seconds, then plunging into cold water to loosen the skin. Peel and cut into small cubes, discarding the seeds.

5 Add the tomato to the chicken, with the mango chutney and lemon juice. Heat through gently and adjust the seasoning to taste. Serve with plenty of boiled rice.

Chicken Korma

A korma is a rich, creamy Moghulai dish that originates from northern India. This recipe uses a combination of yogurt and cream which gives the sauce a delicious, subtle flavour.

Serves 4

675g/1½lb chicken breast fillets, skinned
25g/1oz/ ¼ cup blanched almonds
2 garlic cloves, crushed
2.5cm/1in piece fresh root ginger, peeled and roughly chopped
30ml/2 tbsp oil
3 green cardamom pods
1 onion, finely chopped
10ml/2 tsp ground cumin
1.5ml/ ¼ tsp salt
150ml/ ¼ pint/ ⅔ cup plain yogurt
175ml/6fl oz/ ¾ cup single cream
toasted flaked almonds and fresh coriander, to garnish
boiled rice, to serve

1 Cut the chicken breasts into 2.5cm/1in cubes. Put the almonds, garlic and ginger into a food processor or blender with 30ml/2 tbsp water, and process to a smooth paste.

2 Heat the oil in a large frying pan and fry the chicken for 8–10 minutes or until browned. Remove using a slotted spoon and set aside.

3 Add the cardamom pods to the pan and fry for 2 minutes. Add the onion and fry for a further 5 minutes.

4 Stir in the almond and garlic paste, cumin and salt, and cook, stirring, for a further 5 minutes.

5 Add the yogurt, a tablespoonful at a time, and cook over a low heat, until it has all been absorbed. Return the chicken to the pan. Cover and simmer over a low heat for 5–6 minutes or until the chicken is tender.

6 Add the cream and simmer for a further 5 minutes. Serve with boiled rice and garnish with toasted flaked almonds and fresh coriander.

Moghul-style Chicken

This delicate curry can be served as a starter followed by stronger curries and rice. Saffron is a crucial ingredient, but as it is very expensive, save the dish for special occasions.

Serves 4–6

4 chicken breasts, rubbed with a little garam masala
2 eggs, beaten with salt and pepper
90ml/6 tbsp ghee or melted butter
1 large onion, finely chopped
5cm/2in piece fresh root ginger, peeled and crushed
4 garlic cloves, crushed
4 cloves
4 green cardamoms
5cm/2in cinnamon stick
2 bay leaves
15–20 saffron strands
150ml/ ¼ pint/ ⅔ cup plain yogurt, beaten with 5ml/ 1 tsp cornflour
salt
75ml/5 tbsp double cream
50g/2oz/ ½ cup ground almonds

1 Brush the chicken breasts with the beaten eggs. Heat the ghee or butter in a frying pan and fry the chicken. Remove from the pan and keep warm.

2 In the remaining fat, fry the onion, ginger, garlic, cloves, cardamoms, cinnamon and bay leaves. When the onion turns golden, remove the pan from the heat, allow to cool a little and stir in the saffron and yogurt.

3 Return the chicken to the pan with any juices and gently cook until the chicken is tender. Taste and adjust the seasoning as necessary.

4 Just before serving, fold in the cream and ground almonds. Serve hot.

Cook's Tip
If you don't have time to make your own ghee, clarified butter and vegetable ghee are available from Indian foodstores and supermarkets.

Special Chicken Curry

Chicken curry is always popular when served at a family dinner. This version is cooked covered, giving a thin consistency. If you would prefer it thicker, cook uncovered for the last 15 minutes.

Serves 4–6

60ml/4 tbsp vegetable oil
4 cloves
4–6 green cardamoms
5cm/2in cinnamon stick
3 whole star anise
6–8 curry leaves
1 large onion, finely chopped
5cm/2in piece fresh root ginger, crushed
4 garlic cloves, crushed
60ml/4 tbsp mild curry paste
5ml/1 tsp ground turmeric
5ml/1 tsp five-spice powder
1.3kg/3lb chicken, skinned and jointed
400g/14oz can chopped tomatoes
115g/4oz block creamed coconut
2.5ml/ ½ tsp sugar
50g/2oz/1 cup fresh coriander, chopped
salt

1 Heat the oil in a frying pan and fry the cloves, cardamoms, cinnamon stick, star anise and curry leaves until the cloves swell and the curry leaves are slightly burnt.

2 Add the onion, ginger and garlic, and fry until the onion turns brown. Add the curry paste, turmeric and five-spice powder, and fry until the oil separates.

3 Add the chicken pieces and mix well. When all the pieces are evenly sealed, cover and cook until the meat is nearly done.

4 Add the chopped tomatoes and the creamed coconut. Simmer gently until the coconut dissolves. Mix well, add the sugar and salt to taste. Fold in the coriander leaves, reheat gently and serve hot.

Cook's Tip
Indian five-spice powder is different from Chinese. Make sure you buy Indian.

Tandoori Chicken

A popular party dish. The chicken is marinated the night before, so all you have to do on the day is to cook it in a very hot oven and serve with wedges of lemon and green salad.

Serves 4

1.5kg/3½lb chicken, cut into 8 pieces
juice of 1 large lemon
150ml/¼ pint/⅔ cup plain yogurt
3 garlic cloves, crushed
30ml/2 tbsp olive oil
5ml/1 tsp ground turmeric
10ml/2 tsp paprika
5ml/1 tsp grated fresh root ginger or 2.5ml/½ tsp ground ginger
10ml/2 tsp garam masala
5ml/1 tsp salt
a few drops of red food colouring (optional)
green salad and lemon wedges, to serve

1 Skin the chicken pieces and cut two slits in each piece. Arrange in a single layer in a non-metallic dish and pour over the lemon juice.

2 Mix together the remaining ingredients and pour over the chicken pieces, turning them to coat thoroughly. Cover with clear film and chill overnight.

3 Preheat the oven to 220°C/425°F/Gas 7. Remove the chicken from the marinade and arrange in a single layer in a shallow ovenproof dish. Bake in the oven for 15 minutes, then turn over and cook for a further 15 minutes or until tender.

4 Serve hot with green salad, plus lemon wedges for squeezing.

Cook's Tip
The red colour of tandoori chicken is traditional, but some people are allergic to food colouring. Fortunately, omitting it has no effect upon the flavour of the dish.

Fragrant Chicken Curry

Tender pieces of chicken breast are lightly cooked with fresh vegetables and aromatic spices in the traditional Balti style.

Serves 4

675g/1½lb chicken breast fillets, skinned
30ml/2 tbsp oil
2.5ml/½ tsp cumin seeds
2.5ml/½ tsp fennel seeds
1 onion, thickly sliced
2 garlic cloves, crushed
2.5cm/1in piece fresh root ginger, finely chopped
15ml/1 tbsp curry paste
225g/8oz broccoli, broken into florets
4 tomatoes, cut into thick wedges
5ml/1 tsp garam masala
30ml/2 tbsp chopped fresh coriander
naan bread, to serve

1 Remove any fat from the chicken and cut the meat into 2.5cm/1in cubes.

2 Heat the oil in a wok or heavy-based frying pan, and fry the cumin and fennel seeds for 2 minutes until the seeds begin to splutter. Add the onion, garlic and ginger, and cook for 5–7 minutes. Stir in the curry paste and cook for a further 2–3 minutes.

3 Add the broccoli florets and fry for about 5 minutes. Add the chicken cubes and fry for 5–8 minutes.

4 Add the tomatoes, garam masala and chopped coriander. Cook for a further 5–10 minutes or until the chicken is tender. Serve with naan bread.

Cook's Tip
Balti dishes are traditionally cooked – and often served – in a karahi, a pan that is very similar to a wok. Karahis are available in a wide range of sizes.

Chicken with Mild Balti Spices

This recipe has a beautifully delicate flavour and is probably the most popular of all Balti dishes.

Serves 4–6

45ml/3 tbsp corn oil
3 medium onions, sliced
3 medium tomatoes, halved and sliced
2.5cm/1in cinnamon stick
2 large black cardamom pods
4 black peppercorns
2.5ml/½ tsp black cumin seeds
5ml/1 tsp grated fresh root ginger
5ml/1 tsp crushed garlic
5ml/1 tsp garam masala
5ml/1 tsp chilli powder
5ml/1 tsp salt
1.3kg/3lb chicken, skinned and cut into 8 pieces
30ml/2 tbsp plain yogurt
60ml/4 tbsp lemon juice
30ml/2 tbsp chopped fresh coriander
2 fresh green chillies, chopped

1 Heat the oil in a wok or heavy-based frying pan. Add the onions and fry until they are golden brown. Add the tomatoes and stir well. Add the cinnamon stick, cardamoms, peppercorns, black cumin seeds, ginger, garlic, garam masala, chilli powder and salt. Lower the heat and stir-fry for 3–5 minutes.

2 Add the chicken pieces, two at a time, and stir-fry for at least 7 minutes or until the spice mixture has completely penetrated the chicken. Add the yogurt and mix well.

3 Lower the heat and cover the pan with a piece of foil, making sure that the foil does not touch the food. Cook very gently for about 15 minutes, checking once to make sure the sauce is not catching on the bottom of the pan. Finally, add the lemon juice, fresh coriander and green chillies, and serve at once.

Cook's Tip
Chicken cooked on the bone is both tender and flavoursome. However, you can substitute the whole chicken with 675g/1½lb boned and cubed chicken, if wished. The cooking time can be reduced at step 3 too.

Balti Butter Chicken

Another favourite mild Balti dish, especially in the West. Cooked in butter, with aromatic spices, cream and almonds, it will be enjoyed by everyone.

Serves 4–6

150ml/¼ pint/⅔ cup plain yogurt
50g/2oz/½ cup ground almonds
7.5ml/1½ tsp chilli powder
1.5ml/¼ tsp crushed bay leaves
1.5ml/¼ tsp ground cloves
1.5ml/¼ tsp ground cinnamon
5ml/1 tsp garam masala
4 green cardamom pods
5ml/1 tsp grated fresh root ginger
5ml/1 tsp crushed garlic
400g/14oz can tomatoes
5ml/1 tsp salt
1kg/2¼lb chicken, skinned, boned and cubed
75g/3oz/6 tbsp butter
15ml/1 tbsp corn oil
2 medium onions, sliced
30ml/2 tbsp chopped fresh coriander
60ml/4 tbsp single cream
fresh coriander sprigs, to garnish

1 Put the yogurt, ground almonds, all the dry spices, the ginger, garlic, tomatoes and salt into a bowl, and blend together.

2 Place the chicken in a large bowl and pour over the yogurt mixture. Set aside.

3 Heat the butter and oil in a medium karahi or deep, round-bottomed frying pan. Add the onions and fry for about 3 minutes.

4 Add the chicken mixture and stir-fry for 7–10 minutes. Stir in about half of the coriander and mix well.

5 Pour over the cream and stir in well. Bring to the boil. Sprinkle with the remaining chopped coriander, garnish with fresh coriander sprigs and serve.

Cook's Tip
Substitute the plain yogurt with Greek-style yogurt for an even richer and creamier flavour.

Chicken Saag

A mildly spiced dish using a popular combination of spinach and chicken. It is best made using fresh spinach, but if this is unavailable, you can substitute frozen. Do not use canned.

Serves 4

225g/8oz spinach leaves, washed but not dried
2.5cm/1in piece fresh root ginger, grated
2 garlic cloves, crushed
1 fresh green chilli, roughly chopped
200ml/7fl oz/scant 1 cup water
30ml/2 tbsp oil
2 bay leaves
1.5ml/¼ tsp black peppercorns
1 onion, finely chopped
4 tomatoes, peeled and finely chopped
10ml/2 tsp curry powder
5ml/1 tsp salt
5ml/1 tsp chilli powder
45ml/3 tbsp plain yogurt
8 chicken thighs, skinned
plain yogurt and chilli powder, to garnish
masala naan bread, to serve

1 Cook the spinach, without water, in a tightly covered saucepan for 5 minutes. Put the spinach, ginger, garlic and chilli with 50ml/2fl oz/¼ cup of the water into a food processor or blender, and process to a thick purée.

2 Heat the oil in a large saucepan, add the bay leaves and peppercorns, and fry for 2 minutes. Add the onion and fry for 6–8 minutes or until the onion has browned.

3 Add the tomatoes and simmer for about 5 minutes. Stir in the curry powder, salt and chilli powder, and cook for 2 minutes.

4 Add the spinach purée and the remaining water, and simmer for 5 minutes. Add the yogurt, 15ml/1 tbsp at a time, and simmer for 5 minutes.

5 Add the chicken. Cover and cook for 25–30 minutes or until the chicken is tender. Serve on masala naan bread, drizzle over some yogurt and dust with chilli powder.

Chicken Dhansak

Dhansak curries originate from the Parsee community and are traditionally made with lentils and meat.

Serves 4

75g/3oz/scant ½ cup green lentils
475ml/16fl oz/2 cups Chicken Stock
45ml/3 tbsp oil
5ml/1 tsp cumin seeds
2 curry leaves
1 onion, finely chopped
2.5cm/1in piece fresh root ginger, chopped
1 fresh green chilli, finely chopped
5ml/1 tsp ground cumin
5ml/1 tsp ground coriander
1.5ml/¼ tsp salt
1.5ml/¼ tsp chilli powder
400g/14oz can chopped tomatoes
8 chicken portions, skinned
60ml/4 tbsp chopped fresh coriander
5ml/1 tsp garam masala
fresh coriander sprigs, to garnish
cooked plain and yellow rice, to serve

1 Rinse the lentils under cold running water. Put them into a large, heavy-based saucepan with the stock. Bring to the boil, lower the heat, cover and simmer for about 15–20 minutes. Set aside without draining.

2 Heat the oil in a large saucepan, and fry the cumin seeds and curry leaves for 2 minutes. Add the onion, ginger and chilli, and fry for about 5 minutes. Stir in the cumin, coriander, salt and chilli powder with 30ml/2 tbsp water.

3 Add the tomatoes and chicken. Cover and cook over a medium heat for 10–15 minutes.

4 Add the lentils and their stock, the fresh coriander and garam masala, and cook for 10 minutes or until the chicken is tender. Garnish with coriander sprigs and serve immediately with plain and yellow rice.

Balti Chicken in a Thick Creamy Coconut Sauce

If you like the flavour of coconut, you will really love this curry, which contains both desiccated coconut and coconut milk.

Serves 4

15ml/1 tbsp ground almonds
15ml/1 tbsp desiccated coconut
85ml/3fl oz/⅓ cup coconut milk
175g/6oz/¾ cup fromage frais
7.5ml/1½ tsp ground coriander
5ml/1 tsp chilli powder
5ml/1 tsp crushed garlic
7.5ml/1½ tsp grated fresh root ginger
5ml/1 tsp salt
15ml/1 tbsp corn oil
225g/8oz boneless chicken, skinned and cubed
3 green cardamom pods
1 bay leaf
1 dried red chilli, crushed
30ml/2 tbsp chopped fresh coriander

1 Using a heavy-based saucepan, dry roast the ground almonds and desiccated coconut until they turn a shade darker. Transfer to a mixing bowl.

2 Add the coconut milk, fromage frais, ground coriander, chilli powder, garlic, ginger and salt to a mixing bowl.

3 Heat the oil in a non-stick wok or frying pan and add the chicken cubes, cardamoms and bay leaf. Stir-fry for about 2 minutes to seal the chicken.

4 Pour in the coconut milk mixture and blend everything together. Lower the heat, add the crushed dried chilli and fresh coriander, cover and cook for 10–12 minutes, stirring occasionally. Uncover, then stir and cook for a further 2 minutes before serving.

Cook's Tip
Cut the chicken into small, equal-size cubes for speedy and even cooking.

Balti Chicken in Hara Masala Sauce

A little fresh and dried fruit with mint, coriander leaves and spring onions flavour the creamy sauce of this chicken dish.

Serves 4

1 crisp green dessert apple, peeled, cored and cut into small cubes
60ml/4 tbsp fresh coriander leaves
30ml/2 tbsp fresh mint leaves
120ml/4fl oz/½ cup plain yogurt
45ml/3 tbsp fromage frais
2 medium fresh green chillies, seeded and chopped
1 bunch spring onions, chopped
5ml/1 tsp salt
5ml/1 tsp sugar
5ml/1 tsp crushed garlic
5ml/1 tsp grated fresh root ginger
15ml/1 tbsp corn oil
225g/8oz chicken breast fillets, skinned and cubed
25g/1oz/¼ cup sultanas

1 Place the apple, 45ml/3 tbsp of the coriander, half the mint, yogurt, fromage frais, chillies, spring onions, salt, sugar, garlic and ginger in a food processor, and process for about 1 minute, using the pulsing action.

2 Heat the oil in a non-stick wok or frying pan, pour in the yogurt mixture and cook over a low heat for about 2 minutes.

3 Add the chicken pieces and blend everything together. Cook over a medium-low heat for 12–15 minutes or until the chicken is fully cooked.

4 Finally, add the sultanas and remaining coriander and mint leaves, and serve immediately.

Cook's Tip
This dish makes a good dinner-party centrepiece.

Jeera Chicken

An aromatic dish with a delicious, distinctive taste of cumin. Serve simply with a cooling cucumber raita.

Serves 4

45ml/3 tbsp cumin seeds
45ml/3 tbsp oil
2.5ml/ ½ tsp black peppercorns
4 green cardamom pods
2 fresh green chillies, finely chopped
2 garlic cloves, crushed
2.5cm/1in piece fresh root ginger, grated
5ml/1 tsp ground coriander
10ml/2 tsp ground cumin
2.5ml/ ½ tsp salt
8 chicken portions, e.g. thighs and drumsticks, skinned
5ml/1 tsp garam masala
fresh coriander and chilli powder, to garnish
cucumber raita, to serve

1 Dry roast 15ml/1 tbsp of the cumin seeds for 5 minutes and set aside.

2 Heat the oil in a large saucepan and fry the remaining cumin seeds, peppercorns and cardamoms for 2–3 minutes. Add the chillies, garlic and ginger, and fry for 2 minutes. Add the ground coriander, cumin and salt, and cook for 2–3 minutes. Add the chicken. Cover and simmer for 20–25 minutes.

3 Add the garam masala and toasted cumin seeds, and cook for a further 5 minutes. Serve with cucumber raita, garnished with chilli powder and fresh coriander.

Cook's Tip

Raitas are very easy to make. For a cucumber raita, mix together 300ml/½ pint/1¼ cups lightly beaten plain yogurt, ½ diced cucumber and 1 seeded and chopped fresh green chilli. Season with salt and a pinch of ground cumin. Cover and chill before serving. For a tomato raita, mix the yogurt with 2 peeled, seeded and finely chopped tomatoes, season with salt and stir in 15ml/1 tbsp chopped fresh coriander.

Chicken in a Spicy Yogurt Marinade

Plan this dish well in advance; the extra-long marinating time is necessary to develop a really mellow, spicy flavour.

Serves 6

6 chicken portions
juice of 1 lemon
5ml/1 tsp salt

For the marinade
5ml/1 tsp coriander seeds
10ml/2 tsp cumin seeds
6 cloves
2 bay leaves
1 onion, quartered
2 garlic cloves
5cm/2in piece fresh root ginger, roughly chopped
2.5ml/ ½ tsp chilli powder
5ml/1 tsp ground turmeric
150ml/ ¼ pint/ ⅔ cup plain yogurt
salad leaves and lemon or lime slices, to serve

1 Skin the chicken portions and make deep slashes in the fleshiest parts with a sharp knife. Place in a dish, sprinkle over the lemon juice and salt, and rub in. Set aside.

2 Spread the coriander and cumin seeds, cloves and bay leaves in the bottom of a large frying pan and dry-fry over a moderate heat until the bay leaves are crispy.

3 Allow the spices to cool, then grind coarsely using a pestle and mortar.

4 Finely mince the onion, garlic and ginger in a food processor or blender. Add the ground spices, the chilli powder, turmeric and yogurt, then strain in the lemon juice from the chicken.

5 Arrange the chicken in a single layer in a roasting tin. Pour over the spice mixture, then cover and leave to marinate for 24–36 hours in the fridge. Turn the chicken pieces occasionally in the marinade.

6 Preheat the oven to 200°C/400°F/Gas 6. Cook the chicken for 45 minutes. Serve hot or cold, with salad leaves and slices of lemon or lime.

Chicken Jalfrezi

A Jalfrezi curry is a stir-fried dish cooked with onions, ginger and garlic in a rich pepper sauce.

Serves 4

675g/1½lb chicken breast fillets, skinned
30ml/2 tbsp oil
5ml/1 tsp cumin seeds
1 onion, finely chopped
1 green pepper, seeded and finely chopped
1 red pepper, seeded and finely chopped
1 garlic clove, crushed
2cm/¾in piece fresh root ginger, finely chopped
15ml/1 tbsp curry paste
1.5ml/¼ tsp chilli powder
5ml/1 tsp ground coriander
5ml/1 tsp ground cumin
2.5ml/½ tsp salt
400g/14oz can chopped tomatoes
30ml/2 tbsp chopped fresh coriander
fresh coriander sprig, to garnish
cooked rice, to serve

1 Remove any visible fat from the chicken and cut the meat into 2.5cm/1in cubes.

2 Heat the oil in a wok or frying pan and fry the cumin seeds for 2 minutes until they splutter. Add the onion, peppers, garlic and ginger, and fry for 6–8 minutes.

3 Add the curry paste and fry for about 2 minutes. Stir in the chilli powder, ground coriander, cumin and salt. Add 15ml/1 tbsp water and fry for a further 2 minutes.

4 Add the chicken and fry for about 5 minutes. Add the tomatoes and chopped fresh coriander. Cover and cook for about 15 minutes or until the chicken is tender. Garnish with coriander and serve with rice.

Cook's Tip

Curry paste is a "wet" blend of spices cooked with oil and vinegar, which helps to preserve them. Many brands are available from supermarkets and Indian foodstores.

Chicken Dopiazza

Dopiazza literally translates as "two onions"; in this chicken dish two types of onions are used at different stages during cooking.

Serves 4

45ml/3 tbsp oil
8 small onions, halved
2 bay leaves
8 green cardamom pods
4 cloves
3 dried red chillies
8 black peppercorns
2 onions, finely chopped
2 garlic cloves, crushed
2.5cm/1in piece fresh root ginger, finely chopped
5ml/1 tsp ground coriander
5ml/1 tsp ground cumin
2.5ml/½ tsp ground turmeric
2.5ml/½ tsp chilli powder
2.5ml/½ tsp salt
4 tomatoes, peeled and finely chopped
120ml/4fl oz/½ cup water
8 chicken pieces, e.g. thighs and drumsticks, skinned
boiled rice, to serve

1 Heat 30ml/2 tbsp of the oil in a large saucepan and fry the small onions for 10 minutes or until golden brown. Remove from the pan and set aside.

2 Add the remaining oil to the pan and fry the bay leaves, cardamoms, cloves, chillies and peppercorns for 2 minutes. Add the chopped onions, garlic and ginger, and fry for 5 minutes. Stir in the ground spices and salt, and cook for 2 minutes.

3 Add the tomatoes and the water, and simmer for 5 minutes until the sauce thickens. Add the chicken and cook for about 15 minutes.

4 Add the reserved small onions, then cover and cook for a further 10 minutes, or until the chicken is tender. Serve with boiled rice.

Chicken & Tomato Balti

If you like tomatoes, you will love this chicken recipe. It makes a semi-dry balti, and is good served with a lentil dish and plain boiled rice.

Serves 4

60ml/4 tbsp corn oil
6 curry leaves
2.5ml/ ½ tsp mixed onion and mustard seeds
8 medium tomatoes, sliced
5ml/1 tsp ground coriander
5ml/1 tsp chilli powder
5ml/1 tsp salt
5ml/1 tsp ground cumin
5ml/1 tsp crushed garlic
675g/1½lb chicken, skinned, boned and cubed
150ml/ ¼ pint/ ⅔ cup water
15ml/1 tbsp sesame seeds, roasted
15ml/1 tbsp chopped fresh coriander

1 Heat the oil in a medium karahi or a deep, round-bottomed frying pan. Add the curry leaves and mixed onion and mustard seeds, and stir thoroughly. Lower the heat slightly and add the sliced tomatoes.

2 While the tomatoes are gently cooking, mix together the ground coriander, chilli powder, salt, ground cumin and garlic in a bowl. Tip the spices on to the tomatoes.

3 Add the chicken pieces and mix together well. Stir-fry for about 5 minutes.

4 Pour on the water and continue cooking, stirring occasionally, until the sauce thickens and the chicken is cooked through.

5 Sprinkle the sesame seeds and fresh coriander over the top of the dish and serve.

Cook's Tip
Although it takes very little time to roast sesame seeds, you may find it more convenient to buy them ready-roasted from an Indian foodstore.

Khara Masala Balti Chicken

Whole spices (*khara*) are used in this recipe, giving it a wonderfully rich flavour. This is a dry dish so it is best served with a refreshing raita and paratha.

Serves 4

3 curry leaves
1.5ml/ ¼ tsp mustard seeds
1.5ml/ ¼ tsp fennel seeds
1.5ml/ ¼ tsp onion seeds
2.5ml/ ½ tsp crushed dried red chillies
2.5ml/ ½ tsp white cumin seeds
1.5ml/ ¼ tsp fenugreek seeds
2.5ml/ ½ tsp crushed pomegranate seeds
5ml/1 tsp salt
5ml/1 tsp grated fresh root ginger
3 garlic cloves, sliced
60ml/4 tbsp corn oil
4 fresh green chillies, slit
1 large onion, sliced
1 medium tomato, sliced
675g/1½lb chicken, skinned, boned and cubed
15ml/1 tbsp chopped fresh coriander

1 Mix together the curry leaves, mustard seeds, fennel seeds, onion seeds, crushed red chillies, cumin seeds, fenugreek seeds, crushed pomegranate seeds and salt in a large bowl. Add the ginger and garlic.

2 Heat the oil in a medium karahi or deep round-bottomed frying pan. Add the spice mixture, then the green chillies. Add the onion and stir-fry over a medium heat for 5–7 minutes.

3 Add the tomato and chicken pieces, and cook over a medium heat for about 7 minutes. The chicken should be cooked through and the sauce reduced.

4 Stir over a medium heat for a further 3–5 minutes, then serve hot, garnished with chopped fresh coriander.

Cook's Tip
Paratha is unleavened bread with a flaky texture rather like chapati. It is available from Indian foodstores.

Balti Chicken with Vegetables

In this recipe the chicken and vegetables are cut into strips, which makes the dish particularly attractive.

Serves 4–6
60ml/4 tbsp corn oil
2 medium onions, sliced
4 garlic cloves, thickly sliced
450g/1lb chicken breast, skinned, boned and cut into strips
5ml/1 tsp salt
30ml/2 tbsp lime juice
3 fresh green chillies, chopped
2 medium carrots, cut into batons
2 medium potatoes, cut into 1cm/½in strips
1 medium courgettes, cut into batons

For the garnish
4 lime slices
15ml/1 tbsp chopped fresh coriander
2 fresh green chillies, cut into strips (optional)

1 Heat the oil in a large karahi or deep, round-bottomed frying pan. Lower the heat slightly and add the onions. Fry until lightly browned.

2 Add half the garlic slices and fry for a few seconds before adding the chicken and salt. Cook, stirring, until all the moisture has evaporated and the chicken is lightly browned.

3 Add the lime juice, chopped chillies and all the vegetables to the pan. Increase the heat and add the rest of the garlic. Stir-fry for 7–10 minutes or until the chicken is cooked through and the vegetables are just tender.

4 Transfer to a serving dish and garnish with the lime slices, chopped coriander and chilli strips, if using.

Cook's Tip
A good rule of thumb – but there are exceptions – is that dark green chillies tend to be hotter than pale green ones and pointed chillies tend to be hotter than those with rounded ends.

Sweet-and-sour Balti Chicken

This dish combines a sweet-and-sour flavour with a creamy texture. It is delicious served with rice or naan bread.

Serves 4
45ml/3 tbsp tomato purée
30ml/2 tbsp Greek-style yogurt
7.5ml/1½ tsp garam masala
5ml/1 tsp chilli powder
5ml/1 tsp crushed garlic
30ml/2 tbsp mango chutney
5ml/1 tsp salt
2.5ml/½ tsp sugar (optional)
60ml/4 tbsp corn oil
675g/1½lb chicken, skinned, boned and cubed
150ml/¼ pint/⅔ cup water
2 fresh green chillies, chopped
30ml/2 tbsp chopped fresh coriander
30ml/2 tbsp single cream

1 Blend together the tomato purée, yogurt, garam masala, chilli powder, garlic, mango chutney, salt and sugar, if using, in a medium mixing bowl.

2 Heat the corn oil in a large karahi or a deep, round-bottomed frying pan. Lower the heat slightly and pour in the spice mixture. Bring to the boil and cook for about 2 minutes, stirring occasionally.

3 Add the chicken pieces and stir until they are well coated. Add the water to thin the sauce slightly. Continue cooking for 5–7 minutes or until the chicken is tender.

4 Finally, add the fresh chillies, coriander and cream, and mix well. Cook for a further 2 minutes until the chicken is cooked through. Serve hot.

Cook's Tip
There is no set recipe for garam masala, but this spice mixture typically contains black cumin seeds, peppercorns, cloves, cinnamon and black cardamom pods.

Balti Chicken with Lentils

This is rather an unusual combination of flavours, but well worth a try. The sour-tasting mango powder gives a delicious tangy flavour to this spicy dish.

Serves 4–6

75g/3oz/scant ½ cup chana dhal (split yellow lentils)
60ml/4 tbsp corn oil
2 medium leeks, chopped
6 large dried red chillies
4 curry leaves
5ml/1 tsp mustard seeds
10ml/2 tsp mango powder
2 medium tomatoes, chopped
2.5ml/ ½ tsp chilli powder
5ml/1 tsp ground coriander
5ml/1 tsp salt
450g/1lb chicken, skinned, boned and cubed
15ml/1 tbsp chopped fresh coriander
paratha, to serve

1 Wash the lentils carefully and remove any stones. Put the lentils into a saucepan with enough water to cover, and boil for about 10 minutes until they are soft but not mushy. Drain and set to one side in a bowl.

2 Heat the oil in a medium karahi or deep, round-bottomed frying pan. Lower the heat slightly and throw in the leeks, dried red chillies, curry leaves and mustard seeds. Stir-fry gently for a few minutes.

3 Add the mango powder, tomatoes, chilli powder, ground coriander, salt and chicken, and stir-fry for 7–10 minutes.

4 Mix in the cooked lentils and fry for a further 2 minutes or until the chicken is cooked right through. Garnish with fresh coriander and serve with paratha.

Cook's Tip
Chana dhal, a split yellow lentil, is available from Asian stores. However, split yellow peas are a good substitute.

Chicken in Spicy Onions

One of the few dishes of India in which onions appear prominently. Chunky onion slices infused with toasted cumin seeds and shredded ginger add a delicious contrast to the flavour of the chicken.

Serves 4–6

1.3kg/3lb chicken, jointed and skinned
2.5ml/ ½ tsp turmeric
2.5ml/ ½ tsp chilli powder
60ml/4 tbsp oil
4 small onions, finely chopped
175g/6oz/2½ cups coriander leaves, coarsely chopped
5cm/2in piece fresh root ginger, finely shredded
2 fresh green chillies, finely chopped
10ml/2 tsp cumin seeds, dry roasted
75ml/5 tbsp plain yogurt
75ml/5 tbsp double cream
2.5ml/ ½ tsp cornflour
salt

1 Rub the chicken joints with the turmeric, chilli powder and salt to taste. Heat the oil in a frying pan and fry the chicken pieces without overlapping until both sides are sealed. Remove from the pan and keep warm.

2 Reheat the oil and fry 3 of the chopped onions, 150g/5oz/ 2¼ cups of the coriander leaves, half the ginger, the green chillies and the cumin seeds until the onions are translucent.

3 Return the chicken to the pan with any juices and mix well. Cover and cook gently for 15 minutes.

4 Remove the pan from the heat and allow to cool a little. Mix together the yogurt, cream and cornflour in a bowl, and gradually fold into the chicken, mixing well.

5 Return the pan to the heat and gently cook until the chicken is tender. Just before serving, stir in the reserved onion, coriander and ginger. Serve hot.

Balti Chicken in Saffron Sauce

A beautifully aromatic chicken dish that is partly cooked in the oven, this is sure to impress your guests.

Serves 4–6

50g/2oz/4 tbsp butter
30ml/2 tbsp corn oil
1.3kg/3lb chicken, skinned and cut into 8 portions
1 medium onion, chopped
5ml/1 tsp crushed garlic
2.5ml/ ½ tsp crushed black peppercorns
2.5ml/ ½ tsp crushed cardamom pods
1.5ml/ ¼ tsp ground cinnamon
7.5ml/1½ tsp chilli powder
150ml/ ¼ pint/ ⅔ cup plain yogurt
50g/2oz/ ½ cup ground almonds
15ml/1 tbsp lemon juice
5ml/1 tsp salt
5ml/1 tsp saffron strands
150ml/ ¼ pint/ ⅔ cup water
150ml/ ¼ pint/ ⅔ cup single cream
30ml/2 tbsp chopped fresh coriander
boiled rice, to serve

1 Preheat the oven to 180°C/350°F/Gas 4. Heat the butter and oil in a medium karahi or deep, round-bottomed frying pan. Add the chicken portions and fry for about 5 minutes until lightly browned. Remove from the pan using a slotted spoon, leaving behind as much of the fat as possible, and set aside.

2 Add the onion to the pan, and fry over a medium heat. Mix together the garlic, peppercorns, cardamom, cinnamon, chilli powder, yogurt, ground almonds, lemon juice, salt and saffron strands in a mixing bowl. When the onions are lightly browned, pour the spice mixture into the pan and stir-fry for about 1 minute. Return the chicken to the pan and continue to stir-fry for a further 2 minutes. Add the water and bring to a simmer.

3 Transfer the contents of the pan to an ovenproof casserole and cover with a lid, or, if using a karahi, cover with foil. Transfer to the oven and cook for 30–35 minutes.

4 When the chicken is cooked through, remove it from the oven. Transfer to a frying pan and stir in the cream. Reheat gently over a low heat for about 2 minutes. Garnish with chopped fresh coriander and serve with boiled rice.

Balti Baby Chicken in Tamarind Sauce

The tamarind in this recipe gives the dish a sweet-and-sour flavour; this is also quite a hot balti.

Serves 4–6

60ml/4 tbsp tomato ketchup
15ml/1 tbsp tamarind paste
60ml/4 tbsp water
7.5ml/1½ tsp chilli powder
7.5ml/1½ tsp salt
15ml/1 tbsp sugar
7.5ml/1½ tsp grated fresh root ginger
7.5ml/1½ tsp crushed garlic
30ml/2 tbsp desiccated coconut
30ml/2 tbsp sesame seeds
5ml/1 tsp poppy seeds
5ml/1 tsp ground cumin
7.5ml/1½ tsp ground coriander
2 x 450g/1lb poussins, skinned and each cut into 6–8 pieces
75ml/5 tbsp corn oil
25g/1oz/8 tbsp curry leaves
2.5ml/ ½ tsp onion seeds
3 large dried red chillies
2.5ml/ ½ tsp fenugreek seeds
10–12 cherry tomatoes
45ml/3 tbsp chopped fresh coriander
2 fresh green chillies, chopped

1 Put the tomato ketchup, tamarind paste and water into a large mixing bowl, and use a fork to blend together. Add the chilli powder, salt, sugar, ginger, garlic, coconut, sesame seeds, poppy seeds, ground cumin and ground coriander to the mixture. Add the poussins and stir until they are well coated with the spice mixture. Set to one side.

2 Heat the oil in a large karahi or deep, round-bottomed frying pan. Add the curry leaves, onion seeds, dried red chillies and fenugreek seeds, and fry for about 1 minute.

3 Lower the heat to medium and add the poussins, two or three pieces at a time, along with their sauce, mixing as you go. When all the pieces are in the pan, stir them around well using a slotted spoon.

4 Simmer gently for about 12–15 minutes or until the poussins are thoroughly cooked. Finally, add the tomatoes, fresh coriander and green chillies, and serve.

Balti Chilli Chicken

Hot and spicy would be the best way of describing this mouth-watering balti dish. The smell of the fresh chillies cooking is quite pungent but delicious.

Serves 4–6

75ml/5 tbsp corn oil
8 large fresh green chillies, slit
2.5ml/ ½ tsp mixed onion and cumin seeds
4 curry leaves
5ml/1 tsp grated fresh root ginger
5ml/1 tsp chilli powder
5ml/1 tsp ground coriander
5ml/1 tsp crushed garlic
5ml/1 tsp salt
2 medium onions, chopped
675g/1½lb chicken, skinned, boned and cubed
15ml/1 tbsp lemon juice
15ml/1 tbsp roughly chopped fresh mint
15ml/1 tbsp roughly chopped fresh coriander
8–10 cherry tomatoes

1 Heat the oil in a medium karahi or deep, round-bottomed frying pan. Lower the heat slightly and add the slit green chillies. Fry until the skin starts to change colour.

2 Add the onion and cumin seeds, curry leaves, ginger, chilli powder, ground coriander, garlic, salt and onions, and fry for a few seconds, stirring continuously.

3 Add the chicken cubes and stir-fry for 7–10 minutes or until the chicken is cooked right through.

4 Sprinkle over the lemon juice, and add the mint and coriander. Add the cherry tomatoes and serve immediately.

Cook's Tip
A good raita to serve with this can be made by mixing together 1 peeled and diced cucumber, 2 finely diced tomatoes, 1 finely chopped onion, 300ml/ ½ pint/1¼ cups plain yogurt, 5ml/1 tsp ground cumin, 5ml/1 tsp lightly fried black mustard seeds and a pinch of salt. Chill before serving.

Chicken & Pasta Balti

This is not a traditional balti dish, as pasta is not eaten widely in India or Pakistan. However, it is no less enjoyable for that. The pomegranate seeds give an unusual, tangy flavour.

Serves 4–6

75g/3oz/ ¾ cup small pasta shells (the coloured ones look most attractive)
75ml/5 tbsp corn oil
4 curry leaves
4 dried red chillies
1 large onion, sliced
5ml/1 tsp crushed garlic
5ml/1 tsp chilli powder
5ml/1 tsp grated fresh root ginger
5ml/1 tsp crushed pomegranate seeds
5ml/1 tsp salt
2 medium tomatoes, chopped
175g/6oz chicken, skinned, boned and cubed
225g/8oz/1cup canned chick-peas, drained
115g/4oz/ ⅔ cup sweetcorn kernels
50g/2oz mangetouts, sliced diagonally
15ml/1 tbsp chopped fresh coriander, to garnish (optional)

1 Cook the pasta in boiling salted water, according to the directions on the packet, until *al dente*. Add 15ml/1 tbsp of the oil to the water to prevent the pasta from sticking together. When it is cooked, drain and set to one side in a sieve.

2 Heat the remaining oil in a large karahi or deep, round-bottomed frying pan. Add the curry leaves, dried chillies and onion, and fry for about 5 minutes.

3 Add the garlic, chilli powder, ginger, pomegranate seeds, salt and tomatoes. Stir-fry for about 3 minutes.

4 Next, add the chicken, chick-peas, sweetcorn and mangetouts to the onion mixture. Cook over a medium heat for about 5 minutes, stirring constantly.

5 Tip the pasta into the chicken mixture and stir well. Cook for a further 7–10 minutes until the chicken is cooked through. Serve, garnished with the fresh coriander, if using.

Balti Chicken Pasanda

Pasanda dishes are firm favourites in Pakistan, but they are also becoming well known in the West.

Serves 4

60ml/4 tbsp Greek-style yogurt
2.5ml/ ½ tsp black cumin seeds
4 cardamom pods
6 black peppercorns
10ml/2 tsp garam masala
2.5cm/1in cinnamon stick
15ml/1 tbsp ground almonds
5ml/1 tsp crushed garlic
5ml/1 tsp grated fresh root ginger
5ml/1 tsp chilli powder
5ml/1 tsp salt
675g/1½lb chicken, skinned, boned and cubed
75ml/5 tbsp corn oil
2 medium onions, diced
3 fresh green chillies, chopped
30ml/2 tbsp chopped fresh coriander, plus extra to garnish
120ml/4fl oz/ ½ cup single cream

1 Mix the yogurt, cumin seeds, cardamoms, peppercorns, garam masala, cinnamon stick, ground almonds, garlic, ginger, chilli powder and salt in a medium mixing bowl. Add the chicken and leave to marinate for about 2 hours.

2 Heat the oil in a large karahi or deep, round-bottomed frying pan. Add the onions and fry for 2–3 minutes.

3 Pour in the chicken mixture and stir until it is well blended with the onions. Cook over a medium heat for 12–15 minutes or until the sauce thickens and the chicken is cooked through.

4 Add the green chillies and fresh coriander, and pour in the cream. Bring to the boil and serve immediately, garnished with more coriander.

Cook's Tip

Ground ginger is no substitute for the fresh root, as it burns very easily. Wrap fresh root ginger, unpeeled, in clear film and store in the fridge for up to six weeks.

Chicken in a Hot Red Sauce

In India, small chickens are used for this dish and served as an individual starter with chapatis. If you wish to serve it as a starter, use four poussins instead of chicken joints. Skin them first and make small gashes with a sharp knife to enable the spices to seep in.

Serves 4–6

20ml/4 tsp kashmiri masala paste
60ml/4 tbsp tomato ketchup
5ml/1 tsp Worcestershire sauce
5ml/1 tsp Indian five-spice powder
5ml/1 tsp sugar
8 chicken portions, skinned but not boned
45ml/3 tbsp vegetable oil
4 garlic cloves, crushed
5cm/2in piece fresh root ginger, finely shredded
juice of 1 lemon
a few fresh coriander leaves, finely chopped
salt

1 In a bowl, mix together the kashmiri masala, tomato ketchup, Worcestershire sauce, five-spice powder, sugar and salt. Allow to rest in a warm place until the sugar has dissolved.

2 Place the chicken portions in a wide, shallow dish and rub with the mixture. Set aside to marinate for 2 hours, or overnight if possible.

3 Heat the oil in a large frying pan and fry the garlic and half the ginger until golden brown. Add the chicken pieces and the marinade, and fry without overlapping until both sides are sealed. Cover the pan and cook gently until the chicken is nearly tender and the gravy clings, with the oil separating.

4 Sprinkle the chicken with the lemon juice, the remaining ginger and coriander leaves. Mix well, reheat and serve hot.

Spicy Chicken Dhal

The chicken is coated in a spiced lentil sauce and finished with a tarka, a seasoned oil, which is poured over the dish just before serving.

Serves 4

30ml/2 tbsp chana dhal (split yellow lentils)
50g/2oz/¼ cup masoor dhal
15ml/1 tbsp corn oil
2 medium onions, chopped
5ml/1 tsp crushed garlic
5ml/1 tsp grated fresh root ginger
2.5ml/½ tsp ground turmeric
7.5ml/1½ tsp chilli powder
5ml/1 tsp garam masala
2.5ml/½ tsp ground coriander
7.5ml/1½ tsp salt
175g/6oz chicken breast fillets, skinned and cubed
45ml/3 tbsp fresh coriander leaves
1–2 fresh green chillies, seeded and chopped
30–45ml/2–3 tbsp lemon juice
300ml/½ pint/1¼ cups water
2 tomatoes, peeled and halved

For the tarka

5ml/1 tsp corn oil
2.5ml/½ tsp cumin seeds
2 garlic cloves
2 dried red chillies
4 curry leaves

1 Boil the chana dhal and masoor dhal together in a saucepan of water until soft and mushy. Set aside.

2 Heat the oil in a wok or frying pan and fry the onions until soft and golden brown. Stir in the garlic, ginger, turmeric, chilli powder, garam masala, ground coriander and salt. Add the chicken cubes and stir-fry for 5–7 minutes.

3 Add half the fresh coriander, the green chillies, lemon juice and water, and cook for a further 3–5 minutes.

4 Pour in the chana dhal and masoor dhal, followed by the tomatoes. Add the remaining fresh coriander. Remove from the heat and set aside.

5 To make the tarka, heat the oil and add the cumin seeds, whole garlic cloves, dried chillies and curry leaves. Heat for about 30 seconds and, while it is still hot, pour it over the top of the chicken and lentils. Serve immediately.

Balti Chicken Vindaloo

This is considered rather a hot curry and is probably one of the best-known Indian dishes, especially in the West.

Serves 4

1 large potato
150ml/¼ pint/⅔ cup malt vinegar
7.5ml/1½ tsp crushed coriander seeds
5ml/1 tsp crushed cumin seeds
7.5ml/1½ tsp chilli powder
1.5ml/¼ tsp ground turmeric
5ml/1 tsp crushed garlic
5ml/1 tsp grated fresh root ginger
5ml/1 tsp salt
7.5ml/1½ tsp paprika
15ml/1 tbsp tomato purée
large pinch of ground fenugreek
300ml/½ pint/1¼ cups water
225g/8oz chicken breast fillets, skinned and cubed
15ml/1 tbsp corn oil
2 medium onions, sliced
4 curry leaves
2 fresh green chillies, chopped

1 Peel the potato, cut it into large, irregular shapes, place in a bowl of water and set aside.

2 In a bowl, mix the vinegar with the coriander and cumin seeds, chilli powder, turmeric, garlic, ginger, salt, paprika, tomato purée, fenugreek and water. Pour this mixture over the chicken and set aside.

3 Heat the oil in a wok or frying pan and fry the onions with the curry leaves for 3–4 minutes.

4 Lower the heat and add the chicken mixture to the pan. Continue to stir for a further 2 minutes. Drain the potato pieces and add to the pan. Cover and cook over a medium to low heat for 5–7 minutes or until the sauce has thickened slightly, and the chicken and potatoes are cooked through. Stir the chopped green chillies into the dish and serve hot.

Cook's Tip

The best thing to drink with a hot curry is either iced water or a yogurt-based lassi.

Hot Chilli Chicken

Not for the weak or faint-hearted, this fiery, hot curry is made with a spicy chilli masala paste.

Serves 4

30ml/2 tbsp tomato purée
2 garlic cloves, roughly chopped
2 fresh green chillies, roughly chopped
5 dried red chillies
2.5ml/ ½ tsp salt
1.5ml/ ¼ tsp sugar
5ml/1 tsp chilli powder
2.5ml/ ½ tsp paprika
15ml/1 tbsp curry paste
30ml/2 tbsp oil
2.5ml/ ½ tsp cumin seeds
1 onion, finely chopped
2 bay leaves
5ml/1 tsp ground coriander
5ml/1 tsp ground cumin
1.5ml/ ¼ tsp ground turmeric
400g/14oz can chopped tomatoes
150ml/ ¼ pint/ ⅔ cup water
8 chicken thighs, skinned
5ml/1 tsp garam masala
sliced fresh green chillies, to garnish
chapatis and plain yogurt, to serve

1 Put the tomato purée, garlic, fresh and dried chillies, salt, sugar, chilli powder, paprika and curry paste into a food processor or blender, and process to a smooth paste.

2 Heat the oil in a large saucepan and fry the cumin seeds for 2 minutes. Add the onion and bay leaves, and fry over a medium heat for about 5 minutes.

3 Add the spice paste and fry for 2–3 minutes. Add the remaining ground spices and cook for 2 minutes. Add the chopped tomatoes and water. Bring to the boil and simmer for 5 minutes until the sauce thickens.

4 Add the chicken and garam masala. Cover and simmer for 25–30 minutes until the chicken is tender. Serve with chapatis and plain yogurt, garnished with sliced green chillies.

Chicken with Ginger & Lemon Grass

This Vietnamese dish can also be prepared using duck legs. Be sure to remove the jointed parts of the drumsticks and thigh bones to make the meat easier to eat with chopsticks.

Serves 4–6

3 chicken legs (thighs and drumsticks)
15ml/1 tbsp vegetable oil
2cm/ ¾in piece fresh root ginger, finely chopped
1 garlic clove, crushed
1 small fresh red chilli, seeded and finely chopped
5cm/2in piece lemon grass, shredded
150ml/ ¼ pint/ ⅔ cup Chicken Stock
15ml/1 tbsp fish sauce (optional)
10ml/2 tsp sugar
2.5ml/ ½ tsp salt
juice of ½ lemon
50g/2oz/ ½ cup raw peanuts
2 spring onions, shredded
thinly pared rind of 1 mandarin orange or satsuma, shredded
30ml/2 tbsp chopped fresh mint
cooked rice or rice noodles, to serve

1 Using the heel of a knife, chop through the narrow end of the chicken drumsticks. Remove the jointed parts of the drumsticks and thigh bones, then remove the skin.

2 Heat the vegetable oil in a large wok or frying pan. Add the chicken, ginger, garlic, chilli and lemon grass, and cook over a medium heat for 3–4 minutes. Add the chicken stock, fish sauce, if using, sugar, salt and lemon juice. Cover and simmer for 30–35 minutes.

3 Grill or roast the peanuts under a steady heat for about 2–3 minutes until evenly browned. Turn the nuts out on to a clean dish towel and, when cool enough to handle, rub briskly to loosen the skins. Discard the skins.

4 Serve the chicken, scattered with the roasted peanuts, shredded spring onions, the shredded rind of the mandarin orange or satsuma and mint. Serve with rice or rice noodles.

Soy-braised Chicken

This chicken is cooked whole and divided after cooking. It can be served hot or cold as part of a buffet-style meal.

Serves 6–8
1.3–1.5kg/3–3½lb chicken
15ml/1 tbsp ground Sichuan peppercorns
30ml/2 tbsp grated fresh root ginger
45ml/3 tbsp light soy sauce
30ml/2 tbsp dark soy sauce
45ml/3 tbsp Chinese rice wine or dry sherry
15ml/1 tbsp light brown sugar
vegetable oil, for deep frying
about 600ml/1 pint/2½ cups water
10ml/2 tsp salt
25g/1oz rock sugar
lettuce leaves, to serve

1 Rub the chicken both inside and out with the ground pepper and fresh ginger. In a bowl, mix together the soy sauces, wine or sherry and sugar. Place the chicken in a bowl, pour over the soy mixture and leave to marinate for at least 3 hours, turning several times.

2 Heat the oil in a preheated wok. Remove the chicken from the marinade and deep fry for 5–6 minutes or until brown all over. Remove and drain.

3 Pour off the excess oil from the wok. Add the marinade with the water, salt and rock sugar, and bring to the boil. Return the chicken to the wok and braise in the sauce for 35–40 minutes, covered, turning once or twice.

4 Remove the chicken from the wok and let it cool a little before cutting it into approximately 30 bite-size pieces. Arrange the pieces on a bed of lettuce leaves, then pour some of the sauce over the chicken and serve. Any leftover sauce can be stored in the fridge for use in another dish.

Cook's Tip
Rock sugar is also known as crystal sugar.

Chicken & Ham with Green Vegetables

This dish originates from China, where its name means "Golden Flower and Jade Tree Chicken". It makes a marvellous buffet-style dish for all occasions.

Serves 6–8
1–1.3kg/2¼–3lb chicken
2 spring onions
2–3 pieces fresh root ginger
15ml/1 tbsp salt
225g/8oz honey-roast ham
275g/10oz broccoli
45ml/3 tbsp vegetable oil
5ml/1 tsp light brown sugar
10ml/2 tsp cornflour

1 Place the chicken in a large pan and add sufficient cold water to cover. Add the spring onions, ginger and about 10ml/2 tsp of the salt. Bring to the boil, then cover with a tight-fitting lid, reduce the heat and simmer for 10–15 minutes. Remove from the heat and set aside to let the chicken cook itself in the hot water for at least 4–5 hours – you must not lift the lid as this will let out the residual heat.

2 Remove the chicken from the pan, reserving the liquid, and carefully cut the meat off the bones, keeping the skin on. Slice both the chicken and ham into pieces, each about the size of a matchbox, and arrange the meats in alternating layers on a serving plate.

3 Cut the broccoli into small florets. Heat the oil in a wok and stir-fry the broccoli with the remaining salt and the sugar for about 2–3 minutes. Arrange the broccoli between the rows of chicken and ham, and around the edge of the plate, making a border around the meat.

4 Heat a small amount of the reserved chicken stock and thicken with the cornflour. Stir until smooth, then pour it evenly all over the chicken and ham so that it forms a thin coat of transparent jelly resembling "jade". Allow to cool before serving.

"Kung Po" Chicken Sichuan Style

Kung Po was the name of a court official in the Sichuan province of China; his cook created this dish.

Serves 4

350g/12oz chicken thighs, boned and skinned
1.5ml/¼ tsp salt
½ egg white, lightly beaten
10ml/2 tsp cornflour
1 medium green pepper
60ml/4 tbsp vegetable oil
3–4 dried red chillies, soaked in water for 10 minutes
1 spring onion, cut into short sections
a few small pieces of fresh root ginger
15ml/1 tbsp sweet bean paste or hoisin sauce
5ml/1 tsp chilli bean paste
15ml/1 tbsp Chinese rice wine or dry sherry
115g/4oz/1 cup roasted cashew nuts
a few drops of sesame oil

1 Cut the chicken meat into small cubes, each about the size of a sugar lump. In a bowl, mix the chicken with the salt and egg white. Mix the cornflour to a thin paste with a little water and stir into the chicken.

2 Cut the green pepper into cubes about the same size as the chicken, discarding the core and seeds.

3 Heat a wok and pour in the oil. When the oil is hot, add the chicken cubes and stir-fry for about 1 minute or until they change colour. Remove from the wok using a slotted spoon and keep warm.

4 Add the green pepper, dried red chillies, spring onion and ginger to the wok, and stir-fry for about 1 minute. Return the chicken and add the sweet bean paste or hoisin sauce, chilli bean paste and wine or sherry. Blend well and cook for another minute. Finally, add the cashew nuts and sesame oil. Serve hot.

Spicy Clay-pot Chicken

Clay-pot cooking stems from the Malaysian practice of burying a glazed pot in the embers of a fire. The gentle heat keeps the liquid inside at a slow simmer.

Serves 4–6

1.5kg/3½lb chicken
45ml/3 tbsp grated fresh coconut
30ml/2 tbsp vegetable oil
2 shallots, finely chopped
2 garlic cloves, crushed
5cm/2in piece lemon grass
2.5cm/1in piece galangal or fresh root ginger, thinly sliced
2 small fresh green chillies, seeded and finely chopped
1cm/½in cube shrimp paste or 15ml/1 tbsp fish sauce
400ml/14fl oz can coconut milk
300ml/½ pint/1¼ cups Chicken Stock
2 kaffir lime leaves (optional)
15ml/1 tbsp sugar
15ml/1 tbsp rice or white wine vinegar
2 ripe tomatoes
15ml/2 tbsp chopped fresh coriander leaves, to garnish
boiled rice, to serve

1 Remove the chicken legs and wings with a chopping knife, skin the pieces and divide the drumsticks from the thighs. Using a pair of kitchen scissors, remove the lower part of the chicken, leaving the breast piece. Remove as many of the bones as you can. Cut the breast piece into four. Set the chicken aside.

2 Dry-fry the coconut in a large wok until evenly brown. Add the oil, shallots, garlic, lemon grass, galangal or ginger, chillies and shrimp paste or fish sauce. Fry briefly to release the flavours.

3 Preheat the oven to 180°C/350°F/Gas 4. Add the chicken joints to the wok and brown evenly with the spices for 2–3 minutes. Strain the coconut milk and add the thin part to the wok with the stock, lime leaves, if using, sugar and vinegar. Transfer to a glazed clay pot, cover and bake for 50–55 minutes. Stir in the thick part of the coconut milk and return to the oven for 5–10 minutes to simmer and thicken.

4 Scald the tomatoes in boiling water, then plunge into cold water. Peel, halve, seed and dice the tomatoes. Add them to the dish, scatter with the coriander and serve with rice.

Bang Bang Chicken

What a descriptive name this special dish from Sichuan has! Use toasted sesame paste to give the sauce an authentic flavour, although crunchy peanut butter can be used instead.

Serves 4

3 chicken breast fillets, total weight about 450g/1lb, skinned
1 garlic clove, crushed
2.5ml/½ tsp black peppercorns
1 small onion, halved
1 large cucumber, peeled, seeded and cut into thin strips
salt

For the sauce

45ml/3 tbsp toasted sesame paste
15ml/1 tbsp light soy sauce
15ml/1 tbsp wine vinegar
2 spring onions, finely chopped
2 garlic cloves, crushed
5 x 1cm/2 x ½in piece fresh root ginger, cut into matchsticks
15ml/1 tbsp Sichuan peppercorns, dry-fried and crushed
about 5ml/1 tsp light brown sugar

For the chilli oil

60ml/4 tbsp groundnut oil
5ml/1 tsp chilli powder

1 Place the chicken in a saucepan. Just cover with water, add the garlic, peppercorns and onion, and bring to the boil. Skim the surface, stir in salt to taste, then cover the pan. Cook for 25 minutes or until the chicken is just tender. Drain, reserving the stock.

2 To make the sauce, mix the toasted sesame paste with 45ml/3 tbsp of the chicken stock, saving the rest for soup. Add the soy sauce, vinegar, spring onions, garlic, ginger and crushed Sichuan peppercorns. Stir in sugar to taste.

3 To make the chilli oil, gently heat the groundnut oil and chilli powder together in a pan until gently foaming. Simmer for 2 minutes, then strain off the red-coloured oil and discard the sediment.

4 Spread out the cucumber batons on a serving platter. Cut the chicken into pieces of about the same size as the cucumber strips and arrange them on top. Pour over the sauce, drizzle on the chilli oil and serve.

Cashew Chicken

In this Chinese-inspired dish, tender pieces of chicken are stir-fried with cashews, red chillies and a touch of garlic for a delicious combination.

Serves 4–6

450g/1lb chicken breast fillets
30ml/2 tbsp vegetable oil
2 garlic cloves, sliced
4 dried red chillies, chopped
1 red pepper, seeded and cut into 2cm/¾in dice
30ml/2 tbsp oyster sauce
15ml/1 tbsp soy sauce
pinch of sugar
1 bunch spring onions, cut into 5cm/2in lengths
175g/6oz/1½ cups cashew nuts, roasted
fresh coriander leaves, to garnish

1 Remove and discard the skin from the chicken breasts. Using a sharp knife, cut the chicken into bite-size pieces. Set aside.

2 Heat the oil in a wok and swirl it around. Add the garlic and dried chillies, and fry until golden.

3 Add the chicken and stir-fry until it changes colour, then add the red pepper. If necessary, add a little water.

4 Stir in the oyster sauce, soy sauce and sugar. Add the spring onions and cashews. Stir-fry for about another 1–2 minutes. Serve, garnished with fresh coriander leaves.

Variations

For an extra-spicy dish, season with cayenne pepper to taste just before serving. For a slightly different flavour, substitute halved walnuts for the cashews. For a more substantial dish, add 150g/5oz/2 cups sliced mushrooms and 150g/5oz mangetouts with the red pepper in step 3.

Fragrant Chicken Curry with Thai Spices

To create this wonderful, aromatic dish you need Thai red curry paste – home-made is best, but for speed you could use ready-made.

Serves 4

45ml/3 tbsp oil
1 onion, roughly chopped
2 garlic cloves, crushed
15ml/1 tbsp Thai red curry paste (see Red Chicken Curry with Bamboo Shoots)
115g/4oz creamed coconut dissolved in about 900ml/ 1½ pints/3¾ cups boiling water
2 lemon grass stalks, roughly chopped
6 kaffir lime leaves, chopped
150ml/¼ pint/⅔ cup Greek-style yogurt
30ml/2 tbsp apricot jam
1 cooked chicken, about 1.5kg/3½lb
30ml/2 tbsp chopped fresh coriander
salt and freshly ground black pepper
kaffir lime leaves, shredded coconut and fresh coriander, to garnish
boiled rice, to serve

1 Heat the oil in a saucepan. Add the onion and garlic, and fry over a low heat for 5–10 minutes until soft. Stir in the curry paste and cook, stirring, for 2–3 minutes. Stir in the diluted creamed coconut, then add the lemon grass, lime leaves, yogurt and apricot jam. Stir well. Cover and simmer for 30 minutes.

2 Process the sauce in a blender or food processor, then strain it back into a clean pan, pressing as much of the puréed mixture as possible through the sieve.

3 Remove the skin from the chicken. Slice the meat off the bones and cut it into bite-size pieces. Add to the sauce. If the sauce seems too thin, add a little more creamed coconut.

4 Bring the sauce back to simmering point. Stir in the fresh coriander, and season to taste with salt and pepper. Serve with boiled rice, garnished with extra lime leaves, shredded coconut and fresh coriander.

Thai Chicken & Vegetable Curry

For this curry, chicken and vegetables are cooked in an aromatic Thai-spiced coconut sauce.

Serves 4

15ml/1 tbsp sunflower oil
6 shallots, finely chopped
2 garlic cloves, crushed
450g/1lb chicken breast fillets, cut into 1cm/½in cubes
5ml/1 tsp ground coriander
5ml/1 tsp ground cumin
20ml/4 tsp Thai green curry paste (see Green Curry Coconut Chicken)
1 green pepper, seeded and diced
175g/6oz baby sweetcorn, halved
115g/4oz French beans, halved
150ml/¼ pint/⅔ cup Chicken Stock
150ml/¼ pint/⅔ cup coconut milk
30ml/2 tbsp cornflour
fresh herb sprigs and toasted cashew nuts, to garnish
boiled rice, to serve

1 Heat the oil in a saucepan, add the shallots, garlic and chicken, and cook for 5 minutes until the chicken is coloured all over, stirring occasionally. Add the coriander, cumin and curry paste, and cook for 1 minute.

2 Add the green pepper, baby sweetcorn, beans, stock and coconut milk, and stir to mix. Bring to the boil, stirring all the time, then cover and simmer for 20–30 minutes until the chicken is tender, stirring occasionally.

3 Blend the cornflour with about 45ml/3 tbsp water in a small bowl. Stir into the curry, then simmer gently for about 2 minutes, stirring all the time, until the sauce thickens slightly. Serve hot, garnished with fresh herb sprigs and toasted cashew nuts, and accompanied by boiled rice.

Chicken Rendang

This marvellous Malaysian dish is great served with prawn crackers or with deep-fried anchovies.

Serves 4

4 chicken breast fillets, skinned
5ml/1 tsp sugar
75g/3oz/1 cup desiccated coconut
4 small red or white onions, roughly chopped
2 garlic cloves, chopped
2.5cm/1in piece fresh root ginger, sliced
1–2 lemon grass stalks, root trimmed
2.5cm/1in piece galangal, peeled and sliced
75ml/5 tbsp groundnut oil or vegetable oil
10–15ml/2–3 tsp chilli powder, or to taste
400ml/14fl oz can coconut milk
about 10ml/2 tsp salt
fresh chives and deep-fried anchovies, to garnish

1 Halve the chicken breast fillets, sprinkle with the sugar and leave to stand for about 1 hour.

2 Dry-fry the coconut in a wok over a low heat, turning all the time until crisp and golden. Transfer to a food processor and process to an oily paste. Transfer to a bowl and reserve.

3 Add the onions, garlic and ginger to the processor. Cut off the lower 5cm/2in of the lemon grass, chop and add to the processor with the galangal. Process to a fine paste.

4 Heat the oil in a wok or large saucepan. Fry the onion mixture for a few minutes. Reduce the heat, stir in the chilli powder and cook for 2–3 minutes, stirring. Spoon in 120ml/4fl oz/½ cup of the coconut milk, with salt to taste. As soon as the mixture bubbles, add the chicken, turning until well coated with the spices. Pour in the remaining coconut milk, stirring. Bruise the top of the lemon grass stalks and add to the wok or pan. Cover and cook over a low heat for 40–45 minutes until the chicken is tender.

5 Stir in the reserved coconut paste. Bring to just below boiling point, then simmer for 5 minutes. Transfer to a serving bowl, and garnish with chives and deep-fried anchovies. Serve immediately.

Stir-fried Chicken with Basil & Chillies

Deep frying the basil adds another dimension to this easy Thai dish. Thai basil, which is sometimes known as Holy basil, has a unique, pungent flavour that is both spicy and sharp. The dull leaves have serrated edges.

Serves 4–6

45ml/3 tbsp vegetable oil
4 garlic cloves, sliced
2–4 fresh red chillies, seeded and chopped
450g/1lb boneless chicken
30–45ml/2–3 tbsp fish sauce
10ml/2 tsp dark soy sauce
5ml/1 tsp sugar
10–12 Thai basil leaves

For the garnish

2 fresh red chillies, finely sliced
20 Thai basil leaves, deep fried (optional)

1 Heat the oil in a wok or large frying pan and swirl it around. Add the garlic and chillies, and stir-fry until golden.

2 Cut the chicken into bite-size pieces, add to the wok or pan and stir-fry until it changes colour.

3 Season with fish sauce, soy sauce and sugar. Continue to stir-fry for 3–4 minutes or until the chicken is cooked.

4 Stir in the fresh Thai basil leaves. Garnish with sliced chillies and the deep-fried basil, if using.

Cook's Tip

To deep fry Thai basil leaves, make sure that the leaves are completely dry. Deep fry in hot oil for about 30–40 seconds, lift out and drain on kitchen paper.

Chicken Cooked in Coconut Milk

Traditionally the chicken for this dish would be part-cooked by frying, but here it is roasted in the oven. This is an unusual recipe in that the sauce is white, as it does not contain chillies or turmeric, unlike many other Indonesian dishes.

Serves 4

1.5kg/3½lb chicken or 4 chicken quarters
4 garlic cloves
1 onion, sliced
4 macadamia nuts or 8 almonds
15ml/1 tbsp coriander seeds, dry-fried, or 5ml/1 tsp ground coriander
45ml/3 tbsp oil
2.5cm/1in piece fresh galangal, peeled and bruised
2 lemon grass stalks, fleshy part bruised
3 kaffir lime leaves
2 bay leaves
5ml/1 tsp sugar
600ml/1 pint/2½ cups coconut milk
salt
boiled rice and Deep-fried Onions, to serve

1 Preheat the oven to 190°C/375°F/Gas 5. If using a whole chicken, cut it into 4 or 8 pieces. Season with salt. Put into an oiled roasting tin and cook in the oven for 25–30 minutes.

2 Meanwhile, prepare the sauce. Grind the garlic, onion, nuts and coriander to a fine paste in a food processor or using a pestle and mortar. Heat the oil in a frying pan and fry the paste to bring out the flavour. Do not allow it to brown.

3 Add the part-cooked chicken pieces to a wok, together with the galangal, lemon grass, lime and bay leaves, sugar, coconut milk and salt to taste. Mix well to coat in the sauce.

4 Bring to the boil, then reduce the heat and simmer gently for 30–40 minutes, uncovered, until the chicken is tender and the coconut sauce is reduced and thickened. Stir the mixture occasionally during cooking.

5 Just before serving, remove and discard the galangal and lemon grass. Serve with boiled rice and sprinkle with crisp deep-fried onions.

Green Curry Coconut Chicken

The recipe given here for green curry paste is a slightly complex one, so allow time to make it properly – your efforts will be well rewarded.

Serves 4–6

1.2kg/2½lb chicken
600ml/1 pint/2½ cups canned coconut milk
450ml/¾ pint/scant 2 cups Chicken Stock
2 kaffir lime leaves
350g/12oz sweet potatoes, peeled and roughly chopped
350g/12oz winter squash, peeled, seeded and roughly chopped
115g/4oz French beans, halved
1 small bunch fresh coriander, shredded, to garnish

For the green curry paste
10ml/2 tsp coriander seeds
2.5ml/½ tsp caraway or cumin seeds
3–4 medium fresh green chillies, finely chopped
20ml/4 tsp sugar
10ml/2 tsp salt
7.5cm/3in piece lemon grass
2cm/¾in piece galangal or fresh ginger, finely chopped
3 garlic cloves, crushed
4 shallots or 1 medium onion, finely chopped
2cm/¾in shrimp paste cube
45ml/3 tbsp finely chopped fresh coriander
45ml/3 tbsp finely chopped fresh fresh mint or basil
2.5ml/½ tsp grated nutmeg
30ml/2 tbsp vegetable oil

1 To prepare the chicken, remove the legs, then separate the thighs from the drumsticks. Separate the lower part of the chicken carcass by cutting through the rib section with kitchen scissors. Divide the breast part in half down the middle, then chop each half in two. Remove the skin from all the pieces. Set the chicken aside.

2 Strain the coconut milk into a bowl, reserving the thick part. Place the chicken in a stainless steel or enamel saucepan, cover with the thin part of the coconut milk and the stock. Add the lime leaves and simmer, uncovered, for 40 minutes. Lift the chicken out of the pan, cut the meat off the bones and set aside. Reserve the stock.

3 To make the green curry paste, dry-fry the coriander and caraway or cumin seeds. Grind the chillies with the sugar and salt in a food processor or using a pestle and mortar to make a smooth paste. Combine the dry-fried seeds with the chillies, add the lemon grass, galangal or ginger, garlic and shallots or onion, then grind smoothly. Add the shrimp paste, chopped herbs, nutmeg and oil.

4 Place 250ml/8fl oz/1 cup of the reserved chicken stock in a large wok. Add 60–75ml/4–5 tbsp of the curry paste to the liquid according to taste. Boil rapidly until the liquid has reduced completely. Add the remaining chicken stock, the chicken meat, sweet potatoes, squash and beans. Simmer for 10–15 minutes until all the vegetables are cooked.

5 Just before serving, stir in the thick part of the coconut milk and simmer gently to thicken. Serve, garnished with the shredded coriander.

Red Chicken Curry with Bamboo Shoots

Bamboo shoots have a lovely, crunchy texture. It is quite acceptable to use canned ones, as fresh bamboo is not readily available in the West. Buy canned whole bamboo shoots, which are crisper and of better quality than sliced shoots. Rinse well before using.

Serves 4–6

1 litre/1¾ pints/4 cups coconut milk
450g/1lb chicken breast fillets, skinned and cut into bite-size pieces
30ml/2 tbsp fish sauce
15ml/1 tbsp sugar
225g/8oz drained canned bamboo shoots, rinsed and sliced
5 kaffir lime leaves, torn
salt and freshly ground black pepper
chopped fresh red chillies and kaffir lime leaves, to garnish

For the red curry paste

5ml/1 tsp coriander seeds
2.5ml/½ tsp cumin seeds
12–15 fresh red chillies, seeded and roughly chopped
4 shallots, thinly sliced
2 garlic cloves, chopped
15ml/1 tbsp chopped galangal
2 lemon grass stalks, chopped
3 kaffir lime leaves, chopped
4 fresh coriander roots
10 black peppercorns
good pinch of ground cinnamon
5ml/1 tsp ground turmeric
2.5ml/½ tsp shrimp paste
5ml/1 tsp salt
30ml/2 tbsp vegetable oil

1 To make the red curry paste, dry-fry the coriander and cumin seeds for 1–2 minutes, then put in a mortar or food processor with all the remaining ingredients except the oil. Pound or process to a paste.

2 Add the oil, a little at a time, mixing or processing well after each addition. Transfer to a jar and place in the fridge until ready to use.

3 Pour half of the coconut milk into a large saucepan. Bring to the boil, stirring constantly until the milk has separated.

4 Stir in 30ml/2 tbsp of the red curry paste and cook the mixture for 2–3 minutes, stirring constantly. (The remaining red curry paste can be stored in the fridge for 3–4 weeks.)

5 Add the chicken pieces, fish sauce and sugar to the pan. Mix well, then cook for 5–6 minutes until the chicken changes colour and is cooked through, stirring constantly to prevent the mixture from sticking to the bottom of the pan.

6 Pour the remaining coconut milk into the pan, then add the bamboo shoots and kaffir lime leaves. Bring back to the boil over a medium heat, stirring constantly to prevent the mixture from sticking, then taste and add salt and pepper if necessary.

7 To serve, spoon the curry into a warmed serving dish and garnish with chopped chillies and kaffir lime leaves.

Chicken with Spices & Soy Sauce

A very simple Indonesian recipe, which often appears on Padang restaurant menus. Any leftovers taste equally good when reheated the following day.

Serves 4

1.5kg/3½lb chicken, jointed and cut into 16 pieces
3 onions, sliced
about 1 litre/1¾ pints/4 cups water
3 garlic cloves, crushed
3–4 fresh red chillies, seeded and sliced, or 15ml/1 tbsp chilli powder
45–60ml/3–4 tbsp oil
2.5ml/½ tsp grated nutmeg
6 cloves
5ml/1 tsp tamarind pulp, soaked in 45ml/3 tbsp warm water
30–45ml/2–3 tbsp dark or light soy sauce
salt
fresh red chilli shreds, to garnish
boiled rice, to serve

1 Place the chicken pieces in a large pan with one of the onions. Pour over enough water just to cover. Bring to the boil, then reduce the heat and simmer gently for 20 minutes.

2 Process the remaining onions, with the garlic and chillies, to a fine paste in a food processor or using a pestle and mortar. Heat a little of the oil in a wok or frying pan and cook the paste to bring out the flavour, but do not allow it to brown.

3 When the chicken has cooked for 20 minutes, lift it out of the stock in the pan using a slotted spoon and put it straight into the spicy mixture. Toss everything together over a fairly high heat so that the spices permeate the chicken pieces. Reserve 300ml/½ pint/1¼ cups of the chicken stock.

4 Stir the nutmeg and cloves into the chicken. Strain the tamarind, and add the tamarind juice and the soy sauce to the chicken. Cook for a further 2–3 minutes, then add the reserved stock.

5 Taste and adjust the seasoning and cook, uncovered, for a further 25–35 minutes until the chicken pieces are tender. Transfer the chicken to a serving bowl, top with shredded chilli and serve with boiled rice.

Thai Fried Rice

This recipe uses Thai fragrant rice, which is sometimes known as jasmine rice.

Serves 4

50g/2oz/ ½ cup coconut milk powder
475ml/16fl oz/2 cups water
350g/12oz/1⅔ cups Thai fragrant rice
30ml/2 tbsp groundnut oil
2 garlic cloves, chopped
1 small onion, finely chopped
115g/4oz/ ⅔ cup baby sweetcorn cobs, sliced
2.5cm/1in piece fresh root ginger, grated
225g/8oz chicken breast fillets, skinned and cut into 1cm/½in dice
1 red pepper, seeded and diced
115g/4oz/ ⅔ cup drained canned sweetcorn kernels
5ml/1 tsp chilli oil
15ml/1 tbsp hot curry powder
salt
2 eggs, beaten
spring onion shreds, to garnish

1 In a saucepan, whisk the coconut milk powder into the water. Add the rice, bring to the boil and stir once. Lower the heat to a gentle simmer, cover and cook for 10 minutes or until the rice is tender and the liquid has been absorbed. Spread the rice on a baking sheet and leave until completely cold.

2 Heat the oil in a wok, add the garlic, onion, sweetcorn cobs and ginger, and stir-fry for 2 minutes. Push the vegetables to the sides of the wok, add the chicken to the centre and stir-fry for 2 minutes. Add the rice and stir-fry over a high heat for 3 minutes.

3 Stir in the red pepper, sweetcorn kernels, chilli oil and curry powder, and season with salt. Toss over the heat for 1 minute. Stir in the beaten egg and cook for 1 minute more. Garnish with spring onion shreds and serve.

Cook's Tips

The rice must be completely cold before it is fried and the oil should be very hot, or the rice will absorb too much oil.
Add sliced baby sweetcorn cobs along with the rice, if you like.

Chicken & Basil Coconut Rice

For this dish the rice is partially boiled before being simmered with coconut so that it fully absorbs the flavour of the chillies, basil and spices. Serve in a halved coconut.

Serves 4

350g/12oz/1⅔ cups Thai fragrant rice
30–45ml/2–3 tbsp groundnut oil
1 large onion, thinly sliced into rings
1 garlic clove, crushed
1 fresh red chilli, seeded and thinly sliced
1 fresh green chilli, seeded and thinly sliced
generous handful of basil leaves
about 350g/12oz chicken breast fillets, skinned and thinly sliced
5mm/ ¼in piece lemon grass, pounded or finely chopped
50g/2oz block creamed coconut dissolved in 600ml/1 pint/ 2½ cups boiling water
salt and freshly ground black pepper

1 Bring a saucepan of water to the boil. Add the rice to the pan and boil for about 6 minutes until partially cooked. Drain and allow to cool.

2 Heat the oil in a frying pan and fry the onion rings for 5–10 minutes until golden and crisp. Lift out using a slotted spoon, drain on kitchen paper and set aside but keep warm.

3 Fry the garlic and chillies in the oil remaining in the pan for 2–3 minutes, then add the basil leaves and fry briefly until they begin to wilt. Remove a few leaves and set them aside for the garnish, then add the chicken slices and lemon grass to the pan and fry for 2–3 minutes until golden.

4 Add the rice. Stir-fry for a few minutes to coat the grains, then pour in the coconut liquid. Cook for 4–5 minutes or until the rice is tender, adding a little more water if necessary.

5 Adjust the seasoning to taste. Pile the rice into a halved coconut or warmed serving dish, scatter with the fried onion rings and reserved basil leaves, and serve immediately.

Indonesian Pineapple Rice

This way of presenting rice not only looks spectacular, it also tastes so delicious that it can easily be served solo.

Serves 4

75g/3oz/¾ cup unsalted peanuts
1 large pineapple
45ml/3 tbsp groundnut or sunflower oil
1 onion, chopped
1 garlic clove, crushed
about 225g/8oz chicken breast fillets, cut into strips
225g/8oz/generous 1 cup Thai fragrant rice
600ml/1 pint/2½ cups Chicken Stock
1 lemon grass stalk, bruised
2 thick slices ham, cut into julienne strips
1 fresh red chilli, seeded and very thinly sliced
salt

1 Dry-fry the peanuts in a non-stick frying pan until golden. When cool, grind one sixth of them in a coffee or spice mill and chop the remainder.

2 Cut a lengthways slice of pineapple, slicing through the leaves, then cut out the flesh to leave a neat shell. Chop 115g/4oz of the pineapple into cubes, saving the remainder for another dish.

3 Heat the oil in a saucepan and fry the onion and garlic for 3–4 minutes until soft. Add the chicken strips and stir-fry over a medium heat for a few minutes until evenly brown.

4 Add the rice to the pan. Toss with the chicken mixture for a few minutes, then pour in the stock, with the lemon grass and a little salt. Bring to just below boiling point, lower the heat, cover the pan and simmer gently for 10–12 minutes until both the rice and the chicken pieces are tender.

5 Stir the chopped peanuts, the pineapple cubes and the ham into the rice, then spoon the mixture into the pineapple shell. Sprinkle the ground peanuts and the sliced chilli over the top, and serve immediately.

Chicken Biryani

A classic rice and chicken dish, prepared with whole and ground spices and finished in the oven.

Serves 4

275g/10oz/1½ cups basmati rice
2.5ml/½ tsp salt
5 whole cardamom pods
2–3 whole cloves
1 cinnamon stick
45ml/3 tbsp vegetable oil
3 onions, sliced
675g/1½lb chicken breast fillets, skinned and cubed
1.5ml ¼ tsp ground cloves
5 cardamom pods, seeds removed and ground
1.5ml/¼ tsp hot chilli powder
5ml/1 tsp ground cumin
5ml/1 tsp ground coriander
2.5ml/½ tsp freshly ground black pepper
3 garlic cloves, finely chopped
5ml/1 tsp finely chopped fresh root ginger
juice of 1 lemon
4 tomatoes, sliced
30ml/2 tbsp chopped fresh coriander
150ml/¼ pint/⅔ cup plain yogurt
2.5ml/½ tsp saffron strands, soaked in 10ml/2 tsp hot milk
150ml/¼ pint/⅔ cup water
45ml/3 tbsp toasted flaked almonds and fresh coriander sprigs, to garnish
plain yogurt, to serve

1 Preheat the oven to 190°C/375°F/Gas 5. Bring a pan of water to the boil and add the rice, salt, whole cardamom pods, whole cloves and cinnamon stick. Boil for 2 minutes and then drain, leaving the whole spices in the rice.

2 Heat the oil in a large frying pan and fry the onions for 8 minutes until browned. Add the chicken, then all the ground spices, the garlic, ginger and lemon juice. Stir-fry for 5 minutes.

3 Transfer the mixture to a casserole. Lay the tomatoes on top, sprinkle with the coriander, spoon over the yogurt and top with the drained rice. Drizzle the saffron and milk over the rice and pour over the water. Cover and bake in the oven for 1 hour.

4 Transfer the rice to a warmed serving platter and discard the whole spices. Garnish with toasted almonds and fresh coriander, and serve with yogurt.

Chicken & Mushroom Donburi

"Donburi" means a one-dish meal that is eaten from a bowl, and takes its name from the eponymous Japanese porcelain food bowl. As in most Japanese dishes, the rice here is completely plain, but is nevertheless an integral part of the dish.

Serves 4

225–275g/8–10oz/generous 1–1½ cups Japanese rice or Thai fragrant rice
10ml/2 tsp groundnut oil
50g/2oz/4 tbsp butter
2 garlic cloves, crushed
2.5cm/1in piece fresh root ginger, grated
5 spring onions, sliced diagonally
1 green fresh chilli, seeded and thinly sliced
3 chicken breast fillets, skinned and cut into thin strips
150g/5oz tofu, cut into small cubes
115g/4oz/1¾ cups shiitake mushrooms, stalks discarded and cups sliced
15ml/1 tbsp Japanese rice wine
30ml/2 tbsp light soy sauce
10ml/2 tsp granulated sugar
400ml/14fl oz/1⅔ cups Chicken Stock

1 Cook the rice following the instructions on the packet.

2 Meanwhile, heat the oil and butter in a large frying pan. Stir-fry the garlic, ginger, spring onions and chilli for 1–2 minutes until slightly softened. Add the chicken and fry, in batches if necessary, until all the pieces are evenly browned.

3 Using a slotted spoon, transfer the chicken mixture to a plate and add the tofu to the pan. Stir-fry for a few minutes, then add the mushrooms. Stir-fry for 2–3 minutes over a medium heat until the mushrooms are tender.

4 Stir in the rice wine, soy sauce and sugar, and cook briskly for 1–2 minutes, stirring. Return the chicken to the pan, toss over the heat for about 2 minutes, then pour in the stock. Stir well and cook over a gentle heat for 5–6 minutes until bubbling.

5 Spoon the rice into individual serving bowls, and pile the chicken mixture and sauce on top.

Caribbean Chicken with Pigeon Pea Rice

Golden, spicy caramelized chicken tops a richly flavoured vegetable rice in this hearty and delicious supper dish.

Serves 4

5ml/1 tsp ground allspice
2.5ml/½ tsp ground cinnamon
5ml/1 tsp dried thyme
pinch of ground cloves
1.5ml/¼ tsp freshly grated nutmeg
4 chicken breast fillets, skinned
45ml/3 tbsp groundnut or sunflower oil
15g/½oz/1 tbsp butter
1 onion, chopped
2 garlic cloves, crushed
1 carrot, diced
1 celery stick, chopped
3 spring onions, chopped
1 fresh red chilli, seeded and thinly sliced
400g/14oz can pigeon peas
225g/8oz/generous 1 cup long-grain rice
120ml/4fl oz/½ cup coconut milk
550ml/18fl oz/2½ cups Chicken Stock
30ml/2 tbsp demerara sugar
salt and cayenne pepper

1 In a small bowl, mix together the ground allspice, cinnamon, dried thyme, cloves and nutmeg. Place the chicken fillets on a plate and rub the spice mixture all over them. Set aside for 30 minutes.

2 Heat 15ml/1 tbsp of the oil with the butter in a saucepan. Fry the onion and garlic until soft and beginning to brown. Add the carrot, celery, spring onions and chilli. Sauté for a few minutes. Stir in the pigeon peas, rice, coconut milk and stock. Season with salt and cayenne pepper. Bring to simmering point, cover and cook over a low heat for about 25 minutes.

3 About 10 minutes before the rice mixture is cooked, heat the remaining oil in a heavy-based frying pan, add the sugar and cook, without stirring, until it begins to caramelize. Add the chicken. Cook for 8–10 minutes until it is browned, glazed and cooked through. Transfer the chicken to a board and slice thickly. Serve the pigeon pea rice in individual bowls, with the chicken on top.

Cajun Chicken Jambalaya

For this dish, the chicken is cooked whole and the resulting tasty stock is used to cook the rice.

Serves 4

1.2kg/2½lb chicken
600ml/1 pint/2½ cups water
1½ onions
1 bay leaf
4 black peppercorns
1 fresh parsley sprig
30ml/2 tbsp vegetable oil
2 garlic cloves, chopped
1 green pepper, seeded and chopped
1 celery stick, chopped
225g/8oz/generous 1 cup long-grain rice
115g/4oz/1 cup chorizo sausage, sliced
115g/4oz/⅔ cup chopped cooked ham
400g/14oz can chopped tomatoes with herbs
2.5ml/½ tsp hot chilli powder
2.5ml/½ tsp cumin seeds
2.5ml/½ tsp ground cumin
5ml/1 tsp dried thyme
115g/4oz/1 cup cooked, peeled prawns
dash of Tabasco sauce
salt and freshly ground black pepper
chopped fresh parsley, to garnish
cooked green beans, to serve

1 Place the chicken in a large, flameproof casserole and add the water, the half onion, the bay leaf, peppercorns and parsley, and bring to the boil. Cover and simmer gently for about 1½ hours.

2 Remove the chicken from the stock, discard the skin and bones and chop the meat. Strain the stock and leave to cool.

3 Chop the remaining onion and heat the oil in a large frying pan. Add the onion, garlic, green pepper and celery. Fry for 5 minutes, then stir in the rice. Add the sausage, ham and chicken, and fry for a further 2–3 minutes, stirring frequently.

4 Pour in the tomatoes and 300ml/½ pint/1¼ cups of the reserved stock. Add the chilli powder, cumin and thyme. Bring to the boil, cover and simmer for 20 minutes. Stir in the prawns and Tabasco, and cook for a further 5 minutes. Adjust the seasoning. Serve hot, garnished with chopped parsley and accompanied by green beans.

Rice Layered with Chicken & Potatoes

In India, this dish is mainly prepared for important occasions. Every cook in the country has a subtle and secret variation.

Serves 4–6

1.3kg/3lb chicken breast fillets, skinned and cut into large pieces
60ml/4 tbsp biryani masala paste
2 fresh green chillies, chopped
15ml/1 tbsp grated fresh root ginger
15ml/1 tbsp crushed garlic
50g/2oz/1 cup chopped fresh coriander leaves
6–8 fresh mint leaves, chopped
150ml/¼ pint/⅔ cup plain yogurt, beaten
30ml/2 tbsp tomato purée
4 onions, finely sliced, deep fried and crushed
450g/1lb/2¼ cups basmati rice
5ml/1 tsp black cumin seeds
5cm/2in cinnamon stick
4 green cardamom pods
2 black cardamom pods
vegetable oil, for shallow frying
4 large potatoes, quartered
175ml/6fl oz/¾ cup milk, mixed with 75ml/5 tbsp water
1 sachet saffron powder, mixed with 90ml/6 tbsp milk
30ml/2 tbsp ghee or unsalted butter

For the garnish

ghee or unsalted butter, for shallow frying
50g/2oz/½ cup cashew nuts
50g/2oz/scant ½ cup sultanas
2 hard-boiled eggs, quartered
Deep-fried Onions

1 In a bowl, mix the chicken with the masala paste, chillies, ginger, garlic, coriander, mint, yogurt, tomato purée, onions and salt to taste. Marinate for about 2 hours. Transfer to a heavy-based pan and cook gently for about 10 minutes. Set aside.

2 Boil a large pan of water and soak the rice with the cumin seeds, cinnamon stick and green and black cardamoms for about 5 minutes. Drain well. Some of the whole spices may be removed at this stage.

3 Heat the oil for shallow frying and fry the potatoes until they are evenly browned on all sides. Drain and set aside.

4 Place half the rice on top of the chicken in the pan in an even layer. Then make an even layer with the potatoes. Put the remaining rice on top of the potatoes and spread to make an even layer.

5 Sprinkle the milk mixed with water all over the rice. Make random holes through the rice with the handle of a spoon and pour into each a little saffron milk. Place a few knobs of ghee or butter on the surface, cover and cook over a low heat for 35–45 minutes.

6 Meanwhile, to make the garnish, heat a little ghee or butter and fry the cashew nuts and sultanas until they swell. Drain and set aside.

7 When the chicken dish is cooked, gently toss the rice, chicken and potatoes together, garnish with the nut mixture, hard-boiled eggs and deep-fried onions, and serve hot.

Chicken Chow Mein

Chow Mein, in which noodles are stir-fried with meat, seafood or vegetables, is arguably China's best-known noodle dish.

Serves 4

350g/12oz noodles
225g/8oz chicken breast fillets, skinned
45ml/3 tbsp soy sauce
15ml/1 tbsp rice wine or dry sherry
15ml/1 tbsp dark sesame oil
60ml/4 tbsp vegetable oil
15 ml/1 tsp Chinese five-spice powder
2 garlic cloves, finely chopped
50g/2oz mangetouts
115g/4oz/½ cup beansprouts
50g/2oz/⅓ cup ham, finely shredded
4 spring onions, finely chopped
salt and freshly ground black pepper

1 Cook the noodles in a saucepan of boiling water according to the packet instructions until tender. Drain, rinse under cold water and drain well again.

2 Slice the chicken into fine shreds about 5cm/2in in length. Place in a bowl and add 10ml/2 tsp of the soy sauce, the rice wine or sherry and sesame oil.

3 Heat half the vegetable oil in a wok or large frying pan over a high heat. When it starts smoking, add the chicken mixture. Stir-fry for 2 minutes until colouring, then transfer the chicken to a plate and keep it hot.

4 Wipe the wok clean and heat the remaining oil. Stir in the five-spice powder, garlic, mangetouts, beansprouts and ham, stir-fry for another minute or so, and add the noodles.

5 Continue to stir-fry until the noodles are heated through. Add the remaining soy sauce to taste, and season with salt and pepper. Return the chicken and any juices to the noodle mixture, add the chopped spring onions and give the mixture a final stir. Serve at once.

Special Chow Mein

This recipe calls for lap cheong, an air-dried Chinese sausage available from most Chinese supermarkets. If you cannot buy it, substitute ham, chorizo or salami.

Serves 4–6

45ml/3 tbsp vegetable oil
2 garlic cloves, sliced
5ml/1 tsp chopped fresh root ginger
2 fresh red chillies, chopped
2 lap cheong, about 76g/3oz, rinsed and sliced (optional)
1 chicken breast fillet, thinly sliced
16 raw tiger prawns, peeled but tails left intact and deveined
115g/4oz green beans
225g/8oz/1 cup beansprouts
50g/2oz/1 cup garlic chives
450g/1lb egg noodles, cooked in boiling water until tender
30ml/2 tbsp soy sauce
15ml/1 tbsp oyster sauce
15ml/1 tbsp sesame oil
salt and freshly ground black pepper
2 spring onions, shredded and 15ml/1 tbsp coriander leaves, to garnish

1 Heat 15ml/1 tbsp of the oil in a wok or large frying pan and fry the garlic, ginger and chillies. Add the lap cheong, chicken, prawns and beans. Stir-fry for about 2 minutes over a high heat or until the chicken and prawns are cooked. Transfer the mixture to a bowl and set aside.

2 Heat the rest of the oil in the wok. Add the beansprouts and garlic chives. Stir-fry for 1–2 minutes.

3 Add the noodles, and toss and stir to mix. Season with soy sauce, oyster sauce, salt and pepper.

4 Return the prawn mixture to the wok. Reheat and mix well with the noodles. Stir in the sesame oil. Serve, garnished with spring onions and coriander leaves.

Cook's Tip
Garlic chives are also known as Chinese or flowering chives. They have a mild garlic and chive flavour.

Chicken Curry with Rice Vermicelli

Lemon grass gives this South-east Asian curry a wonderful, lemony flavour and fragrance.

Serves 4

1.5kg/3½lb chicken
225g/8oz sweet potatoes
60ml/4 tbsp oil
1 onion, finely sliced
3 garlic cloves, crushed
30–45ml/2–3 tbsp Thai curry powder
5ml/1 tsp sugar
10ml/2 tsp fish sauce
600ml/1 pint/2½ cups coconut milk
1 lemon grass stalk, cut in half
350g/12oz rice vermicelli, soaked in hot water until soft
salt

For the garnish

115g/4oz/½ cup beansprouts
2 spring onions, thinly sliced diagonally
2 fresh red chillies, seeded and finely sliced
8–10 mint leaves

1 Skin the chicken and cut it into small pieces. Peel the sweet potatoes and cut them into large chunks.

2 Heat half the oil in a large, heavy-based saucepan. Add the onion and garlic, and fry until the onion softens. Add the chicken pieces and stir-fry until they change colour.

3 Stir in the curry powder. Season with salt and sugar, and mix thoroughly, then add the fish sauce, coconut milk and lemon grass. Cook over a low heat for 15 minutes.

4 Meanwhile, heat the remaining oil in a large frying pan. Fry the sweet potatoes until lightly golden.

5 Using a slotted spoon, add the sweet potato pieces to the chicken. Cook for 10–15 minutes more or until both the chicken and sweet potatoes are tender.

6 Drain the rice vermicelli and cook them in a saucepan of boiling water for 3–5 minutes. Drain well. Place in shallow serving bowls with the chicken curry. Garnish with beansprouts, spring onions, chillies and mint leaves, and serve.

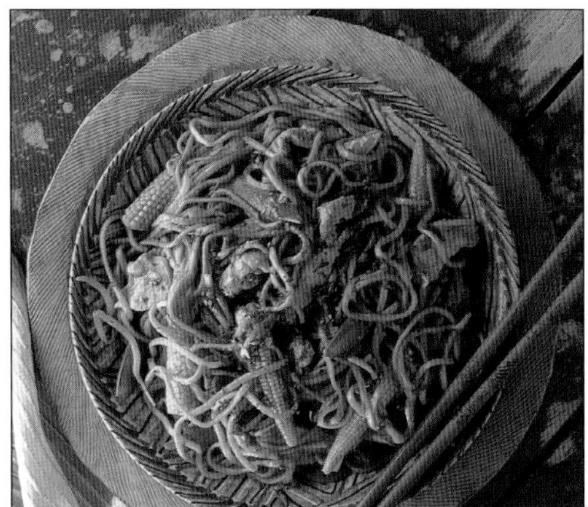

Stir-fried Sweet-&-sour Chicken

A quickly cooked, all-in-one stir-fry meal with a South-east Asian influence.

Serves 4

275g/10oz Chinese egg noodles
30ml/2 tbsp vegetable oil
3 spring onions, chopped
1 garlic clove, crushed
2.5cm/1in piece fresh root ginger, grated
5ml/1 tsp hot paprika
5ml/1 tsp ground coriander
3 chicken breast fillets, sliced
115g/4oz sugar snap peas, topped and tailed
115g/4oz baby sweetcorn, halved
225g/8oz/1 cup beansprouts
15ml/1 tbsp cornflour
45ml/3 tbsp soy sauce
45ml/3 tbsp lemon juice
15ml/1 tbsp sugar
salt
45ml/3 tbsp chopped fresh coriander or spring onion tops, to garnish

1 Bring a large saucepan of salted water to the boil. Add the noodles and cook according to the packet instructions. Drain, cover and keep warm.

2 Heat the oil in a wok or frying pan. Add the spring onions and cook over a gentle heat. Mix in the garlic, ginger, paprika and ground coriander, and stir for a minute or so. Add the chicken and stir-fry for 3–4 minutes.

3 Add the peas, sweetcorn and beansprouts, cover the wok and steam briefly. Stir in the noodles.

4 Combine the cornflour, soy sauce, lemon juice and sugar in a small bowl. Add to the wok and simmer briefly to thicken. Serve, garnished with chopped coriander or spring onion tops.

Cook's Tip

Large wok lids are cumbersome and can be difficult to store in a small kitchen. Consider placing a circle of greaseproof paper against the food surface to keep cooking juices in.

Spicy Sichuan Noodles

Cooked noodles, chicken and roasted cashew nuts tossed in a spicy dressing and served cold.

Serves 4

350g/12oz thick noodles
175g/6oz cooked chicken, shredded
50g/2oz/½ cup roasted cashew nuts
salt

For the dressing

4 spring onions, chopped
30ml/2 tbsp chopped fresh coriander
2 garlic cloves, chopped
30ml/2 tbsp smooth peanut butter
30ml/2 tbsp sweet chilli sauce
15ml/1 tbsp soy sauce
15ml/1 tbsp sherry vinegar
15ml/1 tbsp sesame oil
30ml/2 tbsp olive oil
30ml/2 tbsp Chicken Stock or water
10 toasted Sichuan peppercorns, ground

1 Bring a large saucepan of salted water to the boil. Add the noodles and cook according to the packet instructions. Drain, rinse under cold running water and drain well.

2 Meanwhile, to make the dressing, combine all the ingredients in a large bowl and whisk together well.

3 Add the noodles, shredded chicken and cashew nuts to the dressing, toss gently to coat and adjust the seasoning to taste. Serve at once.

Variation

You could substitute cooked turkey or duck for the chicken.

Mee Krob

The basis of this dish is fried rice vermicelli: take care when frying, as it has a tendency to spit when added to hot oil.

Serves 4

120ml/4fl oz/½ cup vegetable oil
225g/8oz rice vermicelli
150g/5oz French beans, topped, tailed and halved lengthways
1 onion, finely chopped
2 chicken breast fillets, about 175g/6oz each, skinned and cut into strips
5ml/1 tsp chilli powder
225g/8oz cooked peeled prawns
45ml/3 tbsp dark soy sauce
45ml/3 tbsp white wine vinegar
30ml/2 tsp caster sugar
fresh coriander sprigs, to garnish

1 Heat a wok, then add 60ml/4 tbsp of the oil. Break up the rice vermicelli into 7.5cm/3in lengths. When the oil is hot, fry the vermicelli in batches. Remove from the wok and keep warm.

2 Heat the remaining oil in the wok, then add the French beans, onion and chicken, and stir-fry for 3 minutes until the chicken is cooked.

3 Sprinkle in the chilli powder. Stir in the prawns, soy sauce, vinegar and sugar, and stir-fry for 2 minutes.

4 Serve the chicken, prawns and vegetables on the vermicelli, garnished with sprigs of fresh coriander.

Variation

Usually served at celebrations, this dish often includes other ingredients. You could add 115g/4oz minced pork and 3–4 seeded and chopped dried chillies in step 2. Brown bean sauce may be substituted for the soy sauce and palm sugar for the caster sugar. For a more elaborate garnish, make an omelette from 2 eggs, roll it up and cut into thin slices. Shredded spring onion and chopped fresh red chillies can also be sprinkled over the finished dish.

Chilli Chicken

This simple supper dish can be prepared in next to no time using ingredients from the store cupboard.

Serves 4

12 chicken thighs
15ml/1 tbsp olive oil
1 medium onion, thinly sliced
1 garlic clove, crushed
1 fresh green chilli, chopped, or 5ml/1 tsp chilli powder
400g/14oz can chopped tomatoes, with their juice
5ml/1 tsp caster sugar
425g/15oz can red kidney beans, drained and rinsed
salt and freshly ground black pepper
fresh parsley sprig, to garnish
cooked rice, to serve

1 Cut the chicken into large cubes, removing all the skin and bones. Heat the oil in a large, flameproof casserole and brown the chicken pieces on all sides. Remove from the casserole and keep warm.

2 Add the onion and garlic to the casserole, and cook gently until tender. Stir in the fresh chilli or chilli powder and cook for 2 minutes. Add the tomatoes with their juice, sugar and seasoning. Bring to the boil.

3 Return the chicken pieces to the casserole, cover and simmer for about 30 minutes until tender.

4 Add the kidney beans and cook over a low heat for a further 5 minutes to heat them through. Serve with rice, garnished with fresh parsley.

Variation
You could substitute canned chick-peas for the kidney beans and add 2 chopped or sliced medium carrots to the casserole with the onion and garlic in step 2. For an extra spicy touch, add a dash of Tabasco sauce with the seasoning.

Chicken Naan Pockets

This quick-and-easy dish is ideal for a snack lunch and makes excellent picnic fare. For speed, use the ready-to-bake naans available in some supermarkets and Asian stores, or try warmed pitta bread instead.

Serves 4

4 naan breads
450g/1lb chicken, skinned, boned and cubed
45ml/3 tbsp plain yogurt
7.5ml/1½ tsp garam masala
5ml/1 tsp chilli powder
5ml/1 tsp salt
45ml/3 tbsp lemon juice
15ml/1 tbsp chopped fresh coriander
1 fresh green chilli, chopped
15ml/1 tbsp vegetable oil
8 onion rings
2 tomatoes, quartered
½ white cabbage, shredded

For the garnish
lemon wedges
2 small tomatoes, halved
mixed salad leaves
fresh coriander

1 Cut into the middle of each naan to make a pocket, then set aside. Place the chicken cubes in a dish.

2 In a small bowl, mix together the plain yogurt, garam masala, chilli powder, salt, lemon juice, chopped fresh coriander and chopped fresh green chilli. Pour the mixture over the cubed chicken pieces and leave to marinate for about 1 hour.

3 Preheat the grill to very hot, then lower the heat to medium. Place the chicken in a flameproof dish and cook under the grill for 15–20 minutes until tender and cooked through, turning the pieces at least twice. Baste frequently with the vegetable oil during cooking.

4 Fill each naan with the chicken and then with the onion rings, tomatoes and cabbage.

5 Serve hot, garnished with lemon wedges, tomato halves, mixed salad leaves and fresh coriander.

Mixed Tostadas

Like little edible plates, these fried Mexican tortillas can support any filling that is not too juicy.

Makes 14

oil, for shallow frying
14 freshly prepared unbaked corn tortillas
225g/8oz/1 cup mashed cooked or canned red kidney or pinto beans
1 iceberg lettuce, shredded
vinaigrette dressing (optional)
2 cooked chicken breast fillets, skinned and thinly sliced
225g/8oz ready-made guacamole
115g/4oz/1 cup coarsely grated Cheddar cheese
pickled jalapeño chillies, seeded and sliced, to taste

1 Heat the oil in a frying pan and fry the tortillas until golden brown on both sides and crisp but not hard.

2 Spread each tortilla with a layer of mashed beans. Put a layer of shredded lettuce (which can be left plain or lightly tossed with a little dressing) over the beans.

3 Arrange pieces of chicken in a layer on top of the lettuce. Carefully spread over a layer of the guacamole and finally sprinkle with the grated cheese. Scatter sliced pickled chillies over the top, to taste.

4 Arrange the mixed tostadas on a large serving platter. Serve on individual plates but eat using your hands.

Cook's Tip

To make a vinaigrette dressing, whisk together 45ml/3 tbsp wine vinegar, 15ml/1 tbsp Dijon mustard, and salt and pepper to taste. Gradually whisk in 150ml/¼ pint/⅔ cup olive oil. Alternatively, put all the ingredients in a screw-top jar and shake vigorously until thoroughly combined.

Mexican Chicken

Warm taco shells filled with chicken in a spicy sauce, served with lettuce, tomatoes, soured cream and grated cheese.

Serves 4

1.3kg/3lb chicken
5ml/1 tsp salt
12 taco shells
1 small iceberg lettuce, shredded
175g/6oz tomatoes, chopped
250ml/8fl oz/1 cup soured cream
115g/4oz/1 cup grated Cheddar cheese

For the sauce
250ml/8fl oz/1 cup fresh tomatoes, peeled, cooked and sieved
1–2 garlic cloves, crushed
2.5ml/½ tsp cider vinegar
2.5ml/½ tsp dried oregano
2.5ml/½ tsp ground cumin
15–30ml/1–2 tbsp mild chilli powder

1 Put the chicken in a large pan, and add the salt and enough water to cover. Bring to the boil. Reduce the heat and simmer for about 45 minutes to 1 hour until the chicken is thoroughly cooked. Remove the chicken from the pan and allow to cool. Reserve 120ml/4fl oz/½ cup of the stock for the sauce.

2 Remove the chicken meat from the bones, discarding all the skin. Chop the meat coarsely.

3 To make the sauce, combine all the ingredients with the reserved chicken stock in a saucepan and bring to the boil. Stir in the chicken meat. Simmer for about 20 minutes until the sauce thickens considerably, stirring from time to time.

4 Preheat the oven to 180°C/350°F/Gas 4. Spread out the taco shells on two baking sheets and heat in the oven for 7 minutes.

5 Meanwhile, put the shredded lettuce, chopped tomatoes, soured cream and grated cheese in individual serving dishes. To serve, spoon a little of the hot chicken mixture into each taco shell. Garnish with the lettuce, tomatoes, soured cream and grated Cheddar cheese.

Tortilla Flutes

These crisply fried rolled tortillas, stuffed with chicken in fresh tomato sauce, look as good as they taste.

Makes about 12

24 freshly prepared unbaked flour tortillas
2 tomatoes, peeled, seeded and chopped
1 small onion, chopped
1 garlic clove, chopped
30–45ml/2–3 tbsp corn oil
2 freshly cooked chicken breast fillets, skinned and shredded
salt

For the garnish

sliced radishes
stuffed green olives
fresh coriander

1 Place the unbaked flour tortillas in pairs on a work surface, with the right-hand tortilla overlapping the left-hand one by about 5cm/2in.

2 Put the tomatoes, onion and garlic into a food processor and process to a purée. Season with salt to taste.

3 Heat 15ml/1 tbsp of the corn oil in a frying pan and cook the tomato purée for a few minutes, stirring constantly to blend the flavours. Remove from the heat and stir in the shredded chicken, mixing well.

4 Spread about 30ml/2 tbsp of the chicken mixture on each pair of tortillas, roll them up into flutes and secure with a cocktail stick.

5 Heat a little more of the oil in a frying pan large enough to hold the flutes comfortably. Cook more than one at a time if possible, but don't overcrowd the pan. Fry the flutes until light brown all over. Add more oil if needed.

6 Drain the cooked flutes on kitchen paper and keep hot. When ready to serve, transfer to a platter and garnish with radishes, olives and coriander.

Chicken Fajitas

Fajitas are warmed soft tortillas, filled and folded like an envelope. They are traditional Mexican fast food, delicious and easy to prepare, and a favourite for family supper.

Serves 4

115g/4oz/generous ½ cup long-grain rice
15g/1oz/3 tbsp wild rice
15ml/1 tbsp olive oil
15ml/1 tbsp sunflower oil
1 onion, cut into thin wedges
4 chicken breast fillets, skinned and cut into thin strips
1 red pepper, seeded and thinly sliced
5ml/1 tsp ground cumin
generous pinch of cayenne pepper
2.5ml/½ tsp ground turmeric
175ml/6fl oz/¾ cup passata
120–175ml/4–6fl oz/½–¾ cup Chicken Stock
12 small or 8 large wheat tortillas, warmed
soured cream, to serve

For the salsa

1 shallot, roughly chopped
1 small garlic clove
½–1 fresh green chilli, seeded and roughly chopped
small bunch of fresh parsley
5 tomatoes, peeled, seeded and chopped
10ml/2 tsp olive oil
15ml/1 tbsp lemon juice
30ml/2 tbsp tomato juice
salt and freshly ground black pepper

For the guacamole

1 large ripe avocado
2 spring onions, chopped
15–30ml/1–2 tbsp fresh lime or lemon juice
generous pinch of cayenne pepper
15ml/1 tbsp chopped fresh coriander

1 Cook the long-grain and wild rice separately, following the instructions on the packets. Drain and set aside.

2 To make the salsa, finely chop the shallot, garlic, chilli and parsley in a blender or food processor. Spoon into a bowl. Stir in the tomatoes, olive oil, lemon juice and tomato juice. Season to taste with salt and pepper. Cover with clear film and chill.

3 To make the guacamole, scoop the avocado flesh into a bowl. Mash it lightly with the spring onions, citrus juice, cayenne, fresh coriander and seasoning, so that small pieces still remain. Cover the surface closely with clear film and chill.

4 Heat the olive and sunflower oils in a frying pan and fry the onion wedges for 4–5 minutes until softened. Add the chicken strips and red pepper slices, and fry until evenly browned.

5 Stir in the cumin, cayenne and turmeric. Fry, stirring, for about 1 minute, then stir in the passata and chicken stock. Bring to the boil, then lower the heat and simmer gently for 5–6 minutes until the chicken is cooked through. Season to taste.

6 Stir both types of rice into the chicken and cook for 1–2 minutes until the rice is warmed through.

7 Spoon a little of the chicken mixture on to each warmed tortilla. Top with salsa, guacamole and soured cream, and roll up. Alternatively, let everyone assemble their own fajita at the table.

Enchiladas with Hot Chilli Sauce

By Mexican standards, this is a low-heat version of the popular chicken enchiladas. If you like your food hot, you can add extra chillies to the sauce.

Serves 4

butter, for greasing
8 wheat tortillas
175g/6oz/1½ cups grated Cheddar cheese
1 onion, finely chopped
350g/12oz cooked chicken, cut into small chunks
300ml/½ pint/1¼ cups soured cream
1 avocado, sliced and tossed in lemon juice, to garnish

For the salsa picante
1–2 fresh green chillies
15ml/1 tbsp vegetable oil
1 onion, chopped
1 garlic clove, crushed
400g/14oz can chopped tomatoes
30ml/2 tbsp tomato purée
salt and freshly ground black pepper

1 To make the salsa picante, halve the chillies, and remove the cores and seeds. Slice the chillies very thinly. Heat the oil in a frying pan, and fry the onion and garlic for 3–4 minutes until softened. Add the tomatoes, tomato purée and chillies. Simmer gently, uncovered, for about 12–15 minutes, stirring frequently.

2 Pour the sauce into a food processor or blender and process until smooth. Return to the heat and cook very gently, uncovered, for a further 15 minutes. Season and set aside.

3 Preheat the oven to 180°C/350°F/Gas 4 and butter a shallow, ovenproof dish. Sprinkle each tortilla with grated cheese and chopped onion, about 40g/1½oz of the chicken and 15ml/1 tbsp of the salsa. Pour over 15ml/1 tbsp of the soured cream, roll up and place, seam side down, in the dish.

4 Pour the remaining salsa picante over the top of the enchiladas and sprinkle with the remaining cheese and onion. Bake in the oven for about 25–30 minutes until the top is golden. Serve with the remaining soured cream either poured over or in a separate jug and garnish with the sliced avocado.

Turkey-chorizo Tacos

Chopped spicy chorizo sausage and minced turkey make a warming filling for Mexican taco shells.

Serves 4

15ml/1 tbsp vegetable oil
450g/1lb minced turkey
5ml/1 tsp salt
5ml/1 tsp ground cumin
12 taco shells
75g/3oz chorizo, finely chopped
3 spring onions, chopped
2 tomatoes, chopped
1 small lettuce, shredded
115g/4oz/2 cups grated Cheddar cheese
tomato salsa and guacamole, to serve

1 Preheat the oven to 180°C/350°F/Gas 4. Heat the oil in a non-stick frying pan and add the turkey, salt and cumin. Sauté over a medium heat for 5–8 minutes until the turkey is cooked through, stirring frequently to break up any lumps.

2 Meanwhile, arrange the taco shells in one layer on a large baking sheet and heat in the oven about 10 minutes or according to the directions on the package.

3 Add the chopped chorizo and spring onions to the turkey, and stir to mix. Cook until just warmed through, stirring the mixture occasionally.

4 To assemble each taco, place 1–2 spoonfuls of the turkey mixture in the bottom of a warmed taco shell. Top with a generous sprinkling of chopped tomato, shredded lettuce and grated cheese.

5 Serve immediately, with tomato salsa and guacamole.

Variation
You can use minced chicken for these tacos, if preferred.

Hot Turkey Chilli

This nutritious and tasty dish, perfect for a family supper, is made economically with minced turkey.

Serves 8

30ml/2 tbsp corn oil
1 medium onion, halved and thinly sliced
1 green pepper, seeded and diced
3 garlic cloves, crushed
900g/2lb minced turkey
30–45ml/2–3 tbsp chilli powder
7.5ml/1½ tsp ground cumin
5ml/1 tsp dried oregano
400g/14oz can chopped tomatoes
30ml/2 tbsp tomato purée
250ml/8fl oz/1 cup Chicken Stock
425g/15oz can red kidney beans, drained and rinsed
1.5ml/¼ tsp salt
boiled rice, to serve

1 Heat the oil in a large saucepan over a medium heat. Add the onion, green pepper and garlic, and cook for about 5 minutes until softened, stirring frequently.

2 Add the turkey and cook for about 5 minutes until it is lightly browned, stirring to break up any lumps.

3 Stir in the chilli powder, cumin and oregano. Add the tomatoes, tomato purée, chicken stock, kidney beans and salt, and stir well.

4 Bring the mixture to the boil, then reduce the heat and simmer for 30 minutes, stirring occasionally. Serve the chilli with boiled rice.

Cook's Tip

Canned kidney beans are quick and convenient, but you could use dried beans, which are more economical. Soak them in cold water to cover for 3–4 hours, drain and place in a saucepan. Add fresh cold water to cover and bring to the boil. Boil vigorously for 15 minutes. This is essential as it destroys a naturally occurring toxin in the skin of the beans. Lower the heat and simmer for 1½–2 hours until tender, then drain.

Turkey Sosaties with a Curried Apricot Sauce

This is a South African way of cooking poultry in a delicious sweet-and-sour sauce that is spiced with curry powder.

Serves 4

15ml/1 tbsp oil
1 onion, finely chopped
1 garlic clove, crushed
2 bay leaves
juice of 1 lemon
30ml/2 tbsp curry powder
60ml/4 tbsp apricot jam
60ml/4 tbsp apple juice
salt
675g/1½lb turkey fillet
60ml/4 tbsp crème fraîche

1 Heat the oil in a saucepan. Add the onion, garlic and bay leaves, and cook over a low heat for 10 minutes until the onions are soft.

2 Add the lemon juice, curry powder, apricot jam and apple juice with salt to taste. Cook gently for 5 minutes. Remove from the heat and leave to cool.

3 Cut the turkey into 2cm/¾in cubes and place in a dish. Add the cooled onion mixture and stir thoroughly. Cover and leave in a cool place to marinate for at least 2 hours or overnight in the fridge.

4 Preheat the grill or prepare a barbecue. Thread the turkey on to skewers, allowing the marinade to run back into the dish. Grill or barbecue the sosaties for 6–8 minutes, turning several times, until cooked.

5 Meanwhile, transfer the marinade to a pan and simmer for 2 minutes. Stir in the créme fraîche and serve with the sosaties.

Variation

This marinade is equally good with cubes of chicken.

Stuffed Turkey in Lemon Sauce

Sweet potatoes and prawns flavoured with herbs and chilli make an unusual stuffing for turkey fillets. Use orange-fleshed potatoes.

Serves 4

175g/6oz sweet potato
1 onion, finely chopped
5ml/1 tsp dried tarragon, crushed
2.5ml/½ tsp dried basil
1 fresh green chilli, seeded and finely chopped
1 garlic clove, crushed
2.5ml/½ tsp dried thyme
115g/4oz cooked peeled prawns, chopped
4 turkey fillets, about 225g/8oz each
butter, for greasing
salt and freshly ground black pepper
cooked root vegetables, bulgur wheat or rice, to serve

For the lemon sauce

15ml/1 tbsp olive oil
½ onion, finely chopped
2 garlic cloves, crushed
300ml/½ pint/1¼ cups Chicken Stock
3.5ml/¾ tsp dried thyme
2.5ml/½ tsp dried basil
30ml/2 tbsp finely chopped fresh parsley
30ml/2 tbsp lemon juice
mint leaves, to garnish

1 Preheat the oven to 180°C/350°F/Gas 4. Cook the sweet potato in boiling water until tender, drain, transfer to a bowl and mash. Add the onion, tarragon, basil, chilli, garlic, thyme and prawns to the sweet potato, season with pepper and mix well.

2 Lay the turkey fillets on a plate and season. Place a little of the sweet potato stuffing in the centre of each, fold over the sides and roll up. Secure with a wooden cocktail stick and place in a buttered ovenproof dish, seam side down.

3 To make the sauce, heat the oil in a frying pan and fry the onion and garlic for 5–7 minutes until soft. Stir in the stock and simmer briefly. Add the herbs and lemon juice, and simmer for 2 minutes. Season to taste.

4 Pour the sauce around the turkey, cover with foil and bake for 1½ hours, basting frequently with the sauce to keep the rolls moist. Garnish with mint and serve with bulgur wheat or rice.

Duck with Sherry & Pumpkin

For this dish, duck is marinated in a mixture of spices and cooked in a smooth pumpkin and tomato sauce enriched with medium-dry sherry.

Serves 6

1 whole duck, about 1.75kg/3lb
1 lemon
5ml/1 tsp garlic granules or 2 garlic cloves, crushed
5ml/1 tsp curry powder
2.5ml/½ tsp paprika
3.5ml/¾ tsp Indian five-spice powder
30ml/2 tbsp soy sauce, plus extra to serve
vegetable oil, for frying
salt and freshly ground black pepper

For the sauce

75g/3oz pumpkin
1 onion, chopped
4 canned plum tomatoes
300ml/½ pint/1¼ cups medium-dry sherry
about 300ml/½ pint/1¼ cups water

1 Cut the duck into 10 pieces and place in a large bowl. Halve the lemon and squeeze the juice all over the duck. Set aside.

2 In a small bowl, mix together the garlic, curry powder, paprika, five-spice powder and salt and pepper, and rub well into the duck pieces. Sprinkle the duck with the soy sauce, cover loosely with clear film and leave to marinate overnight.

3 To make the sauce, cook the pumpkin in boiling water until tender. Blend to a purée with the onion and tomatoes in a food processor or blender.

4 Pat the duck pieces dry with kitchen paper. Heat a little oil in a wok or large frying pan and fry the duck for 15 minutes until crisp and brown. Remove from the pan and set aside.

5 Wipe away the excess oil from the wok or frying pan with kitchen paper and pour in the pumpkin purée. Add the sherry and a little of the water, then bring to the boil and add the fried duck. Simmer for about 1 hour until the duck is cooked, adding more water if the sauce becomes too thick. Serve hot and hand soy sauce separately.

Hot Chilli Duck with Crab Meat & Cashew Nut Sauce

Perhaps a surprising partner for duck, crab meat nonetheless makes a wonderful rich sauce with Thai spices and coconut.

Serves 4–6

2.75kg/6lb duck
about 1.2 litres/2 pints/5 cups water
2 kaffir lime leaves
2–3 small fresh red chillies, seeded and finely chopped
25ml/5 tsp sugar
30ml/2 tbsp coriander seeds
5ml/1 tsp caraway seeds
115g/4oz/1 cup cashew nuts, chopped
7.5cm/3in piece lemon grass, shredded
2.5cm/1in piece galangal or fresh root ginger, finely chopped
2 garlic cloves, crushed
4 shallots or 1 medium onion, finely chopped
2cm/¾in cube shrimp paste
25g/1oz/½ cup coriander white root or stem, finely chopped
175g/6oz frozen white crab meat, thawed
50g/2oz creamed coconut
salt
1 small bunch fresh coriander, chopped, to garnish
cooked Thai fragrant rice, to serve

1 To portion the duck into manageable pieces, first remove the legs. Separate the thighs from the drumsticks and chop each thigh and drumstick into two pieces. Trim away the lower half of the duck with kitchen scissors. Cut the breast piece in half down the middle, then chop each half into four pieces.

2 Put the duck flesh and bones into a large saucepan and add the water – it should just cover the meat. Add the lime leaves and 5ml/1 tsp salt, bring to the boil and simmer, uncovered, for 35–40 minutes until the duck is tender. Discard the bones, skim off the fat from the stock and place in a clean pan.

3 Grind the chillies together with the sugar and 2.5ml/½ tsp salt using a food processor. Dry-fry the coriander and caraway seeds and the cashews in a wok for about 1–2 minutes. Add to the food processor with the lemon grass, galangal or ginger, garlic and shallots or onion, and process to a smooth paste. Add the shrimp paste and coriander root or stem.

4 Add 250ml/8fl oz/1 cup of the duck stock to the spicy mixture in the food processor and blend to make a thin paste.

5 Pour the spicy paste from the food processor in with the duck, bring to the boil and simmer, uncovered, for about 20–25 minutes.

6 Add the crab meat and creamed coconut, and simmer briefly. Turn out on to a serving dish, garnish with chopped coriander and serve, accompanied by Thai fragrant rice.

Cook's Tip

Shrimp paste is made from dried shrimp fermented in brine. It both smells and tastes strongly, so add it with caution. It is used widely throughout South-east Asia, where it is known as blacan *or* blachan. *The Japanese variety is called* terasi.

Hot Sweet-&-Sour Duck Casserole

This dish has a distinctively sweet, sour and hot flavour, and is best eaten with rice as an accompaniment.

Serves 4–6

1.3kg/3lb duck, jointed and skinned
4 bay leaves
45ml/3 tbsp salt
75ml/5 tbsp vegetable oil
juice of 5 lemons
8 medium onions, finely chopped
50g/2oz garlic, crushed
50g/2oz chilli powder
300ml/½ pint/1¼ cups pickling vinegar
115g/4oz fresh root ginger, thinly sliced or shredded
115g/4oz/generous ½ cup sugar
50g/2oz garam masala

1 Place the duck, bay leaves and salt in a large pan, and cover with cold water. Bring to the boil, then simmer until the duck is fully cooked: the juices should run clear when the thickest part of the thigh is pierced with a skewer or knife. Remove the duck from the pan and keep warm. Reserve the liquid to use as a base for stock or soups.

2 In a large pan, heat the oil and lemon juice until it reaches smoking point. Add the onions, garlic and chilli powder, and fry until the onions are golden brown.

3 Add the vinegar, ginger and sugar, and simmer until the sugar dissolves and the oil has separated.

4 Add the duck to the pan with the garam masala. Mix well, then reheat until the masala clings to the pieces of duck and the gravy is thick. Taste and adjust the seasoning as necessary. If you prefer a thinner gravy, add a little of the reserved stock. Serve hot.

Variation

This recipe also works well with most game birds. Try it with guinea fowl, pheasant or partridge – or, of course, wild duck, such as teal or widgeon.

Chicken Pittas with Red Coleslaw

Pittas are convenient for simple snacks and packed lunches and it's easy to cram in lots of fresh, healthy ingredients.

Serves 4
¼ red cabbage
1 small red onion
2 radishes
1 red dessert apple
15ml/1 tbsp lemon juice
45ml/3 tbsp low-fat fromage frais
1 cooked chicken breast without skin, about 175g/6oz
4 large or 8 small pitta breads
salt and freshly ground black pepper
chopped fresh parsley, to garnish

1 Remove the tough central spine from the cabbage leaves, then finely shred the leaves using a large, sharp knife. Thinly slice the onion. Thinly slice the radishes. Peel, core and grate the apple. Place the cabbage, onion, radishes and apple in a bowl and stir in the lemon juice.

2 Stir the fromage frais into the shredded cabbage mixture, and season well with salt and pepper.

3 Thinly slice the cooked chicken breast and stir into the shredded cabbage mixture until well coated in fromage frais.

4 Preheat the grill. Warm the pittas under the grill, then split them along one edge using a round-bladed knife. Spoon the filling into the pittas, garnish with chopped fresh parsley and serve immediately.

Cook's Tip
If the filled pitta breads need to be made more than an hour in advance, line them with crisp lettuce leaves before adding the filling.

Caribbean Chicken Kebabs

These kebabs have a rich, sunshine Caribbean flavour and the marinade keeps them moist without the need for oil. Serve with a colourful salad and rice.

Serves 4
500g/1¼ lb chicken breast fillet, skinned
finely grated rind of 1 lime
30ml/2 tbsp lime juice
15ml/1 tbsp rum or sherry
15ml/1 tbsp light muscovado sugar
5ml/1 tsp ground cinnamon
2 mangoes, peeled and cubed
rice and salad, to serve

1 Cut the chicken into bite-size chunks and place in a non-metallic bowl with the lime rind and juice, rum or sherry, sugar and ground cinnamon. Toss well to coat, cover and leave to stand for 1 hour.

2 Drain the chicken and reserve the marinade. Thread the chicken on to four wooden skewers, alternating with the mango cubes. Preheat the grill or prepare the barbecue.

3 Cook the chicken skewers under the grill or on the barbecue for 8–10 minutes, turning occasionally and basting frequently with the reserved marinade until the chicken is tender and golden brown. Serve at once with rice and salad.

Cook's Tip
The rum or sherry adds a wonderfully rich flavour, but it can be omitted if you prefer or if you are preparing the kebabs for children. In which case, you might wish to add an extra 15ml/1 tbsp lime juice.

Chicken Tortellini

These tasty little parcels, with a chicken and ham filling, are poached in stock.

Serves 4–6

115g/4oz smoked lean ham, diced
115g/4oz chicken breast fillet, skinned and diced
900ml/1½ pint/3¾ cups vegetable or Chicken Stock
fresh coriander stalks
30ml/2 tbsp grated Parmesan cheese, plus extra to serve
1 egg, beaten, plus egg white for brushing
30ml/2 tbsp chopped fresh coriander
1 quantity Basic Pasta Dough
flour, for dusting
salt and freshly ground black pepper
fresh coriander leaves, to garnish

1 Put the ham and chicken into a saucepan with 150ml/¼ pint/⅔ cup of the stock and some coriander stalks. Bring to the boil, cover and simmer for 20 minutes. Set aside to cool slightly.

2 Drain the ham and chicken, reserving the stock, and mince finely. Put the meat into a bowl with the Parmesan, beaten egg and chopped coriander. Season with salt and pepper.

3 Roll the pasta into thin sheets and cut into 4cm/1½in squares. Put 2.5ml/½ tsp of the meat mixture on each. Brush the edges with egg white and fold each square into a triangle; press out any air and seal firmly. Curl each triangle around the tip of a forefinger and press the two ends together firmly. Lay on a lightly floured dish towel to rest for 30 minutes before cooking.

4 Strain the reserved stock and add to the remainder. Put into a pan and bring to the boil. Lower the heat and add the tortellini. Cook for 5 minutes. Turn off the heat, cover and leave to stand for 20–30 minutes. Ladle into soup plates with some of the stock and garnish with coriander leaves. Serve, with extra grated Parmesan handed separately.

Lasagne

You can still enjoy classic pasta dishes even if you are reducing the fat content of your diet, as this version of lasagne, made with minced chicken or turkey, shows.

Serves 6–8

1 large onion, chopped
2 garlic cloves, crushed
500g/1¼ lb minced chicken or turkey
450g/1lb carton passata
5ml/1 tsp dried mixed herbs
225g/8oz frozen leaf spinach, thawed
200g/7oz lasagne verdi
200g/7oz/scant 1 cup low-fat cottage cheese
salt and freshly ground black pepper
mixed salad, to serve

For the sauce

25g/1oz/2 tbsp low-fat margarine
25g/1oz/¼ cup plain flour
300ml/½ pint/1¼ cups skimmed milk
1.5ml/¼ tsp grated nutmeg
25g/1oz/⅓ cup grated Parmesan cheese

1 Put the onion, garlic and minced chicken or turkey into a non-stick saucepan. Brown quickly for 5 minutes, stirring with a wooden spoon to break up any lumps.

2 Add the passata, herbs and seasoning. Bring to the boil, cover and simmer for 30 minutes.

3 To make the sauce, put all the ingredients, except the Parmesan cheese, into a saucepan. Heat to thicken, whisking constantly until bubbling and smooth. Season to taste, add the cheese to the sauce and stir.

4 Preheat the oven to 190°C/375°F/Gas 5. Lay the spinach leaves out on kitchen paper and pat dry.

5 Layer the chicken or turkey mixture, dried lasagne, cottage cheese and spinach in a 2 litre/3½ pint/9 cup ovenproof dish, starting and ending with a layer of chicken or turkey.

6 Spoon the sauce over the top to cover and bake for 45–50 minutes or until bubbling. Serve with a mixed salad.

Rolled Stuffed Cannelloni

These cannelloni are made by rolling cooked lasagne sheets around the herby chicken filling.

Serves 4

12 sheets lasagne
30ml/2 tbsp grated Parmesan cheese
fresh basil leaves, to garnish

For the filling

2–3 garlic cloves, crushed
1 small onion, finely chopped
150ml/ ¼ pint/ ⅔ cup white wine
450g/1lb minced chicken
15ml/1 tbsp dried basil
15ml/1 tbsp dried thyme
40g/1½ oz/ ¾ cup fresh white breadcrumbs
salt and freshly ground black pepper

For the sauce

25g/1oz/2 tbsp low-fat margarine
25g/1oz/ ¼ cup plain flour
300ml/ ½ pint/1¼ cups skimmed milk
4 sun-dried tomatoes, chopped
15ml/1 tbsp chopped mixed fresh herbs (basil, parsley, marjoram)

1 To make the filling, put the garlic, onion and half the wine into a pan. Cover and cook for 5 minutes. Add the chicken and break up with a spoon. Cook until all the liquid has evaporated and the chicken begins to brown, stirring constantly. Add the remaining wine, seasoning and herbs. Cover and simmer for 20 minutes. Remove from the heat and stir in the breadcrumbs.

2 Cook the lasagne sheets in a large pan of boiling salted water according to the packet instructions until *al dente*. Drain and rinse in cold water. Pat dry on a clean dish towel.

3 Spread out the lasagne. Spoon the chicken mixture along one short edge and roll up into a tube. Cut the tubes in half.

4 Preheat the oven to 200°C/400°F/Gas 6. To make the sauce, put the margarine, flour and milk into a pan, heat and whisk until thickened. Add the tomatoes and herbs. Season to taste.

5 Spoon a layer of sauce into an ovenproof dish and place a layer of cannelloni on top. Repeat, then sprinkle with Parmesan. Bake for 10–15 minutes. Garnish and serve.

Minty Yogurt Chicken

Marinating skinned chicken in yogurt infused with fresh mint and lime or lemon juice is an excellent way to give it flavour with the minimum of fat.

Serves 4

8 chicken thighs, skinned
15ml/1 tbsp clear honey
30ml/2 tbsp lime or lemon juice
30ml/2 tbsp plain yogurt
60ml/4 tbsp chopped fresh mint
salt and freshly ground black pepper
boiled new potatoes and tomato salad, to serve

1 Slash the flesh of the chicken thighs at intervals with a sharp knife. Place in a bowl.

2 In another small bowl, mix the honey, lime or lemon juice, yogurt, seasoning and half the mint.

3 Spoon the yogurt mixture over the chicken and leave to marinate for 30 minutes. Preheat the grill and line a grill pan with foil.

4 Cook the chicken under a moderately hot grill until thoroughly cooked and golden brown, turning occasionally during cooking.

5 Sprinkle the chicken with the remaining mint and serve at once with new potatoes and tomato salad.

Cook's Tip

There are several different types of yogurt. Ordinary plain yogurt is made by adding a culture to full-fat milk. Its fat content varies, but can be as high as 7.5 per cent. Low-fat yogurt is made from concentrated skimmed milk and has a fat content of 0.5–2 per cent. Very low-fat yogurt, made from skimmed milk, contains less than 0.5 per cent fat.

Chicken with Mixed Vegetables

A riot of colour, this delectable dish has plenty of contrasts in terms of texture and taste.

Serves 4

350g/12oz chicken breast fillets, skinned
20ml/4 tsp vegetable oil
300ml/ ½ pint/1 ¼ cups Chicken Stock
75g/3oz/ ¾ cup drained, canned straw mushrooms
50g/2oz/ ½ cup drained, canned bamboo shoots, sliced
50g/2oz/ ⅓ cup drained, canned water chestnuts, sliced
1 small carrot, sliced
50g/2oz mangetouts
15ml/1 tbsp dry sherry
15ml/1 tbsp oyster sauce
5ml/1 tsp caster sugar
5ml/1 tsp cornflour
15ml/1 tbsp cold water
salt and freshly ground white pepper

1 Put the chicken in a shallow bowl. Add 5ml/1 tsp of the oil, 1.5ml/¼ tsp salt and a pinch of pepper. Cover and set aside for 10 minutes in a cool place.

2 Bring the stock to the boil in a saucepan. Add the chicken and cook for 12 minutes or until tender. Drain, reserving 75ml/5 tbsp of the stock. Slice the chicken.

3 Heat the remaining oil in a non-stick frying pan or wok, add all the vegetables and stir-fry for 2 minutes. Stir in the sherry, oyster sauce, caster sugar and reserved stock. Add the chicken to the pan and cook for 2 minutes more.

4 Mix the cornflour to a smooth, thin paste with the water. Add the mixture to the pan and cook, stirring constantly, until the sauce thickens slightly. Season to taste with salt and pepper, and serve immediately.

Cook's Tip
Popular in Chinese and South-east Asian cuisine, straw mushrooms are valued less for their flavour than for their slippery texture.

Chicken Baked with Butter Beans & Garlic

A one-pot meal that combines chicken with leeks, fennel and garlic-flavoured butter beans.

Serves 6

2 leeks
1 small fennel bulb
4 garlic cloves
2 x 400g/14oz cans butter beans, drained and rinsed
2 large handfuls fresh parsley, chopped
300ml/ ½ pint/1 ¼ cups dry white wine
300ml/ ½ pint/1 ¼ cups vegetable stock
1.5kg/3 ½ lb chicken
fresh parsley sprigs, to garnish
lightly cooked green vegetables, to serve

1 Preheat the oven to 180°C/350°F/Gas 4. Slit the leeks, wash out any grit, then slice them thickly. Cut the fennel into quarters, remove the core and chop the flesh roughly. Peel the garlic cloves, leaving them whole.

2 Mix the leeks, fennel, whole garlic cloves, butter beans and parsley in a bowl. Spread out the mixture on the base of a heavy-based flameproof casserole that is large enough to hold the chicken. Pour in the white wine and vegetable stock, and stir well.

3 Place the chicken on top of the vegetable mixture. Bring to the boil, cover the casserole and transfer it to the oven. Bake for 1–1½ hours until the chicken is cooked and so tender that it falls off the bone. Garnish with parsley and serve with lightly cooked green vegetables.

Cook's Tip
Stock can be made with almost any vegetables, but not green leafy ones. Add a few fresh herbs, garlic and a strip of lemon rind, cover with water and simmer for about 30 minutes.

Two-way Chicken with Vegetables

This tender, slow-cooked chicken makes a tasty lunch or supper, with the stock and remaining vegetables providing a nourishing soup for a second meal.

Serves 6

1.5kg/3½ lb chicken
2 onions, quartered
3 carrots, thickly sliced
2 celery sticks, chopped
1 parsnip or turnip, thickly sliced
50g/2oz/¾ cup button mushrooms, with stalks, roughly chopped
1–2 fresh thyme sprigs or 5ml/1 tsp dried thyme
4 bay leaves
large bunch of fresh parsley
115g/4oz/1 cup wholemeal pasta shapes
salt and freshly ground black pepper
cooked new potatoes or pasta and mangetouts or French beans, to serve (optional)

1 Trim the chicken of any extra fat. Put it into a flameproof casserole and add the vegetables and herbs. Pour in sufficient water to cover. Bring to the boil over a medium heat, skimming off any scum. When the water boils, lower the heat and simmer for 2–3 hours.

2 Lift the chicken out of the stock and carve the meat neatly, discarding the skin and bones, and returning any small pieces of meat to the pan. Serve the chicken with some of the vegetables from the pan, plus new potatoes or pasta and mangetouts or French beans, if you like.

3 Remove the bay leaves and any large pieces of parsley and thyme from the pan, and discard. Set the remaining mixture aside to cool, then chill it overnight in the fridge. Next day, lift off the fat that has solidified on the surface. Reheat the soup over a low heat.

4 When the soup comes to the boil, add the pasta shapes, with salt if required, and cook for 10–12 minutes or until the pasta is *al dente*. Adjust the seasoning to taste, and serve.

Chicken Kiev with Ricotta

Cut through the crispy-coated chicken to reveal a creamy filling with just a hint of garlic – proof that a lower-fat chicken Kiev can be delicious.

Serves 4

4 large chicken breast fillets, skinned
15ml/1 tbsp lemon juice
115g/4oz/½ cup ricotta cheese
1 garlic clove, crushed
30ml/2 tbsp chopped fresh parsley
1.5ml/¼ tsp grated nutmeg
30ml/2 tbsp plain flour
pinch of cayenne pepper
1.5ml/¼ tsp salt
2 egg whites, lightly beaten
115g/4oz/2 cups fresh white breadcrumbs
duchesse potatoes, French beans and grilled tomatoes, to serve

1 Place the chicken breasts between two sheets of clear film and gently beat with a meat mallet or rolling pin until flattened. Sprinkle with the lemon juice.

2 Mix the ricotta cheese with the garlic, 15ml/1 tbsp of the parsley and the nutmeg. Shape into four 5cm/2in long cylinders. Put one portion of the cheese and herb mixture in the centre of each chicken breast and fold the meat over, tucking in the edges to enclose the filling completely. Secure the chicken with wooden cocktail sticks pushed through the centre of each.

3 Mix together the flour, cayenne pepper and salt on a plate. Place the egg whites in a bowl. Mix together the breadcrumbs and remaining parsley on another plate.

4 Dust the chicken with the seasoned flour, dip into the egg whites, then coat with the breadcrumbs. Chill for 30 minutes in the fridge. Preheat the oven to 200°C/400°F/Gas 6. Dip the chicken into the egg white and breadcrumbs for a second time.

5 Put the chicken on a non-stick baking sheet and spray with non-stick cooking spray. Bake in the oven for 25 minutes or until the coating is golden brown and the chicken completely cooked. Remove the cocktail sticks, and serve with duchesse potatoes, French beans and grilled tomatoes.

Chicken in Creamy Orange Sauce

This sauce is deceptively creamy – in fact it is made with low-fat fromage frais, which is virtually fat-free. The brandy adds a richer flavour, but is optional – omit it if you prefer and use orange juice alone.

Serves 4
8 chicken thighs or drumsticks, skinned
45ml/3 tbsp brandy
300ml/ ½ pint/1 ¼ cups orange juice
3 spring onions, chopped
10ml/2 tsp cornflour
90ml/6 tbsp low-fat fromage frais
salt and freshly ground black pepper
boiled rice or pasta and green salad, to serve

1 Fry the chicken pieces without fat in a non-stick or heavy-based pan, turning until evenly browned.

2 Stir in the brandy, orange juice and spring onions. Bring to the boil, then cover and simmer for 15 minutes or until the chicken is tender and the juices run clear, not pink, when the thickest part is pierced with a skewer or knife.

3 In a small bowl, blend the cornflour with a little water, then mix into the fromage frais. Stir this into the sauce and stir over a moderate heat until boiling.

4 Adjust the seasoning to taste, and serve with boiled rice or pasta and green salad.

Cook's Tip
Adding a thin cornflour paste to the fromage frais stabilizes it and helps prevent it from curdling. This is also a good technique with yogurt, which will also curdle if it is added to a dish that is going to be boiled.

Oat-crusted Chicken with Sage

A smooth sauce, lightly flavoured with sage, makes a fine contrast to the crunchy oats coating these tender chicken pieces.

Serves 4
45ml/3 tbsp skimmed milk
10ml/2 tsp English mustard
40g/1½oz/ ½ cup rolled oats
45ml/3 tbsp chopped fresh sage
8 chicken thighs or drumsticks, skinned
115g/4oz/ ½ cup low-fat fromage frais
5ml/1 tsp wholegrain mustard
salt and freshly ground black pepper
fresh sage leaves, to garnish

1 Preheat the oven to 200°C/400°F/Gas 6. Mix together the milk and English mustard in a small bowl.

2 Mix the oats with 30ml/2 tbsp of the chopped sage, and salt and freshly ground black pepper to taste on a plate. Brush the chicken with the milk and press into the oats to coat evenly.

3 Place the chicken on a baking sheet and bake for about 40 minutes or until the juices run clear, not pink, when the meat is pierced through the thickest part with a skewer or the point of a knife.

4 Meanwhile, in a bowl, mix together the low-fat fromage frais, wholegrain mustard, the remaining sage and seasoning. Garnish the chicken with fresh sage and serve hot or cold, accompanied by the mustard sauce.

Cook's Tip
If fresh sage is not available, choose another fresh herb such as thyme or parsley, instead of using a dried alternative. Although sage can be dried successfully, unlike some herbs, it quickly loses its volatile aromatic oils and becomes very crumbly and dusty with little flavour.

Chicken & Bean Bake

A delicious combination of chicken, fresh tarragon and mixed beans, topped with a layer of tender potatoes.

Serves 6

900g/2lb potatoes
50g/2oz/ ½ cup reduced-fat mature Cheddar cheese, finely grated
600ml/1 pint/2½ cups plus 30–45ml/2–3 tbsp skimmed milk
30ml/2 tbsp snipped fresh chives
2 leeks, sliced
1 onion, sliced
30ml/2 tbsp dry white wine
40g/1½oz/3 tbsp half-fat spread
40g/1½oz/⅓ cup plain flour
300ml/ ½ pint/1¼ cups Chicken Stock
350g/12oz cooked skinless chicken breast fillet, diced
225g/8oz/3 cups brown-cap mushrooms, sliced
300g/11oz can red kidney beans
400g/14oz can flageolet beans
400g/14oz can black-eyed beans
30–45ml/2–3 tbsp chopped fresh tarragon
salt and freshly ground black pepper

1 Preheat the oven to 200°C/400°F/Gas 6. Cut the potatoes into chunks and cook in boiling salted water for 15–20 minutes. Drain and mash. Add the cheese, 30–45ml/2–3 tbsp milk and the chives, season and mix well. Set aside and keep warm.

2 Meanwhile, put the leeks and onion in a saucepan with the wine. Cover and cook gently for 10 minutes until the vegetables are just tender, stirring occasionally.

3 Put the half-fat spread, flour, remaining milk and the stock in another pan. Heat gently, whisking, until the sauce boils and thickens. Simmer for 3 minutes, stirring. Remove the pan from the heat and stir in the leek mixture, chicken and mushrooms.

4 Drain and rinse all the canned beans. Stir into the sauce with the tarragon and seasoning. Heat gently, stirring, until piping hot.

5 Transfer the mixture to an ovenproof dish and spoon or pipe the mashed potatoes over the top. Bake for about 30 minutes until the potato topping is crisp and golden brown, and serve.

Chicken with a Herb Crust

The chicken breasts can be brushed with melted low-fat spread instead of Dijon mustard before being coated in the breadcrumb mixture, if you prefer.

Serves 4

4 chicken breast fillets, skinned
a little oil, for greasing
15ml/1 tbsp Dijon mustard
30ml/2 tbsp chopped fresh parsley
50g/2oz/1 cup fresh breadcrumbs
15ml/1 tbsp dried mixed herbs
25g/1oz/2 tbsp low-fat spread, melted
salt and freshly ground black pepper
boiled new potatoes and salad, to serve

1 Preheat the oven to 180°C/350°F/Gas 4. Lay the chicken breast fillets in a single layer in a greased ovenproof dish and spread with the mustard. Season with salt and pepper.

2 In a bowl, mix the parsley, breadcrumbs and dried mixed herbs together thoroughly.

3 Sprinkle the breadcrumb mixture over the chicken to coat it and press in well. Spoon over the low-fat spread.

4 Bake in the oven, uncovered, for 20 minutes or until the chicken is tender and the topping is crisp. Serve with new potatoes and salad.

Cook's Tip

Dijon mustard is made from black mustard seeds, spices and white wine. It has a clean, medium-hot flavour and a creamy texture. It is the type most widely used in cooking. However, if you prefer a hotter taste, you could use English mustard or for a sweet-sour flavour, use German mustard. American mustard is very mild and quite sweet.

Tuscan Chicken

This simple peasant casserole has all the flavours of traditional Tuscan ingredients. The wine can be replaced by chicken stock.

Serves 4

8 chicken thighs, skinned
5ml/1 tsp olive oil
1 medium onion, thinly sliced
2 red peppers, seeded and sliced
1 garlic clove, crushed
300ml/½ pint/1¼ cups passata
150ml/¼ pint/⅔ cup dry white wine
1 large fresh oregano sprig or 5ml/1 tsp dried oregano
400g/14oz can cannellini beans, drained and rinsed
45ml/3 tbsp fresh breadcrumbs
salt and freshly ground black pepper

1 Fry the chicken in the oil in a large non-stick or heavy-based frying pan until golden brown. Remove from the pan, set aside and keep hot.

2 Add the onion and peppers to the pan, and gently sauté until softened but not brown. Stir in the garlic.

3 Return the chicken to the pan, and add the passata, wine and oregano. Season well, bring to the boil, then cover the pan tightly. Lower the heat and simmer gently, stirring occasionally, for 30–35 minutes or until the chicken is tender and the juices run clear, not pink, when the thickest part is pierced with the point of a knife or skewer.

4 Stir in the cannellini beans and simmer for a further 5 minutes until heated through. Sprinkle with the breadcrumbs and cook under a hot grill until golden brown.

Cook's Tip
Passata is a pasteurized, sieved tomato sauce which, unlike tomato purée, has not been concentrated. It has a fine, full flavour, as it is usually made from sun-ripened tomatoes. It is available in bottles and cans from most supermarkets.

Chicken with Orange & Mustard Sauce

The beauty of this recipe is its simplicity; the chicken breasts continue to cook in their own juices while you prepare the sauce.

Serves 4

2 large oranges
4 chicken breast fillets, skinned
5ml/1 tsp sunflower oil
salt and freshly ground black pepper
new potatoes and sliced courgettes tossed in parsley, to serve

For the orange and mustard sauce
10ml/2 tsp cornflour
150ml/¼ pint/⅔ cup plain low-fat yogurt
5ml/1 tsp Dijon mustard

1 Peel the oranges using a sharp knife, removing all the white pith. Remove the segments by cutting between the membranes, holding the fruit over a small bowl to catch any juice. Set aside with the juice until required.

2 Season the chicken with salt and pepper to taste. Heat the sunflower oil in a non-stick frying pan, add the chicken and cook for 5 minutes on each side. Remove the chicken from the frying pan and wrap it in foil; the meat will continue to cook for a while.

3 To make the orange and mustard sauce, blend the cornflour with the juice from the orange to a smooth paste. Add the yogurt and mustard, and mix well. Pour the mixture into the frying pan and bring to the boil over a low heat. Simmer for 1 minute.

4 Add the orange segments to the sauce and heat gently. Unwrap the chicken and add any excess juices to the sauce. Slice the chicken on the diagonal and serve with the sauce, new potatoes and sliced courgettes tossed in parsley.

Chicken Provençal

A richly flavoured dish in which the chicken and vegetables are simmered slowly together until wonderfully tender.

Serves 4

1 medium aubergine, diced
10ml/2 tsp olive oil
8 chicken thighs, skinned
1 medium red onion, cut into wedges
1 green pepper, seeded and thickly sliced
2 garlic cloves, sliced
1 small fresh green chilli, sliced
2 courgettes, thickly sliced
2 beefsteak tomatoes, cut into wedges
1 bouquet garni
salt and freshly ground black pepper

1 Sprinkle the aubergine with salt, then leave to drain for 30 minutes. Rinse and pat dry with kitchen paper.

2 Heat the oil in a large, non-stick pan and fry the chicken until golden. Add the aubergine, onion, green pepper and garlic, and fry gently until the vegetables are soft.

3 Add the chilli, courgettes, tomatoes, bouquet garni and seasoning. Cover tightly and cook over a low heat for 25–30 minutes until the chicken and vegetables are tender. Remove the bouquet garni and serve immediately.

Cook's Tip

In the past, it was always necessary to sprinkle aubergines with salt to remove the bitter and unpalatable juices – a process known as degorging. Modern varieties, especially those grown under glass, have been selectively bred so that this is rarely essential. Nevertheless, it is worth doing if the aubergine is to be fried as dégorging helps to reduce the amount of oil absorbed and improves the texture. Always rinse the aubergines thoroughly to get rid of all traces of salt and then pat dry before using. Baby aubergines never require salting.

Caribbean Ginger Chicken

Pineapple helps to keep the chicken moist during cooking, as well as providing flavour along with the other ingredients, without the addition of any fat. Pineapple also contains an enzyme that helps to tenderize meat.

Serves 4

4 chicken breasts, skinned
½ small fresh pineapple, peeled and sliced
2 spring onions, chopped
30ml/2 tbsp chopped fresh root ginger
1 garlic clove, crushed
15ml/1 tbsp dark muscovado sugar
15ml/1 tbsp lime juice
5ml/1 tsp hot pepper sauce
5ml/1 tsp tomato purée
salt and freshly ground black pepper
cooked plain and wild rice, and salad, to serve

1 Preheat the oven to 200°C/400°F/Gas 6. Slash the chicken at intervals with a sharp knife. Place in an ovenproof dish with the pineapple slices.

2 In a bowl, mix together the spring onions, ginger, garlic, sugar, lime juice, pepper sauce, tomato purée, salt and pepper. Spread the mixture over the chicken.

3 Cover and bake in the oven for 30 minutes or until the chicken juices run clear when the thickest part is pierced with a skewer or knife. Serve with plain and wild rice, and salad.

Cook's Tip

To prepare fresh pineapple, cut off the green spiky top and take a thin slice from the base, so that it will stand upright. Using a sharp, long-bladed knife, cut off the skin downwards in wide strips. Carefully remove the hard brown "eyes" from the pineapple flesh with the point of the knife. Cut the flesh into slices, then remove the woody core from each slice with a knife.

Yakitori Chicken

These Japanese-style kebabs are easy to eat and ideal for barbecues or parties. Make extra yakitori sauce if you would like to serve it with the kebabs. For an authentic touch, serve the kebabs with *shichimi* – seven-spice flavour, usually made from ground chilli, anise pepper, sesame seeds, rape seeds, poppy seeds, dried citrus peel and ground nori seaweed.

Serves 4

6 boneless chicken thighs, skinned
1 bunch spring onions
shichimi (seven-flavour spice), to serve (optional)

For the yakitori sauce

150ml/ 1/4 pint/ 2/3 cup Japanese soy sauce
90g/3 1/2 oz/ 1/2 cup sugar
25ml/1 1/2 tbsp sake or dry white wine
15ml/1 tbsp plain flour

1 To make the sauce, stir the soy sauce, sugar and sake or wine into the flour in a small saucepan and bring to the boil, stirring. Lower the heat and simmer the mixture for 10 minutes until the sauce is reduced by a third. Set aside.

2 Cut the chicken into bite-size pieces. Cut the spring onions into 3cm/1¼in pieces. Preheat the grill or prepare the barbecue.

3 Thread the chicken and spring onions alternately on to 12 bamboo skewers. Grill under medium heat or cook on the barbecue for 5–10 minutes until the chicken is cooked but still moist, brushing generously several times with the sauce.

4 Serve with a little extra yakitori sauce, offering shichimi with the kebabs if you wish.

Cook's Tip

There are several types of Japanese soy sauce – shoyu. Tamari is a thick, mellow-flavoured sauce that is a popular choice for dips. Usukuchi is lighter, but quite salty. Do not substitute Chinese soy sauce, as it is much stronger than Japanese.

Chicken Couscous

This simple-to-prepare, all-in-one main dish has a low fat content and needs no accompaniment.

Serves 4

225g/8oz/1 1/3 cups couscous
1 litre/1 3/4 pints/4 cups boiling water
5ml/1 tsp olive oil
400g/14oz skinless boneless chicken, diced
1 yellow pepper, seeded and sliced
2 large courgettes, thickly sliced
1 small fresh green chilli, thinly sliced, or 5ml/1 tsp chilli sauce
1 large tomato, diced
425g/15oz can chick-peas, drained and rinsed
salt and freshly ground black pepper
fresh coriander or parsley sprigs to garnish

1 Place the couscous in a large bowl and pour over the boiling water. Cover and leave to stand for 30 minutes.

2 Heat the oil in a large, non-stick pan and stir-fry the chicken quickly to seal, then reduce the heat.

3 Stir in the yellow pepper, courgettes and fresh chilli or chilli sauce and cook for 10 minutes until the vegetables are softened, stirring frequently.

4 Add the tomato and chick-peas, followed by the couscous. Adjust the seasoning to taste and stir over a moderate heat until heated through.

5 Transfer to a serving platter, garnish with sprigs of fresh coriander or parsley and serve hot.

Variation

For a spicier dish, add 2.5ml/ ½ tsp each ground coriander, paprika, ground cumin, ground turmeric and ground cinnamon, together with 115g/4oz/ ⅔ cup sultanas with the vegetables in step 3.

Moroccan Spiced Roast Poussins

A flavoursome stuffing of rice, apricots and fresh mint keeps these baby chickens moist inside while a coating of spicy yogurt does the same outside.

Serves 4

75g/3oz/scant ½ cup cooked long-grain rice
1 small onion, finely chopped
finely grated rind and juice of 1 lemon
30ml/2 tbsp chopped fresh mint
45ml/3 tbsp chopped dried apricots
30ml/2 tbsp plain yogurt
10ml/2 tsp ground turmeric
10ml/2 tsp ground cumin
2 x 450g/1lb poussins
salt and freshly ground black pepper
lemon slices and fresh mint sprigs, to garnish
cooked rice and wild rice, to serve

1 Preheat the oven to 200°C/400°F/Gas 6. Mix together the rice, onion, lemon rind, mint and apricots. Stir in half each of the lemon juice, yogurt, turmeric and cumin. Season to taste with salt and pepper.

2 Stuff the poussins with the rice mixture at the neck end only. Any spare stuffing can be cooked with the chicken in foil parcels and served separately. Place the poussins on a rack in a roasting tin.

3 In a small bowl, mix together the remaining lemon juice, yogurt, turmeric and cumin, then brush this mixture all over the poussins. Cover them loosely with foil and cook in the oven for 30 minutes.

4 Remove the foil and roast the poussins for a further 15 minutes or until they are golden brown and the juices run clear when the thickest part of the thigh is pierced with a skewer or the point of a knife.

5 Cut the poussins in half with a knife or poultry shears. Transfer to serving plates, garnish with the lemon slices and mint, and serve with the reserved rice stuffing and mixed rice.

Curried Chicken Salad

The chicken is tossed in a curried yogurt dressing and served on a colourful bed of pasta and vegetables.

Serves 4

2 cooked chicken breast fillets
175g/6oz French beans
350g/12oz/3 cups multi-coloured penne
150ml/¼ pint/⅔ cup plain low-fat yogurt
5ml/1 tsp mild curry powder
1 garlic clove, crushed
1 fresh green chilli, seeded and finely chopped
30ml/2 tbsp chopped fresh coriander
4 firm ripe tomatoes, peeled, seeded and cut into strips
salt and freshly ground black pepper
fresh coriander leaves, to garnish

1 Remove the skin from the chicken and cut the meat into strips. Cut the French beans into 2.5cm/1in lengths and cook in boiling water for 5 minutes. Drain and rinse under cold water.

2 Cook the pasta in a large pan of boiling salted water according to the packet instructions until *al dente*. Drain and rinse thoroughly.

3 Mix the yogurt, curry powder, garlic, chilli and chopped coriander together in a bowl. Stir in the chicken pieces and leave to stand for 30 minutes.

4 Transfer the pasta to a large glass bowl and toss with the beans and tomatoes. Spoon over the chicken and sauce. Garnish with coriander leaves and serve.

Variations

For herbed chicken salad, substitute 30ml/2 tbsp each finely chopped fresh parsley and watercress and 3 finely chopped spring onions for the curry powder, chilli and coriander. For lemon chicken salad, substitute the juice of ½ lemon, 1 bunch snipped chives and 30ml/2 tbsp finely chopped fresh mixed herbs for the same ingredients and omit the garlic.

Gingered Chicken Noodles

A blend of ginger, spices and coconut milk flavours this delicious supper dish, which is made in minutes. For a real oriental touch, add a little fish sauce to taste, just before serving.

Serves 4

350g/12oz chicken breast fillets, skinned
225g/8oz courgettes
275g/10oz aubergine
10ml/2 tsp oil
5cm/2in piece fresh root ginger, finely chopped
6 spring onions, sliced
10ml/2 tsp Thai green curry paste
400ml/14fl oz/1⅔ cups coconut milk
475ml/16fl oz/2 cups Chicken Stock
115g/4oz medium egg noodles
45ml/3 tbsp chopped fresh coriander, plus extra to garnish
15ml/1 tbsp lemon juice
salt and freshly ground black pepper

1 Cut the chicken into bite-size pieces. Cut the courgettes in half lengthways and roughly chop them. Cut the aubergine into similar-size pieces.

2 Heat half the oil in a large, non-stick saucepan. Add the chicken and fry over a medium heat, stirring frequently, until golden all over. Remove from the pan using a slotted spoon and drain well on kitchen paper.

3 Add the remaining oil to the pan and cook the ginger and spring onions, stirring frequently, for 3 minutes. Add the courgettes and cook for 2–3 minutes or until they are beginning to turn golden. Stir in the curry paste and cook over a low heat for 1 minute.

4 Add the coconut milk, stock, aubergine and chicken, and simmer for 10 minutes. Add the noodles and cook for a further 5 minutes or until the chicken is cooked and the noodles are tender. Stir in the coriander and lemon juice, and adjust the seasoning to taste. Serve, garnished with more coriander.

Chicken with Pineapple

This chicken has a delicate tang. The pineapple not only tenderizes the chicken, but also gives it a hint of sweetness.

Serves 6

225g/8oz/1 cup canned pineapple, in natural juice
5ml/1 tsp ground cumin
5ml/1 tsp ground coriander
2.5ml/½ tsp crushed garlic
5ml/1 tsp chilli powder
5ml/1 tsp salt
30ml/2 tbsp plain low-fat yogurt
15ml/1 tbsp chopped fresh coriander
a few drops of orange food colouring
275g/10oz boneless chicken, skinned
½ red pepper
½ yellow or green pepper
1 large onion, chopped
6 cherry tomatoes
15ml/1 tbsp vegetable oil
salad, to serve

1 Drain the pineapple juice into a bowl. Reserve eight chunks of pineapple and squeeze the juice from the remaining chunks into the bowl and set aside. You should have about 120ml/4fl oz/½ cup pineapple juice.

2 In a large mixing bowl, blend the cumin, ground coriander, garlic, chilli powder, salt, yogurt, fresh coriander and food colouring. Pour in the reserved pineapple juice and mix well.

3 Cut the chicken into bite-size cubes, add to the yogurt and spice mixture, and leave to marinate for about 1–1½ hours.

4 Cut the peppers into bite-size chunks, discarding the seeds.

5 Preheat the grill to medium. Arrange the chicken pieces, peppers, onion, tomatoes and reserved pineapple chunks alternately on six wooden or metal skewers.

6 Brush the kebabs with the oil, then place the skewers on a flameproof dish or in a grill pan. Grill, turning and basting the chicken with the marinade regularly, for about 15 minutes. Serve with salad.

Chicken Tikka

The red food colouring gives this dish its traditional bright colour. Serve with lemon wedges.

Serves 4
1.5kg/3½ lb chicken
mixed salad leaves, e.g. frisée and oakleaf lettuce or radicchio, and lemon wedges, to serve

For the marinade
150ml/ ¼ pint/ ⅔ cup plain low-fat yogurt
5ml/1 tsp ground paprika
10ml/2 tsp grated fresh root ginger
1 garlic clove, crushed
10ml/2 tsp garam masala
2.5ml/ ½ tsp salt
red food colouring (optional)
juice of 1 lemon

1 Joint the chicken and cut it into eight pieces, using a sharp knife.

2 To make the marinade, mix all the ingredients in a large dish. Add the chicken pieces and turn to coat them thoroughly. Chill for 4 hours or overnight in the fridge to allow the flavours to penetrate the flesh.

3 Preheat the oven to 200°C/400°F/Gas 6. Remove the chicken pieces from the marinade and arrange them in a single layer in a large, ovenproof dish. Bake for 30–40 minutes or until tender, basting with a little of the marinade while cooking.

4 Arrange the chicken on a bed of salad leaves and serve hot or cold with lemon wedges for squeezing.

Cook's Tip
Poppadums can be a healthy accompaniment to a low-fat Indian meal. Instead of frying them, put them, one at a time, on the turntable of a microwave oven and cook on HIGH for 40–60 seconds. They will not be quite so puffed up as fried poppadums, but will still be crisp – and much healthier.

Tandoori Chicken

Although the authentic tandoori flavour is very difficult to achieve in conventional ovens, this low-fat version still makes a very tasty dish.

Serves 4
4 chicken quarters
175ml/6fl oz/ ¾ cup plain low-fat yogurt
5ml/1 tsp garam masala
5ml/1 tsp grated fresh root ginger
5ml/1 tsp crushed garlic
7.5ml/1½ tsp chilli powder
1.5ml/ ¼ tsp ground turmeric
5ml/1 tsp ground coriander
15ml/1 tbsp lemon juice
5ml/1 tsp salt
a few drops of red food colouring
15ml/1 tbsp corn oil

For the garnish
mixed salad leaves
lime wedges

1 Skin and rinse the chicken quarters, then pat dry with kitchen paper. Make two slits into the flesh of each piece, place in a dish and set aside.

2 In a bowl, mix together the yogurt, garam masala, ginger, garlic, chilli powder, turmeric, coriander, lemon juice, salt, red food colouring and oil. Beat well so that all the ingredients are thoroughly mixed together.

3 Cover the chicken quarters with the yogurt and spice mixture, turning them to coat well and set aside to marinate for about 3 hours.

4 Preheat the oven to 240°C/475°F/Gas 9. Transfer the chicken pieces to an ovenproof dish. Bake in the oven for about 20–25 minutes or until the chicken is cooked right through, browned on top, and the juices run clear when the thickest part is pierced with a skewer or the point of a knife.

5 Remove from the oven and transfer to a serving dish. Garnish with the salad leaves and lime, and serve.

Kashmiri Chicken Curry

This mild yet flavoursome dish is given a special lift by the addition of apples.

Serves 4

10ml/2 tsp corn oil
2 medium onions, diced
1 bay leaf
2 cloves
2.5cm/1in cinnamon stick
4 black peppercorns
1 baby chicken, about 675g/ 1½ lb skinned and cut into 8 pieces
5ml/1 tsp garam masala
5ml/1 tsp grated fresh root ginger
5ml/1 tsp crushed garlic
5ml/1 tsp salt
5ml/1 tsp chilli powder
15ml/1 tbsp ground almonds
150ml/ ¼ pint/ ⅔ cup plain low-fat yogurt
2 green dessert apples, peeled, cored and roughly sliced
15ml/1 tbsp chopped fresh coriander
15g/ ½ oz flaked almonds, lightly toasted, and fresh coriander leaves, to garnish

1 Heat the oil in a non-stick wok or frying pan, and fry the onions with the bay leaf, cloves, cinnamon and peppercorns for about 3–5 minutes. Add the chicken pieces and continue to stir-fry for at least 3 minutes.

2 Lower the heat and add the garam masala, ginger, garlic, salt, chilli powder and ground almonds, and continue to stir for 2–3 minutes. Pour in the yogurt and stir over a low heat for a further 2–3 minutes. Add the apples and chopped coriander, cover and cook for about 10–15 minutes.

3 Check that the chicken is cooked through, and serve immediately, garnished with toasted flaked almonds and whole coriander leaves.

Cook's Tip
While less fat may be required, a wok with a non-stick lining cannot be heated to high temperatures. A well-seasoned cast-iron wok also works in a "non-stick" way.

Karahi Chicken with Mint

For this tasty dish, the chicken is first boiled before being quickly stir-fried in a little oil, to ensure that it is cooked through despite the short cooking time.

Serves 4

275g/10oz chicken breast fillet, skinned and cut into strips
300ml/ ½ pint/1¼ cups water
15ml/1 tbsp soya oil
2 small bunches spring onions, roughly chopped
5ml/1 tsp grated fresh root ginger
5ml/1 tsp crushed dried red chillies
30ml/2 tbsp lemon juice
15ml/1 tbsp chopped fresh coriander
15ml/1 tbsp chopped fresh mint
3 tomatoes, seeded and roughly chopped
5ml/1 tsp salt
fresh mint and coriander sprigs, to garnish

1 Put the chicken and water into a saucepan, bring to the boil and lower the heat to medium. Cook for about 10 minutes or until the water has evaporated and the chicken is cooked. Remove from the heat and set aside.

2 Heat the soya oil in a heavy-based non-stick frying pan or saucepan and add the spring onions. Stir-fry over a medium heat for about 2 minutes until soft and translucent. Add the boiled chicken strips and stir-fry for a further 3 minutes over a medium heat.

3 Gradually add the ginger, dried chillies, lemon juice, coriander, mint, tomatoes and salt, and gently stir for a few minutes to blend all the flavours together. Transfer to a serving dish, garnish with mint and coriander sprigs, and serve immediately.

Cook's Tip
If fresh mint is not available, use a jar of mint that has been shredded and preserved in salt and vinegar, rather than the dried herb. Once opened, the jar should be stored in the fridge.

Balti Minced Chicken with Green & Red Chillies

Minced chicken is seldom cooked in Indian or Pakistani homes. However, it works very well in this low-fat recipe.

Serves 4

275g/10oz chicken breast fillet, skinned and cubed
2 thick fresh red chillies
3 thick fresh green chillies
30ml/2 tbsp corn oil
6 curry leaves
3 medium onions, sliced
7.5ml/1½ tsp crushed garlic
7.5ml/1½ tsp ground coriander
7.5ml/1½ tsp grated fresh root ginger
5ml/1 tsp chilli powder
5ml/1 tsp salt
15ml/1 tbsp lemon juice
30ml/2 tbsp chopped fresh coriander
chapatis and lemon wedges, to serve

1 Place the chicken cubes in a saucepan, cover with water and bring to the boil. Lower the heat and simmer for about 10 minutes until tender and cooked through. Drain thoroughly. Place the chicken in a food processor and mince.

2 Cut the chillies in half lengthways and, if desired, remove the seeds. Cut the flesh into strips.

3 Heat the oil in a non-stick wok or frying pan, and fry the curry leaves and onions until the onions are a soft golden brown. Lower the heat and add the garlic, ground coriander, ginger, chilli powder and salt.

4 Add the minced chicken and stir-fry for 3–5 minutes. Add the lemon juice, chilli strips and most of the fresh coriander. Stir for a further 3–5 minutes.

5 Transfer to a warmed serving dish and serve immediately, garnished with the remaining fresh coriander and accompanied by chapatis and lemon wedges.

Balti Chicken Pieces with Cumin & Coriander Potatoes

The spicy potatoes are cooked separately in the oven first.

Serves 4

150ml/¼ pint/⅔ cup plain low-fat yogurt
25g/1oz/¼ cup ground almonds
7.5ml/1½ tsp ground coriander
2.5ml/½ tsp chilli powder
5ml/1 tsp garam masala
15ml/1 tbsp coconut milk
5ml/1 tsp crushed garlic
5ml/1 tsp grated fresh root ginger
30ml/2 tbsp chopped fresh coriander
1 fresh red chilli, seeded and chopped
225g/8oz chicken breast fillets, skinned and cubed
15ml/1 tbsp corn oil
2 medium onions, sliced
3 green cardamom pods
2.5cm/1in cinnamon stick
2 cloves

For the potatoes

15ml/1 tbsp corn oil
8 baby potatoes, thickly sliced
1.5ml/¼ tsp cumin seeds
15ml/1 tbsp finely chopped fresh coriander

1 In a bowl, mix together the yogurt, ground almonds, ground coriander, chilli powder, garam masala, coconut milk, garlic, ginger, half the fresh coriander and half the chilli. Add the chicken cubes, mix well and leave to marinate for 2 hours.

2 Meanwhile, for the potatoes, preheat the oven to 180°C/350°F/Gas 4. Heat the oil in a non-stick wok or frying pan and stir-fry the potatoes, cumin seeds and coriander for 2–3 minutes. Transfer to an ovenproof dish, cover and cook in the oven for about 30 minutes or until the potatoes are cooked through.

3 Increase the oven temperature to 200°C/400°F/Gas 6. Wipe out the wok or frying pan and add the oil with the onions, cardamoms, cinnamon and cloves. Heat for about 1½ minutes. Pour the chicken mixture into the onions and stir-fry for 5–7 minutes. Lower the heat, cover and cook gently for a further 5–7 minutes. Serve, topped with the cooked potatoes, and garnished with the remaining chopped fresh coriander and red chilli.

Spicy Masala Chicken

These grilled chicken pieces have a sweet-and-sour taste. They can be served either hot or cold.

Serves 6

12 chicken thighs, skinned
90ml/6 tbsp lemon juice
5ml/1 tsp grated fresh root ginger
5ml/1 tsp crushed garlic
5ml/1 tsp crushed dried red chillies
5ml/1 tsp salt
5ml/1 tsp soft brown sugar
30ml/2 tbsp clear honey
30ml/2 tbsp chopped fresh coriander
1 fresh green chilli, finely chopped
30ml/2 tbsp vegetable oil
fresh coriander sprigs, to garnish
boiled rice and salad, to serve

1 Prick the chicken thighs with a fork. Rinse them in cold water, pat dry with kitchen paper and set aside in a bowl.

2 In a large mixing bowl, thoroughly mix together the lemon juice, grated ginger, garlic, crushed dried red chillies, salt, brown sugar and honey.

3 Transfer the chicken thighs to the spice mixture, turning to coat all over. Set aside in a cool place to marinate for about 45 minutes.

4 Preheat the grill to medium. Add the chopped coriander and fresh green chilli to the chicken thighs, and place them in a flameproof dish.

5 Pour any remaining marinade over the chicken and baste with the oil, using a pastry brush.

6 Grill the chicken thighs for 15–20 minutes, turning and basting with the oil occasionally, until golden brown and the juices run clear when the thickest part is pierced with a skewer or the point of a knife.

7 Transfer to a serving dish, garnish with fresh coriander sprigs and serve with rice and salad.

Hot Chicken Curry

This curry has a lovely, thick sauce and is made using red and green peppers for extra colour. It can be served with either chapatis or plain boiled rice.

Serves 4

30ml/2 tbsp corn oil
1.5ml/ ¼ tsp fenugreek seeds
1.5ml/ ¼ tsp onion seeds
2 medium onions, chopped
2.5ml/ ½ tsp crushed garlic
2.5ml/ ½ tsp grated fresh root ginger
5ml/1 tsp ground coriander
5ml/1 tsp chilli powder
5ml/1 tsp salt
400g/14oz can tomatoes
30ml/2 tbsp lemon juice
350g/12oz skinless boneless chicken, cubed
30ml/2 tbsp chopped fresh coriander
3 fresh green chillies, chopped
½ red pepper, seeded and cut into chunks
½ green pepper, seeded and cut into chunks
fresh coriander sprigs, to garnish

1 Heat the oil in a heavy-based saucepan, and fry the fenugreek and onion seeds until they turn a shade darker. Add the onions, garlic and ginger, and fry for about 5 minutes until the onions turn golden brown.

2 Meanwhile, in a separate bowl, mix together the ground coriander, chilli powder, salt, tomatoes and lemon juice. Pour the tomato mixture into the saucepan and stir-fry over a medium heat for about 3 minutes.

3 Add the chicken cubes and stir-fry for 5–7 minutes. Add the chopped fresh coriander, green chillies and chopped peppers. Lower the heat, cover and simmer for about 10 minutes until the chicken is cooked. Serve hot, garnished with coriander sprigs.

Cook's Tip

Known as methi *in Indian, fenugreek seeds look like small, light brown pebbles and have a pungent smell. It is these seeds that give curry powder its characteristic aroma.*

Spaghetti with Turkey Ragout

Minced turkey is low in fat and makes a very tasty and economical sauce to serve with spaghetti.

Serves 4

450g/1lb minced turkey
1 medium onion, diced
1 medium carrot, diced
1 celery stick, diced
400g/14oz can tomatoes
15ml/1 tbsp tomato purée
5ml/1 tsp dried oregano
2 bay leaves
225g/8oz spaghetti
salt and freshly ground black pepper

1 In a non-stick pan, dry-fry the turkey and onion until lightly coloured. Stir in the carrot and celery and cook, stirring constantly, for 5–8 minutes.

2 Add the tomatoes, tomato purée, oregano, bay leaves and seasoning, and bring to the boil. Cover and simmer gently for 40 minutes until the turkey is tender and the sauce is reduced.

3 Meanwhile, cook the spaghetti in boiling salted water according to the packet instructions until *al dente*. Drain well.

4 Place the spaghetti in a large bowl or on individual plates and spoon the turkey ragout over the top. Serve at once.

Cook's Tip
Always use a large saucepan of lightly salted boiling water for cooking pasta. Allow about 2 litres/3½ pints/8 cups of water for every 225g/8oz of pasta. Start timing it from the moment the water in the pan comes back to the boil after the pasta has been added. Cook dried pasta for 8–12 minutes and fresh pasta for 2–3 minutes, but remember that these are only guidelines. Start testing the pasta to see if it is done by biting a small piece between your front teeth. When it is tender but still firm to the bite, it is ready – al dente. *Drain the pasta immediately and do not delay before serving or it will dry out and become sticky and inedible.*

Turkey & Pasta Bake

A sauce of minced and smoked turkey is combined with cooked rigatoni and finished in the oven under a Parmesan cheese topping.

Serves 4

275g/10oz minced turkey
150g/5oz smoked turkey rashers, chopped
1–2 garlic cloves, crushed
1 onion, finely chopped
2 carrots, diced
30ml/2 tbsp concentrated tomato purée
300ml/½ pint/1¼ cups Chicken Stock
225g/8oz/2 cups rigatoni
30ml/2 tbsp grated Parmesan cheese
salt and freshly ground black pepper

1 Dry-fry the minced turkey in a non-stick saucepan, breaking up any large pieces with a wooden spoon, until it is crumbly and well browned all over.

2 Add the chopped turkey rashers, garlic, onion, carrots, tomato purée, stock and seasoning. Bring to the boil, cover and simmer for 1 hour until tender.

3 Preheat the oven to 180°C/350°F/Gas 4. Cook the pasta in a large pan of boiling salted water according to the packet instructions until *al dente*. Drain thoroughly and mix with the turkey sauce.

4 Transfer to a shallow, ovenproof dish and sprinkle with the grated Parmesan cheese. Bake in the oven for 20–30 minutes until lightly browned. Serve hot.

Cook's Tip
Parmesan cheese has quite a high fat content, but as it is strongly flavoured, a little goes long way. This is especially true if you use freshly grated mature Parmesan. Reduced-fat versions of traditional cheeses are constantly improving in quality, but, as a rule, do not brown under the grill, although they melt. If you want a browned topping, mix the cheese with breadcrumbs.

Turkey Pastitsio

A traditional Greek pastitsio is a rich, high-fat dish made with minced beef, but this lighter version is just as tasty.

Serves 4–6

450g/1lb minced turkey
1 large onion, finely chopped
60ml/4 tbsp tomato purée
250ml/8fl oz/1 cup red wine or Chicken Stock
5ml/1 tsp ground cinnamon
350g/12oz/3 cups macaroni
oil, for greasing
300ml/ ½ pint/1 ¼ cups skimmed milk
25g/1oz/2 tbsp low-fat sunflower margarine
25g/1oz/ ¼ cup plain flour
5ml/1 tsp grated nutmeg
2 tomatoes, sliced
60ml/4 tbsp wholemeal breadcrumbs
salt and freshly ground black pepper
green salad, to serve

1 Preheat the oven to 220°C/425°F/Gas 7. Dry-fry the turkey and onion in a non-stick pan over a medium heat, stirring constantly, until lightly browned.

2 Stir in the tomato purée, red wine or stock and cinnamon. Season to taste with salt and pepper, then cover and simmer for 5 minutes.

3 Cook the macaroni in boiling salted water according to the packet instructions until *al dente*, then drain. Make layers of the macaroni and the meat mixture in a lightly greased, wide, ovenproof dish, ending with a layer of macaroni.

4 Place the milk, margarine and flour in a saucepan, and whisk over a moderate heat until thickened and smooth. Stir in the nutmeg, and season with salt and pepper to taste.

5 Pour the sauce evenly over the pasta and meat to cover the surface completely. Arrange the tomato slices on top and sprinkle lines of breadcrumbs over the surface.

6 Bake for 30–35 minutes or until golden brown and bubbling. Serve hot with a green salad.

Mediterranean Turkey Rolls

Turkey breast steaks have less than 2 per cent fat and they are very quick to cook.

Serves 4

4 thin turkey breast steaks
30ml/2 tbsp Pesto Sauce
25g/1oz/½ cup large basil leaves
120ml/4fl oz/½ cup Chicken Stock
250ml/8fl oz/1 cup passata
garlic salt and freshly ground black pepper
cooked noodles or rice, to serve

1 Place the turkey steaks between two sheets of clear film and beat with a meat mallet or rolling pin until thin. Spread with the pesto sauce. Lay the basil leaves over each steak, then roll them up like Swiss rolls. Secure with wooden cocktail sticks.

2 Bring the stock and passata to the boil in a large saucepan. Add the turkey rolls, cover and simmer for 15–20 minutes or until the turkey is cooked through.

3 Adjust the seasoning and remove the cocktail sticks. Serve the turkey rolls hot with noodles or rice.

Pesto Sauce

A low-fat version of this Italian sauce is quick and easy.

Makes about 225g/8oz

50g/2oz/1 cup fresh basil leaves
25g/1oz/½ cup fresh parsley sprigs
1 garlic clove, crushed
25g/1oz/¼ cup pine nuts
115g/4oz/½ cup curd cheese
30ml/2 tbsp freshly grated Parmesan cheese
salt and freshly ground black pepper

1 Process half the herbs, the garlic, pine nuts and curd cheese in a food processor until smooth.

2 Add the remaining herbs and the Parmesan, season to taste with salt and pepper, and process until all the herbs are finely chopped.

Turkey Tonnato

This low-fat version of the popular Italian dish *vitello tonnato* is garnished with fine strips of sweet red pepper instead of the traditional anchovy fillets.

Serves 4

450g/1lb turkey fillets
1 small onion, sliced
1 bay leaf
4 black peppercorns
350ml/12fl oz/1½ cups Chicken Stock
200g/7oz can tuna in brine, drained
75ml/5 tbsp reduced-fat mayonnaise
30ml/2 tbsp lemon juice
2 red peppers, seeded and thinly sliced
about 25 capers, drained
salt
mixed salad and lemon wedges, to serve

1 Put the turkey fillets in a single layer in a large, heavy-based saucepan. Add the onion, bay leaf, peppercorns and stock. Bring to the boil and reduce the heat. Cover and simmer for about 12 minutes or until the turkey is tender.

2 Turn off the heat and leave the turkey to cool in the stock, then lift it out with a slotted spoon. Slice thickly and arrange on a serving plate.

3 Boil the stock until reduced to about 75ml/5 tbsp. Strain and set aside to cool.

4 Put the tuna, mayonnaise, lemon juice, 45ml/3 tbsp of the reduced stock and a pinch of salt into a blender or food processor, and process until smooth. Stir in enough of the remaining stock to reduce the sauce to the thickness of double cream. Spoon over the turkey.

5 Arrange the strips of red pepper in a lattice pattern over the turkey. Put a caper in the centre of each diamond shape. Chill in the fridge for 1 hour, then serve with a mixed salad and lemon wedges.

Turkey Picadillo

Using minced turkey rather than beef for this Mexican-style dish makes it much lower in fat. Serve as a filling for soft wheat tortillas or baked potatoes and then top with some plain low-fat yogurt for a tasty meal.

Serves 4

15ml/1 tbsp sunflower oil
1 onion, chopped
450g/1lb minced turkey
1–2 garlic cloves, crushed
1 fresh green chilli, seeded and finely chopped
6 tomatoes, peeled and chopped
15ml/1 tbsp tomato purée
2.5ml/½ tsp ground cumin
1 yellow or orange pepper, seeded and chopped
50g/2oz/⅓ cup raisins
50g/2oz/½ cup flaked almonds, toasted
45ml/3 tbsp chopped fresh coriander
150ml/¼ pint/⅔ cup plain low-fat yogurt
2–3 spring onions, finely chopped
4 soft tortillas
salt and freshly ground black pepper
shredded lettuce, to serve
lime wedges, to garnish

1 Heat the oil in a large frying pan and add the chopped onion. Cook gently for 5 minutes until soft. Stir in the minced turkey and garlic, and cook gently for a further 5 minutes.

2 Add the chilli, tomatoes, tomato purée, cumin, yellow or orange pepper and raisins. Cover and cook over a low heat for 15 minutes, stirring occasionally and adding a little water if necessary.

3 Stir in the toasted almonds, with about two thirds of the chopped coriander. Season to taste.

4 Tip the yogurt into a bowl. Stir in the remaining chopped coriander and the spring onions.

5 Heat the tortillas in a dry frying pan, without oil, for 15–20 seconds. Place some shredded lettuce and turkey mixture on each tortilla, roll up like a pancake and transfer to a plate. Top with a generous spoonful of the yogurt and coriander mixture, and serve immediately garnished with lime wedges.

Mandarin Sesame Duck

Duck is a high-fat meat, but it is possible to get rid of a good proportion of the fat by cooking it in this way. (If you remove the skin completely, the meat can be dry.) For a special occasion duck breasts are a good choice, though they are more expensive.

Serves 4

4 duck leg or boneless breast portions
30ml/2 tbsp light soy sauce
45ml/3 tbsp clear honey
15ml/1 tbsp sesame seeds
4 mandarin oranges
5ml/1 tsp cornflour
salt and freshly ground black pepper
lightly cooked mangetouts, carrots and beansprouts, to serve

1 Preheat the oven to 180°C/350°F/Gas 4. Prick the duck skin all over. Slash the breast skin (if using) diagonally at intervals.

2 Place the duck on a rack in a roasting tin and roast for 1 hour. Mix 15ml/1 tbsp of the soy sauce with 30ml/2 tbsp of the honey and brush over the duck. Sprinkle with sesame seeds. Roast for 15–20 minutes until golden brown.

3 Meanwhile, grate the rind from 1 mandarin and squeeze the juice from 2 of them. Place in a small saucepan. Mix in the cornflour, then stir in the remaining soy sauce and honey. Heat, stirring, until thickened and clear. Season to taste.

4 Peel and slice the remaining mandarins. Place the duck on individual plates, and top with the mandarin slices and the sauce. Serve with mangetouts, carrots and beansprouts.

Variations

If liked, you could substitute black or white poppy seeds for the sesame seeds, satsumas for the mandarin oranges and tamari for the soy sauce.

Udon Pot

A quick and easy Japanese dish, this combines chicken with king prawns, vegetables and noodles in a flavoursome stock.

Serves 4

350g/12oz dried udon noodles
1 large carrot, cut into bite-size chunks
225g/8oz chicken breast fillets or boneless thighs, skinned and cut into bite-size pieces
8 raw king prawns, peeled and deveined
4–6 Chinese cabbage leaves, cut into short strips
8 shiitake mushrooms, stems removed
50g/2oz mangetouts
1.5 litres/2½ pints/6¼ cups Chicken Stock or instant bonito stock
30ml/2 tbsp mirin
soy sauce, to taste

To serve

1 bunch spring onions, finely chopped
30ml/2 tbsp grated fresh root ginger
lemon wedges
fresh coriander sprigs
soy sauce

1 Cook the noodles until just tender, following the directions on the packet. Drain, rinse under cold water and drain thoroughly again.

2 Blanch the carrot in boiling water for 1 minute, then drain.

3 Spoon the noodles and carrot chunks into a large saucepan or flameproof casserole and arrange the chicken breasts or thighs, prawns, Chinese cabbage leaves, mushrooms and mangetouts on top.

4 Bring the stock to the boil in another saucepan. Add the mirin and soy sauce to taste. Pour the stock over the noodles. Cover the pan or casserole, bring to the boil over a moderate heat, then simmer gently for 5–6 minutes until all the ingredients are cooked.

5 Transfer to a serving dish and serve with chopped spring onions, grated ginger, lemon wedges, fresh coriander sprigs and a little soy sauce.

Poached Chicken

An organic free-range bird is the best choice for this simply cooked dish.

Serves 4

1 leek, roughly chopped
1 large carrot, roughly chopped
1 celery stick, roughly chopped
1 medium onion, roughly chopped
1.5kg/3½lb chicken
15ml/1 tbsp roughly chopped fresh parsley
10ml/2 tsp roughly chopped fresh thyme
6 fresh green peppercorns
Mustard Mayonnaise, green salad and lightly cooked baby carrots, to serve

1 Put the leek, carrot, celery and onion in a large saucepan. Place the chicken on top, cover with water and bring to the boil. Remove any scum that comes to the surface.

2 Add the herbs and peppercorns. Simmer gently for 1 hour. Remove from the heat and let the chicken cool in the stock.

3 Transfer the chicken to a board or plate and carve, discarding the skin. (Save the stock for another dish.) Arrange the slices on a serving platter. Serve with mustard mayonnaise, green salad and lightly cooked baby carrots.

Mustard Mayonnaise

Home-made mayonnaise is a really special treat.

Makes 350ml/12fl oz/1½ cups

2 egg yolks
15–30ml/1–2 tbs lemon juice
15–30ml/1–2 tbsp Dijon mustard
350ml/12fl oz/1½ cups olive oil
salt and freshly ground black pepper

1 Process the egg yolks, lemon juice and mustard in a food processor.

2 With the motor running, add the oil, a few drops at a time at first, then in a thin stream. Season to taste with salt and pepper.

Chicken with Lemon Sauce

Succulent chicken with a light, refreshing, lemony sauce and just a hint of lime is a sure winner.

Serves 4

4 chicken breast fillets, skinned
5ml/1 tsp sesame oil
15ml/1 tbsp dry sherry
1 egg white, lightly beaten
30ml/2 tbsp cornflour
15ml/1 tbsp vegetable oil
salt and freshly ground white pepper
chopped fresh coriander leaves, chopped spring onions and lemon wedges, to garnish

For the sauce

45ml/3 tbsp lemon juice
30ml/2 tbsp lime cordial
45ml/3 tbsp caster sugar
10ml/2 tsp cornflour
90ml/6 tbsp cold water

1 Arrange the chicken fillets in a single layer in a shallow bowl. Mix the sesame oil with the sherry, and season with salt and pepper. Pour over the chicken, cover and leave to marinate for 15 minutes. Mix together the egg white and cornflour. Add the mixture to the chicken and turn to coat thoroughly.

2 Heat the vegetable oil in a heavy-based frying pan or wok and fry the chicken fillets for about 15 minutes until they are golden brown on both sides.

3 Meanwhile, to make the sauce, combine all the ingredients in a small pan. Add a pinch of salt. Bring to the boil over a low heat, stirring constantly until the sauce is smooth and has thickened slightly.

4 Cut the chicken into pieces and arrange on a warmed serving plate. Pour the sauce over, garnish with the coriander leaves, spring onions and lemon wedges, and serve.

Variation

You can replace the dry sherry with white port or dry Madeira, if wished.

Chicken with Asparagus

Canned asparagus may be used, but will not require any cooking – simply add at the very end to warm through.

Serves 4

4 large chicken breast fillets, skinned
15ml/1 tbsp ground coriander
30ml/2 tbsp olive oil
20 slender asparagus spears, cut into 7.5–10cm/3–4in lengths
300ml/½ pint/1¼ cups Chicken Stock
15ml/1 tbsp cornflour
15ml/1 tbsp lemon juice
salt and freshly ground black pepper
15ml/1 tbsp chopped fresh parsley, to garnish

1 Divide each chicken breast fillet into two natural pieces. Place each between two sheets of clear film and flatten to a thickness of 5mm/¼in with a rolling pin. Cut into 2.5cm/1in strips diagonally across the fillets. Sprinkle over the ground coriander and toss to coat each piece.

2 Heat the oil in a large frying pan and fry the chicken very quickly in small batches for 3–4 minutes until lightly coloured. Season each batch with a little salt and pepper. Remove from the pan and keep warm while frying the rest of the chicken.

3 Add the asparagus and chicken stock to the pan, and bring to the boil. Cook for a further 4–5 minutes or until the asparagus is tender.

4 Mix the cornflour to a thin paste with a little cold water and stir into the sauce to thicken. Return the chicken to the pan together with the lemon juice. Reheat and then serve immediately, garnished with the chopped parsley.

Cook's Tip
You can use green or white asparagus for this dish, but whichever you choose, the buds should be plump and the stems evenly coloured.

Chicken with White Wine, Olives & Garlic

The chicken portions are browned without fat before being simmered in a rich white wine sauce.

Serves 4

1.5kg/3½ lb chicken, cut into serving portions
15ml/1 tbsp olive oil
1 onion, sliced
3–5 garlic cloves, to taste, crushed
5ml/1 tsp dried thyme
475ml/16fl oz/2 cups dry white wine
16–18 green olives, stoned
1 bay leaf
15ml/1 tbsp lemon juice
15–30ml/1–2 tbsp butter
salt and freshly ground black pepper

1 Heat a deep, heavy-based, non-stick frying pan, add the chicken portions, skin side down, and cook over a medium heat for about 10 minutes until browned. Turn the chicken portions and cook for a further 5–8 minutes to brown the other side. (Work in batches if necessary.) Transfer the chicken to a plate and set aside.

2 Heat the oil in the same pan. Add the onion and a pinch of salt, and cook for 5 minutes, stirring occasionally until just soft. Add the garlic and thyme, and cook for 1 minute.

3 Add the wine and stir, scraping up any sediment that clings to the base of the pan. Bring to the boil and boil for 1 minute. Stir in the green olives.

4 Return the chicken to the pan. Add the bay leaf and season lightly with pepper. Lower the heat, cover and simmer for 20–30 minutes until the chicken is cooked through.

5 Transfer the chicken portions to a warmed platter. Stir the lemon juice into the sauce. Whisk in the butter, a little at a time, to thicken the sauce slightly. Spoon the sauce over the chicken and serve immediately.

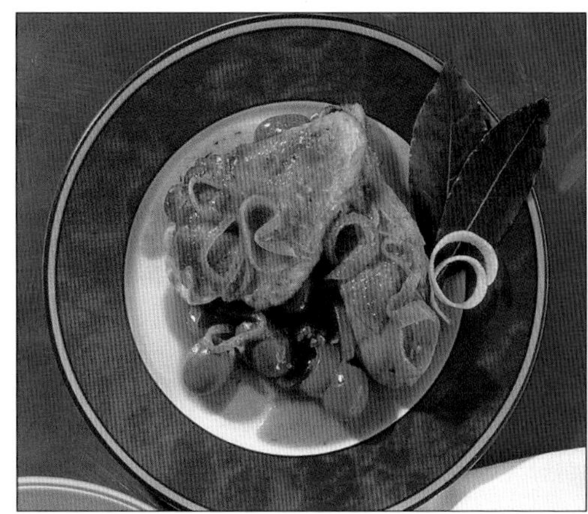

Lemon Chicken with Guacamole Sauce

Guacamole, which is very easy to prepare and looks stunning on the plate, is a great partner for chicken.

Serves 4

juice of 2 lemons
45ml/3 tbsp olive oil
2 garlic cloves, finely chopped
4 chicken breasts, about 200g/7oz each
2 tomatoes, cored and cut in half
salt and freshly ground black pepper
chopped fresh coriander and frisée lettuce, to garnish

For the guacamole sauce

1 ripe avocado
60ml/4 tbsp soured cream
45ml/3 tbsp fresh lemon juice
2.5ml/ ½ tsp salt
about 50ml/2fl oz/ ¼ cup water

1 Combine the lemon juice, oil, garlic, 2.5ml/ ½ tsp salt and a little pepper in a bowl. Arrange the chicken breasts, in one layer, in a shallow non-metallic dish. Pour over the lemon mixture and turn to coat evenly. Cover and leave to marinate for at least 1 hour at room temperature or chill overnight.

2 To make the sauce, halve the avocado, remove the stone and scrape the flesh into a food processor. Add the soured cream, lemon juice and salt, and process until smooth. Add the water and process to blend. If necessary, add a little more water to thin the sauce. Transfer to a bowl and set aside.

3 Preheat the grill and heat a ridged frying pan. Remove the chicken breasts from the marinade and pat dry. When the frying pan is hot add the chicken breasts and cook for about 10 minutes, turning frequently, until they are cooked through.

4 Meanwhile, arrange the tomato halves, cut sides up, on a baking sheet and season lightly. Grill for about 5 minutes until hot and bubbling.

5 To serve, place a chicken breast, tomato half and a spoon of sauce on each plate. Garnish with coriander and lettuce.

Chicken Breasts with Prunes & Almonds

An excellent dish for a winter dinner party. Chicken is cooked in a lightly spiced, fruity sauce that is thickened with ground almonds.

Serves 4

25g/1oz/2 tbsp butter or margarine
15ml/1 tbsp vegetable oil
about 1.2kg/2½ lb chicken breast halves
750ml/1¼ pints/3 cups Chicken Stock
115g/4oz/ ¾ cup raisins
15ml/1 tbsp fresh thyme or 5ml/1 tsp dried thyme
3 fresh sage leaves, chopped
45ml/3 tbsp chopped fresh parsley
15ml/1 tbsp chopped fresh marjoram or 5ml/1 tsp dried marjoram
50g/2oz/1 cup fresh breadcrumbs
50g/2oz/ ½ cup ground almonds
12 prunes, stoned
4–6 cloves
2.5ml/ ½ tsp ground mace
pinch of saffron strands, crumbled
salt and freshly ground black pepper
40g/1½ oz/ ⅓ cup flaked almonds, toasted, to garnish
lightly cooked courgettes and baby carrots, to serve

1 Heat the butter or margarine with the oil in a frying pan. Add the chicken and fry for 10 minutes until browned on all sides. Transfer the chicken pieces to a large, flameproof casserole.

2 Pour the stock into the casserole and bring to the boil. Add all the remaining ingredients, up to the toasted almonds, and stir well to mix. Simmer over a low heat for 45 minutes until the chicken is tender.

3 Lift the chicken out of the casserole and leave until cool enough to handle. Bring the cooking liquid back to the boil and boil for about 10 minutes until well reduced, stirring frequently.

4 Remove the bones from the chicken and return the meat to the sauce. Heat through. Serve, sprinkled with the toasted almonds and accompanied by lightly cooked courgettes and baby carrots.

Chicken with Red Wine Vinegar

This is an easy version of the modern classic invented by a French master chef.

Serves 4

4 chicken breast fillets, about 200g/7oz each, skinned
50g/2oz/4 tbsp unsalted butter
8–12 shallots, halved
60ml/4 tbsp red wine vinegar
2 garlic cloves, finely chopped
60ml/4 tbsp dry white wine
120ml/4fl oz/ ½ cup Chicken Stock
15ml/1 tbsp chopped fresh parsley
freshly ground black pepper
green salad, to serve

1 Cut each chicken breast in half crossways to make 8 pieces. Melt half the butter in a large, heavy-based frying pan over a medium heat. Add the chicken and cook for 3–5 minutes until golden brown, turning once, then season with pepper.

2 Add the shallot halves to the pan, cover and cook over a low heat for 5–7 minutes, shaking the pan and stirring occasionally.

3 Transfer the chicken pieces to a plate. Add the vinegar to the pan and cook, stirring frequently, for about 1 minute until the liquid is almost evaporated. Add the garlic, wine and stock, and stir to blend.

4 Return the chicken to the pan with any juices. Cover and simmer for 2–3 minutes until the chicken is tender.

5 Transfer the chicken and shallots to a serving dish and keep warm. Increase the heat and boil the cooking liquid until it has reduced by half. Remove the pan from the heat. Gradually add the remaining butter, whisking until the sauce is slightly thickened and glossy. Stir in the parsley, and pour the sauce over the chicken pieces and shallots. Serve with a green salad.

Variation
You could use different flavoured vinegars. Try tarragon vinegar and substitute fresh tarragon for the parsley.

Chicken Cordon Bleu

Perennially popular, this dish consists of breasts of chicken stuffed with smoked ham and Gruyère cheese, then coated in egg and breadcrumbs, and fried.

Serves 4

4 chicken breast fillets, about 130g/3½ oz each, skinned
4 very thin slices smoked ham, halved and rind removed
about 90g/3½ oz Gruyère cheese, thinly sliced
plain flour, for coating
2 eggs, beaten
75g/3oz/generous 1 cup natural-coloured dried breadcrumbs
5ml/1 tsp dried thyme
40g/1½ oz/3 tbsp butter
30ml/2 tbsp olive oil
salt and freshly ground black pepper
mixed leaf salad, to serve

1 Slit the chicken breasts about three quarters of the way through, then open them up and lay them flat. Place a slice of ham on each cut side of the chicken, trimming to fit if necessary.

2 Top with the Gruyère slices, making sure that they are well within the ham slices. Fold over the chicken and reshape, pressing well to seal and ensuring that no cheese is visible.

3 Put the flour into a shallow bowl. Pour the beaten eggs into another bowl, and mix the breadcrumbs with the thyme and seasoning in a third bowl. Toss each stuffed breast in the flour, then coat in egg and breadcrumbs, shaking off any excess. Lay the crumbed breasts flat on a plate, cover and chill for 1 hour.

4 To cook, heat the butter and oil in a frying pan. Slide in the coated breasts, two at a time. Fry over a medium-low heat for about 5 minutes on each side, turning carefully with a fish slice. Drain on kitchen paper and keep hot while you cook the remaining breasts. Serve with a side salad.

Variation
Instead of Gruyère, try one of the herb-flavoured hard cheeses, such as double Gloucester with chives.

Chicken Breasts with Grapes

Reducing the sauce is important for really concentrating the flavour, so take the time to do this fully before adding the cream.

Serves 4

4 chicken breast fillets, about 200g/7oz each, well trimmed
25g/1oz/2 tbsp butter
1 large or 2 small shallots, chopped
120ml/4fl oz/ ½ cup dry white wine
250ml/8fl oz/1 cup Chicken Stock
120ml/4fl oz/ ½ cup whipping cream
150g/5oz seedless green grapes
salt and freshly ground black pepper
fresh parsley sprigs, to garnish

1 Season the chicken breast fillets. Melt half the butter in a frying pan over a medium-high heat and cook the chicken for 4–5 minutes on each side until golden.

2 Transfer the chicken to a plate and cover to keep warm. Add the remaining butter to the pan and sauté the shallots until just softened, stirring frequently.

3 Add the wine, bring to the boil and boil to reduce by half, then add the stock and continue boiling to reduce by half again.

4 Add the cream to the sauce, bring back to the boil and pour in any juices from the chicken. Add the grapes and cook gently for 5 minutes. Slice the chicken and serve with the sauce, garnished with parsley.

Variation

This recipe also works well with poussins. Cook 4 poussins and the shallots as in steps 1 and 2 in a flameproof casserole. After adding the wine and stock in step 3, return the poussins to the casserole and simmer for 20–25 minutes. Transfer to a serving platter and finish the sauce as above.

Tarragon Chicken Breasts

The original version of this dish, created in France, uses a whole chicken, but boneless breasts are quick to cook and elegant. The combination of dried and fresh tarragon makes a wonderfully aromatic sauce.

Serves 4

4 chicken breast fillets, about 150–175g/5–6oz each, skinned
120ml/4fl oz/ ½ cup dry white wine
about 300ml/ ½ pint/1 ¼ cups Chicken Stock
15ml/1 tbsp dried tarragon
1 garlic clove, finely chopped
175ml/6fl oz/ ¾ cup whipping cream
15ml/1 tbsp chopped fresh tarragon
salt and freshly ground black pepper
fresh tarragon sprigs, to garnish

1 Season the chicken breast fillets lightly with salt and pepper, and put them in a saucepan just large enough to hold them in one layer. Pour over the wine and stock, adding more stock to cover, if necessary, then add the dried tarragon and garlic.

2 Bring the stock just to a simmer over a medium heat and cook gently for 8–10 minutes until the chicken juices run clear when the thickest part is pierced with a knife or skewer.

3 Using a slotted spoon, transfer the chicken to a plate and cover to keep warm. Strain the cooking liquid into a small saucepan, skim off any fat and boil to reduce by two thirds.

4 Add the cream and boil to reduce by half. Stir in the fresh tarragon and adjust the seasoning to taste. Slice the chicken, spoon over a little sauce, garnish with fresh tarragon sprigs and serve immediately.

Cook's Tip

Tarragon is traditionally paired with chicken, but you could, of course, use chopped fresh basil or parsley instead. Do not use dried versions of these two herbs.

Stuffed Chicken Breasts with Cream Sauce

The chicken meat encloses a delicately flavoured leek filling with a hint of lime.

Serves 4

4 large chicken breast fillets, skinned, or chicken suprêmes
50g/2oz/4 tbsp butter
3 large leeks, white and pale green parts only, thinly sliced
5ml/1 tsp grated lime rind
250ml/8fl oz/1 cup Chicken Stock or half stock and half dry white wine
120ml/4fl oz/½ cup double cream
15ml/1 tbsp lime juice
salt and freshly ground black pepper
lime twists and fresh parsley sprigs, to garnish

1 Cut horizontally into the thickest part of each chicken fillet or suprême to make a deep, wide pocket. Take care not to cut all the way through. Set the chicken aside.

2 Melt half the butter in a large, heavy-based frying pan over a low heat. Cook the leeks and lime rind, stirring occasionally, for 15–20 minutes or until the leeks are soft but not coloured. Turn them into a bowl, season and leave to cool.

3 Divide the leeks among the chicken pockets, packing them full. Secure the openings with wooden cocktail sticks.

4 Melt the remaining butter in a clean frying pan over a moderate heat. Add the chicken pockets and brown lightly on both sides. Pour in the stock, and wine if using, and bring to the boil. Cover and simmer for about 10 minutes or until the chicken is cooked through.

5 Using a slotted spoon, remove the chicken from the pan and keep warm. Boil the cooking liquid until it is reduced by half. Stir the cream into the cooking liquid and boil until reduced by about half again. Stir in the lime juice and season to taste.

6 Remove the cocktail sticks. Cut each pocket into 1cm/½in slices. Pour the sauce over and garnish with lime and parsley.

Lavender Chicken

Here, lavender flowers are used to perfume and flavour chicken cooked with red wine, oranges and thyme. The heady aroma of this dish will be a talking point among your guests.

Serves 4

15ml/1 tbsp butter
15ml/1 tbsp olive oil
8 chicken portions
8 shallots
30ml/2 tbsp flour
250ml/8fl oz/1 cup red wine
250ml/8fl oz/1 cup Chicken Stock
4 fresh thyme sprigs
10ml/2 tsp fresh thyme flowers, removed from stalk
10ml/2 tsp tsp lavender flowers
grated rind and juice of 1 orange
salt and freshly ground black pepper

To garnish

1 orange, divided into segments
12 fresh lavender sprigs
20ml/4 tsp fresh lavender flowers

1 Heat the butter and oil in a heavy-based pan and add the chicken portions. Fry until brown all over, then transfer to a large casserole. Add the shallots to the frying pan and cook for 2 minutes. Transfer to the casserole.

2 Add the flour to the frying pan and cook, stirring constantly, for 2 minutes. Pour in enough wine and stock to make a thin sauce, bring to the boil, stirring all the time, and season to taste.

3 Stir in the thyme sprigs, thyme and lavender flowers, orange rind and juice. Pour the sauce over the chicken. Cover and simmer for 30–40 minutes until the chicken is tender.

4 Remove the thyme sprigs. Serve, garnished with orange segments and lavender sprigs and flowers.

Cook's Tip

Do not use lavender flowers that may have been sprayed with a toxic substance, or that grow near a busy road and so may have been polluted by traffic fumes.

Roly Poly Chicken & Chanterelle Pudding

A warming dish for misty autumn days, this pudding is cooked in the old-fashioned way, wrapped in muslin.

Serves 4

1 medium onion, chopped
1 celery stick, sliced
10ml/2 tsp chopped fresh thyme
30ml/2 tbsp vegetable oil
2 chicken breast fillets, skinned
115g/4oz/1½ cups chanterelles, trimmed and sliced
40g/1½ oz/⅓ cup plain flour
300ml/½ pint/1¼ cups boiling Chicken Stock
5ml/1 tsp Dijon mustard
10ml/2 tsp wine vinegar
salt and freshly ground black pepper

For the roly poly dough

350g/12oz/3 cups self-raising flour, plus extra
2.5ml/½ tsp salt
150g/5oz/10 tbsp chilled unsalted butter, diced
75ml/5 tbsp cold water

1 Fry the onion, celery and thyme gently in the oil without colouring. Cut the chicken into bite-size pieces, add to the pan with the mushrooms and cook briefly. Stir in the flour, then remove from the heat. Gradually stir in the chicken stock. Return to the heat, simmer to thicken, then add the mustard, vinegar and seasoning. Set aside to cool.

2 To make the dough, sift the flour and salt into a bowl. Add the butter and rub in until it resembles coarse breadcrumbs. Add the water all at once and combine without over-mixing.

3 Roll out the dough on a floured surface into a 25 × 30cm/ 10 × 12in rectangle. Rinse a piece of muslin, about twice as big as the dough, in a little water and lay it on a clean, flat surface. Spread the chicken filling over the dough and roll up from the short end, using the muslin to help, to make a fat sausage. Enclose in the muslin and tie each end with cooking string.

4 Lower the pudding into a pan of boiling water, cover and simmer for 1½ hours. Lift out, untie and discard the muslin. Slice the pudding and serve hot.

Stuffed Chicken Rolls

These are simple to make, but sophisticated enough to serve at a dinner party.

Serves 4

25g/1oz/2 tbsp butter
1 garlic clove, chopped
150g/5oz/1¼ cups cooked white long-grain rice
45ml/3 tbsp ricotta cheese
10ml/2 tsp chopped fresh flat leaf parsley
5ml/1 tsp chopped fresh tarragon
4 chicken breast fillets, skinned
3–4 slices Parma ham
15ml/1 tbsp olive oil
120ml/4fl oz/½ cup white wine
salt and freshly ground black pepper
fresh flat leaf parsley sprigs, to garnish
cooked tagliatelle and sautéed blewit mushrooms, to serve (optional)

1 Preheat the oven to 180°C/350°F/Gas 4. Melt about 10g/¼oz/1½ tsp of the butter in a small pan and fry the garlic for a few seconds without browning. Spoon into a bowl. Add the rice, ricotta, parsley and tarragon to the garlic, and season with salt and pepper. Stir to mix.

2 Place each chicken breast fillet in turn between two sheets of clear film and flatten by beating lightly, but firmly, with a rolling pin or meat mallet.

3 Lay a slice of Parma ham over each chicken breast, trimming it to fit if necessary. Place a spoonful of the rice stuffing at the wider end of each breast. Roll up carefully and tie in place with cooking string or secure with a wooden cocktail stick.

4 Heat the oil and the remaining butter in a frying pan and lightly fry the chicken rolls until browned on all sides. Place side by side in a shallow, ovenproof dish and pour over the wine.

5 Cover the dish with greaseproof paper and cook in the oven for 30–35 minutes until the chicken is tender.

6 Cut the rolls into slices and serve on a bed of tagliatelle with sautéed blewit mushrooms, if you like. Garnish with fresh, flat leaf parsley.

Chicken with Wild Mushrooms & Vermouth

Tender chicken slices are folded into a rich soured-cream sauce, spiked with dry white vermouth.

Serves 4
30ml/2 tbsp oil
1 leek, finely chopped
4 chicken breast fillets, skinned and sliced
225g/8oz/3 cups wild mushrooms, sliced if large
15ml/1 tbsp brandy
pinch of grated nutmeg
1.5ml/¼ tsp chopped fresh thyme
150ml/¼ pint/⅔ cup dry white vermouth
150ml/¼ pint/⅔ cup Chicken Stock
6 green olives, stoned and quartered
150ml/¼ pint/⅔ cup soured cream
salt and freshly ground black pepper
fresh thyme sprigs and croûtons, to garnish

1 Heat the oil and fry the leek until softened but not browned. Add the chicken slices and mushrooms. Fry, stirring occasionally, until just beginning to brown.

2 Pour over the brandy and ignite. When the flames have died down, stir in the nutmeg, chopped thyme, vermouth and stock, with salt and pepper to taste.

3 Bring to the boil, lower the heat and simmer for 5 minutes. Stir in the olives and most of the soured cream. Reheat gently, but do not let the mixture boil.

4 Garnish with the remaining soured cream, the thyme sprigs and croûtons. Serve immediately.

Cook's Tip
Chinese dried mushrooms work well in this dish. Soak them for 1 hour in cold water before use.

Whisky Chicken with Onion Marmalade

Whisky-flavoured roasted chicken portions are served with meltingly tender onions and green pepper.

Serves 4
25g/1oz/4 tbsp sesame seeds, crushed
2 garlic cloves, crushed
pinch of paprika
30ml/2 tbsp oil
30ml/2 tbsp whisky
30ml/2 tbsp clear honey
4 chicken portions
salt and freshly ground black pepper

For the onion marmalade
30ml/2 tbsp oil
2 large onions, finely sliced
1 green pepper, seeded and sliced
150ml/¼ pint/⅔ cup vegetable stock

1 Preheat the oven to 190°C/375°F/Gas 5. In a bowl, make a paste with the sesame seeds, garlic, paprika, oil, whisky and honey. Season and add a little water if the paste is too thick.

2 Make several cuts in the chicken portions and place them in an ovenproof dish. Spread the paste over. Roast for 40 minutes or until cooked through.

3 Meanwhile, to make the marmalade, heat the oil in a frying pan and fry the onions over a medium heat for 15 minutes. Add the green pepper and fry for 5 minutes more. Stir in the stock, season with salt and pepper, and cook gently, stirring occasionally, for about 20 minutes.

4 Transfer the chicken to warmed plates and serve with the warm onion marmalade.

Variation
Instead of making cuts in the chicken portions, ease the skin away from the flesh and push the paste underneath.

Chicken with Sloe Gin & Juniper

Juniper is used in the manufacture of gin, and the reinforcement of the flavour by using both sloe gin and juniper berries is delicious. Sloe gin is easy to make, but can also be bought.

Serves 8
30ml/2 tbsp butter
30ml/2 tbsp sunflower oil
8 chicken breast fillets
350g/12oz carrots, cooked
1 garlic clove, crushed
15ml/1 tbsp finely chopped fresh parsley
50ml/2fl oz/¼ cup Chicken Stock
50ml/2fl oz/¼ cup red wine
50ml/2fl oz/¼ cup sloe gin
5ml/1 tsp crushed juniper berries
salt and freshly ground black pepper
chopped fresh basil, to garnish

1 Heat the butter with the oil in a pan and sauté the chicken until browned on all sides.

2 In a food processor, combine all the remaining ingredients except the basil and process to a smooth purée. If the mixture seems too thick, add a little more red wine or water until a thinner consistency is reached.

3 Put the chicken breasts in a heavy-based pan, pour the sauce over the top and cook for about 15 minutes until the chicken is cooked through.

4 Adjust the seasoning to taste and serve, garnished with chopped fresh basil.

Variation
Instead of sloe gin, you could make this dish with a herb-flavoured liqueur, such as Benedictine or Galliano, a plum brandy, such as slivovitz or kirsch, or a herb- or plum-flavoured vodka, but still using the juniper berries.

Herbed Chicken with Apricot & Pecan Potato Baskets

The potato baskets make a pretty addition to the chicken and could easily have different fillings when you need a change.

Serves 8
8 chicken breast fillets, skinned
30ml/2 tbsp butter
6 mushrooms, chopped
15ml/1 tbsp chopped pecan nuts
115g/4oz/⅓ cup chopped cooked ham
50g/2oz/1 cup wholemeal breadcrumbs
15ml/1 tbsp chopped fresh parsley, plus a few whole leaves to garnish
salt and freshly ground black pepper

For the sauce
10ml/2 tsp cornflour
120ml/4fl oz/½ cup white wine
50g/2oz/4 tbsp butter
50g/2oz apricot chutney

For the potato baskets
4 large baking potatoes
175g/6oz pork sausagemeat
225g/8oz can apricots in natural juice, drained and quartered
1.5ml/¼ tsp ground cinnamon
2.5ml/½ tsp grated orange rind
30ml/2 tbsp maple syrup
25g/1oz/2 tbsp butter
25g/1oz/¼ cup chopped pecan nuts, plus some pecan halves to garnish

1 Preheat the oven to 160°C/325°F/Gas 3. Place the potatoes in the oven to bake. Place the chicken breast fillets between two sheets of clear film and beat lightly with a rolling pin or meat mallet to flatten.

2 Melt the butter in a pan and sauté the mushrooms, pecans and ham. Stir in the breadcrumbs and parsley, and season.

3 Divide the mushroom mixture among the chicken fillets. Roll up and secure each one with a wooden cocktail stick. Chill while making the sauce.

4 To make the sauce, mix the cornflour with a little of the wine to make a smooth paste. Put the remaining wine in a pan and add the paste. Simmer until smooth, then add the butter and chutney, and cook for about 5 minutes, stirring constantly.

5 Place the chicken breasts in a shallow, ovenproof dish and pour over the sauce. Bake in the oven (do not adjust the temperature) for 20 minutes, basting several times.

6 To make the potato baskets, cut the baked potatoes in half and scoop out the inside, leaving a reasonable layer within the shell. Mash the potato and place in a mixing bowl.

7 Fry the sausagemeat, discarding some of the fat that comes off. Add the remaining ingredients and cook for 1 minute. Add the mixture to the mashed potato, blend and use to fill the potato shells. Sprinkle the pecan halves over the top, place in the oven with the chicken and bake for another 30 minutes.

8 Remove the chicken from the oven and drain the sauce into a jug. Slice the chicken, arrange on plates and pour the sauce over. Garnish with parsley and serve with the potato baskets.

Persian Chicken with Walnut Sauce

This distinctive dish is traditionally served on festive occasions in Iran.

Serves 4

30ml/2 tbsp oil
4 chicken portions (leg or breast)
1 large onion, grated
250ml/8fl oz/1 cup water
115g/4oz/1 cup finely chopped walnuts
75ml/4 tbsp pomegranate purée
15ml/1 tbsp tomato purée
30ml/2 tbsp lemon juice
15ml/1 tbsp sugar
3–4 saffron strands dissolved in 15ml/1 tbsp boiling water
salt and freshly ground black pepper
rice and salad leaves, to serve

1 Heat 15ml/1 tbsp of the oil in a large saucepan or flameproof casserole and sauté the chicken portions until golden brown. Add half of the grated onion and fry until slightly softened.

2 Add the water and seasoning, and bring to the boil. Cover the pan, reduce the heat and simmer for 15 minutes.

3 Heat the remaining oil in a small saucepan or frying pan and fry the rest of the onion for 2–3 minutes until soft. Add the walnuts and fry for a further 2–3 minutes over a low heat, stirring frequently and taking care that the walnuts do not burn.

4 Stir in the pomegranate and tomato purées, lemon juice, sugar and the dissolved saffron. Season to taste and then simmer over a low heat for 5 minutes.

5 Pour the walnut sauce over the chicken, ensuring that it is well covered. Cover and simmer for 30–35 minutes until the meat is cooked and the oil of the walnuts has risen to the top. Serve at once with rice and salad leaves.

Cook's Tip
Pomegranate purée is available from Middle Eastern delicatessens and specialist foodstores.

Chicken with Parma Ham & Cheese

An Italian way of making a special meal of chicken, using Fontina cheese and cured ham.

Serves 4

2 thin slices Parma ham
2 thin slices Fontina cheese
4 part-boned chicken breasts
4 fresh basil sprigs
30ml/2 tbsp olive oil
15g/½oz/1 tbsp butter
120ml/4fl oz/ ½ cup dry white wine
salt and freshly ground black pepper
tender young salad leaves, to serve

1 Preheat the oven to 200°C/400°F/Gas 6. Lightly oil an ovenproof dish. Cut the ham and cheese slices in half crossways.

2 Skin the chicken breasts and open out the slit in the centre of each one. Fill each cavity with half a ham slice and a fresh basil sprig.

3 Heat the oil and butter in a wide, heavy-based frying pan until foaming. Cook the chicken breasts over a medium heat for 1–2 minutes on each side until they change colour.

4 Transfer the chicken to the ovenproof dish. Add the wine to the pan juices, stir until sizzling, then pour over the chicken and season to taste.

5 Top each chicken breast with a slice of Fontina. Bake for 20 minutes or until the chicken is tender. Serve hot, with tender young salad leaves.

Cook's Tip
There is nothing quite like the buttery texture and nutty flavour of Fontina cheese, and it also has superb melting qualities, but you could use a Swiss or French mountain cheese, such as Gruyère or Emmental. Ask for the cheese to be sliced thinly on the machine slicer, as you will find it difficult to slice it sufficiently thinly yourself.

Chicken Kiev

This popular recipe is a modern Russian invention. These chicken breasts filled with garlic butter should be prepared in advance to allow time for chilling.

Serves 4

115g/4oz/ ½ cup butter, softened
2 garlic cloves, crushed
finely grated rind of 1 lemon
30ml/2 tbsp chopped fresh tarragon
pinch of grated nutmeg
4 chicken breast fillets with wing bones attached, skinned
1 egg, lightly beaten
115g/4oz/2 cups fresh breadcrumbs
oil, for deep frying
salt and freshly ground black pepper
lemon wedges, to garnish
potato wedges, to serve

1 Mix the butter in a bowl with the garlic, lemon rind, tarragon and nutmeg. Season to taste with salt and pepper. Shape the butter into a rectangular block about 5cm/2in long, wrap in foil and chill for 1 hour.

2 Place the chicken on a piece of oiled clear film. Cover with a second piece of clear film and gently beat the pieces with a meat mallet or rolling pin until fairly thin.

3 Cut the butter lengthways into four pieces and put one in the centre of each chicken fillet. Fold the edges over the butter and secure with wooden cocktail sticks.

4 Put the beaten egg and the breadcrumbs into separate dishes. Dip the chicken pieces first in the beaten egg and then in the breadcrumbs to coat evenly. Dip them a second time in egg and crumbs, then put them on a plate and chill for at least 1 hour.

5 Heat the oil in a large pan or deep-fat fryer to 180°C/350°F. Deep fry the chicken for 6–8 minutes or until the chicken is cooked and the coating golden brown and crisp. Drain on kitchen paper and remove the cocktail sticks. Garnish with wedges of lemon and serve with potato wedges.

Chicken with Tomatoes & Prawns

This dish was created especially for Napoleon after the battle of Marengo.

Serves 4

120ml/4fl oz/ ½ cup olive oil
8 chicken thighs on the bone, skinned
1 onion, finely chopped
1 celery stick, finely chopped
1 garlic clove, crushed
350g/12oz ripe Italian plum tomatoes, peeled and roughly chopped
250ml/8fl oz/1 cup dry white wine
2.5ml/ ½ tsp finely chopped fresh rosemary
15g/½oz/1 tbsp butter
8 small triangles thinly sliced white bread, without crusts
175g/6oz large raw prawns, peeled
salt and freshly ground black pepper
finely chopped flat leaf parsley, to garnish

1 Heat 30ml/2 tbsp of the oil in a frying pan and sauté the chicken over a medium heat for 5 minutes until it has changed colour on all sides. Transfer to a flameproof casserole.

2 Add the onion and celery to the pan and cook gently, stirring frequently, for 3 minutes until softened. Add the garlic, tomatoes, wine, rosemary and seasoning. Bring to the boil, stirring.

3 Pour the tomato sauce over the chicken. Cover and cook gently for 40 minutes or until the chicken juices run clear when the thickest part is pierced with a knife or skewer.

4 About 10 minutes before serving, heat the remaining oil and the butter in the frying pan. Add the triangles of bread and fry until crisp and golden on each side. Drain on kitchen paper.

5 Add the prawns to the casserole and heat until they are cooked. Taste the sauce and adjust the seasoning as necessary.

6 Dip one of the tips of each fried bread triangle in the chopped parsley. Serve the chicken dish hot, garnished with the bread triangles.

Bisteeya

This intriguing dish is a simplified version of a Moroccan speciality.

Serves 4

30ml/2 tbsp sunflower oil, plus extra for brushing
25g/1oz/2 tbsp butter
3 chicken quarters, preferably breasts
1½ Spanish onions, grated or very finely chopped
good pinch of ground ginger
good pinch of saffron powder
10ml/2 tsp ground cinnamon, plus extra for dusting
40g/1½ oz/4 tbsp flaked almonds
1 large bunch fresh coriander, finely chopped
1 large bunch fresh parsley, finely chopped
3 eggs, beaten
about 175g/6oz filo pastry
5–10ml/1–2 tsp icing sugar (optional), plus extra for dusting
salt and freshly ground black pepper

1 Heat the oil and butter in a large, flameproof casserole or saucepan and brown the chicken pieces for about 4 minutes. Add the onions, ginger, saffron, 2.5ml/ ¼ tsp of the cinnamon and enough water (about 300ml/ ½ pint/1¼ cups) so that the chicken braises, rather than boils. Season well.

2 Bring to the boil, then cover and simmer very gently for 45–55 minutes or until the chicken is tender. Meanwhile, dry-fry the almonds until golden and set aside.

3 Transfer the chicken to a plate. When cool enough to handle, remove the skin and bones and cut the flesh into pieces.

4 Stir the coriander and parsley into the pan, and simmer the sauce until well reduced and thick. Add the beaten eggs and cook over a very gentle heat until they are lightly scrambled.

5 Preheat the oven to 180°C/350°F/Gas 4. Oil a shallow, round ovenproof dish, about 25cm/10in in diameter. Place one or two sheets of filo pastry in a single layer over the base of the dish (it will depend on the size of your filo pastry), so that it is completely covered and the edges of the pastry sheets hang over the sides. Brush lightly with oil and make two more layers of filo, brushing with oil between the layers.

6 Place the chicken on the pastry and then spoon the egg and herb mixture on top.

7 Place a single layer of filo pastry on top of the filling (you may need to use more than one sheet of filo pastry) and scatter with the almonds. Sprinkle with the remaining cinnamon and the icing sugar, if using.

8 Fold the edges of the filo over the almonds and then make four further layers of filo (using one or two sheets per layer, depending on size), brushing each layer with a little oil. Tuck the filo edges under the pie (as if you were making a bed) and brush the top layer with oil.

9 Bake in the oven for 40–45 minutes until golden. Dust the top with icing sugar and use the extra cinnamon to make criss-cross or diagonal lines. Serve immediately.

Chicken in Badacsonyi Wine

A Hungarian recipe, originally made with a Balatan wine called *Badacsonyi Kĕkryalii* ("Blue Handled"), which has a full body and distinctive bouquet.

Serves 4

50g/2oz/4 tbsp butter
4 spring onions, chopped
115g/4oz rindless smoked bacon, diced
2 bay leaves
1 fresh tarragon sprig
1.5kg/3½ lb corn-fed chicken
60ml/4 tbsp sweet sherry or mead
115g/4oz/1½ cups button mushrooms, sliced
300ml/ ½ pint/1¼ cups Badacsonyi or dry white wine
salt
fresh tarragon and bay leaves, to garnish
steamed rice, to serve

1 Heat the butter in a large, heavy-based pan or flameproof casserole and sweat the spring onions for 1–1½ minutes. Add the bacon, bay leaves and tarragon, stripping the leaves from the stem. Cook for a further 1 minute.

2 Add the whole chicken to the pan and pour in the sherry or mead. Cook, covered, over a very low heat for 15 minutes.

3 Sprinkle the mushrooms into the pan and pour in the wine. Cook, covered, for 1 hour. Remove the lid, baste the chicken with the wine mixture and cook, uncovered, for a further 30 minutes, until almost all the liquid has evaporated.

4 Skim the fat from the cooking liquid remaining in the pan. Taste and adjust the seasoning as necessary. Transfer the chicken, vegetables and bacon to a serving dish. Garnish with tarragon and bay leaves, and serve with rice.

Cook's Tip

Traditionally, this recipe also used a sweet drink with a honeyed caramel flavour called marc. If you can obtain this, use it instead of the sweet sherry or mead.

Chicken with Morels

Morels are among the tastiest dried mushrooms and, although they are expensive, a small quantity goes a long way and is certainly worth investing in for this wonderful dinner party dish.

Serves 4

40g/1½oz dried morel mushrooms
250ml/8fl oz/1 cup Chicken Stock
50g/2oz/4 tbsp butter
5 or 6 shallots, thinly sliced
115g/4oz/1½ cups button mushrooms, thinly sliced
1.5ml/¼ tsp dried thyme
30–45ml/2–3 tbsp brandy
175ml/6fl oz/¾ cup double or whipping cream
4 chicken breast fillets, about 200g/7oz each, skinned
15ml/1 tbsp vegetable oil
175ml/6fl oz/¾ cup Champagne or dry sparkling wine
salt and freshly ground black pepper

1 Put the morels in a sieve and rinse well under cold running water, shaking to remove as much grit as possible. Put them in a saucepan with the stock and bring to the boil over a medium heat. Remove the pan from the heat and set aside for 1 hour.

2 Remove the morels from the cooking liquid. Strain the liquid through a very fine, muslin-lined sieve and set aside. Reserve a few whole morels and slice the rest.

3 Melt half the butter in a frying pan over a medium heat. Add the shallots and cook for 2 minutes until softened, then add the morels and button mushrooms and cook, stirring frequently, for 2–3 minutes.

4 Season and add the thyme, brandy and 100ml/3½fl oz/⅓ cup of the cream. Reduce the heat and simmer gently for 10–12 minutes until any liquid has evaporated, stirring occasionally. Remove the mixture from the pan and set aside.

5 Pull off the small fillet (the finger-shaped piece on the underside) from each chicken breast and reserve for another use. Make a pocket in each breast by cutting a slit along the thicker edge, taking care not to cut all the way through.

6 Using a small spoon, fill each pocket with one quarter of the mushroom mixture, then, if necessary, close with a wooden cocktail stick.

7 Melt the remaining butter with the oil in a heavy-based frying pan over a medium-high heat and cook the chicken breasts on one side for 6–8 minutes until golden. Transfer to a plate. Add the Champagne or sparkling wine to the pan and boil to reduce by half. Add the reserved strained morel cooking liquid and boil to reduce by half again.

8 Add the remaining cream and cook over a medium heat for 2–3 minutes until the sauce thickens slightly and coats the back of a spoon. Adjust the seasoning. Return the chicken to the pan with any accumulated juices and the reserved whole morels, and simmer for 3–5 minutes over a medium-low heat until the chicken is hot and the juices run clear when the thickest part is pierced with a knife or skewer. Serve immediately.

Pan-fried Marinated Poussin

These small birds are full of flavour when marinated for several hours before they are cooked.

Serves 3–4

2 poussins, about 450g/1lb each
5–6 fresh mint leaves, torn into pieces
1 leek, sliced into thin rings
1 garlic clove, finely chopped
60ml/4 tbsp olive oil
30ml/2 tbsp lemon juice
50ml/2fl oz/¼ cup dry white wine
salt and freshly ground black pepper
fresh mint leaves, to garnish

1 Cut the poussins in half down the backbone, dividing the breast. Flatten the four halves with a meat mallet. Place them in a bowl with the mint, leek and garlic. Season with pepper, and sprinkle with oil and half the lemon juice. Cover and leave to stand in a cool place for 6 hours.

2 Heat a large, heavy-based frying pan. Place the poussins and their marinade in the pan, cover and cook over moderate heat for about 45 minutes, turning them occasionally. Season with salt during the cooking. Transfer the poussins to a warmed serving platter.

3 Tilt the pan and spoon off any fat on the surface of the liquid. Pour in the white wine and the remaining lemon juice, and cook until the sauce reduces by about half.

4 Strain the sauce, pressing the vegetables to extract all the juices. Place the poussins on individual plates and spoon over the sauce. Garnish with mint and serve.

Cook's Tip

While bottled lemon juice is very convenient, it does not have the same flavour as freshly squeezed juice. Let citrus fruits come to room temperature before squeezing for the maximum quantity of juice.

Steamboat

This Malaysian dish is named after the utensil in which it is cooked – a type of fondue with a funnel and a moat. The moat is filled with stock, which traditionally is kept hot with charcoal. An electric steamboat or any traditional fondue pot can be used instead.

Serves 8

8 Chinese dried mushrooms, soaked for 30 minutes in warm water to cover
1.5 litres/2½ pints/6¼ cups Chicken Stock
10ml/2 tsp rice wine or medium-dry sherry
10ml/2 tsp sesame oil
225g/8oz lean pork, thinly sliced
225g/8oz rump steak, thinly sliced
1 chicken breast fillet, skinned and thickly sliced
2 chicken livers, trimmed and sliced
225g/8oz raw prawns, peeled
450g/1lb white fish fillets, skinned and cubed
200g/7oz fish balls
115g/4oz fried tofu, each piece halved
leafy green vegetables, such as lettuce, Chinese leaves, spinach leaves and watercress, cut into 15cm/6in lengths
225g/8oz Chinese rice vermicelli
8 eggs
selection of sauces, including soy with sesame seeds; soy with crushed ginger; chilli; plum and hot mustard
½ bunch spring onions, chopped
salt and freshly ground white pepper

1 Drain the mushrooms, reserving the soaking liquid. Cut off and discard the stems; slice the caps thinly.

2 Pour the stock into a large saucepan and add the rice wine or sherry, sesame oil and reserved mushroom liquid. Bring the mixture to the boil, then season with salt and pepper. Reduce the heat and simmer gently.

3 Put the meat, fish, tofu, green vegetables and mushrooms in bowls on the table. Soak the vermicelli in hot water for about 5 minutes, drain and place in 8 soup bowls on a small side table. Crack an egg in a small bowl for each diner; place on the side table. Put the sauces in bowls beside each other.

4 Add the spring onions to the pan of stock, bring it to a full boil and fuel the steamboat. Pour the stock into the moat and seat your guests at once. Each guest lowers a few chosen morsels into the boiling stock, using chopsticks or fondue forks, leaves them for a minute or two, then removes them with a small wire mesh ladle, a fondue fork or pair of chopsticks.

5 When all the meat, fish, tofu and vegetables have been cooked, the stock will be concentrated and wonderfully enriched. Add a little boiling water if necessary. Bring the soup bowls containing the soaked noodles to the table, pour in the hot soup and slide a whole egg into each, stirring until it cooks and forms threads.

Cook's Tip
Fresh or frozen fish balls are available from Asian foodstores and Chinese supermarkets.

Drunken Chicken

In China, "drunken" foods are usually served cold as part of an appetizer to a Chinese meal or as canapés.

Serves 4–6

1 chicken, about 1.3kg/3lb
1cm/½ in piece fresh root ginger, thinly sliced
2 spring onions, trimmed
1.75 litres/3 pints/7½ cups water or to cover
15ml/1 tbsp salt
300ml/½ pint/1¼ cups dry sherry
15–30ml/1–2 tbsp brandy
shredded spring onions and fresh herbs, to garnish

1 Rinse and dry the chicken inside and out. Place the ginger and spring onions in the body cavity. Put the chicken in a large saucepan or flameproof casserole and just cover with water. Bring to the boil, skim and cook for 15 minutes.

2 Turn off the heat, cover the pan or casserole tightly and leave the chicken in the cooking liquid for 3–4 hours, by which time it will be cooked. Drain well. Pour 300ml/½ pint/1¼ cups of the stock into a jug. Freeze the remaining stock for another dish.

3 Leaving the skin on the chicken, joint it neatly. Divide each leg into a drumstick and thigh. Make two more portions from the wings and some from the breast. Finally cut away the remainder of the breast pieces (still on the bone) and divide each breast into two even-size portions.

4 Arrange the chicken portions in a shallow dish. Rub salt into the skin and cover with clear film. Leave in a cool place for several hours or overnight in the fridge.

5 Next day, lift off and discard any fat from the stock. Mix the sherry and brandy in a jug, add the stock and pour over the chicken. Cover again and leave in the fridge to marinate for 2–3 days, turning occasionally.

6 When ready to serve remove the chicken skin. Cut the chicken through the bone into chunky pieces and arrange on a serving platter, garnished with spring onion shreds and herbs.

Poussins Véronique

A double poussin is six to ten weeks old and weighs about 1kg/2lb, so one bird is large enough to serve two people.

Serves 4

2 fresh tarragon or thyme sprigs
2 double poussins
25g/1oz/2 tbsp butter
60ml/4 tbsp white wine
grated rind and juice of ½ lemon
15ml/1 tbsp olive oil
15ml/1 tbsp plain flour
150ml/ ¼ pint/ ⅔ cup Chicken Stock
115g/4oz seedless green grapes, cut in half if large
salt and freshly ground black pepper
chopped fresh parsley, to garnish
lightly cooked green beans, to serve

1 Preheat the oven to 180°C/350°F/Gas 4. Put a sprig of tarragon or thyme inside the cavity of each poussin and tie the birds into a neat shape.

2 Heat the butter in a flameproof casserole, add the poussins and brown them lightly all over. Pour in the white wine, season with salt and pepper to taste, cover and transfer the casserole to the oven. Cook for 20–30 minutes or until tender and the juices run clear when the thickest part is pierced with a skewer or the point of knife.

3 Remove the poussins from the casserole and cut in half with a pair of kitchen scissors, removing the backbones and small rib-cage bones. Arrange in a shallow, ovenproof dish (that will slide under the grill). Sprinkle with lemon juice and brush with oil. Grill until lightly browned. Keep warm.

4 Mix the flour into the butter and wine in the casserole, and blend in the stock. Bring to the boil, adjust the seasoning to taste and add the lemon rind and grapes, then simmer for 2–3 minutes.

5 Spoon the sauce over the poussins, garnish with chopped fresh parsley and serve immediately with lightly cooked green beans.

Baby Chickens with Lime & Chilli

Kept succulent with a sun-dried tomato-flavoured butter, these poussins make a splendid barbecued meal for friends, though they also cook well under the grill.

Serves 4

4 poussins, about 450g/1lb each
45ml/3 tbsp butter
30ml/2 tbsp sun-dried tomato purée
finely grated rind of 1 lime
10ml/2 tsp chilli sauce
juice of ½ lime
fresh flat leaf parsley sprigs, to garnish
lime wedges, to serve

1 Prepare the barbecue or preheat the grill. Spatchcock the poussins and turn the flattened birds breast side up. Lift the breast skin carefully and gently ease your fingertips underneath, to loosen it from the flesh.

2 In a bowl, mix together the butter, tomato purée, lime rind and chilli sauce. Spread about three quarters of the mixture under the skin of each poussin, smoothing it evenly.

3 To hold the poussins flat during cooking, thread two skewers through each bird, crossing at the centre. Each skewer should pass through a wing and then out through a drumstick.

4 Combine the remaining butter mixture with the lime juice and brush it over the skin of the poussins. Cook on a medium-hot barbecue or under the grill, turning occasionally, for 25–30 minutes or until the juices run clear when the thickest part of the thigh is pierced with a skewer or knife. Garnish with flat leaf parsley and serve with lime wedges.

Cook's Tip

If you wish to serve half a poussin per portion, you may find it easier simply to cut the birds in half lengthways. Use poultry shears or a large, sharp knife to cut through the breastbone and backbone.

Poussins with Courgette & Apricot Stuffing

If possible, buy very small poussins for this recipe. If these are not available, buy slightly larger poussins and serve half per person.

Serves 4

4 small poussins
about 40g/1½ oz/3 tbsp butter
5–10ml/1–2 tsp ground coriander
1 large red pepper, seeded and cut into strips
1 fresh red chilli, seeded and thinly sliced
15–30ml/1–2 tbsp olive oil
120ml/4fl oz/½ cup Chicken Stock
30ml/2 tbsp cornflour
salt and freshly ground black pepper
fresh flat leaf parsley, to garnish

For the stuffing

550ml/18fl oz/2½ cups vegetable or Chicken Stock
275g/10oz/1⅔ cups couscous
2 small courgettes
8 ready-to-eat dried apricots
15ml/1 tbsp chopped fresh flat leaf parsley
15ml/1 tbsp chopped fresh coriander
juice of ½ lemon

1 To make the stuffing, bring the stock to the boil and pour it over the couscous in a large bowl. Stir once and then set aside for 10 minutes.

2 Meanwhile, top and tail the courgettes and then grate coarsely. Roughly chop the apricots and add to the courgettes. Preheat the oven to 200°C/400°F/Gas 6.

3 When the couscous has swollen, fluff up with a fork and then spoon 90ml/6 tbsp into a separate bowl and add the courgettes and chopped apricots. Add the herbs, seasoning and lemon juice, and stir to make a fairly loose stuffing. Set aside the remaining couscous for serving.

4 Spoon the apricot stuffing loosely into the body cavities of the poussins and secure with cooking string or wooden cocktail sticks. Place the birds in a roasting tin so that they fit comfortably but not too closely. Rub the butter into the skins, and sprinkle with ground coriander and a little salt and pepper. Place the red pepper and chilli in the roasting tin around the poussins and spoon over the olive oil.

5 Roast in the oven for 20 minutes, then reduce the temperature to 180°C/350°F/Gas 4. Pour the stock around the poussins and baste them with the stock and red pepper/chilli mixture. Return the tin to the oven and cook for a further 30–35 minutes until the poussins are cooked through. Baste occasionally with the stock.

6 Transfer the poussins to a warmed serving plate. Steam the reserved couscous to reheat. Blend the cornflour with 45ml/3 tbsp cold water, stir into the stock and peppers in the roasting tin and heat gently on top of the stove, stirring, until the sauce is slightly thickened. Taste and adjust the seasoning.

7 Pour the sauce into a jug or over the poussins. Garnish the birds with parsley and serve with the reserved couscous.

Chicken Liver Risotto

The combination of chicken livers, bacon, parsley and thyme gives this risotto a wonderfully rich flavour. Serve it as a starter for four or a lunch for two or three.

Serves 2–4

175g/6oz chicken livers
about 15ml/1 tbsp olive oil
about 25g/1oz/2 tbsp butter
3 rindless streaky bacon rashers, finely chopped
2 shallots, finely chopped
1 garlic clove, crushed
1 celery stick, finely sliced
275g/10oz/1½ cups risotto rice
175ml/6fl oz/¾ cup dry white wine
900ml–1 litre/1½–1¾ pints/3¾–4 cups simmering Chicken Stock
5ml/1 tsp chopped fresh thyme
15ml/1 tbsp chopped fresh parsley
salt and freshly ground black pepper
fresh parsley and thyme sprigs, to garnish

1 Clean the chicken livers, removing any fat or membrane. Rinse, pat dry with kitchen paper and cut into small pieces.

2 Heat the oil and butter in a frying pan and fry the bacon for 2–3 minutes. Add the shallots, garlic and sliced celery, and fry for 3–4 minutes over a low heat until the vegetables are softened.

3 Increase the heat and add the livers. Stir-fry for a few minutes until they are brown all over but still slightly pink in the centre.

4 Add the rice. Cook, stirring, for a few minutes, then pour over the wine. Bring to the boil, stirring frequently, taking care not to break up the livers. When all the wine has been absorbed, add the hot stock, a ladleful at a time, stirring constantly. About halfway through the cooking, add the thyme and season with salt and pepper. Continue to add the stock, making sure that each quantity has been absorbed before adding more.

5 When the risotto is creamy and the rice is tender, stir in the parsley. Adust the seasoning. Remove the pan from the heat, cover and leave to rest for a few minutes before serving, garnished with parsley and thyme sprigs.

Mushroom Picker's Chicken Paella

A good paella is based on a few well-chosen ingredients. Here, chicken combines with mixed wild mushrooms and vegetables.

Serves 4

45ml/3 tbsp olive oil
1 medium onion, chopped
1 small fennel bulb, sliced
225g/8oz/generous 3 cups assorted wild and cultivated mushrooms, trimmed and sliced
1 garlic clove, crushed
3 chicken legs, chopped through the bone
350g/12oz/1⅔ cups short-grain Spanish or Italian rice
900ml/1½ pints/3¾ cups Chicken Stock, boiling
pinch of saffron strands or 1 sachet saffron powder
1 fresh thyme sprig
400g/14oz can butter beans, drained and rinsed
75g/3oz/¾ cup frozen peas

1 Heat the oil in a 35cm/14in paella pan or a large frying pan. Add the onion and fennel, and fry over a gentle heat for 3–4 minutes.

2 Add the mushrooms and garlic, and cook until the juices begin to run, then increase the heat to evaporate them. Push the vegetables to one side. Add the chicken and fry briefly.

3 Stir in the rice, add the stock, saffron, thyme, butter beans and peas. Bring to simmering point and cook gently for 15 minutes without stirring.

4 Remove the pan from the heat and cover the surface of the paella with a circle of greased greaseproof paper. Cover the paper with a clean dish towel and allow the paella to finish cooking in its own heat for about 5 minutes. Bring to the table, uncover and serve.

Cook's Tip
Suitable mushrooms for this dish include ceps, bay boletus. chanterelles, saffron milk-caps, hedgehog fungus, St George's, Caesar's and oyster mushrooms.

Seven-vegetable Couscous

In this glorious, magically numbered Moroccan dish, chicken is partnered with lamb, carrots, parsnips, turnips, onions, courgettes, tomatoes and French beans. You can substitute different vegetables if you wish.

Serves 6

30ml/2 tbsp sunflower or olive oil
450g/1lb lean lamb, cut into bite-size pieces
2 chicken breast quarters, halved
2 onions, chopped
350g/12oz carrots, cut into chunks
225g/8oz parsnips, cut into chunks
115g/4oz turnips, cut into cubes
6 tomatoes, peeled and chopped
900ml/1½ pints/3¾ cups Chicken Stock
good pinch of ground ginger
1 cinnamon stick
400g/14oz can chick-peas, drained
400g/14oz/2⅓ cups couscous
2 small courgettes, cut into julienne strips
115g/4oz French beans, halved if necessary
50g/2oz/⅓ cup raisins
a little harissa or Tabasco sauce
salt and freshly ground black pepper

1 Heat half the oil in a large, heavy-based saucepan or flameproof casserole and add the lamb, in batches if necessary, and fry until evenly browned, stirring frequently. Transfer to a plate using a slotted spoon. Add the chicken pieces to the pan and cook, turning occasionally, until evenly browned. Transfer to the plate with the lamb.

2 Heat the remaining oil and add the onions. Fry over a gentle heat for 2–3 minutes, stirring occasionally, until softened, but not coloured. Add the carrots, parsnips and turnips. Stir well, cover with a lid and sweat over a gentle heat for 5–6 minutes, stirring once or twice.

3 Add the tomatoes, and return the lamb and chicken to the pan. Pour in the chicken stock. Season with salt and pepper to taste, and add the ground ginger and cinnamon stick. Bring to the boil and simmer gently for 35–45 minutes until the meat is nearly tender.

4 Skin the chick-peas by placing them in a bowl of cold water and rubbing them between your fingers. The skins will rise to the surface. Discard the skins and drain. Prepare the couscous according to the instructions on the packet.

5 Add the skinned chick-peas, courgettes, beans and raisins to the meat mixture, stir gently and continue cooking for about 10–15 minutes until the vegetables and meat are tender. Pile the couscous on to a large warmed serving platter, making a slight well in the centre.

6 Transfer the chicken to a plate, and remove the skin and bones, if you wish. Spoon 3–4 large spoonfuls of stock into a separate saucepan. Stir the chicken back into the stew, add harissa or Tabasco sauce to taste to the separate pan of stock and heat both gently. Remove and discard the cinnamon stick, spoon the stew over the couscous and serve. Hand the harissa sauce in a separate bowl.

Turkey Escalopes with Capers

These thin slices of turkey, coated in breadcrumbs, cook very quickly. Here they are enhanced with the fresh, sharp flavours of lemon, capers and sage.

Serves 2

4 thin turkey breast escalopes, about 75g/3oz each
1 large unwaxed lemon
2.5ml/ ½ tsp chopped fresh sage
60–75ml/4–5 tbsp extra virgin olive oil
50g/2oz/ ¾ cup fine dry breadcrumbs
15ml/1 tbsp capers, rinsed and drained
salt and freshly ground black pepper
fresh sage leaves and lemon wedges, to garnish

1 Place the turkey escalopes between two sheets of clear film and pound with the flat side of a meat mallet or rolling pin to flatten to a thickness of about 5mm/ ¼in.

2 With a vegetable peeler, remove four thin pieces of rind from the lemon. Cut them into fine julienne strips, cover with clear film and set aside. Grate the remainder of the lemon rind and squeeze the lemon.

3 Put the grated rind in a large, non-metallic shallow dish and add the chopped sage, salt and pepper. Stir in 15ml/1 tbsp of the lemon juice, reserving the rest, and about 15ml/1 tbsp of the oil, then add the turkey, turn to coat and leave to marinate for 30 minutes.

4 Place the breadcrumbs in another shallow dish. Dip the turkey escalopes in the crumbs, coating them on both sides.

5 In a heavy-based frying pan, heat 30ml/2 tbsp of the oil over a high heat, add the escalopes and cook for 2–3 minutes, turning once, until golden. Transfer to warmed plates and keep warm.

6 Wipe out the pan, add the remaining oil, the lemon julienne strips and the capers, and heat through, stirring. Spoon a little sauce over the turkey, garnish with sage leaves and lemon wedges, and serve.

Turkey Breasts with Wine & Grapes

Good stock and wine provide the flavour in this velvety sauce.

Serves 3

450g/1lb turkey breast, thinly sliced
45ml/3 tbsp flour
45–60ml/3–4 tbsp oil
120ml/4fl oz/ ½ cup white wine or sherry
120ml/4fl oz/ ½ cup Chicken Stock
150g/5oz white grapes
salt and freshly ground black pepper
fresh flat leaf parsley, to garnish
boiled new potatoes or rice, to serve

1 Put the turkey slices between two sheets of clear film and flatten them with a rolling pin or meat mallet. Spread out the flour on a plate, and season with salt and pepper. Toss each turkey slice in it so that both sides are thoroughly coated and shake off any excess.

2 Heat the oil in a large frying pan and sauté the turkey slices for about 3 minutes on each side. Pour in the wine or sherry and boil rapidly to reduce it slightly.

3 Stir in the chicken stock, lower the heat and cook for another few minutes until the turkey is cooked through.

4 Halve and seed the grapes, and stir them into the sauce. Adjust the seasoning to taste. Transfer to a warmed serving platter and serve, garnished with flat leaf parsley, accompanied by new potatoes or rice.

Cook's Tip

For a dark sauce you could use red wine and black grapes, and also add 115g/4oz/scant 2 cups sliced chestnut mushrooms. Sauté them in the oil before you cook the turkey in Step 2.

Turkey with Fig, Orange & Mint Marmalade

This unusual fruity sauce gives a tremendous lift to the rather bland flavour of turkey breast fillets.

Serves 4

450g/1lb dried figs
½ bottle sweet, fruity white wine
15ml/1 tbsp butter
4 turkey breast fillets, about 175–225g/6–8oz each
30ml/2 tbsp dark orange marmalade
10 fresh mint leaves, finely chopped, plus extra to garnish
juice of ½ lemon
salt and freshly ground black pepper

1 Place the dried figs in a saucepan with the white wine and bring to the boil, then simmer very gently for about 1 hour. Leave the figs to cool in the cooking liquid and chill overnight.

2 Melt the butter in a frying pan and fry the turkey fillets, turning them once, until they are cooked through. Transfer to a warmed serving dish and keep warm.

3 Drain any fat from the pan and pour in the cooking liquid from the figs. Bring to the boil and reduce until about 150ml/¼ pint/⅔ cup remains.

4 Add the marmalade, chopped mint and lemon juice, and simmer for a few minutes. Season to taste with salt and pepper. Add the figs and heat through.

5 When the sauce is thick and shiny, pour it over the meat and serve, garnished with plenty of mint leaves.

Cook's Tip
Some of the more unusual varieties of mint would be ideal for this dish. Try apple or pineapple, for example. A variety with variegated leaves would make an attractive garnish.

Turkey with Marsala Cream Sauce

Marsala makes a very rich and tasty sauce. The addition of lemon juice gives it a sharp edge, which helps to balance the richness.

Serves 6

6 turkey breast steaks
45ml/3 tbsp plain flour
30ml/2 tbsp olive oil
25g/1oz/2 tbsp butter
175ml/6fl oz/¾ cup dry Marsala
60ml/4 tbsp lemon juice
175ml/6fl oz/¾ cup double cream
salt and freshly ground black pepper
lemon wedges and chopped fresh parsley, to garnish
steamed mangetouts and French beans, to serve

1 Put each turkey steak between two sheets of clear film and pound with a meat mallet or rolling pin to flatten and stretch. Cut each steak in half or into quarters, discarding any sinew.

2 Spread out the flour in a shallow dish and season well. Dip the turkey steaks in the flour, turning them to coat thoroughly.

3 Heat the oil and butter in a wide saucepan or frying pan. Add as many pieces of turkey as the pan will hold in a single layer and sauté over a medium heat for 3 minutes on each side until coloured on the outside and cooked. Transfer to a warmed serving dish and keep hot. Repeat with the remaining turkey.

4 Lower the heat. Mix the Marsala and lemon juice in a jug, add to the pan and raise the heat. Bring to the boil, stirring in the sediment, then add the cream. Simmer, stirring constantly, until the sauce is reduced and glossy. Taste and adjust the seasoning. Spoon over the turkey, garnish with lemon wedges and parsley, and serve at once with mangetouts and French beans.

Variations
Chicken breast fillets can be used instead of the turkey, and 50g/2oz/¼ cup mascarpone cheese can be substituted for the double cream.

Turkey Zador with Mlinces

In this Croatian recipe for special occasions, the unusual *mlinces* are used to soak up the juices from a roast turkey.

Serves 10–12

3kg/6½ lb turkey
2 garlic cloves, halved
115g/4oz smoked bacon, finely chopped
30ml/2 tbsp chopped fresh rosemary
120ml/4fl oz/ ½ cup olive oil
250ml/8fl oz/1 cup dry white wine
fresh rosemary sprigs, to garnish
grilled bacon, to serve

For the mlinces

350g/12oz/3 cups plain flour, sifted
120–150ml/4–5fl oz/ ½– ⅔ cup warm water
30ml/2 tbsp oil
salt

1 Preheat the oven to 200°C/400°F/Gas 6. Dry the turkey well inside and out. Rub all over with the garlic cloves.

2 Toss the bacon and rosemary together, and use to stuff the turkey neck flap. Secure the skin with a wooden cocktail stick. Brush the bird with the oil. Place in a roasting tin and cover loosely with foil. Roast for 45–50 minutes. Remove the foil and reduce the oven temperature to 160°C/325°F/Gas 3. Baste the turkey with the juices and pour over the wine. Cook for 1 hour, basting occasionally. Reduce the temperature to 150°C/300°F/Gas 2 and cook for a further 45 minutes, basting occasionally.

3 Meanwhile, to make the *mlinces*, sift the flour with a little salt into a bowl. Add the water and oil, and mix to a soft but pliable dough. Knead briefly and divide equally into four. Roll out thinly on a lightly floured surface into 40cm/16in circles. Sprinkle with salt. Bake on baking sheets alongside the turkey for 25 minutes until crisp. Crush into pieces about 6–10cm/2½–4in.

4 About 6–8 minutes before the end of the cooking time for the turkey, add the *mlinces* to the meat juices in the roasting tin alongside the bird. Leave the turkey to rest for 10–15 minutes before carving, then serve, garnished with rosemary and accompanied by the *mlinces* and grilled bacon.

Turkey with Sage, Prunes & Brandy

This stir-fry has a very rich sauce based on a good-quality brandy – use the best you can afford.

Serves 4

115g/4oz/ ½ cup prunes
675g/1½ lb turkey breast fillet
300ml/ ½ pint/1¼ cups brandy
15ml/1 tbsp chopped fresh sage
150g/5oz smoked bacon, in one piece
50g/2oz/4 tbsp butter
24 baby onions, peeled and quartered
salt and freshly ground black pepper
fresh sage sprigs, to garnish

1 Stone the prunes and cut them into slivers. Remove the skin from the turkey and cut the breast into thin pieces.

2 Mix together the prunes, turkey, brandy and chopped sage in a non-metallic dish. Cover and set aside to marinate overnight in the fridge.

3 Next day, strain the turkey and prunes, reserving the marinade, and pat dry with kitchen paper. Dice the bacon.

4 Heat a wok or heavy-based frying pan and add half the butter. When the butter is hot, add the onions and stir-fry for 4 minutes until crisp and golden. Set aside.

5 Add the bacon to the wok and stir-fry for 1 minute until it begins to release some fat. Add the remaining butter, and stir-fry the turkey and prunes for 3–4 minutes until the turkey and bacon are crisp and golden.

6 Push the turkey mixture to one side of the wok, add the reserved marinade and simmer until thickened. Stir the turkey into the sauce, season well with salt and pepper, and serve, garnished with sage.

Cook's Tip
"VSOP" on the label is a guarantee of the quality of the brandy.

Breast of Turkey with Mango & Wine

Fresh mango gives this Caribbean-inspired dish a truly tropical taste.

Serves 4

4 turkey breast steaks, about 175g/6oz each
2 garlic cloves, crushed
1.5ml/ ¼ tsp ground cinnamon
15ml/1 tbsp finely chopped fresh parsley, plus extra to garnish
15ml/1 tbsp crushed cream crackers
25g/1oz/2 tbsp diced ripe mango, plus extra to garnish
40g/1½ oz/3 tbsp butter or margarine
6 shallots, sliced
150ml/ ¼ pint/ ⅔ cup white wine
salt and freshly ground black pepper

1 Cut a slit horizontally into each turkey steak to make a "pocket".

2 Put half the garlic, the cinnamon, parsley, cracker crumbs, mango, 15ml/1 tbsp of the butter or margarine and salt and pepper in a bowl, and mash together.

3 Spoon a little of the mango mixture into each of the "pockets". If necessary, secure with a wooden cocktail stick. Season the turkey with a little extra pepper.

4 Melt the remaining butter or margarine in a large frying pan, and sauté the remaining garlic and the shallots for 5 minutes. Add the turkey and cook for 15 minutes, turning once.

5 Add the wine, cover and simmer gently until the turkey is fully cooked. Add the extra diced mango, heat through for a minute or two, then serve, garnished with chopped parsley.

Cook's Tip
If a mango "gives" when gently squeezed in the palm of the hand, it is ripe, regardless of the colour of its skin.

Vine-leaf Wrapped Turkey with Noilly Prat

Pretty vine-leaf parcels conceal turkey escalopes filled with a delicious wild rice and pine nut stuffing flavoured with Noilly Prat.

Serves 4

115g/4oz drained vine leaves in brine
4 turkey escalopes, about 115–175g/4–6oz each
300ml/ ½ pint/1 ¼ cups Chicken Stock

For the stuffing
30ml/2 tbsp sunflower oil
3 shallots, chopped
75g/3oz/ ¾ cup cooked wild rice
4 tomatoes, peeled and chopped
45ml/3 tbsp Noilly Prat
25g/1oz/ ¼ cup pine nuts, chopped
salt and freshly ground black pepper

1 Preheat the oven to 190°C/375°F/Gas 5. Rinse the vine leaves a few times in cold water and drain.

2 To make the stuffing, heat the oil in a frying pan. Add the shallots and fry gently until soft. Remove the pan from the heat and stir in the cooked rice, tomatoes, Noilly Prat and pine nuts. Season with salt and pepper to taste.

3 Put the turkey escalopes between sheets of clear film and flatten with a rolling pin or meat mallet. Top each escalope with a quarter of the stuffing and roll the meat over the filling.

4 Overlap a quarter of the vine leaves to make a rectangle. Centre a turkey roll on top, roll up and tie with raffia or string. Repeat with the remaining leaves and turkey rolls.

5 Pack the rolls snugly in an ovenproof dish, pour over the stock and bake for 40 minutes. Skim any surface fat from the stock and pour the stock into a jug. Serve immediately with the turkey parcels.

Stuffed Turkey Breast with Lemon

This elegant dish of rolled turkey breast makes an impressive but economical main course.

Serves 4–5

675g/1½ lb boneless turkey breast, in one piece
1 carrot, cut into matchsticks
1 medium courgette, cut into matchsticks
75g/3oz ham, cut into matchsticks
2 thick slices white bread, crusts removed, softened in a little milk
10 green olives, stoned and finely chopped
1 large garlic clove, finely chopped
60ml/4 tbsp chopped fresh parsley
60ml/4 tbsp finely chopped fresh basil
1 egg
1.5ml/¼ tsp grated lemon rind
30ml/2 tbsp grated Parmesan cheese
60ml/4 tbsp olive oil
250ml/8fl oz/1 cup hot Chicken Stock
½ lemon, cut into thin wedges
25g/1oz/2 tbsp butter
salt and freshly ground black pepper

1 Remove any skin or fat from the turkey. Using a sharp knife, cut part of the way through the turkey breast and open the two halves out like a book. Pound the meat with a mallet or rolling pin to obtain one large piece of meat of as even a thickness as possible.

2 Preheat the oven to 200°C/400°F/Gas 6. Blanch the carrot and courgette pieces in a small saucepan of boiling water for 2 minutes, then drain. Combine with the ham.

3 Squeeze the bread and place in a mixing bowl, breaking it up with a fork. Stir in the olives, garlic, herbs and egg. Add the lemon rind and Parmesan. Season to taste with salt and pepper.

4 Spread the bread mixture over the meat, leaving a small border all around. Cover with the ham and vegetable mixture. Roll up the turkey and tie in several places with cooking string.

5 Heat the oil in a flameproof casserole slightly larger than the turkey roll. Brown the meat on all sides. Remove the casserole from the heat, add the stock and arrange the lemon wedges around the meat. Cover and place in the oven.

6 After 15 minutes remove the lid, discard the lemon and baste the meat. Continue cooking, uncovered, for 25–30 minutes, basting occasionally. Transfer the turkey to a warmed serving plate and allow to rest for at least 10 minutes before slicing.

7 Strain the sauce. Stir in the butter and adjust the seasoning. Serve the sliced turkey roll warm with the sauce. If you wish to serve it cold, slice it just before serving and omit the sauce.

Variation

Substitute 75g/3oz/generous 1 cup sliced mushrooms, sautéed lightly in 40g/1½oz/3 tbsp butter, for the ham in Step 2. Omit the lemon wedges during cooking.

Turkey Rolls with Cranberries

Cranberry sauce is traditionally served with roast turkey, but here the berries are incorporated into a lovely stuffing.

Serves 4

4 turkey escalopes
30ml/2 tbsp vegetable oil
120ml/4fl oz/½ cup cranberry juice or fruity red wine
2.5ml/½ tsp each arrowroot and water, mixed
salt and freshly ground black pepper
salad, to serve

For the stuffing

90g/3½ oz/¾ cup cranberries
175g/6oz seedless red grapes
1 large red dessert apple, quartered and cored
15ml/1 tbsp honey
10ml/2 tsp finely chopped fresh root ginger
2.5ml/½ tsp ground allspice

1 To make the stuffing, process the cranberries, grapes and apple in a food processor until finely chopped. Drain, pressing to extract the juice. Reserve the juice. Mix the fruit with the honey, ginger and allspice.

2 Place each turkey escalope between two sheets of clear film and beat with a meat mallet or rolling pin until 5mm/¼in thick. Season, then divide the stuffing among them, spreading almost to the edges. Roll up, tucking in the sides. Tie in two or three places with cooking string or secure with cocktail sticks.

3 Heat the oil in a large frying pan and brown the rolls on all sides over a moderately high heat for 5–7 minutes. Add the reserved fruit juice and the cranberry juice or wine, and bring to the boil. Cover and simmer for 20 minutes until tender and cooked through. Turn the rolls halfway through the cooking.

4 Remove the turkey rolls from the pan and keep warm. Boil the cooking liquid until it has reduced to about 175ml/6fl oz/¾ cup. Stir in the arrowroot mixture and boil for 2 minutes.

5 Remove the string or cocktail sticks from the turkey rolls and cut into slices. Serve the sliced rolls with the cooking liquid as a sauce and accompanied by salad.

Stir-fried Duck with Blueberries

Serve this conveniently quick dinner-party dish with sprigs of fresh mint, which will give a wonderful fresh aroma as you bring the meal to the table.

Serves 4

2 duck breast fillets, about 175g/6oz each
30ml/2 tbsp sunflower oil
15ml/1 tbsp red wine vinegar
5ml/1 tsp sugar
5ml/1 tsp red wine
5ml/1 tsp crème de cassis
115g/4oz/1 cup fresh blueberries
15ml/1 tbsp chopped fresh mint
salt and freshly ground black pepper
fresh mint sprigs, to garnish

1 Cut the duck breast fillets into neat slices. Season well with salt and pepper.

2 Heat a wok, then add the oil. When the oil is hot, add the duck and stir-fry for 3 minutes.

3 Add the red wine vinegar, sugar, red wine and crème de cassis. Bubble for 3 minutes to reduce to a thick syrup.

4 Stir in the blueberries, sprinkle over the chopped mint and serve, garnished with sprigs of mint.

Variations

You could substitute blackcurrants, redcurrants or cranberries for the blueberries. If using cranberries – and if you can obtain a bottle – substitute Karpi, a Finnish liqueur made from cranberries, for the crème de cassis. Otherwise, use crème de cassis, which is a classic French liqueur made form blackcurrants.

Duck with Peppercorns

Thick, meaty duck breast, like steak, should be served medium-rare. Green peppercorns make a zingy sauce, but choose pink peppercorns if you prefer a milder flavour.

Serves 2

5ml/1 tsp vegetable oil
2 duck breast fillets, about 225g/8oz each, skinned
60ml/4 tbsp duck or Chicken Stock
90ml/6 tbsp whipping cream
5ml/1 tsp Dijon mustard
15ml/1 tbsp green or pink peppercorns in vinegar, drained
salt
fresh parsley, to garnish

1 Heat the oil in a heavy-based frying pan. Add the duck breast fillets and cook over a medium-high heat for about 3 minutes on each side.

2 Transfer the duck to a plate and cover to keep warm. Pour off any fat from the pan and stir in the stock, cream, mustard and peppercorns. Boil for 2–3 minutes until the sauce thickens slightly, then season with salt.

3 Pour any accumulated juices from the duck into the sauce, then slice the fillets diagonally.

4 Arrange the sliced duck on two warmed individual serving plates, pour over a little of the sauce, garnish with parsley and serve at once.

Cook's Tip

Green peppercorns are the unripe berries of the same plant from which both black and white peppercorns come, Piper nigrum, although they have a milder flavour. They have a special affinity with poultry, especially duck. Pink peppercorns, however, are not really peppercorns at all, but the processed berries of a South American plant that is related to poison ivy.

Duck Risotto

This makes an excellent starter for six or could be served for half that number as a lunch or supper dish.

Serves 3–6

2 duck breast fillets
30ml/2 tbsp brandy
30ml/2 tbsp orange juice
15ml/1 tbsp olive oil (optional)
1 onion, finely chopped
1 garlic clove, crushed
275g/10oz/1½ cups risotto rice
1–1.2 litres/1¾–2 pints/4–5 cups simmering Chicken Stock
5ml/1 tsp chopped fresh thyme
5ml/1 tsp chopped fresh mint
10ml/2 tsp grated orange rind
40g/1½ oz/½ cup grated Parmesan cheese
salt and freshly ground black pepper
strips of thinly pared orange rind, to garnish

1 Score the fatty sides of the duck and rub with salt. Dry-fry, fat side down, in a heavy-based frying pan over a medium heat for 6–8 minutes to render the fat. Transfer to a plate, and pull away and discard the fat. Cut the flesh into 2cm/¾in wide slices.

2 Pour all but 15ml/1 tbsp of the rendered duck fat from the pan into a jug, then reheat the fat in the pan. Fry the duck slices for 2–3 minutes over a medium-high heat until evenly browned.

3 Add the brandy, heat to simmering point and then ignite. When the flames have died down, add the orange juice and season. Remove from the heat and set aside.

4 In a saucepan, heat either 15ml/1 tbsp of the remaining duck fat or the olive oil. Fry the onion and garlic over a gentle heat until the onion is soft but not browned. Add the rice and cook, stirring all the time, until the grains are coated in oil.

5 Add the stock, a ladle at a time, waiting for each addition to be absorbed completely before adding the next. Just before adding the final ladleful, stir in the duck with the thyme and mint. Continue cooking until the risotto is creamy and the rice is tender. Add the grated orange rind and Parmesan. Adjust the seasoning, then remove from the heat, cover and leave to stand for a few minutes. Serve, garnished with the pared orange rind.

Peruvian Duck with Rice

This is a very rich dish, brightly coloured with tomatoes, squash and fresh herbs.

Serves 4–6

4 duck breast fillets
1 Spanish onion, chopped
2 garlic cloves, crushed
10ml/2 tsp grated fresh root ginger
4 tomatoes (peeled, if liked), chopped
225g/8oz kabocha or acorn squash, cut into 1cm/½ in cubes
275g/10oz/1½ cups long-grain rice
750ml/1¼ pints/3 cups Chicken Stock
15ml/1 tbsp finely chopped fresh coriander
15ml/1 tbsp finely chopped fresh mint
salt and freshly ground black pepper

1 Heat a heavy-based frying pan or flameproof casserole. Using a sharp knife, score the fatty side of the duck breast fillets in a criss-cross pattern, rub the fat with a little salt, then dry-fry, skin side down, for 6–8 minutes to render some of the fat.

2 Pour all but 15ml/1 tbsp of the fat into a jar or cup, then fry the duck fillets, meat side down, in the fat remaining in the pan for 3–4 minutes until brown all over. Transfer to a board, slice thickly and set aside in a shallow dish. Deglaze the pan with a little water and pour this liquid over the duck.

3 Fry the onion and garlic in the same pan for 4–5 minutes until the onion is fairly soft, adding a little extra duck fat if necessary. Stir in the ginger, cook for 1–2 minutes more, then add the tomatoes and cook, stirring, for another 2 minutes. Add the squash, stir-fry for a few minutes, then cover and allow to steam for about 4 minutes.

4 Stir in the rice and cook, stirring, until it is well coated. Pour in the stock, return the slices of duck to the pan and season.

5 Bring to the boil, then lower the heat, cover and simmer for 30–35 minutes until the rice is tender. Stir in the coriander and mint, and serve.

Roasted Duckling on a Bed of Honeyed Potatoes

The rich flavour of duck combined with sweetened potatoes glazed with honey makes an excellent treat for a dinner party.

Serves 4

1 duckling
60ml/4 tbsp light soy sauce
150ml/ ¼ pint/ ⅔ cup orange juice
3 large floury potatoes, cut into chunks
30ml/2 tbsp clear honey
15ml/1 tbsp sesame seeds
salt and freshly ground black pepper

1 Preheat the oven to 200°C/400°F/Gas 6. Place the duckling, breast side up, in a roasting tin. Prick the skin well.

2 Mix the soy sauce and orange juice together and pour over the bird. Cook in the oven for 20 minutes.

3 Place the potato chunks in a bowl, stir in the honey and toss to mix well. Remove the duckling from the oven and spoon the potatoes all around and under the bird.

4 Roast for 35 minutes, then remove from the oven. Toss the potatoes in the duckling juices and turn the duckling over so that the underside will be cooked. Return to the oven and cook for a further 30 minutes.

5 Remove the duckling from the oven and carefully scoop off the excess fat, leaving the juices behind.

6 Sprinkle the sesame seeds over the potatoes, season and turn the duckling back over, breast side up, and cook for a further 10 minutes. Remove the duckling and potatoes from the oven and keep warm, allowing the bird to rest for 10–15 minutes.

7 Pour off the excess fat from the roasting tin and simmer the juices on top of the stove for a few minutes. Serve the juices with the carved duckling and potatoes.

Duck with Orange Sauce

This is the classic French recipe.

Serves 2–3

2kg/4½ lb duck
2 oranges
90g/3½ oz/ ½ cup caster sugar
90ml/6 tbsp white wine vinegar
120ml/4fl oz/ ½ cup Grand Marnier or orange liqueur
salt and freshly ground black pepper
watercress and orange slices, to garnish

1 Preheat the oven to 150°C/300°F/Gas 2. Trim off the excess fat and skin from the duck, and prick the skin all over with a fork. Season the duck inside and out and tie the legs with cooking string. Place the duck on a rack in a large roasting tin. Cover tightly with foil and cook in the oven for 1½ hours.

2 With a vegetable peeler, remove the orange rind in wide strips, then slice into thin strips. Squeeze the juice from the oranges.

3 Place the sugar and vinegar in a small, heavy-based saucepan and stir to dissolve the sugar. Boil over a high heat, without stirring, until the mixture is a rich caramel colour. Remove from the heat and carefully add the orange juice, pouring it down the side of the pan. Swirl the pan to blend, bring back to the boil, and add the orange rind and liqueur. Simmer for 2–3 minutes.

4 Remove the duck from the oven and pour off all the fat from the tin. Raise the oven temperature to 200°C/400°F/Gas 6. Return the duck to the oven and continue to roast, uncovered, for 25–30 minutes, basting a few times with some of the sauce, until the duck is brown and the juices run clear when the thickest part of the thigh is pierced with a knife or skewer.

5 Pour the juices from the duck cavity into the tin and transfer the bird to a carving board. Cover with foil and rest for 10 minutes.

6 Pour the roasting juices into the saucepan with the remaining caramel mixture, skim off the fat and simmer gently. Serve the duck, garnished with watercress and orange slices, and accompanied by the sauce.

Spiced Duck with Pears

A delicious casserole based on a Catalan dish that uses goose or duck. The sautéed pears are added towards the end of cooking, along with picarda sauce, a pounded pine nut and garlic paste which both flavours and thickens.

Serves 6

15ml/1 tbsp olive oil
6 duck portions
1 large onion, thinly sliced
1 cinnamon stick, halved
2 fresh thyme sprigs
475ml/16fl oz/2 cups Chicken Stock

To finish

3 firm ripe pears
30ml/2 tbsp olive oil
2 garlic cloves, sliced
25g/1oz/ ¼ cup pine nuts
2.5ml/ ½ tsp saffron strands
25g/1oz/2 tbsp raisins
salt and freshly ground black pepper
fresh thyme or parsley sprigs, to garnish
mashed potatoes, to serve (optional)

1 Preheat the oven to 180°C/350°F/Gas 4. Heat the oil in a flameproof casserole and fry the duck portions for about 5 minutes until the skin is golden. Transfer the duck to a plate and drain off all but 15ml/1 tbsp of the fat left in the pan.

2 Add the onion to the casserole and fry for 5 minutes. Add the cinnamon stick, thyme and stock. Return the duck to the casserole and bring the stock to the boil. Transfer to the oven and bake for 1¼ hours.

3 Meanwhile, peel, core and halve the pears. Heat the olive oil in a large frying pan and fry the pears until just golden on the cut sides.

4 Pound the garlic, pine nuts and saffron in a mortar with a pestle to make a thick, smooth paste. Add the paste to the casserole together with the raisins and pears. Bake for a further 15 minutes until the pears are tender.

5 Season to taste and garnish with thyme or parsley. Serve with mashed potatoes, if liked.

Duck Breasts with a Walnut & Pomegranate Sauce

This is an extremely exotic sweet-and-sour dish which originally came from Persia.

Serves 4

60ml/4 tbsp olive oil
2 onions, very thinly sliced
2.5ml/ ½ tsp ground turmeric
400g/14oz/3½ cups walnuts, roughly chopped
1 litre/1¾ pints/4 cups duck or Chicken Stock
6 pomegranates
30ml/2 tbsp caster sugar
60ml/4 tbsp lemon juice
4 duck breast fillets, about 225g/8oz each
salt and freshly ground black pepper

1 Heat half the oil in a frying pan. Add the onions and turmeric, and cook gently until soft. Transfer to a pan, add the walnuts and stock, then season with salt and pepper. Stir, bring to the boil and simmer, uncovered, for 20 minutes.

2 Cut the pomegranates in half and scoop out the seeds into a bowl. Reserve the seeds of 1 pomegranate. Transfer the remaining seeds to a blender or food processor and process to break them up. Strain through a sieve, to extract the juice, and stir in the sugar and lemon juice.

3 Score the skin of the duck breast fillets in a lattice fashion. Heat the remaining oil in a frying pan and place the duck in it, skin side down. Cook gently for 10 minutes, pouring off the fat from time to time, until the skin is dark golden and crisp. Turn over the fillets and cook for a further 3–4 minutes. Transfer to a plate and leave to rest.

4 Deglaze the frying pan with the pomegranate juice mixture, stirring with a wooden spoon, then add the walnut and stock mixture and simmer for 15 minutes until slightly thickened.

5 Slice the duck breast fillets, drizzle with a little sauce and serve, garnished with the reserved pomegranate seeds. Serve the remaining sauce separately.

Apple-stuffed Duck

Stuffing the duck breast fillets with whole apples keeps the meat moist and gives an attractive appearance when they are served cold, perhaps as part of a celebration buffet.

Serves 4

40g/1½ oz/¼ cup raisins or sultanas
30ml/2 tbsp brandy
3 large onions
30ml/2 tbsp oil
175g/6oz/3 cups fresh breadcrumbs
2 small dessert apples
2 large duck breast fillets
salt and freshly ground black pepper
mixed leaf salad, to serve

1 Place the dried fruit in a bowl, pour over the brandy and leave to soak. Preheat the oven to 220°C/425°F/Gas 7.

2 Chop one of the onions finely and sauté it in the oil until golden. Season with salt and pepper, and add 50–120ml/ 2–4fl oz/ ¼–½ cup water. Bring to the boil and then add breadcrumbs until the stuffing is moist but not sloppy.

3 Core and peel the apples. Drain the raisins and press them into the centre of the apples. Flatten the duck breast fillets and spread them out, skin side down.

4 Divide the stuffing among the duck fillets and spread it over the meat. Place an apple at one end of each fillet and carefully roll up to enclose the apple and stuffing. Secure with fine cooking string. Quarter the remaining onions. Prick the duck skin in several places to release the fat.

5 Arrange the duck on a rack in a roasting tin with the onions underneath. Roast for about 35 minutes. Pour off the fat, then reduce the oven temperature to 150°C/325°F/Gas 3 and roast for a further 30–45 minutes.

6 Serve hot or cold. If serving cold, leave to cool, then chill and cut each breast into five or six thin slices. Arrange on a platter and bring to room temperature before serving with a salad.

Duck with Chestnut Sauce

This autumnal dish makes use of delicious sweet chestnuts that can be gathered in the woods.

Serves 4–5

1 fresh rosemary sprig, plus extra to garnish
1 garlic clove, thinly sliced
30ml/2 tbsp olive oil
4 duck breast fillets, skin and fat removed

For the sauce

450g/1lb chestnuts
5ml/1 tsp oil
350ml/12fl oz/1½ cups milk
1 small onion, finely chopped
1 carrot, finely chopped
1 small bay leaf
salt and freshly ground black pepper
30ml/2 tbsp cream, warmed

1 Pull the leaves from the sprig of rosemary. Combine them with the garlic and oil in a shallow bowl. Pat the duck fillets dry with kitchen paper and lay them in a shallow dish. Brush with the flavoured oil and leave to marinate for at least 2 hours.

2 Preheat the oven to 180°C/350°F/Gas 4. To make the sauce, cut a cross in the flat side of each chestnut with a sharp knife. Place the chestnuts in a roasting tin with the oil and shake the tin until the nuts are well coated. Bake in the oven for about 20 minutes, then peel.

3 Place the chestnuts in a heavy-based saucepan with the milk, onion, carrot and bay leaf. Cook for about 10–15 minutes until the chestnuts are very tender. Season with salt and pepper. Discard the bay leaf. Press the mixture through a sieve.

4 Return the chestnut sauce to the pan and heat gently while the duck is cooking. Preheat the grill or prepare a barbecue.

5 Grill the duck for about 6–8 minutes until medium rare. The meat should be pink when sliced. Slice into rounds and arrange on warmed plates.

6 Stir the cream into the sauce just before serving. Garnish the sliced duck with rosemary and serve with the sauce.

Anita Wong's Duck

A Chinese recipe, which would be served at celebrations, such as weddings where it denotes marital harmony.

Serves 4–6

60ml/4 tbsp vegetable oil
2 garlic cloves, chopped
2.25kg/5–5¼ lb duck, with giblets (if making your own stock)
2.5cm/1in piece fresh root ginger, thinly sliced
45ml/3 tbsp bean paste
30ml/2 tbsp light soy sauce
15ml/1 tbsp dark soy sauce
15ml/1 tbsp sugar
2.5ml/½ tsp Chinese five-spice powder
3 pieces star anise
450ml/¾ pint/scant 2 cups duck stock (see Cook's Tip)
salt
shredded spring onions, to garnish

1 Heat the oil in a large pan. Fry the garlic without browning, then add the duck. Turn frequently until the outside is slightly brown all over. Transfer to a plate.

2 Add the ginger to the pan, then stir in the bean paste. Cook for 1 minute, then add both soy sauces, the sugar and the five-spice powder. Return the duck to the pan and fry, turning, until the outside is coated. Add the star anise and stock, and season to taste. Cover tightly and simmer gently for 2–2½ hours or until the duck is tender. Skim off the excess fat. Leave the bird in the sauce to cool.

3 Cut the duck into serving portions and pour over the sauce. Garnish with shredded spring onions and serve cold.

Cook's Tip

To make stock, put the duck giblets in a pan with a small onion and a piece of bruised fresh root ginger. Cover with 600ml/1 pint/2½ cups water, bring to the boil and then simmer, covered, for 20 minutes. Strain and blot with kitchen paper to remove excess fat.

Pheasant Breast with Apples

This luxurious dish bears the signature of Normandy: Calvados, the regional apple brandy, and rich cream.

Serves 2

2 pheasant breast fillets
25g/1oz/2 tbsp butter
1 onion, thinly sliced
1 dessert apple, peeled and quartered
10ml/2 tsp sugar
60ml/4 tbsp Calvados
60ml/4 tbsp Chicken Stock
1.5ml/¼ tsp dried thyme
120ml/4fl oz/½ cup whipping cream
salt and freshly ground white pepper
sautéed potatoes, to serve

1 Score the thick end of each pheasant breast fillet.

2 In a heavy-based frying pan, melt half of the butter over a medium heat. Add the onion and cook for 8–10 minutes until golden, stirring occasionally. Transfer to a plate.

3 Cut each apple quarter crossways into thin slices. Melt half the remaining butter in the pan and add the apple. Sprinkle with the sugar and cook for 5–7 minutes until caramelized, turning occasionally. Transfer to the plate with the onion.

4 Wipe out the pan, add the remaining butter and increase the heat to medium-high. Add the pheasant breast fillets, skin side down, and cook for 3–4 minutes until golden. Turn and cook for a further 1–2 minutes until the juices run slightly pink when the thickest part of the meat is pierced with a knife or skewer. Transfer to a board and cover to keep warm.

5 Add the Calvados to the pan and boil until reduced by half. Add the stock and thyme, season and reduce by half again. Stir in the cream, bring to the boil and cook for 1 minute. Return the onion and apple slices to the pan, and cook for 1 minute.

6 Slice the pheasant breasts diagonally and arrange on warmed plates. Spoon over a little sauce with the onion and apples.

Index

NOTES

Notes